Anonymous

The people's guide, a business, political and religious directory of Morgan Co., Ind.:

Also, a historical sketch of Morgan County and a brief history of each township

Anonymous

The people's guide, a business, political and religious directory of Morgan Co., Ind.:
Also, a historical sketch of Morgan County and a brief history of each township

ISBN/EAN: 9783337713355

Printed in Europe, USA, Canada, Australia, Japan

Cover: Foto ©ninafisch / pixelio.de

More available books at **www.hansebooks.com**

THE PEOPLE'S GUIDE

A BUSINESS, POLITICAL AND RELIGIOUS

Directory of Morgan Co., Ind.

TOGETHER WITH A COLLECTION OF VERY IMPORTANT
DOCUMENTS AND STATISTICS CONNECTED
WITH OUR MORAL, POLITICAL
AND SCIENTIFIC
HISTORY

ALSO, A

HISTORICAL SKETCH OF MORGAN COUNTY, *Indiana*

AND A

BRIEF HISTORY OF EACH TOWNSHIP.

By CLINE & McHAFFIE.

INDIANAPOLIS:
INDIANAPOLIS PRINTING AND PUBLISHING HOUSE.
1874.

Entered according to the act of Congress, in the year 1874, in the office of the Librarian of Congress at Washington, D. C., by CLINE & McHAFFIE.

DECLARATION OF INDEPENDENCE.

IN CONGRESS, TUESDAY, JULY 4, 1776.

Agreeably to the order of the day, the Congress resolved itself into a committee of the whole, to take into their further consideration the Declaration; and, after some time, the President resumed the chair, and Mr. Harrison reported that the committee had agreed to a declaration, which they desired him to report. (The committee consisted of Jefferson, Franklin, John Adams, Sherman, and R. R. Livingston.)

The Declaration being read, was agreed to, as follows:

A DECLARATION

BY THE REPRESENTATIVES OF THE UNITED STATES OF AMERICA,
IN CONGRESS ASSEMBLED.

When, in the course of human events, it becomes necessary for one people to dissolve the political bands which have connected them with another, and to assume among the powers of the earth the separate and equal station to which the laws of nature and of nature's God entitle them, a decent respect for the opinions of mankind requires that they should declare the causes which impel them to the separation.

We hold these truths to be self-evident: that all men are created equal; that they are endowed by their Creator with certain inalienable rights; that among these are life, liberty, and the pursuit of happiness. That, to secure these rights, governments are instituted among men, deriving their just powers from the consent of the governed; that, whenever any form of government becomes destructive of these ends, it is the right of the people to alter or to abolish it, and to institute a new government, laying its foundation on such principles, and organizing its powers in such form, as to them shall seem most likely to effect their safety and happiness. Prudence, indeed, will dictate that governments long established should not be changed for light and transient causes; and, accordingly, all experience hath shown that mankind are more disposed to suffer, while evils are sufferable, than to right themselves by abolishing the forms to which they are accustomed. But, when a long train of abuses and usurpations, pursuing invariably the same object, evinces a design to reduce them under absolute despotism, it is their right, it is their duty, to throw off such government, and to provide new guards for their future security. Such has been the patient sufferance of these colonies, and such is now the necessity which constrains them to alter their former systems of government. The history of the present King of Great Britain is a history of repeated injuries and usurpations, all having, in direct object, the establishment of an absolute tyranny over these States. To prove this, let facts be submitted to a candid world:

He has refused his assent to laws the most wholesome and necessary for the public good.

He has forbidden his Governors to pass laws of immediate and pressing importance, unless suspended in their operation till his assent should be obtained; and, when so suspended, he has utterly neglected to attend to them.

He has refused to pass other laws for the accommodation of large districts of people unless those people would relinquish the right of representation in the legislature—a right inestimable to them, and formidable to tyrants only.

He has called together legislative bodies at places unusual, uncomfortable, and distant from the depository of their public records, for the sole purpose of fatiguing them into compliance with his measures.

He has dissolved representative houses repeatedly for opposing, with manly firmness, his invasions on the rights of the people.

He has refused, for a long time after such dissolutions, to cause others to be elected; whereby the legislative powers, incapable of annihilation, have returned to the people at large for their exercise, the State remaining, in the meantime, exposed to all the danger of invasion from without, and convulsions within.

He has endeavored to prevent the population of these States; for that purpose, obstructing the laws for naturalization of foreigners; refusing to pass others to encourage their emigration hither, and raising the conditions of new appropriations of lands.

He has obstructed the administration of justice, by refusing his assent to laws for establishing judiciary powers.

He has made judges dependent on his will alone for the tenure of their offices and the amount and payment of their salaries.

He has erected a multitude of new offices, and sent hither swarms of officers to harass our people, and eat out their substances.

He has kept among us, in times of peace, standing armies, without the consent of our legislature.

He has affected to render the military independent of, and superior to, the civil power.

He has combined, with others, to subject us to a jurisdiction foreign to our constitution, and unacknowledged by our laws; giving his assent to their acts of pretended legislation:

For quartering large bodies of armed troops among us;

For protecting them, by mock trial, from punishment, for any murders which they should commit on the inhabitants of these States;

For cutting off our trade with all parts of the world;

For imposing taxes on us without our consent;

For depriving us, in many cases, of the benefits of trial by jury.

For transporting us beyond seas to be tried for pretended offenses.

For abolishing the free system of English laws in a neighboring province, establishing therein an arbitary government, and enlarging its boundaries, so as to render it at once an example and fit instrument for introducing the same absolute rule into these colonies;

For taking away our charters, abolishing our most valuable

laws, and altering, fundamentally, the powers of our governments;

For suspending our own legislature, and declaring themselves invested with power to legislate for us in all cases whatsoever.

He has abdicated government here, by declaring us out of his protection, and waging war against us.

He has plundered our seas, ravaged our coast, burnt our towns, and destroyed the lives of our people.

He is, at this time, transporting large armies of foreign mercenaries to complete the works of death, desolation, and tyranny, already begun, with circumstances of cruelty and perfidy scarcely paralleled in the most barbarous ages, and totally unworthy the head of a civilized nation.

He has constrained our fellow-citizens, taken captive on the high seas, to bear arms against their country, to become the executioners of their friends and brethren, or to fall themselves by their hands.

He has excited domestic insurrections amongst us, and has endeavored to bring on the inhabitants of our frontiers, the merciless Indian savages, whose known rule of warfare is an undistinguished destruction, of all ages, sexes, and conditions.

In every stage of these oppressions, we have petitioned for redress, in the most humble terms; our repeated petitions have been answered only by repeated injury. A prince, whose character is thus marked by every act which may define a tyrant, is unfit to be the ruler of a free people.

Nor have we been wanting in attention to our British brethren. We have warned them, from time to time, of attempts made by their legislature to extend an unwarrantable jurisdiction over us. We have reminded them of the circumstances of our emigration and settlement here. We have appealed to their native justice and magnanimity, and we have conjured them, by the ties of our common kindred, to disavow these usurpations, which would inevitably interrupt our connections and correspondence. They, too, have been deaf to the voice of justice and consanguinity. We must, therefore, acquiesce in the necessity, which denounces our separation, and hold them, as we hold the rest of mankind, enemies in war—in peace, friends.

We, therefore, the representatives of the UNITED STATES OF AMERICA, in GENERAL CONGRESS assembled, appealing to the Supreme Judge of the World for the rectitude of our intentions, do, in the name, and by the authority of the good people of these colonies, solemnly publish and declare, That these United Colonies are, and of right ought to be, FREE AND INDEPENDENT STATES; that they are absolved from all allegiance to the British crown, and that all political connections between them and the State of Great Britain, is, and ought to be, totally dissolved; and that, as *FREE AND INDEPENDENT STATES*, they have full power to levy war, conclude peace, contract alliances, establish commerce, and to do all other acts and things which INDEPENDENT STATES may of right do. And for the support of this Declaration, with a firm reliance on the protection of DIVINE PROVIDENCE, we mutually pledge to each other, our lives, our fortunes, and our sacred honor.

The foregoing Declaration was, by order of Congress, engrossed, and signed by the following members:

JOHN HANCOCK.

New Hampshire.
JOSIAH BARTLETT.
WILLIAM WHIPPLE,
MATTHEW THORNTON.

Massachusetts Bay.
SAMUEL ADAMS,
JOHN ADAMS,
ROBERT TREAT PAYNE,
ELBRIDGE GERRY.

Connecticut.
ROGER SHERMAN,
SAMUEL HUNTINGTON,
WILLIAM WILLIAMS,
OLIVER WOLCOTT.

Rhode Island.
STEPHEN HOPKINS.
WILLIAM ELLERY,

New York.
WILLIAM FLOYD,·
PHILIP LIVINGSTON,
FRANCIS LEWIS,
LEWIS MORRIS.

New Jersey.
RICHARD STOCKTON,
JOHN WITHERSPOON,
FRANCIS HOPKINSON,
JOHN HART,
ABRAHAM CLARK.

Pennsylvania.

ROBERT MORRIS,
BENJAMIN RUSH,
BENJAMIN FRANKLIN,
JOHN MORTON,
GEORGE CLYMER,
JAMES SMITH,
GEORGE TAYLOR,
JAMES WILSON,
GEORGE ROSS.

Delaware.

CÆSAR RODNEY,
GEORGE READ,
THOMAS M'KEEN.

Maryland.

SAMUEL CHASE,
WILLIAM PACA,
THOMAS STONE,
CHARLES CARROLL, of Car'n.

Georgia.

BUTTON GWINNETT,
LYMAN HALL,
GEORGE WALTON.

Virginia.

GEORGE WYTHE,
RICHARD HENRY LEE,
THOMAS JEFFERSON,
BENJAMIN HARRISON,
THOMAS NELSON, Jun.,
FRANCIS LIGHTFOOT LEE,
CARTER BRAXTON.

North Carolina.

WILLIAM HOOPER,
JOSEPH HEWES,
JOHN PENN.

South Carolina.

EDWARD RUTLEDGE,
THOMAS HAYWARD, Jun.,
THOMAS LYNCH, Jun.,
ARTHUR MIDDLETON.

CONSTITUTION

OF THE

UNITED STATES OF AMERICA.

We, the People of the United States, in order to form a more perfect Union, establish justice, insure domestic tranquility, provide for the common defense, promote the general welfare, and secure the blessings of liberty to ourselves and our posterity, do ordain and establish this Constitution for the United States of America.

ARTICLE I.

SECTION 1. All the legislative powers herein granted shall be vested in a Congress of the United States, which shall consist of a Senate and House of Representatives.

SEC. 2. The House of Representatives shall be composed of members chosen every second year by the people of the several States; and the electors in each State shall have the qualifications requisite for electors of the most numerous branch of the State Legislature.

No person shall be a Representative who shall not have attained to the age of twenty-five years, and been seven years a citizen of the United States, and who shall not, when elected, be an inhabitant of that State in which he shall be chosen.

Representatives and direct taxes shall be apportioned among the several States which may be included within this Union, according to their respective numbers, which shall be determined by adding to the whole number of free persons, including those bound to service for a term of years, and excluding Indians not taxed, three-fifths of all other persons. The actual enumeration shall be made within three years after the first meeting of the Congress of the United States, and within every subsequent term of ten years, in such manner as they shall by law direct. The number of Representatives shall not exceed one for every thirty thousand, but each State shall have at least one Representative; and until such enumeration shall be made, the State of New Hampshire shall be entitled to choose three, Massachusetts eight, Rhode Island and Providence Plantations one, Connecticut five, New York six, New Jersey four, Pennsylvania eight, Delaware one, Maryland six, Virginia ten, North Carolina five, South Carolina five, and Georgia three.

When vacancies happen in the representation from any State, the Executive authority thereof shall issue Writs of Election to fill such vacancies.

The House of Representatives shall choose their Speaker and other officers; and shall have the sole power of impeachment.

SEC. 3. The Senate of the United States shall be composed of two Senators from each State, chosen by the Legislature thereof, for six years; and each Senator shall have one vote.

Immediately after they shall be assembled in consequence of the first election, they shall be divided as equally as may be into three classes. The seats of the Senators of the first class shall be vacated at the expiration of the second year, of the second class at the expiration of the fourth year, and of the third class at the expiration of the sixth year, so that one-third may be chosen every second year; and if vacancies happen by resignation, or otherwise, during the recess of the Legislature of any State, the Executive thereof may make temporary appointments until the next meeting of the Legislature, which shall then fill such vacancies.

No person shall be a Senator who shall not have attained to the age of thirty years, and been nine years a citizen of the United States, and who shall not, when elected, be an inhabitant of that State for which he shall be chosen.

The Vice-President of the United States shall be President of the Senate, but shall have no vote, unless they be equally divided.

The Senate shall choose their other officers, and also a President *pro tempore*, in the absence of the Vice-President, or when he shall exercise the office of President of the United States.

The Senate shall have the sole power to try all impeachments. When sitting for that purpose, they shall be on oath or affirmation. When the President of the United States is being tried, the Chief Justice shall preside; and no person shall be convicted without the concurrence of two-thirds of the members present.

Judgment in cases of impeachment shall not extend further than to removal from office, and disqualification to hold and enjoy any office of honor, trust or profit under the United States; but the party convicted shall nevertheless be liable and subject to indictment, trial, judgment and punishment, according to law.

SEC. 4. The times, places, and manner of holding elections for Senators and Representatives, shall be prescribed in each State by the Legislature thereof; but the Congress may, at any time, by law make or alter such regulations, except as the places of choosing Senators.

The Congress shall assemble at least once in every year, and such meeting shall be on the first Monday in December, unless they shall by law appoint a different day.

SEC. 5. Each House shall be the judge of the elections, returns, and qualifications of its own members, and a majority of each shall constitute a quorum to do business; but a smaller number may adjourn from day to day, and may be authorized to compel the attendance of absent members, in such manner and under such penalties as each House may provide.

Each House may determine the Rules of its Proceedings, punish its members for disorderly behavior, and with the concurrence of two-thirds, expel a member.

Each House shall keep a Journal of its Proceedings, and from time to time publish the same, excepting such parts as may, in their judgment, require secrecy; and the yeas and nays of the members of either House on any question shall, at the desire of one-fifth of those present, be entered on the journal.

Neither House, during the session of Congress, shall, without the consent of the other, adjourn for more than three days, nor to any other place than that in which the two Houses shall be sitting.

SEC. 6. The Senators and Representatives shall receive a compensation for their services, to be ascertained by law and paid out of the treasury of the United States. They shall in all cases, except treason, felony, and breach of the peace, be privileged from arrest during their attendance at the session of their respective Houses, and in going to and returning from the same; and for any speech or debate in either House, they shall not be questioned in any other place.

No Senator or Representative shall, during the time for which he was elected, be appointed to any civil office under the authority of the United States, which shall have been created, or the emoluments whereof shall have been increased during such time, and no person holding any office under the United States shall be a member of either House during his continuance in office.

SEC. 7. All bills for raising revenue shall originate in the House of Representatives; but the Senate may propose or concur with amendments as on other bills.

Every bill which shall have passed the House of Representatives and the Senate, shall, before it becomes a law, be presented to the President of the United States: If he approve, he shall sign it; but if not, he shall return it, with his objections, to that House in which it shall have originated, who shall enter the objections at large on their Journal, and proceed to reconsider it. If, after such reconsideration, two-thirds of that House shall agree to pass the bill, it shall be sent, together with the objections, to the other House, by which it shall likewise be reconsidered, and if approved by two-thirds of that House, it shall become a law. But in all such cases the votes of both Houses shall be determined by yeas and nays, and the names of persons voting for and against the bill shall be entered on the Journal of each House respectively. If any bill shall not be returned by the President within ten days (Sundays excepted) after it shall have been presented to him, the same shall be a law, in like manner as if he had signed it, unless the Congress, by their adjournment, prevent its return, in which case it shall not be a law.

Every order, resolution, or vote to which the concurrence of the Senate and House of Representatives may be necessary (except on a question of adjournment) shall be presented to the President of the United States; and before the same shall take effect, shall be approved by him; or, being disapproved by him, shall be repassed by two-thirds of the Senate and

House of Representatives, according to the rules and limitations prescribed in the case of a bill.

SEC. 8. The Congress shall have power—

To lay and collect Taxes, Duties, Imposts and Excises, to pay the debts and provide for the common defense and general welfare of the United States: but all Duties, Imposts and Excises shall be uniform throughout the United States;

To borrow money on the credit of the United States;

To regulate commerce with foreign nations, and among the several States, and with the Indian tribes;

To establish an uniform rule of naturalization, and uniform laws on the subject of bankruptcies throughout the United States;

To coin money, regulate the value thereof and of foreign coin, and fix the standard of weights and measures;

To provide for the punishment of counterfeiting the securities and current coin of the United States;

To establish post-offices and post roads;

To promote the progress of science and useful arts, by securing for limited times to authors and inventors the exclusive right to their respective writings and discoveries;

To constitute tribunals inferior to the Supreme Court;

To define and punish piracies and felonies committed on the high seas, and offenses against the law of nations;

To declare war, grant letters of marque and reprisal, and make rules concerning captures on land and water;

To raise and support armies, but no appropriation of money to that use shall be for a longer term than two years;

To provide and maintain a navy;

To make rules for the government and regulation of the land and naval forces;

To provide for calling forth the militia to execute the laws of the Union, suppress insurrections, and repel invasions;

To provide for organizing, arming, and disciplining the militia, and for governing such part of them as may be employed in the service of the United States, reserving to the States respectively the appointment of the officers, and the authority of training the militia according to the discipline prescribed by Congress;

To exercise exclusive legislation, in all cases whatsoever, over such district (not exceeding ten miles square) as may.

by cession of particular States, and the acceptance of Congress, become the Seat of the Government of the United States, and to exercise like authority over all places purchased by the consent of the Legislature of the State in which the same shall be, for the erection of forts, magazines, arsenals, dock-yards, and other needful buildings; and

To make all laws which shall be necessary and proper for carrying into execution the foregoing powers, and all other powers vested by this Constitution in the Government of the United States, or in any department or officer thereof.

Sec. 9. The migration or importation of such persons as any of the States now existing shall think proper to admit, shall not be prohibited by the Congress prior to the year one thousand eight hundred and eight, but a tax or duty may be imposed on such importation, not exceeding ten dollars for each person.

The privilege of the Writ of Habeas Corpus shall not be suspended, unless when, in cases of rebellion or invasion, the public safety may require it.

No bill of attainder or ex post facto law shall be passed.

No capitation, or other direct tax shall be laid, unless in proportion to the census or enumeration hereinbefore directed to be taken.

No tax or duty shall be laid on articles exported from any State.

No preference shall be given by any regulation of commerce or revenue to the ports of one State over those of another; nor shall vessels bound to or from one State, be obliged to enter, clear, or pay duties in another.

No money shall be drawn from the treasury but in consequence of appropriations made by law; and a regular statement and account of the receipts and expenditures of all public money shall be published from time to time.

No title of nobility shall be granted by the United States: And no person holding any office of profit or trust under them shall, without the consent of the Congress, accept of any present, emolument, office, or title, of any kind whatever, from any king, prince, or foreign State.

Sec. 10. No State shall enter into any treaty, alliance, or confederation: grant letters of marque or reprisal; coin money; emit bills of credit; make anything but gold and silver coin a tender in payment of debts; pass any bill of attainder, ex post facto law, or law impairing the obligation of contracts, or grant any title of nobility.

No State shall, without the consent of the Congress, lay any imposts or duties on imports or exports, except what may be absolutely necessary for executing its inspection laws; and the net produce of all duties and imposts, laid by any State on imports or exports, shall be for the use of the treasury of the United States; and all such laws shall be subject to the revision and control of the Congress.

No State shall, without the consent of Congress, lay any duty of tonnage, keep troops, or ships of war in time of peace, enter into any agreement or compact with another State, or with a foreign power, or engage in war, unless actually invaded, or in such imminent danger as will not admit of delay.

ARTICLE II.

SECTION 1. The Executive Power shall be vested in a President of the United States of America. He shall hold his office during the term of four years, and, together with the Vice-President, chosen for the same term, be elected as follows:

Each State shall appoint, in such manner as the Legislature thereof may direct, a number of electors equal to the number of Senators and Representatives to which the State may be entitled in the Congress; but no Senator or Representative, or person holding an office of trust or profit under the United States, shall be appointed an elector.

[The electors shall meet in their respective States, and vote by ballot for two persons—of one at least shall not be an inhabitant of the same State with themselves. And they shall make a list of all the persons voted for, and of the number of votes for each; which list they shall sign and certify, and transmit, sealed, to the seat of the Government of the United States, directed to the President of the Senate. The President of the Senate shall, in the presence of the Senate and House of Representatives, open all the certificates, and the votes shall then be counted. The person having the greatest number of votes shall be the President, if such number be a majority of the whole number of electors appointed; and if there be more than one who have such majority, and have an equal number of votes, then the House of Representatives shall immediately choose by ballot one of them for President;

and if no person have a majority, then from the five highest on the list the said House shall, in like manner, choose the President. But, in choosing the President, the votes shall be taken by States, the representation from each State having one vote. A quorum for this purpose shall consist of a member or members from two-thirds of the States, and a majority of all the States shall be necessary to a choice. In every case, after the choice of the President, the person having the greatest number of votes of the electors shall be the Vice-President. But if there should remain two or more who have equal votes, the Senate shall choose from them by ballot the Vice-President.*]

The Congress may determine the time of choosing the electors, and the day on which they shall give their votes; which day shall be the same throughout the United States.

No person, except a natural born citizen, or a citizen of the United States at the time of the adoption of this Constitution, shall be eligible to the office of President; neither shall any person be eligible to that office who shall not have attained to the age of thirty-five years, and been fourteen years a resident within the United States.

In case of the removal of the President from office, or of his death, resignation or inability to discharge the powers and duties of the said office, the same shall devolve on the Vice President; and the Congress may by law provide for the case of removal, death, resignation, or inability, both of the President and Vice President, declaring what officer shall then act as President; and such officer shall act accordingly until the disability be removed, or a President shall be elected.

The President shall, at stated times, receive for his services a compensation, which shall neither be increased nor diminished during the period for which he shall have been elected; and he shall not receive within that period any other emolument from the United States, or any of them.

Before he enter on the execution of his office, he shall take the following oath or affirmation:

"I do solemnly swear (or affirm) that I will faithfully execute the office of President of the United States, and will, to the best of my ability, preserve, protect, and defend the Constitution of the United States."

SEC. 2. The President shall be Commander-in-Chief of the

---

*This clause has been repealed and annulled by the 12th amendment.

Army and Navy of the United States, and of the militia of the several States when called into the actual service of the United States; he may require the opinion, in writing, of the principal officer in each of the Executive Departments upon any subject relating to the duties of their respective offices; and he shall have power to grant reprieves and pardons for offenses against the United States, except in cases of impeachment.

He shall have power, by and with the advice and consent of the Senate, to make treaties, provided two-thirds of the Senate present concur; and he shall nominate, and by and with the advice and consent of the Senate, shall appoint Embassadors, other Public Ministers and Consuls, Judges of the Supreme Court, and all other officers of the United States whose appointments are not herein otherwise provided for, and which shall be established; but the Congress may by law vest the appointment of such inferior officers as they think proper in the President alone, in the Courts of Law, or in the Heads of Departments.

The President shall have power to fill up all vacancies that may happen during the recess of the Senate, by granting commissions, which shall expire at the end of their next session.

Sec. 3. He shall, from time to time, give to the Congress information of the state of the Union, and recommend to their consideration such measures as he shall judge necessary and expedient; he may, on extraordinary occasions, convene both Houses, or either of them; and, in case of disagreement between them with respect to the time of adjournment, he may adjourn them to such time as he shall think proper; he shall receive Embassadors and other public Ministers; he shall take care that the laws be faithfully executed, and shall commission all the officers of the United States.

Sec. 4. The President, Vice-President, and all Civil Officers of the United States, shall be removed from office on impeachment for, and conviction of, Treason, Bribery, or other high Crimes and Misdemeanors.

ARTICLE III.

Section 1. The judicial power of the United States shall be vested in one Supreme Court, and in such inferior Courts as the Congress may from time to time ordain and establish. The Judges, both of the Supreme and inferior courts, shall hold their offices during good behavior, and shall, at stated times, receive for their services a compensation, which shall not be diminished during their continuance in office.

SEC. 2. The judicial power shall extend to all cases, in Law and Equity, arising under this Constitution, the Laws of the United States, and Treaties made, or which shall be made, under their authority; to all cases affecting Embassadors, other public Ministers and Consuls; to all cases of admiralty and maritime jurisdiction; to controversies to which the United States shall be a party; to controversies between two or more States; between a State and citizens of another State; between citizens of different States; between citizens of the same State claiming lands under grants of different States; and between a State, or the citizens thereof, and foreign States, citizens or subjects.

In all cases affecting Embassadors, other public Ministers and Consuls, and those in which a State shall be a party, the Supreme Court shall have original jurisdiction. In all the other cases before mentioned, the Supreme Court shall have appellate jurisdiction, both as to law and fact, with such exceptions and under such regulations as the Congress shall make.

The trial of all crimes, except in cases of Impeachment, shall be by jury; and such trial shall be held in the State where the said crimes shall have been committed; but when not committed within any State, the trial shall be at such place or places as the Congress may by law have directed.

SEC. 3. Treason against the United States shall consist only in levying war against them, or adhering to their enemies, giving them aid and comfort. No person shall be convicted of treason unless on the testimony of two witnesses to the same overt act, or on confession in open Court.

The Congress shall have power to declare the punishment of treason, but no Attainder of Treason shall work corruption of blood, or forfeiture, except during the life of the person attainted.

ARTICLE IV.

SECTION 1. Full faith and credit shall be given in each State to the public acts, records, and judicial proceedings of every other State. And the Congress may by general laws prescribe the manner in which such acts, records, and proceedings shall be proved, and the effect thereof.

SEC. 2. The citizens of each State shall be entitled to all privileges and immunities of citizens in the several States.

A person charged in any State with treason, felony, or other crime, who shall flee from justice, and be found in another State, shall, on demand of the executive authority of the State from which he fled, be delivered up, to be removed to the State having jurisdiction of the crime.

No person held to service or labor in one State, under the laws thereof, escaping into another, shall, in consequence of any law or regulation therein, be discharged from such service or labor, but shall be delivered up on claim of the party to whom such service or labor may be due.

SEC. 3. New States may be admitted by the Congress into this Union; but no new State shall be formed or erected within the jurisdiction of any other State; nor any State be formed by the junction of two or more States or parts of States without the consent of the Legislatures of the States concerned, as well as of the Congress.

The Congress shall have power to dispose of and make all needful rules and regulations respecting the territory or other property belonging to the United States; and nothing in this Constitution shall be so construed as to prejudice any claims of the United States, or any particular State.

SEC. 4. The United States shall guarantee to every State in this Union a republican form of Government, and shall protect each of them against invasion; and on application of the Legislature, or of the Executive (when the Legislature can not be convened), against domestic violence.

ARTICLE V.

The Congress, whenever two-thirds of both Houses shall deem it necessary, shall propose amendments to the Constitution, or, on the application of the Legislatures of two-thirds of the several States, shall call a convention for proposing amendments, which, in either case, shall be valid to all intents and purposes, as part of this Constitution, when ratified by the Legislatures of three-fourths of the several States, or by conventions in three-fourths thereof, as the one or the other mode of ratification may be proposed by the Congress; *Provided*, That no amendment which may be made prior to the year one thousand eight hundred and eight shall in any manner affect the first and fourth classes in the ninth section of the first article; and that no State, without its consent, shall be deprived of its equal suffrage in the Senate.

ARTICLE VI.

All debts contracted and engagements entered into before the adoption of this Constitution, shall be as valid against the United States, under this Constitution, as under the Confederation.

This Constitution and the laws of the United States which shall be made in pursuance thereof; and all Treaties made, or which shall be made, under the authority of the United States, shall be the supreme law of the land; and the Judges in every State shall be bound thereby, anything in the Constitution or laws of any State to the contrary notwithstanding.

The Senators and Representatives before mentioned, and the members of the several State Legislatures, and all executive and judicial officers, both of the United States and of the several States, shall be bound by oath or affirmation to support this Constitution; but no religious test shall ever be required as a qualification to any office or public trust under the United States.

ARTICLE VII.

The ratification of the conventions of nine States shall be sufficient for the establishment of this Constitution between the States so ratifying the same.

DONE in convention, by the unanimous consent of the States present, the seventeenth day of September, in the year of our Lord one thousand seven hundred and eighty-seven, and of the Independence of the United States of America the twelfth. In Witness whereof, we have hereunto subscribed our names.

GEO. WASHINGTON,
Pres't and Deputy from Virginia.

New Hampshire.

JOHN LANGDON,   NICHOLAS GILMAN.

Massachusetts.

NATHANIEL GORHAM, RUFUS KING.

Connecticut.

WM. SAML. JOHNSON, ROGER SHERMAN.

New York.

ALEXANDER HAMILTON.

New Jersey.

WIL. LIVINGSTON, DAVID BREARLEY,
WM. PATERSON, JONA. DAYTON.

Pennsylvania.

B. FRANKLIN, THOMAS MIFFLIN,
ROBT. MORRIS, GEO. CLYMER,
THO. FITZSIMONS, JARED INGERSOLL,
JAMES WILSON, GOUV. MORRIS.

Delaware.

GEO. READ, GUNNING BEDFORD, JR.
JOHN DICKINSON, RICHARD BASSETT.
JACO. BROOM,

Maryland.

JAMES M'HENRY, DAN. OF ST. THOS. JENIFER,
DANL. CARROLL,

Virginia.

JOHN BLAIR, JAMES MADISON, JR.

North Carolina.

WM. BLOUNT, RICH'D DOBBS SPAIGHT.
HU. WILLIAMSON,

South Carolina.

J. RUTLEDGE, CHARLES C. PINCKNEY.
CHARLES PINCKNEY, PIERCE BUTLER.

Georgia.

WILLIAM FEW, ABR. BALDWIN.

Attest: **WILLIAM JACKSON,** *Secretary.*

ARTICLES.

In addition to, and amendment of, the Constitution of the United States of America, proposed by Congress, and ratified by the Legislatures of the several States, pursuant to the fifth article of the original Constitution.

ARTICLE I.

Congress shall make no law respecting an establishment of religion, or prohibiting the free exercise thereof; or abridging the freedom of speech or of the press; or the right of the people peaceably to assemble, and to petition the Government for a redress of grievances.

ARTICLE II.

A well-regulated Militia being necessary to the security of a free State, the right of the people to keep and bear arms shall not be infringed.

ARTICLE III.

No soldier shall, in time of peace, be quartered in any house, without the consent of the owner, nor in time of war, but in a manner to be prescribed by law.

ARTICLE IV.

The right of the people to be secure in their persons, houses, papers, and effects, against unreasonable searches and seizures, shall not be violated, and no warrant shall issue but upon probable cause, supported by oath or affirmation, and particularly describing the place to be searched, and the persons or things to be seized.

ARTICLE V.

No person shall be held to answer for a capital, or otherwise infamous crime, unless on a presentment or indictment of a Grand Jury, except in cases arising in the land or naval forces, or in the militia, when in actual service in time of war or public danger; nor shall any person be subject for the same offense to be twice put in jeopardy of life or limb; nor shall be compelled in any criminal case to be a witness against himself, nor be deprived of life, liberty, or property, without due process of law; nor shall private property be taken for public use without just compensation.

ARTICLE VI.

In all criminal prosecutions, the accused shall enjoy the right to a speedy and public trial, by an impartial jury of the State and district wherein the crime shall have been committed, which district shall have been previously ascertained by law, and to be informed of the nature and cause of the accusation to be confronted with the witnesses against him; to have compulsory process for obtaining witnesses in his favor, and to have the assistance of counsel for his defense.

ARTICLE VII.

In suits at common law, where the value in controversy shall exceed twenty dollars, the right of trial by jury shall be preserved, and no fact tried by a jury shall be otherwise re-examined in any Court of the United States, than according to the rules of the common law.

ARTICLE VIII.

Excessive bail shall not be required, nor excessive fines imposed, nor cruel and unusual punishments inflicted.

ARTICLE IX.

The enumeration in the Constitution of certain rights, shall not be construed to deny or disparage others retained by the people.

ARTICLE X.

The powers not delegated to the United States by the Constitution, nor prohibited by it to the States, are reserved to the States respectively, or to the people.

ARTICLE XI.

The judicial power of the United States shall not be construed to extend to any suit in law or equity, commenced or prosecuted against one of the United States by citizens of another State, or by citizens or subjects of any foreign State.

ARTICLE XII.

The Electors shall meet in their respective States, and vote by ballot for President and Vice-President, one of whom, at least, shall not be an inhabitant of the same State with themselves; they shall name in their ballot the person voted for as President, and in distinct ballots the person voted for as Vice-President, and they shall make distinct lists of all persons voted for as President, and all persons voted for as Vice-President, and of the number of votes for each, which lists they shall sign and certify, and transmit sealed to the seat of government of the United States, directed to the President of the Senate:—The President of the Senate shall, in presence of the Senate and House of Representatives, open all the certificates, and the votes shall then be counted; The person having the greatest number of votes for President shall be the President, if such number be a majority of the whole number of Electors appointed; and if no person have such majority, then from the persons having the highest numbers, not exceeding three, on the list of those voted for as President, the House of Representatives shall choose immediately by ballot the President. But in choosing the President, the votes shall be taken by States, the representation from each State having one; a quorum for this shall consist of a member or members from two-thirds of the States, and a majority of all the States shall be necessary to a choice. And if the House of Representatives shall not choose a President, whenever the right of choice shall devolve upon them, before the fourth day of March next following, then the Vice-President shall act as President, as in the case of the death or other constitutional disability of the President. The person having the greatest number of votes as Vice-President, shall be the Vice-President, if such number be a majority of the whole number of electors appointed; and if no person have a majoaity, then from the two highest numbers on the list, the Senate shall choose the Vice-President; a quorum for the purpose shall consist of two-thirds of the whole number of Senators, and a majority of the whole number shall be necessary to a choice. But no person constitutionally ineligible to the office of President, shall be eligible to that of Vice-President of the United States.

ARTICLE XIII.

"SECTION 1. Neither slavery nor involuntary servitude, except as a punishment for crime, whereof the party shall have been duly convicted, shall exist within the United States, or any place subject to their jurisdiction.

"SECTION 2. Congress shall have power to enforce this Article by appropriate legislation, approved February 1, 1863."

The Constitution was adopted on the 17th of September, 1787, by the convention appointed in pursuance of the Resolution of the Congress of the Confederation, of the 21st February, 1787, and ratified by the conventions of the several States, as follows:

By Convention of	Delaware	7th December,	1787
"	"	Pennsylvania	12th December, 1787
"	"	New Jersey	18th December, 1787
"	"	Georgia	2d January, 1788
"	"	Connecticut	9th January, 1788
"	"	Massachusetts	6th February, 1788
"	"	Maryland	28th April, 1788
"	"	South Carolina	28th May, 1788
"	"	New Hampshire	21st June, 1788
"	"	Virginia	26th June, 1788
"	"	New York	26th July, 1788
"	"	North Carolina	21st November, 1789
"	"	Rhode Island	29th May, 1790

The first ten of the Amendments were proposed on the 25th of September, 1789, and ratified by the constitutional number of States on the 15th December, 1791; the eleventh, on the 8th of January, 1798; and the twelfth, on the 25th September, 1804; and the thirteenth, on the ——, 186—.

CONSTITUTION

OF THE

STATE OF INDIANA.

———:o:———

PREAMBLE.

To THE END, that justice be established, public order maintained, and liberty perpetuated; WE the People of the State of Indiana, grateful to ALMIGHTY GOD for the free exercise of the right to choose our own form of government, do ordain this Constitution.

ARTICLE I.
BILL OF RIGHTS.

SECTION 1. WE DECLARE, That all men are created equal; that they are endowed by their Creator with certain unalienable rights; that among these are life, liberty, and the pursuit of happiness; that all power is inherent in the people; and that all free governments are, and of right ought to be, founded on their authority, and instituted for their peace, safety, and well being. For the advancement of these ends, the People have, at all times, an indefeasible right to alter and reform their government.

Sec. 2. All men shall be secured in their natural right to worship Almighty God, according to the dictates of their own consciences.

Sec. 3. No law shall, in any case whatever, control the free exercise and enjoyment of religious opinions, or interfere with the rights of conscience.

Sec. 4. No preference shall be given, by law, to any creed, religious society, or mode of worship; and no man shall be compelled to attend, erect, or support any place of worship, or to maintain any ministry, against his consent.

Sec. 5. No religious test shall be required, as a qualification for any office of trust or profit.

Sec. 6. No money shall be drawn from the treasury, for the benefit of any religious or theological institution.

Sec. 7. No person shall be rendered incompetent as a witness, in consequence of his opinions on matters of religion.

Sec. 8. The mode of administering an oath or affirmation, shall be such as may be most consistent with, and binding upon, the conscience of the person to whom such oath or affirmation may be administered.

Sec. 9. No law shall be passed, restraining the free interchange of thought and opinion, or restricting the right to speak, write, or print freely, on any subject whatever; but for the abuse of that right every person shall be responsible.

Sec. 10. In all prosecutions for libel, the truth of the matters alleged to be libelous may be given in justification.

Sec. 11. The right of the people to be secure in their persons, houses, papers, and effects, against unreasonable search or seizure, shall not be violated; and no warrant shall issue, but upon probable cause, supported by oath or affirmation, and particularly describing the place to be searched, and the person or thing to be seized.

Sec. 12. All courts shall be open; and every man, for injury done to him in his person, property or reputation, shall have remedy by due course of law. Justice shall be administered freely, and without purchase; completely, and without denial; speedily, and without delay.

Sec. 13. In all criminal prosecutions, the accused shall have the right to a public trial, by an impartial jury, in the county in which the offense shall have been committed; to be heard by himself and counsel; to demand the nature and cause of the accusation against him, and to have a copy thereof; to meet the witnesses face to face, and to have compulsory process for obtaining witnesses in his favor.

Sec. 14. No person shall be put in jeopardy twice for the same offense. No person, in any criminal prosecution, shall be compelled to testify against himself.

Sec. 15. No person arrested, or confined in jail, shall be treated with unnecessary rigor.

Sec. 16. Excessive bail shall not be required. Excessive fines shall not be imposed. Cruel and unusual punishment shall not be inflicted. All penalties shall be proportioned to the nature of the offense.

Sec. 17. Offenses, other than murder or treason, shall be bailable by sufficient sureties. Murder or treason shall not be bailable, when the proof is evident, or the presumption strong.

Sec. 18. The penal code shall be founded on the principles of reformation, and not of vindictive justice.

Sec. 19. In all criminal cases whatever, the jury shall have the right to determine the law and the facts.

Sec. 20. In all civil cases, the right of trial by jury shall remain inviolate.

Sec. 21. No man's particular services shall be demanded without just compensation. No man's property shall be taken by law, without just compensation; nor, except in case of the State, without such compensation first assessed and tendered.

Sce. 22. The privilege of the debtor to enjoy the necessary comforts of life, shall be recognized by wholesome laws, exempting a reasonable amount of property from seizure or sale for the payment of any debt or liability hereafter contracted; and there shall be no imprisonment for debt, except in case of fraud.

Sec. 23. The General Assembly shall not grant to any citizen, or class of citizens, privileges or immunities which, upon the same terms, shall not equally belong to all citizens.

Sec. 24. No *ex-post-facto* law, or law impairing the obligation of contracts, shall ever be passed.

Sec. 25. No law shall be passed, the taking effect of which shall be made to depend upon any authority, except as provided in this Constitution.

Sec. 26. The operation of the laws shall never be suspended, except by the authority of the General Assembly.

Sec. 27. The privilege of the writ of *habeas corpus* shall not be suspended, except in case of rebellion or invasion; and then, only if the public safety demand it.

Sec. 28. Treason against the State shall consist only in levying war against it, and in giving aid and comfort to its enemies.

Sec. 29. No person shall be convicted of treason, except on the testimony of two witnesses to the same overt act, or upon his confession in open court.

Sec. 30. No conviction shall work corruption of blood, or forfeiture of estate.

Sec. 31. No law shall restrain any of the inhabitants of the State from assembling together in a peaceable manner, to consult for their common good; nor from instructing their representatives; nor from applying to the General Assembly for redress of grievances.

Sec. 32. The people shall have a right to bear arms, for the defense of themselves and the State.

Sec. 33. The military shall be kept in strict subordination to the civil power.

Sec. 34. No soldier shall, in time of peace, be quartered in any house, without the consent of the owner; nor, in time of war, but in a manner to be prescribed by law.

Sec. 35. The General Assembly shall not grant any title of nobility, nor confer hereditary distinctions.

Sec. 36. Emigration from the State shall not be prohibited.

Sec. 37. There shall be neither slavery, nor involuntary servitude, within the State, otherwise than for the punishment of crimes, whereof the party shall have been duly convicted. No indenture of any Negro or Mulatto, made and executed out of the bounds of the State, shall be valid within the State.

ARTICLE II.

SUFFRAGE AND ELECTION.

Sec. 1. All elections shall be free and equal.

Sec. 2. In all elections, not otherwise provided for by this Constitution, every white male citizen of the United States, of the age of twenty-one years and upwards, who shall have resided in the State during the six months immediately preceding such election; and every white male, of foreign birth, of the age of twenty-one years and upwards, who shall have resided in the United States one year, and shall have resided in this State during the six months immediately preceding such election, and shall have declared his intention to become a citizen of the United States, conformably to the laws of the United States on the subject of naturalization, shall be entitled to vote in the township or precinct where he may reside.

Sec. 3. No soldier, seaman, or marine, in the army or navy of the United States, or of their allies, shall be deemed to have acquired a residence within the State, in consequence of having been stationed within the same; nor shall any such soldier, seaman, or marine have the right to vote.

Sec. 4. No person shall be deemed to have lost his residence in the State by reason of his absence, either on business of this State or of the United States.

Sec. 5. No Negro or Mulatto shall have the right of suffrage.

Sec. 6. Every person shall be disqualified from holding office during the term for which he may have been elected, who shall have given or offered a bribe, threat, or reward to procure his election.

Sec. 7. Every person who shall give or accept a challenge to fight a duel, or who shall knowingly carry to another person such challenge, or who shall agree to go out of the State to fight a duel, shall be ineligible to any office of trust or profit.

Sec. 8. The General Assembly shall have power to deprive of the right of suffrage, and to render ineligible, any person convicted of an infamous crime.

Sec. 9. No person holding a lucrative office or appointment under the United States, or under this State, shall be eligible to a seat in the General Assembly; nor shall any person hold more than one lucrative office at the same time, except as in this Constitution expressly permitted: *Provided*, that officers in the militia, to which there is attached no annual salary, and the office of Deputy Postmaster, where the compensation does not exceed ninety dollars per annum, shall not be deemed lucrative: *And provided, also*, that counties containing less than one thousand polls, may confer the office of Clerk, Recorder, and Auditor, or any two of said offices, upon the same person.

Sce. 10. No person who may hereafter be a collector or holder of public moneys, shall be eligible to any office of trust or profit, until he shall have accounted for, and paid over, according to law, all sums for which he may be liable.

Sec. 11. In all cases in which it is provided that an office shall not be filled by the same person more than a certain number of years continuously, an appointment *pro tempore*, shall not be reckoned a part of that term.

Sec. 12. In all cases, except treason, felony, and breach of the peace, electors shall be free from arrest, in going to elections, during their attendance there, and in returning from the same.

Sec. 13. All elections by the people shall be by ballot; and all elections by the General Assembly, or by either branch thereof, shall be *viva voce*.

Sec. 14. All general elections shall be held on the second Tuesday in October.

ARTICLE III.
DISTRIBUTION OF POWERS.

SECTION 1. The powers of the Government are divided into three separate departments; the Legislative, the Executive, including the Administrative, and the Judicial; and no person, charged with official duties under one of these departments, shall exercise any of the functions of another, except as in this Constitution expressly provided.

ARTICLE IV.
LEGISLATIVE.

SECTION 1. The Legislative authority of the State shall be vested in the General Assembly, which shall consist of a Senate and a House of Representatives. The style of every law shall be: "Be it enacted by the General Assembly of the State of Indiana;" and no law shall be enacted except by bill.

Sec. 2. The Senate shall not exceed fifty, nor the House of Representatives one hundred members; and they shall be chosen by the electors of the respective counties or districts, into which the State may, from time to time, be divided.

Sec. 3. Senators shall be elected for the term of four years and Representatives for the term of two years, from the day next after their general election: *Provided, however,* that the Senators elect, at the second meeting of the General Assembly under this Constitution, shall be divided, by lot into two equal classes, as nearly as may be; and the seats of Senators of the first class shall be vacated at the expiration of two years, and those of the second class at the expiration of four years; so that one-half as nearly as possible, shall be chosen biennially forever thereafter. And in case of increase in the number of Senators. they shall be annexed, by lot, to one or the other of the two classes, as to keep them as nearly equal as practicable.

Sec. 4. The General Assembly shall, at its second session after the adoption of this Constitution, and every six years thereafter, cause an enumeration to be made of all the white male inhabitants over the age of twenty-one years.

Sec. 5. The number of Senators and Representatives shall, at the session next following each period of making such enumeration, be fixed by law, and apportioned among the several counties, according to the number of white male inhabitants above twenty-one years of age in each: *Provided*, that the first and second election of members of the General Assembly under this Constitution shall be according to the apportionment last made by the General Assembly, before the adoption of this Constitution.

Sec. 6. A senatorial or representative district, where more than one county shall constitute a district, shall be composed of contiguous counties; and no county for senatorial apportionment shall ever be divided.

Sec. 7. No person shall be a senator or a representative who at the time of his election is not a citizen of the United States; nor any one who has not been, for two years next preceding his election, an inhabitant of this State, and, for one year next preceding his election, an inhabitant of the county or district whence he may be chosen. Senators shall be at least twenty-five, and Representatives at least twenty-one years of age.

Sec. 8. Senators and Representatives, in all cases except treason, felony, and breach of the peace, shall be privileged from arrest during the session of the General Assembly, and in going to and returning from the same, and shall not be subject to any civil process during the session of the General Assembly, nor during the fifteen days next before the commencement thereof. For any speech or debate in either house, a member shall not be questioned in any other place.

Sec. 9. The session of the General Assembly shall be held biennially at the capital of the State, commencing on the Thursday next after the first Monday of January, in the year one thousand eight hundred and fifty-three, and on the same day of every second year thereafter, unless a different day or place shall have been appointed by law. But if, in the opinion of the Governor, the public welfare shall require it, he may, at any time, by proclamation, call a special session.

Sec. 10. Each house when assembled shall choose its own officers (the President of the Senate excepted), judge of the elections, qualifications, and returns of its own members, determine its rules of proceeding, and sit upon its own adjournment. But neither house shall, without the consent of the other, adjourn for more than three days, nor to any place other than that in which it may be sitting.

Sec. 11. Two-thirds of each house shall constitute a quorum to do business, but a smaller number may meet, adjourn from day to day, and compel the attendance of absent members. A quorum being in attendance, if either house fail to effect an organization within the first five days thereafter, the members of the house so failing shall be entitled to no compensation from the end of the said five days, until an organization shall have been effected.

Sec. 12. Each house shall keep a journal of its proceedings, and publish the same. The yeas and nays, on any question, shall, at the request of any two members, be entered, together with the names of the members demanding the same, on the journal : *Provided*, that on a motion to adjourn, it shall reqire one-tenth of the members present to order the yeas and nays.

Sec. 13. The doors of each house, and of committees of the whole, shall be kept open, except in such cases, as, in the opinion of either house, may require secrecy.

Sec. 14. Either house may punish its members for disorderly behavior, and may, with the concurrence of two-thirds, expel a member; but not a second time for the same cause.

Sec. 15. Either house, during its session, may punish by imprisonment, any person not a member, who shall have been guilty of disrespect to the house, by disorderly or contemptuous behavior in its presence; but such imprisonment shall not at any time exceed twenty-four hours.

Sec. 16. Each house shall have all powers necessary for a branch of the legislative department of a free and independent State.

Sec. 17. Bills may originate in either house, but may be amended or rejected in the other, except that bills for raising revenue shall originate in the House of Representatives.

Sec. 18. Every bill shall be read, by sections, on three several days, in each house; unless, in case of emergency, two-thirds of the house where such bill may be depending shall, by a vote of yeas and nays, deem it expedient to dispense with this rule; but the reading of a bill by sections, on its final passage, shall, in no case, be dispensed with; and the vote on the passage of every bill or joint resolution shall be taken by yeas and nays.

Sec. 19. Every act shall embrace but one subject and matters properly connected therewith; which subject shall be expressed in the title. But if any subject shall be embraced in an act which shall not be expressed in the title, such act shall be void only as to so much thereof as shall not be expressed in the title.

Sec. 20. Every act and joint resolution shall be plainly worded, avoiding, as far as practicable, the use of technical terms.

Sec. 21. No act shall ever be revised or amended by mere reference to its title; but the act revised, or section amended, shall be set forth and published at full length.

Sec. 22. The General Assembly shall not pass local or special laws, in any of the following enumerated cases, that is to say:

Regulating the jurisdiction and duties of justices of the peace and of constables;

For the punishment of crimes and misdemeanors;

Regulating the practice in courts of justice;

Providing for changing the venue in civil and criminal cases;

Granting divorces;

Changing the names of persons;

For laying out, opening and working on, highways, and for the election or appointment of supervisors;

Vacating roads, town plats, streets, alleys, and public squares;

Summoning and empanneling grand and petit juries, and providing for their compensation;

Regulating the election of county and township officers, and their compensation;

For the assessment and collection of taxes for State, county, township, or road purposes;

Providing for supporting common schools, and the preservation of school funds;

In relation to fees or salaries;

In relation to interest on money;

Providing for opening and conducting elections of State, county, or township officers, and designating the places of voting;

Providing for the sale of real estate belonging to minors or other persons laboring under legal disabilities, by executors, administrators, guardians, or trustees.

Sec. 23. In all the cases enumerated in the preceding section, and in all other cases where a general law can be made applicable, all laws shall be general, and of uniform operation throughout the State.

Sec. 24. Provisions may be made, by general law, for bringing suit against the State, as to all liabilities originating after the adoption of this Constitution; but no special act authorizing such suit to be brought, or making compensation to any person claiming damages against the State, shall ever be passed.

Sec. 25. A majority of all the members elected to each house, shall be necessary to pass every bill or joint resolution; and all bills and joint resolutions so passed, shall be signed by the presiding officers of the respective houses.

Sec. 26. Any member of either house shall have the right to protest, and to have his protest, with his reasons for dissent, entered on the journal.

Sec. 27. Every statute shall be a public law, unless otherwise declared in the statute itself.

Sec. 28. No act shall take effect, until the same shall have been published and circulated in the several counties of this State, by authority, except in case of emergency; which emergency shall be declared in the preamble, or in the body of the law.

Sec. 29. The members of the General Assembly shall receive for their services, a compensation, to be fixed by law; but no increase of compensation shall take effect during the session at which such increase may be made. No session of the General Assembly, except the first under this Constitution, shall extend beyond the term of sixty-one days, nor any special session beyond the term of forty days.

Sec. 30. No Senator or Representative shall, during the term for which he may have been elected, be eligible to any office, the election to which is vested in the General Assembly; nor shall he be appointed to any civil office of profit, which shall have been created, or the emoluments of which have been increased, during such term; but this latter provision shall not be construed to apply to any office elective by the people.

ARTICLE V

EXECUTIVE.

SECTION 1. The executive power of the State shall be vested in a Governor. He shall hold his office during four years, and shall not be eligible more than four years in any period of eight years.

Sec. 2. There shall be a Lieutenant-Governor, who shall hold his office during four years.

Sec. 3. The Governor and Lieutenant-Governor shall be elected at the times and places of choosing members of the General Assembly.

Sec. 4. In voting for Governor and Lieutenant-Governor the electors shall designate for whom they vote as Governor, and for whom as Lieutenant-Governor. The returns of every election for Governor and Lieutenant-Governor shall be sealed up and transmitted to the seat of Government, directed to the Speaker of the House of Representatives, who shall open and publish them in the presence of both Houses of the General Assembly.

Sec. 5. The person, respectively, having the highest number of votes for Governor and Lieutenant-Governor, shall be elected; but in case two or more persons shall have an equal, and the highest, number of votes for either office, the General Assembly shall, by joint vote, forthwith proceed to elect one of the said persons Governor or Lieutenant, as the case may be.

Sec. 6. Contested elections for Governor or Lieutenant-Governor, shall be determined by the General Assembly, in such manner as may be prescribed by law.

Sec. 7. No person shall be eligible to the office of Governor or Lieutenant-Governor, who shall not have been five years a citizen of the United States, and also a resident of the

State of Indiana during the five years next preceding his election, nor shall any person be eligible to either of the said offices, who shall not have attained the age of thirty years.

Sec. 8. No member of Congress, or person holding any office under the United States or under this State, shall fill the office of Governor or Lieutenant-Governor.

Sec. 9. The official term of the Governor and Lieutenant-Governor shall commence on the second Monday of January, in the year one thousand eight hundred and fifty-three; and on the same day every fourth year thereafter.

Sec. 10. In case of the removal of the Governor from office, or of his death, resignation, or inability to discharge the duties of the office, the same shall devolve on the Lieutenant-Governor; and the General Assembly shall, by law, provide for the case of removal from office, death, resignation, or inability, both of the Governor and Lieutenant-Governor, declaring what officer shall then act as Governor; and such officer shall act accordingly, until the disability be removed, or a Governor be elected.

Sec. 11. Whenever the Lieutenant-Governor shall act as Governor, or shall be unable to attend as President of the Senate, the Senate shall elect one of its own members as President for the occasion.

Sec. 12. The Governor shall be commander-in-chief of the military and naval forces, and may call out such forces to execute the laws, or to suppress insurrection or to repel invasion.

Sec. 13. He shall from time to time, give to the General Assembly information touching the condition of the State, and recommend such measures as he shall judge to be expedient.

Sec. 14. Every bill which shall have passed the General Assembly, shall be presented to the Governor; if he approve, he shall sign it; but if not, he shall return it, with his objections, to the house in which it shall have originated; which house shall enter the objections, at large, upon its journals, and proceed to reconsider the bill. If, after such reconsideration, a majority of all the members elected to that house, shall agree to pass the bill, it shall be sent, with the Governor's objections, to the other house, by which it shall likewise be reconsidered; and, if approved by a majority of all the members elected to that house, it shall be a law. If any bill shall not be returned by the Governor within three days, Sundays excepted, after it shall have been presented to him, it shall be a law, without his signature, unless the general adjournment shall prevent its return; in which case it shall be a law, unless the Governor, within five days next after such adjournment, shall file such bill, with his objections thereto, in the office of Secretary of State; who shall lay the same before the General Assembly, at its next session, in like manner as if it had been returned by the Governor. But no bill shall be presented to the Governor, within two days next previous to the final adjournment of the General Assembly.

Sec. 15. The Governor shall transact all necessary business with the officers of the government, and may require information, in writing, from the officers of the administrative department, upon any subject relating to the duties of their respective offices.

Sec. 16. He shall take care that the laws be faithfully executed.

Sec. 17. He shall have the power to grant reprieves, commutations, and pardons, after conviction, for all offenses, except treason and cases of impeachment, subject to such regulations as may be provided by law. Upon conviction for treason, he shall have power to suspend the execution of the sentence, until the case shall be reported to the General Assembly, at its next meeting; when the General Assembly shall either grant a pardon, commute the sentence, direct the execution of a sentence, or grant a further reprieve. He shall have power to remit fines and forfeitures, under such regulations as may be prescribed by law; and shall report to the General Assembly, at its next meeting, each case of reprieve, commutation, or pardon granted, and also the names of all persons in whose favor remission of fines and forfeitures shall have been made, and the several amounts remitted: *Provided, however,* that the General Assembly may, by law, constitute a council, to be composed of officers of State, without whose advice and consent the Governor shall not have power to grant pardons, in any case, except such as may, by law, be left to his sole power.

Sec. 18. When, during a recess of the General Assembly, a vacancy shall happen in any office, the appointment to which is vested in the General Assembly; or when, at any time, a vacancy shall have occurred in any other State office, or in the office of judge of any court; the Governor shall fill such vacancy by appointment, which shall expire when a successor shall have been elected and qualified.

Sec. 19. He shall issue writs of election, to fill such vacancies as may have occurred in the General Assembly.

Sec. 20. Should the seat of government become dangerous from disease, or a common enemy, he may convene the General Assembly at any other place.

Sec. 21. The Lieutenant Governor shall, by virtue of his office, be President of the Senate; have a right, when in committee of the whole, to join in debate, and to vote on all subjects; and, whenever the Senate shall be equally divided, he shall give the casting vote.

Sec. 22. The Governor shall, at stated times, receive for his services a compensation, which shall neither be increased nor diminished during the term for which he shall have been elected.

Sec. 23. The Lieutenant Governor, while he shall act as President of the Senate, shall receive for his services the same compensation as the Speaker of the House of Representatives; and any person acting as Governor, shall receive the compensation attached to the office of Governor.

Sec. 24. Neither the Governor nor the Lieutenant Governor shall be eligible to any other office, during the term for which he shall have been elected.

ARTICLE VI.

ADMINISTRATIVE.

SECTION 1. There shall be elected by the voters of the State an Auditor, a Treasurer of State, who shall, severally, hold their offices for two years. They shall perform such duties, as may be enjoined by law; and no person shall be eligible to either of said offices, more than four years in any period of six years.

Sec. 2. There shall be elected, in each county, by the voters thereof, at the time of holding general elections, a clerk of the circuit court, auditor, recorder, treasurer, sheriff, coroner, and surveyor. The clerk, auditor, and recorder shall continue in office four years; and no person shall be eligible to the office of clerk, recorder, or auditor, more than eight years, in any period of twelve years. The treasurer, sheirff, coroner, and surveyor, shall continue in office two years; and no person shall be eligible to the office of treasurer or sheriff more than four years in any period of six years.

Sec. 3. Such other county and township officers as may be necessary, shall be elected, or appointed, in such manner as may be prescribed by law.

Sec. 4. No person shall be elected, or appointed as a county officer, who shall not be an elector of the county; nor any one who shall not have been an inhabitant thereof during one year next preceding his appointment, if the county shall have been so long organized, but if the county shall not have been so long organized, then within the limits of the county or counties, out of which the same shall have been taken.

Sec. 5. The Governor, and the Secretary, Auditor, and Treasurer of State shall, severally, reside and keep the public records, books and papers, in any manner relating to their respective offices, at the seat of government.

Sec. 6. All county, township, and town officers shall reside within their respective counties, townships, and towns; and shall keep their respective offices at such places therein, and perform such duties, as may be directed by law.

Sec. 7. All State officers shall, for crime, incapacity, or negligence, be liable to be removed from office, either by impeachment by the House of Representatives, to be tried by the Senate, or by a joint resolution of the General Assembly; two-thirds of the members elected to each branch voting, in either case, therefor.

Sec. 8. All State, county, township, and town officers, may be impeached, or removed from office, in such manner as may be prescribed by law.

Sec. 9. Vacancies in county, township, and town offices shall be filled in such manner as may be prescribed by law.

Sec. 10. The General Assembly may confer upon the boards doing county business in the several counties, powers of a local administrative character.

ARTICLE VII.
JUDICIAL

Section 1. The Judicial power of the State shall be vested in a Supreme Court, in Circuit Courts, and in such inferior Courts as the General Assembly may establish.

Sec. 2. The Supreme Court shall consist of not less than three, nor more than five Judges; a majority of whom shall form a quorum. They shall hold their offices for six years, if they so long behave well.

Sec. 3. The State shall be divided into as many districts as there are judges of the Supreme Court; and such districts shall be formed of contiguous territory, as nearly equal in population, as, without dividing a county, the same can be made. One of said judges shall be elected from each district, and reside therein; but said judge shall be elected by the electors of the State at large.

Sec. 4. The Supreme Court shall have jurisdiction, co-extensive with the limits of the State, in appeals and writs of error, under such regulations and restrictions as may be prescribed by law. It shall also have such original jurisdiction as the General Assembly may confer.

Sec. 5. The Supreme Court shall, upon the decision of every case, give a statement in writing of each question arising in the record of such case, and the dicision of the court thereon.

Sec. 6. The General Assembly shall provide, by law, for the speedy publication of the decisions of the Supreme Court, made under this Constitution; but no judge shall be allowed to report such decisions.

Sec. 7. There shall be elected by the voters of the State, a Clerk of the Supreme Court, who shall hold his office four years, and whose duties shall be prescribed by law.

Sec. 8. The circuit courts shall each consist of one judge, and shall have such civil and criminal jurisdiction as may be prescribed by law.

Sec. 9. The State shall from time to time. be divided into judicial circuits; and a judge for each circuit shall be elected by the voters thereof. He shall reside within the circuit, and shall hold his office for the term of six years, if he so long behave well.

Sec. 10. The General Assembly may provide by law, that the judge of one circuit may hold the courts of another circuit, in cases of necessity or convenience; and in case of temporary inability of any judge, from sickness or other cause, to hold the courts in his circuit, provision may be made, by law, for holding such courts.

Sec. 11. There shall be elected in each judicial circuit, by the voters thereof, a prosecuting attorney, who shall hold his office for two years.

Sec. 12. Any judge or prosecuting attorney, who shall have been convicted of corruption or other high crime, may, on information in the name of the State, be removed from office by the Supreme Court, or in such other manner as may be prescribed by law.

Sec. 13. The judges of the Supreme Court and circuit courts shall, at stated times, receive a compensation, which shall not be diminished during their continuance in office.

Sec. 14. A conpetent number of justices of the peace shall be elected, by the voters in each township in the several counties. They shall continue in office four years, and their powers and duties shall be prescribed by law.

Sec. 15. All judicial officers shall be conservators of the peace in their respective jurisdictions.

Sec. 16. No person elected to any judicial office, shall, during the term for which he shall have been elected, be eligible to any office of trust or profit, under the State, other than a judicial office.

Sec. 17. The General Assembly may modify, or abolish, the grand jury system.

Sec. 18. All criminal prosecutions shall be carried on in the name, and by the authority of the State; and the style of all process shall be: "The State of Indiana."

Sec. 19. Tribunals of conciliation may be established, with such powers and duties as shall be prescribed by law; or the powers and duties of the same may be conferred upon other courts of justice; but such tribunals or other courts, when sitting as such, shall have no power to render judgment to be obligatory on the parties, unless they voluntarily submit their matters of difference, and agree to abide the judgment of such tribunal or court.

Sec. 20. The General Assembly, at its first session after the adoption of this Constitution, shall provide for the appointment of three commissioners, whose duty it shall be to revise, simplify, and abridge the rules, practice, pleadings, and forms of the courts of justice. And they shall provide for abolishing the distinct forms of action at law, now in use, and that justice shall be administered in a uniform mode of pleading, without distinction between law and equity. And the General Assembly may, also, make it the duty of said commissioners to reduce into a systematic code, the general statute law of the State; and said commissioners shall report the result of their labors to the General Assembly, with such recommendations and suggestions, as to abridgment and amendment, as to said commissioners, may seem necessary or proper. Provision shall be made, by law, for filling vacancies, regulating the tenure of office and the compensation of said commissioners.

Sec. 21. Every person of good moral character, being a voter, shall be entitled to admission to practice law in all courts of justice.

ARTICLE VIII.

EDUCATION.

Section 1. Knowledge and learning, generally diffused throughout a community, being essential to the preservation of a free government, it shall be the duty of the General Assembly to encourage, by all suitable means, moral intellectual, scientific, and agricultural improvement; to provide, by law, for a general and uniform system of common schools, wherein tuition shall be without charge, and equally open to all.

Sec. 2. The common school fund shall consist of the congressional township fund, and the lands belonging thereto;

The surplus revenue fund;

The saline fund and the lands belonging thereto;

The bank tax fund, and the funds arising from the one hundred and fourteenth section of the charter of the State Bank of Indiana;

The fund to be derived from the sale of county seminaries, and the moneys and property heretofore held for such seminaries; from the fines assessed for breaches of the penal laws of the State; and from all forfeitures which may accrue;

All lands and other estate which shall escheat to the State, for want of heirs or kindred entitled to the inheritance;

All lands that have been, or may hereafter be, granted to the State, where no special purpose is expressed in the grant, and the proceeds of the sales thereof; including the proceeds of the sales of the Swamp Lands, granted to the State of Indiana by the act of Congress of the 28th of September, 1850, after deducting the expenses of selecting and draining the same;

Taxes on the property of corporations, that may be assessed by the General Assembly for common school purposes.

Sec. 3. The principal of the common school fund shall remain a perpetual fund, which may be increased, but shall never be diminished; and the income thereof shall be inviolably appropriated to the support of common schools, and to no other purpose whatever.

Sec. 4. The General Assembly shall invest, in some safe and profitable manner, all such portions of the common school fund as have not heretofore been entrusted to the several counties; and shall make provision, by law, for the distribution among the several counties of the interest thereof.

Sec. 5. If any county shall fail to demand its proportion of such interest for common school purposes, the same shall be reinvested for the benefit of such county.

Sec. 6. The several counties shall be held liable for the preservation of so much of the said fund as may be intrusted to them, and for the payment of the annual interest thereon.

Sec. 7. All trust funds held by the State shall remain inviolate, and be faithfully, and exclusively applied to the purpose for which the trust was created.

Sec. 8. The General Assembly shall provide for the election, by the voters of the State, of a State Superintendent of Public Instruction, who shall hold his office for two years, and whose duties and compensation shall be prescribed by law.

ARTICLE IX.

STATE INSTITUTIONS.

SECTION 1. It shall be the duty of the General Assembly to provide by law for the support of Institututions for the education of the Deaf and Dumb, and of the Blind; and also for the treatment of the Insane.

Sec. 2. The General Assembly shall provide Houses of Refuge for the correction and reformation of juvenile offenders.

Sec. 3. The county boards shall have power to provide farms, as an asylum for those persons who, by reason of age, infirmity or other misfortune, have claims upon the sympathies and aid of society.

ARTICLE X.
FINANCE.

Section 1. The General Assembly shall provide by law for a uniform and equal rate of assessment and taxation; and shall prescribe such regulations as shall secure a just valuation for taxation of all property, both real and personal, excepting such only for municipal, educational, literary, scientific, religious or charitable purposes, as may be specially exempted by law.

Sec. 2. All the revenues derived from the sale of any of the public works belonging to the State, and from the net annual income thereof, and any surplus that may at any time remain in the treasury, derived from taxation for general State purposes, after the payment of the ordinary expenses of the government, and of the interest on bonds of the State, other than bank bonds, shall be annually applied, under the direction of the General Assembly, to the payment of the principal of the public debt.

Sec. 3. No money shall be drawn from the treasury but in pursuance of appropriations made by law.

Sec. 4. An accurate statement of the receipts and expenditures of the public money, shall be published with the laws of each regular session of the General Assembly.

Sec. 5. No law shall authorize any debt to be contracted, on behalf of the State, except in the following cases: To meet casual deficits in the revenue; to pay the interest on the State Debt; to repel invasion, suppress insurrection, or if hostilities be threatened, provide for the public defense.

Sec. 6. No county shall subscribe for stock in any incorporated company, unless the same be paid for at the time of such subscription; nor shall any county loan its credit to any incorporated company, nor borrow money for the purpose of taking stock in any such company; nor shall the General Assembly ever, on behalf of the State, assume the debts of any county, city, town, or township, nor of any corporation whatever.

ARTICLE XI.

CORPORATIONS.

SECTION 1. The General Assembly shall not have power to establish, or incorporate, any bank or banking company, or moneyed institution, for the porpose of issuing bills of credit, or bills payable to order or bearer, except under the conditions prescribed in this Constitution.

Sec. 2. No banks shall be established otherwise than under a general banking law, except as provided in the fourth section of this article.

Sec. 3. If the General Assembly shall enact a general banking law, such law shall provide for the registry and countersigning, by an officer of State, of all paper credit designed to be circulated as money; and ample collateral security, readily convertible into specie, for the redemption of the same in gold or silver, shall be required; which collateral security shall be under the control of the proper officer or officers of State.

Sec. 4. The General Assembly may also charter a bank with branches, without collateral security, as required in the preceding section.

Sec. 5. If the General Assembly shall establish a bank with branches, the branches shall be mutually responsible for each other's liabilities, upon all paper credit issued as money.

Sec. 6. The stockholders in every bank, or banking company, shall be individually responsible to an amount over and above their stock, equal to their respective shares of stock, for all debts or liabilities of said bank or banking company.

Sec. 7. All bills or notes issued as money, shall be, at all times, redeemable in gold or silver; and no law shall be passed, sanctioning, directly or indirectly, the suspension, by any bank or banking company, of specie payments.

Sec. 8. Holders of bank notes shall be entitled, in case of insolvency, to preference of payment over all other creditors.

Sec. 9. No bank shall receive, directly or indirectly, a greater rate of interest than shall be allowed, by law, to individuals loaning money.

Sec. 10. Every bank or banking company shall be required to cease all banking operations within twenty years from the time of its organization, and promptly thereafter to close its business.

Sec. 11. The General Assembly is not prohibited from investing the Trust Funds in a bank with branches; but in case of such investment, the safety of the same shall be guaranteed by unquestionable security.

Sec. 12. The State shall not be a stockholder in any bank after the expiration of the present bank charter; nor shall the credit of the State ever be given, or loaned, in aid of any person, association or corporation; nor shall the State hereafter become a stockholder in any corporation or association.

Sec. 13. Corporations, other than banking, shall not be created by special act, but may be formed under general laws.

Sec. 14. Dues from corporations, other than banking, shall be secured by such individual liability of the corporators, or other means, as may be prescribed by law.

ARTICLE XII.
MILITIA.

SECTION 1. The militia shall consist of all able-bodied white male persons, between the ages of eighteen and forty-five years, except such as may be exempted by the laws of the United States, or of this State; and shall be organized, officered, armed, equipped, and trained, in such manner as may be provided by law.

Sec. 2. The Governor shall appoint the Adjutant, Quartermaster and Commissary Generals.

Sec. 3. All militia officers shall be commissioned by the Governor, and shall hold their offices not longer than six years.

Sec. 4. The General Assembly shall determine the method of dividing the militia into divisions, brigades, regiments, batalions and companies, and fix the rank of all staff officers.

Sec. 5. The militia may be divided into classes of sedentary and active militia, in such manner as shall be prescribed by law.

Sec. 6. No person conscientiously opposed to bearing arms shall be compelled to do militia duty; but such person shall pay an equivalent for exemption; the amount to be prescribed by law.

ARTICLE XIII.

NEGROES AND MULATTOES.

Sec. 1. No Negro or Mulatto shall come into, or settle in, the State, after the adoption of this Constitution.

Sec. 2. All contracts made with any Negro or Mulatto coming into the State, contrary to the provisions of the foregoing section, shall be void; and any person who shall employ such Negro or Mulatto, or otherwise encourage him to remain in the State, shall be fined in any sum not less than ten dollars, nor more than five hundred dollars.

Sec. 3. All fines which may be collected for a violation of the provisions of this article, or of any law which may hereafter be passed for the purpose of carrying the same into execution, shall be set apart and appropriated for the colonization of such Negroes and Mulattoes, and their descendants, as may be in the State at the adoption of this Constitution, and may be willing to emigrate.

Sec. 4. The General Assembly shall pass laws to carry out the provisions of this article.

ARTICLE XIV.

BOUNDARIES

SECTION 1. In order that the boundaries of the State may be known and established, it is hereby ordained and declared, that the State of Indiana is bounded, on the east, by the meridian line which forms the western boundary of the State of Ohio; on the south, by the Ohio River, from the mouth of the Great Miami River to the mouth of the Wabash River; on the west, by a line drawn along the middle of the Wabash River, from its mouth to a point where a due north line, drawn from the town of Vincennes, would last touch the north-western shore of said Wabash River; and, thence, by a due north line, until the same shall intersect an east and west line, drawn through a point ten miles north of the southern extreme of Lake Michigan; on the north, by said east and west line, until the same shall intersect the first mentioned meridian line, which forms the western boundary of the State of Ohio.

Sec. 2. The State of Indiana shall possess jurisdiction and sovereignty co-extensive with the boundaries declared in the preceding section; and shall have concurrent jurisdiction, in civil and criminal cases, with the State of Kentucky on the Ohio River, and with the State of Illinois on the Wabash River, so far as said rivers form the common boundary between this State and said States respectively.

ARTICLE XV.

MISCELLANEOUS.

SECTION 1. All officers whose appointment is not otherwise provided for in this Constitution, shall be chosen in such manner as now is, or hereafter may be, prescribed by law.

Sec. 2. When the duration of any office is not provided for by this Constitution, it may be declared by law; and, if not so declored, such office shall be held during the pleasure of the authority making the appointment. But the General Assembly shall not create any office, the tenure of which shall be longer than four years.

Sec. 3. Whenever it is provided in this Constitution, or in any law which may be hereafter passed, that any officer other than a member of the General Assembly, shall hold his office for any given term, the same shall be construed to mean, that such officer shall hold his office for such term, and until his successor shall have been elected and qualified.

Sec. 4 Every person elected or appointed to any office under this Constitution shall, before entering on the duties thereof, take an oath or affirmation, to support the Constitution of this State, and of the United States, and also an oath of office.

Sec. 5. There shall be a seal of State kept by the Governor for official purposes, which shall be called the seal of the State of Indiana.

Sec. 6. All commissions shall issue in the name of the State, shall be signed by the Governor, sealed with the State seal, and attested by the Secretary of State.

Sec. 7. No county shall be reduced to an area less than four hundred square miles; nor shall any county under that area be further reduced.

Sec. 8. No lottery shall be authorized; nor shall the sale of lottery tickets be allowed.

Sec. 9. The following grounds, owned by the State in Indianapolis, namely: the State House Square, the Governor's

Circle, and so much of out-lot numbered one hundred and forty-seven, as lies uorth of the arm of the Central Canal, shall not be sold or leased.

Sec. 10. It shall be the duty of the General Assembly to provide for the permanent enclosure and preservation of the Tippecanoe Battle Ground.

ARTICLE XVI.

AMENDMENTS.

SECTION 1. Any amendment or amendments to this Constitution may be proposed in either branch of the General Assembly, and if the same shall be agreed to by a majority of the members elected to each of the two houses, such proposed amendment or amendments, shall with the yeas and nays thereon, be entered on their journals, and referred to the General Assembly to be chosen at the next general election; and if in the General Assembly so next chosen, such proposed amendment or amendments shall be agreed to by a majority of all the members elected to each house, then it shall be the duty of the General Assembly to submit such amendment or amendments to the electors of the State; and if a majority of said electors shall ratify the same, such amendment or amendments shall become a part of this Constitution.

Sec. 2. If two or more amendments shall be submitted at the same time, they shall be submitted in such manner that the electors shall vote for or against each of such amendments separately; and while an amendment or amendments which shall have been agreed upon by one General Assembly shall be awaiting the action of a succeeding General Assembly, or of the electors, no additional amendment or amendments shall be proposed.

SCHEDULE.

This Constitution, if adopted, shall take effect on the first day of November, in the year one thousand eight hundred and fifty-one, and shall supersede the Constitution adopted in the year one thousand eight hundred and sixteen. That no inconvenience may arise from the change in the government, it is hereby ordained as follows:—

First. All laws now in force, and not inconsistent with this

Constitution, shall remain in force, until they shall expire or be repealed.

Second. All indictments, prosecutions, suits, pleas, plaints, and other proceedings, pending in any of the Courts, shall be prosecuted to final judgment and execution; and all appeals, writs of error, certiorari, and injunctions, shall be carried on in the several Courts, in the same manner as is now provided by law.

Third. All fines, penalties, and forfeitures, due or accruing to the State, or to any county therein, shall inure to the State, or to such county, in the manner prescribed by law. All bonds executed to the State, or to any officer, in his official capacity, shall remain in force and inure to the use of those concerned.

Fourth. All acts of incorporation for municipal purposes shall continue in force under this Constitution, until such time as the General Assembly shall, in its discretion, modify or repeal the same.

Fifth. The Governor, at the expiration of the present official term, shall continue to act until his successor shall have been sworn into office.

Sixth. There shall be a session of the General Assembly, commencing on the first Monday of December, in the year one thousand eight hundred and fifty-one.

Seventh. Senators now in office and holding over, under the existing Constitution, and such as may be elected at the next general election, and the Representatives then elected, shall continue in office until the first general election under this Constitution.

Eighth. The first general election under this Constitution, shall be held in the year one thousand eight hundred and fifty-two.

Ninth. The first election for Governor, Lieutenant Governor, Judges of the Supreme Courts and Circuit Courts, Clerk of the Supreme Court, Prosecuting Attorney, Secretary, Auditor, and Treasurer of State, and State Superintendent of Public Instruction, under this Constitution, shall be held at the general election in the year one thousand eight hundred and fifty-two; and such of said officers as may be in office, when this Constitution shall go into effect, shall continue in their respective offices, until their successors shall have been elected and qualified.

Tenth. Every person elected by popular vote, and now in any office which is continued by this Constitution, and every person who shall be so elected to any such office before the taking effect of this Constitution, (except as in this Constitution otherwise provided,) shall continue in office until the term for which such person has been, or may be, elected, shall expire: *Provided,* That no such person shall continue in office after the taking effect of this Constitution, for a longer period than the term of such office in this Constitution prescribed.

Eleventh. On the taking effect of this Constitution, all officers thereby continued in office, shall, before proceeding in the further discharge of their duties, take an oath, or affirmation, to support this Constitution.

Twelfth. All vacancies that may occur in existing offices, prior to the first general election under this Constitution, shall be filled in the manner now prescribed by law.

Thirteenth. At the time of submitting this Constitution to the electors for their approval or disapproval, the article numbered thirteen, in relation to Negroes and Mulattoes, shall be submitted as a distinct proposition, in the following form: "Exclusion and Colonization of Negroes and Mulattoes," "Aye" or "No." And if a majority of the votes cast shall be in favor of said article, then the same shall form a part of this Constitution; otherwise, it shall be void. and form no part thereof.

Fourteenth. No Article or Section of this Constitution shall be submitted, as a distinct proposition, to a vote of the electors, otherwise than as herein provided.

Fifteenth. Whenever a portion of the citizens of the counties of Perry and Spencer shall deem it expedient to form, of the contiguous territory of said counties, a new county, it shall be the duty of those interested in the organization of such new county, to lay off the same by proper metes and bounds, of equal portions as nearly as practicable, not to exceed one-third of the territory of each of said counties. The proposal to create such new county shall be submitted to the voters of said counties, at a general election, in such manner as shall be prescribed by law. And if a majority of all the votes given at said election shall be in favor of the organization of said new county, it shall be the duty of the General Assembly to organize the same out of the territory thus designated.

Sixteenth. The General Assembly may alter or amend the charter of Clarksville, and make such regulations as may be necessary for carrying into effect the objects contemplated in granting the same; and the funds belonging to said town shall be applied according to the intention of the grantor.

Done in Convention, at Indianapolis, the tenth day of February, in the year of our Lord one thousand eight hundred and fifty-one; and of the Independence of the United State, the seventy-fifth.

GEORGE WHITFIELD CARR,

President, and Delegate from the County of Lawrence.

Attest: WM. H. ENGLISH,
    Principal Secretary.

GEORGE L. SITES,
HERMAN G. BARKWELL, } *Assistant Secretaries.*
ROBERT M. EVANS,

EMANCIPATION PROCLAMATION.

Whereas, On the twenty-second day of September, in the year of our Lord, one thousand eight hundred and sixty-two, a proclamation was issued by the President of the United States, containing among other things the following, to-wit:

That, on the first day of January, in the year of our Lord, one thousand eight hundred and sixty-three, all persons held as slaves within any State, or designated part of a State, the people whereof shall then be in rebellion against the United States, shall be then, henceforth and forever free, and the Executive Government of the United States, including the military and naval authorities thereof, will recognize and maintain the freedom of such persons, or any of them, in any efforts they may make for their actual freedom.

That the Executive will, on the first day of January aforesaid, by proclamation, designate the States and parts of States, if any, in which the people therein respectively shall then be in rebellion against the United States, and the fact that any State, or the people thereof, shall on that day be in good faith represented in the Congress of the United States by members chosen thereto, at elections wherein a majority of the qualified voters of such States shall have participated, shall, in the absence of strong countervailing testimony, be deemed conclusive that such State and the people thereof are not then in rebellion against the United States.

Now, therefore, I, Abraham Lincoln, President of the United States, by virtue of the power in me vested as Commander-in-Chief of the Army and Navy of the United States, in time of actual armed rebellion against the authority and Government of the United States, and as a fit necessary war measure for suppressing said rebellion, do, on this first day of January, in the year of our Lord, one thousand eight hundred and sixty-three, and in accordance with my purpose so to do, publicly proclaimed for the full period of one hundred days from the day of the first above-mentioned order, and designate, as the States and parts of States wherein the people thereof respectively are this day in rebellion againt the United States, the following to-wit: Arkansas, Texas, Louisiana, except the parishes of St. Bernard, Plaquemines, Jefferson, St. John, St. Charles, St. James, Ascension, Assumption, Terre Bonne, Lafourche, St. Mary, St. Martin and Orleans, including the city of New Orleans. Mississippi, Alabama, Florida, Georgia, South Carolina, North Carolina, and Virginia, except the forty-eight counties designated as West Virginia, and also the counties of Berkeley, Accomac, Northampton. Elizabeth City, York, Princess Ann, and Norfolk, including the cities of Norfolk and Portsmouth, and which excepted parts are, for the present, left precisely as if this proclamation were not issued.

And by virtue of the power, and for the purpose aforesaid, I do order and declare that all persons held as slaves within said designated States and parts of States are, and henceforward, shall be free; and that the Executive Government of the United States, including the military and naval authorities thereof, will recognize and maintain the freedom of said persons.

And I hereby enjoin upon the people so declared to be free to abstain from all violence, unless in necessary self-defense; and I recommend to them that, in all cases, when allowed, they labor faithfully for reasonable wages.

And I further declare and make known that such persons of suitable condition will be received into the armed service of the United States, to garrison forts, positions, stations, and other places, and to man vessels of all sorts in said service.

And upon this, sincerely believed to be an act of justice, warranted by the Constitution upon military necessity, I invoke the considerate judgment of mankind and the gracious favor of Almighty God.

In witness whereof I have hereunto set my hand and caused the seal of the United States to be affixed.

Done at the City of Washington, this first day of January, {SEAL} in the year of our Lord one thousand eight hundred and sixty-three, and of the Independence of the United States of America the eighty-seventh.

By the President: ABRAHAM LINCOLN.
WILLIAM H. SEWARD, *Secretary of State.*

POLITICAL PLATFORMS.

―――:o:―――

PLATFORM OF THE BRECKINRIDGE PARTY OF 1860.

Resolved, That the platform adopted by the Democratic party at Cincinnati be affirmed, with the following explanatory resolutions:

1. That the government of a territory organized by an act of Congress is provisional and temporary, and during its existence all citizens of the United States have an equal right to settle with their property in the territory, without their rights, either in person or property, being destroyed by congressional or territorial legislation.

2. That it is the duty of the Federal Government, in all its departments, to protect the rights of persons and property in the territories, and wherever else its constitutional authority extends.

3. That when the settlers in a territory, having an adequate population, form a State Constitution, the right of sovereignty commences, and being consummated by their admission into the Union, they stand on an equality with the people of other States, and a State thus organized ought to be admitted into the Federal Union, whether its constitution prohibits or recognizes the institution of slavery.

4. That the Democratic party are in favor of the acquisition of Cuba, on such terms as shall be honorable to ourselves and just to Spain, at the earliest practicable moment.

5. That the enactments of State Legislatures to defeat the faithful execution of the Fugitive Slave Law are hostile in character, subversive of the Constitution, and revolutionary in their effect.

6. That the Democracy of the United States recognize it as an imperative duty of the government to protect the natural-

ized citizen in all his rights, whether in home or in foreign lands, to the same extent as its native born citizens.

WHEREAS, One of the greatest necessities of the age, in a political, commercial, postal, and military point of view, is a speedy communication between the Pacific and Atlantic coasts; therefore, be it resolved,

7. That the National Democratic party do hereby pledge themselves to use every means in their power to secure the passage of some bill, to the extent of the Constitutional authority by Congress, for the construction of a railroad to the Pacific Ocean at the earliest practicable moment.

PLATFORM OF THE DOUGLAS PARTY OF 1860.

Resolved, That we, the Democracy of the Union in Convention assembled, hereby declare our affirmation of the resolutions unanimously adopted and declared as a platform of principles by the Democratic Convention at Cincinnati, in the year 1856, believing that Democratic principles are unchangable in their nature when applied to the same subject matter, and we recommend as our only further resolutions the following:

That inasmuch as differences of opinion exist in the Democratic party as to the nature and extent of the powers of a Territorial Legislature, and as to the powers and duties of Congress, under the Constitution of the United States, over the institution of slavery in the territories;

Resolved, That the Democratic party will abide by the decision of the Supreme Court of the United States over the institution of slavery in the territories.

Resolved, That it is the duty of the United States to afford ample and complete protection to all its citizens, at home or abroad, and whether native or foreign born.

Resolved, That one of the necessities of the age, in a military, commercial, and postal point of view, is a speedy communication between the Atlantic and Pacific States, and the Democratic party pledge such constitutional enactment as will insure the construction of a railroad to the Pacific coast at the earliest practical period.

Resolved, That the Democratic party are in favor of the acquisition of the Island of Cuba, on such terms as shall be honorable to ourselves and just to Spain.

Resolved, That the enactments of State Legislatures to defeat the faithful execution of the Fugitive Slave Law are hostile in character, subversive to the Constitution, and revolutionary in their effect.

Resolved, That it is in accordance with the Cincinnati Platform, that during the existence of Territorial Governments, the measure of restriction, whatever it may be, imposed by the Federal Constitution on the power of the Territorial Legislature over the subject of the domestic relations, as the same has been or shall hereafter be decided by the Supreme Court of the United States, should be respected by all good citizens, and enforced with promptness and fidelity by every branch of the General Government.

THE REPUBLICAN PLATFORM OF 1860.

Resolved, That we, the delegated representatives of the Republican electors of the United States, in Convention assembled, in the discharge of the duty we owe to our constituents and our country, unite in the following resolutions:

1. That the history of the nation during the last four years has fully established the propriety and necessity of the organization and perpetuation of the Republican party, and that the causes which called it into existence are permanent in their nature, and now, more than ever, demand its peaceful and constitutional triumph.

2. That the maintenance of the principles promulgated in the Declaration of Independence, and embodied in the Federal Constitution, that "all men are created equal; that they are endowed by their Creator with certain inalienable rights, among which are those of life, liberty and the pursuit of happiness, and that Governments are instituted among men to secure the enjoyment of these rights, deriving their just power from the consent of the governed"—are essential to the preservation of our republican institutions, and that the Federal Constitution, the rights of the States, and the union of the States, must and shall be preserved.

3. That to the union of the States this nation owes its unprecedented increase in population, its surprising developments of material resources; its rapid augmentation of wealth; its happiness at home and its honor abroad; and we hold in abhorrence all schemes for disunion, come from whatever source they may; and we congratulate the country that no Republican member of Congress has uttered or countenanced the threats of disunion as often made by the Democratic members of Congress, without rebuke and with applause from their political associates; and we denounce those threats of disunion in case of a popular overthrow of their ascendency, as denying the vital principles of a free Government, and as an avowal of contemplated treason which it is the imperative duty of an indignant people sternly to rebuke and forever silence.

4. That the maintenance inviolate, of the rights of the States, and especially of each State, to order and control its own domestic institutions according to its own judgment exclusively, is essential to that balance of power on which the perfection and endurance of our political fabric depends; and we denounce the lawless invasion by armed force of the soil of any State or Territory, no matter under what pretext, as one of the gravest of crimes.

5. That the present Democratic Administration has far exceeded our worst apprehensions in the measureless subserviency to the exactions of a sectional interest, as especially evinced in its desperate exertions to force the infamous Lecompton Constitution upon the protesting people of Kansas, construing the relation between master and servant to involve an unqualified property in persons; in its attempted enforcement every where, on land and sea, through the intervention of Congress and of the Federal Courts, of the extreme pretensions of a purely local interest; and in its general and unvarying abuse of the power entrusted to it by a confiding people.

6. That the people justly view with alarm the reckless extravagance which pervades every department of the Federal Government. That a return to right economy and accountability is indispensible to arrest the plunder of the public treasury by favored partisans, while the recent startling developments of frauds and corruption at the Federal metropolis show that an entire change of administration is imperatively demanded.

7. That the new dogma that the Constitution of its own force carries slavery into any or all the Territories of the United States, is a dangerous political heresy, at variance with the explicit provisions of that instrument itself, with cotemporaneous exposition, and with legislative and judicial precedents, that it is revolutionary in its tendency and subversive of the peace and harmony of the country.

8. That the nominal condition of all the territory of the United States is that of freedom; that as our Republican fathers, when they had abolished slavery in all our national territory, ordained that no person should be deprived of life, liberty or property without due process of law, it becomes our duty by legislation, whenever such legislation is necessary, to maintain this provision of the Constitution against all attempts to violate it; and we deny the authority of Congress, or a Territorial Legislature, or of any individual, to give legal existence to slavery in any Territory of the United States.

9. That we brand the recent re-opening of the African Slave Trade, under the cover of our national flag, aided by perversions of judicial power, as a crime against humanity, and a burning shame to our country and age; and we call upon Congress to take prompt and efficient measures for the total and final suppression of that exercrable traffic.

10. That in the recent vetoes by their Federal Governors of the acts of the Legislatures of Kansas and Nebraska, prohibiting slavery in these Territories, we find a practical illustration of the boasted Democratic principles of non-intervention and Popular Sovereignty, embodied in the Kansas-Nebraska bill, and a demonstration of the deception and fraud involved therein.

11. That Kansas should, of right, be immediately admitted as a State under the Constitution recently formed and adopted by her people, and accepted by the House of Representatives.

12. That while providing revenue for the support of the General Government, by duties upon imports, sound policy requires such an adjustment of these imports as to encourage the development of the industrial interests of the whole country, and we commend that policy of National Exchange which secures to the working men liberal wages, agriculture remunerative prices, to merchants and manufacturers an ade-

quate reward for their skill, labor and enterprise, and to the nation commercial prosperity and independence.

13. That we protest against any sale or alienation to others of the public lands held by actual settlers, and against any view of the free homestead policy, which regards the settlers as paupers or suppliants for public bounty, and we demand the passage by Congress of the complete and satisfactory homestead measure which has already passed the House.

14. That the National Republican party is opposed to any change in our naturalization laws, or any State Legislation, by which the rights of citizenship hitherto accorded to immigrants from foreign lands shall be abridged or impaired, and in favor of giving a full and efficient protection to the rights of all classes of citizens, whether native or naturalized, both at home and abroad.

15. That appropriations by Congress for river and harbor improvements of a national character, is required for the accommodation and security of an existing commerce, or authorized by the Constitution and justified by the obligation of the Government to protect the lives and property of its citizens.

16. That a railroad to the Pacific ocean is imperatively demanded by the interests of the whole country; and that the Federal Government ought to render immediate and efficient aid in its construction, and that preliminary thereto, a daily overland mail should be promptly established.

17. Finally, having thus set forth our distinctive principles and views, we invite the co-operation of all citizens, however differing in other questions, who substantially agree with us, in their affirmance and support.

PLATFORM OF THE NATIONAL CONSTITUTIONAL PARTY OF 1860.

The Union, the Constitution and the Laws.

UNION PLATFORM, ADOPTED AT BALTIMORE, JUNE 8, 1864.

Resolved, That it is the highest duty of every American citizen to maintain against all its enemies, the integrity of the Union, and the paramount authority of the Constitution and laws of the United States, and that, laying all political opinions aside, we pledge ourselves, as Union men, animated by a common sentiment, and aiming at a common object, to do everything in our power to aid the Government in quelling, by force of arms, the rebellion now raging against its authority, and bringing to the punishment due to their crimes, the rebels and traitors arrayed against it.

Resolved, That we approve the determination of the Government of the United States not to compromise with rebels or to offer any terms of peace, except such as may be based upon an unconditional surrender of their hostility, &c., and a return to their just allegiance to the Constitution and laws of the United States, and that we call upon the Government to maintain this position, and to prosecute the war with the utmost possible vigor to the complete suppression of the rebellion, in full reliance upon the self-sacrifices, the patriotism, the heroic valor, and the undying devotion of the American people to their country and its free institutions.

Resolved, That slavery was the cause, and now constitutes the strength of the rebellion. and that as it must be always and everywhere hostile to the principles of Republican Governments, justice and the national safety demand its utter and complete extirpation from the soil of the Republic, and that we uphold and maintain the acts and proclamations by which the Government, in its own defence, has aimed a death blow at this gigantic evil. We are in favor, furthermore, of such an amendment to the Constitution, to be made by the people in conformity with its provisions, as shall terminate and forever prohibit the existence of slavery within the limits of the jurisdiction of the United States.

Resolved, That the thanks of the American people are due to the soldiers and sailors of the army and navy, who have periled their lives in defence of their country, and in vindication of the honor of the flag; that the nation owes them some permanent recognition of their patriotism and their valor, and ample and permanent provision for those of their survivors who have received disabling and honorable wounds in the service of their country, and that the memories of those who have fallen in its defense, shall be held in grateful and everlasting remembrance.

Resolved, That we approve and applaud the political wisdom, the unselfish patriotism and unswerving fidelity to the Constitution and the principles of American liberty with which Abraham Lincoln has discharged, under circumstances of unparalelled difficuly, the great duties and responsibilities of the Presidential office; that we approve and endorse, as demanded by the emergency and essential to the preservation of the nation, and as within the Constitution, the measures and acts which he has adopted to defend the nation against its open and secret foes; especially the Proclamation of Emancipation, and the employment, as Union soldiers, of men heretofore held in slavery, and that we have full confidence in his determination to carry these and all other Constitutional measures, essential to the salvation of the country, into full and complete effect.

Resolved, That we deem it essential to the general welfare, that harmony should prevail in the national councils, and we regard as worthy of public confidence and official trust those only who cordially endorse the principles proclaimed in these resolutions, and which should characterize the administration of the Government.

Resolved, That the Government owes to all men employed in its armies, without distinction of color, the full protection of the laws of war, and any violation of these laws and of the usages of civilized nations in the time of war, by the rebels now in arms, should be made the subject of full and prompt redress.

Resolved, That the foreign immigration, which in the past has added so much to the wealth and development of resources and increase of power to this nation, the asylum of the oppressed of all nations, should be fostered and encouraged by a liberal and just policy.

Resolved, That we are in favor of the speedy construction of the railroad to the Pacific.

Resolved, That the national faith is pledged for the redemption of the public debt and must be kept inviolate; and that for this purpose we recommend economy and rigid responsibilities in the public expenditures, and a vigorous and just system of taxation; that it is the duty of every loyal State to sustain the use of the national currency.

Resolved, That we approve the position taken by the Government, that the people of the United States can never regard with indifference the attempt of European power to overthrow by force, or to supplant by fraud, the institutions of any Republican government on the Western Continent, and that they will view with extreme jealousy, as menacing to the peace and independence of this our country, the efforts of any such power to obtain new footholds for monarchial governments sustained by a foreign military force in near proximity to the United States.

FREMONT PLATFORM, ADOPTED AT CLEVELAND, MAY 31, 1864.

1. That the Federal Union must be preserved.

2. That the Constitution and laws of the United States must be observed and obeyed.

3. That the rebellion must be suppressed by the force of arms, and without compromise.

4. That the rights of Free Speech, Free Press, and the Habeas Corpus must be held inviolate, save in districts where martial law has been proclaimed.

5. That the rebellion has destroyed slavery, and the Federal Constitution should be amended to prohibit its re-establishment.

6. That the right for asylum, except for crime, and subject to law, is a recognized principle—a principle of American liberty; that any violation of it must not be overlooked, and must not go unrebuked.

7. That the National policy known as the Monroe doctrine has become a recognized principle, and that the establishment of an anti-republican form of government on this continent by a foreign power can not be tolerated.

8. That the gratitude and support of the nation is due to the faithful soldiers, and the earnest leaders of the Union army and navy, for their heroic achievements and valor in defense of our imperiled country and of civil liberty.

9. That the one term policy for the Presidency adopted by

the people is strengthened by the existing crisis, and shall be maintained by constitutional amendments.

10. That the Constitution shall be so amended that the President and Vice President shall be elected by a direct vote of the people.

11. That the reconstruction of the rebellious States belongs to the people through their representatives in Congress, and not to the Executive.

12. That the confiscation of the lands of the rebels and their distribution among the soldiers and actual settlers is a measure of justice; that integrity and economy are demanded at all times in the measures of the government, and that now the want of this is criminal.

NATIONAL DEMOCRATIC PLATFORM OF 1864.

Resolved, That in the future, as in the past, we will adhere with unswerving fidelity to the Union under the Constitution as the only solid foundation of our strength, security and happiness as a people, and as a framework of government equally conducive to the welfare and prosperity of all the States, both Northern and Southern.

Resolved, That this Convention does explicitly declare, as the sense of the American people, that after four years of failure to restore the Union by experiment of war, during which, under the pretence of military necessity or war power higher than the Constitution, the Constitution itself has been disregarded in every part, and public liberty and private right alike trodden down, and the material prosperity of the country essentially impaired, justice, humanity, liberty and the public welfare demand that immediate efforts be made for a cessation of hostilities with a view to an ultimate convention of the States, or other peaceable means, to the end that at the earliest practical moment peace may be restored on the basis of the Federal Union of the States.

Resolved, That the direct interference of the military authorities of the United States in the recent elections held in Kentucky, Maryland, Missouri and Delaware was a shameful violation of the Constitution, and a repetition of such acts in the approaching election will be held as revolutionary, and resisted with all the means and power under our control.

Resolved, That the aim and object of the Democratic party is to preserve the Federal Union and the rights of the States unimpaired, and they hereby declare that they consider that the administrative usurpation of extraordinary and dangerous powers not granted by the Constitution, the subversion of the civil by military law in States not in insurrection, the arbitrary military arrest, imprisonment, trial and sentence of American citizens in States where the civil law exists in full force, the suppression of freedom of speech and of the press, the denial of the right of asylum, the open and avowed right of disregard of State rights, the employment of unusual test oaths, and the interference with, and denial of the right of the people to bear arms in their defense, is calculated to prevent a restoration of the Union and a perpetuation of the Government deriving its just powers from the consent of the governed.

Resolved, That the shameful disregard of the Administration to its duty in respect to our fellow-citizens who now are, and long have been, prisoners of war in a suffering condition, deserves the severest reprobation on the score alike of public policy and common humanity.

Resolved, That the sympathy of the Democratic party is heartily and earnestly extended to the soldiery of our army and sailors of our navy who are and have been in the field and on the sea, under the flag of their country, and in the event of its attaining power, they will receive all the care, protection and regard that the brave soldiers and sailors of the Republic have so nobly earned.

THE CHICAGO PLATFORM, 1868.

The following is the platform as adopted:

The National Republican Party of the United States, assembled in National Convention, in the city of Chicago, on the 20th day of May, 1868, make the following declaration of principles:

1. We congratulate the country on the assured success of

the reconstruction policy of Congress, as evinced by the adoption, in the majority of the States lately in rebellion, of constitutions securing equal civil and political rights to all; and it is the duty of the Government to sustain those constitutions and to prevent the people of such States from being remitted to a state of anarchy.

2. The guarantee by Congress of equal suffrage to all loyal men at the South was demanded by every consideration of public safety, of gratitude, and of justice, and must be maintained, while the question of suffrage in all the loyal States properly belongs to the people of those States.

3. We denounce all forms of repudiation as a national crime, and the national honor requires the payment of the public indebtedness in the utmost good faith to all creditors at home and abroad, not only according to the letter but the spirit of the laws under which it was contracted.

4. It is due to the labor of the nation that taxation should be equalized and reduced as rapidly as the national faith will permit.

5. The national debt, contracted as it has been for the preservation of the Union for all time to come, should be extended over a fair period for redemption; and it is the duty of Congress to reduce the rate of interest thereon whenever it can be honestly done.

6. That the best policy to diminish our burden of debt is to so improve our credit that capitalists will seek to loan us money at lower rates of interest than we now pay, and must continue to pay, so long as repudiation, partial or total, open or covert, is threatened or suspected.

7. The Government of the United States should be administered with the strictest economy, and the corruptions which have been so shamefully nursed and fostered by ANDREW JOHNSON call loudly for radical reform.

8. We professedly deplore the untimely and tragic death of ABRAHAM LINCOLN, and regret the accession of ANDREW JOHNSON to the Presidency, who has acted treacherously to the people who elected him, and the cause he was pledged to support—who has usurped high legislative and judicial functions—who has refused to execute the laws—who has used his high office to induce other officers to ignore and violate the laws—who has employed his executive powers to render inse-

cure the property, the peace, liberty, and life of the citizen—who has abused the pardoning power—who has denounced the National Legislature as unconstitutional—persistently and corruptly resisted, by every measure in his power, every proper attempt at the reconstruction of the States lately in rebellion—who has perverted the public patronage into an engine of wholesale corruption, and who has been justly impeached for high crimes and misdemeanors, and properly pronounced guilty thereof by the vote of thirty-five Senators.

9. The doctrine of Great Britain and other European Powers, that because a man is once a subject he is always so, must be resisted at every hazard by the United States as a relic of the feudal times, not authorized by the law of nations, and at war with our national honor and independence. Naturalized citizens are entitled to be protected in all their rights of citizenship as though they were native born; and no citizen of the United States, native or naturalized, must be liable to arrest and imprisonment by any foreign power for acts done or words spoken in this country; and if so arrested and imprisoned it is the duty of the Government to interfere in his behalf.

10. Of all who were faithful in the trials of the late war there were none entitled to more especial honor than the brave soldiers and seamen who endured the hardships of campaign and cruise, and imperiled their lives in the service of the country. The bounties and pensions provided by the laws for these brave defenders of the nation are obligations never to be forgotten. The widows and orphans of the gallant dead are the wards of the people, a sacred legacy bequeathed to the nation's protecting care.

11. Foreign emigration, which in the past has added so much to the wealth, development, and resources and increase of power to this nation, the asylum of the oppressed of all nations, should be fostered and encouraged by a liberal and just policy.

12. This Convention declares itself in sympathy with all the oppressed people which are struggling for their rights.

The following resolutions were also adopted unanimously, and are added to the declaration of principles:

Resolved, That we highly commend the spirit of magnanimity and forgiveness with which the men who have served in the rebellion, but now frankly and honestly co-operate with us in restoring the peace of the country and reconstructing the Southern State governments upon the basis of impartial justice and equal rights, are received back into the communion of the loyal people. And we favor the removal of the disqualifications and restrictions placed upon the late rebels in the same measure as the spirit of loyalty will direct, and as may be consistent with the safety of the loyal people.

Resolved, That we recognize the great principles laid down in the immortal Declaration of Independence as the true foundation of Democratic government; and we hail with gladness every effort toward making these principles a living reality on every inch of American soil.

DEMOCRATIC PLATFORM OF 1868.

The Democratic party, in National Convention assembled, reposing its trust in the intelligence, patriotism, and discriminating justice of the people, standing upon the Constitution as the foundation and limitation of the powers of the Government and the guarantee of the liberties of the citizen, and recognizing the questions of slavery and secession as having been settled for all time to come by the war or the voluntary action of the Southern States in Constitutional Conventions assembled, and never to be revived or re-agitated, do, with the return of peace, demand:

1. The immediate restoration of all the States to their rights in the Union under the Constitution of the civil Government and in the American people.

2. Amnesty for all past political offenses; the regulation of the elective franchise in the States by their citizens.

3. Payment of the public debt of the United States as rapidly as practicable, all money drawn from the people by taxation, except so much as is requisite for the necessities of the Government economically administered being honestly applied to such payment, and where the obligations of the Government do not expressly state upon their face or the law under which they were issued does not provide that they shall be paid in coin they ought, in right and justice, be paid in the lawful money of the United States.

4. Equal taxation of every species of property according to the value; reducing Government bonds and other public securities.

5. One currency for the Government and the people, the laborer and the office-holder, pensioner and the soldier, the producer and the bondholder.

6. Economy in the administration of the Government; the reduction of the standing army and navy; the abolition of the Freedmen's Bureau, and all political instrumentalities designed to secure negro supremacy; simplification of the system and discontinuance of inquisitorial modes of assessing and collecting internal revenue, that the burden of taxation may be equalized and lessened, and the credit of the Government and the currency made good; the repeal of all enactments for enrolling the State militia into a national force in time of peace; and a tariff for revenue upon foreign imports and such equal taxation under the internal revenue laws as will afford incidental protection to domestic manufactures as well, without impairing the revenue, impose the least burden upon and best promote and encourage the great industrial interests of the country.

7. Reform of abuses in the Administration; the expulsion of corrupt men from office; the abrogation of useless offices; the restoration of the rightful authority to and the independence of the Executive and Judicial Departments of the Government; the subordination of the military to the civil power, to the end that the usurpation of Congress and the despotism of the sword may cease.

8. Equal rights and protection for naturalized and native born citizens at home and abroad; the assertion of American nationality, which will command the respect of foreign powers furnish an example and encouragement to people struggling for national integrity, constitutional liberty, and individual rights; and the maintenance of the rights of naturalized citizens against the absolute doctrine of immutable allegiance and the claims of foreign powers to punish them for alleged crimes committed beyond their jurisdiction. In demanding these measures and reforms, we arraign the radical party for its disregard of right and the unparalleled oppression and tyranny which have marked its career, after the most solemn and unanimous pledge of both houses of Congress to prose-

cute the war exclusively for the maintenance of the Government and the preservation of the Union under the Constitution. It has repeatedly violated that most sacred pledge under which was rallied that noble volunteer army which carried our flag to victory. Instead of restoring the Union it has, so far as it is in its power, dissolved it, and subjected ten States in time of peace to military despotism and negro supremacy. It has nullified there the right of trial by jury; it has abolished the writ of habeas corpus, that most sacred writ of liberty; it has overthrown the freedom of speech and of the press; it has substituted arbitrary seizures and arrests, military trials, secret star chambers, and inquisitions for constitutional tribunals; it has disregarded, in time of peace, the right of the people to be free from search and seizure; it has entered the post-office and telegraph office, and even the private rooms of individuals and seized there their private papers and letters, without any specification or notice of affidavit, as required by the organic law. It has converted the American Capitol into a bastile; it has established a system of spies and official espionage to which the constitutional monarchies of Europe never dare to resort. It has abolished the right of appeal on important constitutional questions to the supreme judicial tribunals, and threatens to curtail or destroy its original jurisdiction, which is irrevocably vested by the Constitution; while the learned Chief Justice has been subjected to the most atrocious calumnies merely because he would not prostitute his high office to the support of the false and partisan charges against the President. Its corruption and extravagance have exceeded anything known in history, and by its frauds and monopolies it has nearly doubled the burden of the debt created during the war. It has stripped the President of his Constitutional power of appointment even of his own Cabinet. Under its repeated assaults the pillars of the Government are rocking to their base; and should it succeed in November next, and inaugurate its President, we will meet as a subjected and conquered people amid the ruins of liberty and the scattered fragments of the Constitution; and we do declare and resolve that ever since the people of the United States threw off all subjection to the British crown, the privilege and trust of suffrage have belonged to the several States, and have been granted, regulated, and controlled exclusively by the political power of each State respectively, and any attempt by Congress, on any pretext whatever, to deprive any State of this right, or interfere with this exercise, is a flagrant usurpation of power which can find no warrant in the Constitution, and if sanctioned by the people will subvert our form of Government, and can only end in a single, centralized and consolidated Government, in which the separate existence of the States will be entirely absorbed, and an unqualified despotism then be established in place of a Federal Union of coequal States, and that we regard the reconstruction acts so called of Congress such usurpations and unconstitutional, revolutionary and void; that our soldiers and sailors who carried the flag of our country to victory against a most gallant and determined foe must ever be gratefully remembered, and all the guarantees given in their favor must be faithfully carried into execution; that the public lands should be distributed widely among the people and should be disposed of either under the pre-emption of the homestead lands and sold in reasonable quantities, and to none but actual occupants, at the price established by the Government. When the grants of the public lands may be allowed necessary for the encouragement of important public improvements, the proceeds of the sale of such lands, and not the lands themselves, should be so applied; that the President of the United States, Andrew Johnson, exercising the power of his high office in resisting the aggressions of Congress on the constitutional rights of the States and the people, is entitled to the gratitude of the whole American people, and on behalf of the Democratic party, we tender him our thanks for his patriotic efforts in that regard.

Upon this platform the Democratic party appeal to every patriot, including all the conservative element, and all who desire to support the Constitution and restore the Union, forgetting all past differences of opinion, to unite with us in the present great struggle for the liberties of the people; and that to all such, to whatever party they may have heretofore belonged, we extend the right hand of fellowship, and hail all such co-operating with us as friends and brothers.

REPUBLICAN PLATFORM, 1872.

The Republican party of the United States, assembled in national convention in the city of Philadelphia on the 5th and 6th days of June, 1872, again declares its faith, appeals to its history, and announces its position upon the questions before the country:

1. During eleven years of supremacy it has accepted with grand courage the solemn duties of the time. It suppressed a gigantic rebellion, emancipated four millions of slaves, decreed the equal citizenship of all, and established universal suffrage. Exhibiting unparalelled magnanimity, it criminally punished no man for political offenses, and warmly welcomed all who proved loyalty by obeying the laws and dealing justly with their neighbors. It has steadily decreased with firm hand the resultant disorders of a great war, and initiated a wise and humane policy toward the Indians. The Pacific railroad and similar vast enterprises have been generously aided and successfully conducted, the public lands freely given to actual settlers, immigration protected and encouraged, and a full acknowledgement of the naturalized citizen's rights secured from European Powers. A uniform national currency has been provided, repudiation frowned down, the national credit sustained under the most extraordinary burdens, and new bonds negotiated at lower rates. The revenues have been carefully collected and honestly applied. Despite annual large reductions of the rates of taxation, the public debt has been reduced during General Grant's Presidency at the rate of a hundred millions a year, great financial crises have been avoided, and peace and plenty prevail throughout the land. Menacing foreign difficulties have been peacefully and honorably composed, and the honor and power of the nation kept in high respect throughout the world. This glorious record of the past is the party's best pledge for the future. We believe the people will not intrust the Government to any party or combination of men composed chiefly of those who have resisted every step of this benificent progress.

2. The recent amendments to the national Constitution should be cordially sustained because they are right, not

merely tolerated because they are law, and should be carried out according to their spirit by appropriate legislation, the enforcement of which can safely be intrusted only to the party that secured those amendments.

3. Complete liberty and exact equality in the enjoyment of all civil, political and public rights should be established and effectually maintained throughout the Union by efficient and appropriate State and Federal legislation. Neither the law nor its administration should admit any discrimination in respect of citizens by reason of race, creed, color, or previous condition of servitude.

4. The national Government should seek to maintain honorable peace with all nations, protecting its citizens everywhere and sympathizing with all peoples who strive for greater liberty.

5. Any system of the civil service under which the subordinate positions of the government are considered rewards for mere party zeal is fatally demoralizing, and we therefore favor a reform of the system by laws which shall abolish the evils of patronage and make honesty, efficiency, and fidelity the essential qualifications for public positions, without creating a life tenure of office.

6. We are opposed to further grants of the public lands to corporations and monopolies, and demand that the national domain be set apart for free homes for the people.

7. The annual revenue, after paying current expenditures, pensions, and the interest on the public debt, should furnish a moderate balance for the reduction of the principal, and that revenue, except so much as may be derived from a tax upon tobacco and liquors, should be raised by duties upon importations, the details of which should be so adjusted as to aid in securing remunerative wages to labor, and promote the industries, prosperity, and growth of the whole country.

8. We hold in undying honor the soldiers and sailors whose valor saved the Union. Their pensions are a sacred debt of the nation, and the widows and orphans of those who died for their country are entitled to the care of a generous and grateful people. We favor such additional legislation as will extend the bounty of the Government to all our soldiers and

sailors who were honorably discharged, and who in the line of duty became disabled, without regard to the length of service or the cause of such discharge.

9. The doctrine of Great Britain and other European Powers concerning allegiance—"once a subject always a subject"—having at last through the efforts of the Republican party been abandoned, and the American idea of the individual's right to transfer allegiance having been accepted by European nations, it is the duty of our Government to guard with jealous care the rights of adopted citizens against the assumption of unauthorized claims by their former Governments, and we urge continued careful encouragement and protection of voluntary immigration.

10. The franking privilege ought to be abolished, and the way prepared for a speedy reduction in the rates of postage.

11 Among the questions which press for attention is that which concerns the relations of capital and labor, and the Republican party recognizes the duty of so shaping legislation as to secure full protection and the amplest field for capital, and for labor, the creator of capital, the largest opportunities and a just share of the mutual profits of these two great servants of civilization.

12. We hold that Congress and the President have only fulfilled an imperative duty in their measures for the suppression of violent and treasonable organizations in certain lately rebellious regions, and for the protection of the ballot-box; and therefore they are entitled to the thanks of the nation.

13. We denounce repudiation of the public debt, in any form or disguise as a national crime. We witness with pride the reduction of the principal of the debt, and the rates of interest upon the balance, and confidently expect that our excellent national currency will be perfected by a speedy resumption of specie payment.

14. The Republican party is mindful of its obligations to the loyal women of America for their noble devotion to the cause of freedom. Their admission to wider fields of usefulness is viewed with satisfaction; and the honest demand of

any class of citizens for additional rights should be treated with respectful consideration.

15. We heartily approve the action of Congress in extending amnesty to those lately in rebellion, and rejoice in the growth of peace and fraternal feeling throughout the land.

16. The Republican party proposes to respect the rights reserved by the people to themselves as carefully as the powers delegated by them to the State and to the Federal Government. It disapproves of the resort to unconstitutional laws for the purpose of removing evils, by interference with rights not surrendered by the people to either the State or national Government.

17. It is the duty of the General Government to adopt such measures as may tend to encourage and restore American commerce and ship-building.

18. We believe that the modest patriotism, the earnest purpose, the sound judgment, the practical wisdom, the incorruptible integrity, and the illustrious services of Ulysses S. Grant have commended him to the heart of the American people, and with him at our head we start to day upon a new march to victory.

19. Henry Wilson, nominated for the Vice-Presidency. known to the whole land from the early days of the great struggle for liberty as an indefatigable laborer in all campaigns, an incorruptible legislator and representative man of American institutions, is worthy to associate with our great leader and share the honors which we pledge our best efforts to bestow upon them.

NATIONAL LIBERAL REPUBLICAN CONVENTION, 1872.

ADDRESS TO THE PEOPLE OF THE UNITED STATES.

The Administration now in power has rendered itself guilty of wanton disregard of the laws of the land, and of usurping powers not granted by the Constitution; it has acted as if the laws had binding force only for those who are governed, and not for those who govern. It has thus struck a blow at the fundamental principles of constitutional government and the liberties of the citizen.

The President of the United States has openly used the powers and opportunities of his high office for the promotion of personal ends.

He has kept notoriously corrupt and unworthy men in places of power and responsibility, to the detriment of the public interest.

He has used the public service of the Government as a machinery of corruption and personal influence, and has interfered with tyrannical arrogance in the political affairs of States and municipalities.

He has rewarded with influential and lucrative offices men who had acquired his favor by valuable presents, thus stimulating the demoralization of our political life by his conspicuous example.

He has shown himself deplorably unequal to the task imposed upon him by the necessities of the country, and culpably careless of the responsibilities of his high office.

The partizans of the Administration, assuming to be the Republican party and controlling its organization, have attempted to justify such wrongs and palliate such abuses to the end of maintaining partisan ascendency.

They have stood in the way of necessary investigations and indispensable reforms, pretending that no serious fault could be found with the present administration of public affairs, thus seeking to blind the eyes of the people.

They have kept alive the passions and resentment of the late civil war, to use them for their own advantage, they have resorted to arbitrary measures in direct conflict with the organic law, instead of appealing to the better instincts and latent patriotism of the Southern people by restoring to them these rights, the enjoyment of which is indispensable to a successful administration of their local affairs, and would tend to revive a patriotic and hopeful national feeling.

They have degraded themselves and the name of their party, once justly entitled to the confidence of the nation, by a base sycophancy to the dispenser of executive power and patronage, unworthy of republican freemen; they have sought to silence the voice of just criticism, and stifle the moral sense of the people, and to subjugate public opinion by tyrannical party discipline.

They are striving to maintain themselves in authority for

selfish ends by an unscrupulous use of the power which rightfully belongs to the people, and should be employed only in the service of the country.

Believing that an organization thus led and controlled can no longer be of service to the best interests of the Republic, we have resolved to make an independent appeal to the sober judgment, conscience, and patriotism of the American people.

RESOLUTIONS.

We, the Liberal Republicans of the United States, in National Convention assembled at Cincinnati, proclaim the following principles as essential to just government:

1. We recognize the equality of all men before the law, and hold that it is the duty of government, in its dealings with the people, to mete out equal and exact justice to all, of whatever nativity, race, color, or persuasion, religious or political.

2. We pledge ourselves to maintain the Union of these States, emancipation and enfranchisement, and to oppose any re-opening of the questions settled by the thirteenth, fourteenth, and fifteenth amendments of the Constitution.

3. We demand the immediate and absolute removal of all disabilities imposed on account of the rebellion, which was finally subdued seven years ago, believing that universal amnesty will result in complete pacification in all sections of the country.

4. Local self-government, with impartial suffrage, will guard the rights of all citizens more securely than any centralized power. The public welfare requires the supremacy of the civil over the military authority, and the freedom of person under the protection of the *habeas corpus*. We demand for the individual the largest liberty consistent with public order, for the State self-government, and for the nation a return to the methods of peace and the constitutional limitations of power.

5. The civil service of the Government has become a mere instrument of partisan tyranny and personal ambition, and an object of selfish greed. It is a scandal and reproach upon free institutions, and breeds a demoralization dangerous to the perpetuity of republican government. We therefore regard a thorough reform of the civil service as one of the most pressing necessities of the hour; that honesty, capacity, and fidelity

constitute the only valid claims to public employment; that the offices of the Government cease to be a matter of arbitrary favoritism and patronage, and that public station shall become again a post of honor. To this end it is imperatively required that no President shall be a candidate for re election.

6. We demand a system of Federal taxation which shall not unnecessarily interfere with the industry of the people, and which shall provide the means necessary to pay the expenses of the Government, economically administered, the pensions, the interest on the public debt, and a moderate reduction annually of the principal thereof; and recognizing that there are in our midst honest but irreconcilable differences of opinion with regard to the respective systems of protection and free trade, we remit the discussion of the subject to the people in their congressional districts and the decision of Congress thereon, wholly free from executive interference or dictation.

7. The public credit must be sacredly maintained, and we denounce repudiation in every form and guise.

8. A speedy return to specie payments is demanded alike by the highest considerations of commercial morality and honest government.

9. We remember with gratitude the heroism and sacrifices of the soldiers and sailors of the Republic, and no act of ours shall ever detract from their justly earned fame or the full rewards of their patriotism.

10. We are opposed to all further grants of lands to railroads or other corporations. The public domain should be held sacred to actual settlers.

11. We hold that is the duty of the Government in its intercourse with foreign nations to cultivate the friendships of peace by treating with all on fair and equal terms, regarding it alike dishonorable either to demand what is not right or submit to what is wrong.

12. For the promotion and success of these vital principles and the support of the candidates nominated by this convention we invite and cordially welcome the co-operation of all patriotic citizens, without regard to previous political affiliations.

NATIONAL DEMOCRATIC CONVENTION, 1872.

We, the Democratic electors of the United States in Convention assembled, do present the following principles, already adopted at Cincinnati, as essential to just government.

1. We recognize the equality of all men before the law, and hold that it is the duty of Government in its dealings with the people to mete out equal and exact justice to all, of whatever nativity, race, color, or persuasion, religious or political.

2. We pledge ourselves to maintain the union of these States, emancipation, and enfranchisement, and to oppose any re-opening of the questions settled by the thirteenth, fourteenth and fifteenth amendments to the Constitution.

3. We demand the immediate and absolute removal of all disabilities imposed on account of the rebellion, which was finally subdued seven years ago, believing that universal amnesty will result in complete pacification in all sections of the country.

4. Local self-government, with impartial suffrage, will guard the rights of all citizens more securely than any centralized power. The public welfare requires the supremacy of the civil over the military authority, and freedom of person under the protection of the *habeas corpus*. We demand for the individual the largest liberty consistent with public order; for the State self-government, and for the nation a return to the methods of peace and the constitutional limitations of power.

5. The civil service of the Government has become a mere instrument of partisan tyranny and personal ambition, and an object of selfish greed. It is a scandal and reproach upon free institutions and breeds a demoralization dangerous to the perpetuity of republican government. We therefore regard a thorough reform of the civil service as one of the most pressing necessities of the hour; that honesty, capacity, and fidelity constitute the only valid claim to public employment; that the offices of the government cease to be a matter of arbitrary favoritism and patronage, and that public station become again a post of honor. To this end it is imperatively required that no President shall be a candidate for re-election.

6. We demand a system of Federal taxation which shall not unnecessarily interfere with the industry of the people, and which shall provide the means necessary to pay the expenses of the Government, economically administered, the pensions, the interest on the public debt, and a moderate reduction annually of the principal thereof; and recognizing that there are in our midst honest but irreconcilable differences of opinion with regard to the respective systems of protection and free trade, we remit the discussion of the subject to the people in their Congressional districts, and to the decision of the Congress thereon, wholly free from executive interference or dictation.

7. The public credit must be sacredly maintained, and we denounce repudiation in every form and guise.

8. A speedy return to specie payment is demanded alike by the highest considerations of commercial morality and honest government.

9. We remember with gratitude the heroism and sacrifices of the soldiers and sailors of the Republic, and no act of ours shall ever detract from their justly earned fame for the full reward of their patriotism.

10. We are opposed to all further grants of lands to railroads or other corporations. The public domain should be held sacred to actual settlers.

11. We hold that it is the duty of the Government in its intercourse with foreign nations to cultivate the friendships of peace, by treating with all on fair and equal terms, regarding it alike dishonorable either to demand what is not right or to submit to what is wrong.

12. For the promotion and success of these vital principles, and the support of the candidates nominated by this convention, we invite and cordially welcome the co-operation of all patriotic citizens, without regard to previous political affiliations.

NATIONAL LABOR REFORM CONVENTION, 1872.

We hold that all political power is inherent in the people, and free government founded on their authority and established for their benefit; that all citizens are equal in political rights, entitled to the largest religious and political liberty compatible with the good order of society, as also the use and enjoyment of the fruits of their labor and talents; and no man or set of men is entitled to exclusive separable endowments and privileges, or immunities from the Government, but in consideration of public services; and any laws destructive of these fundamental principles are without moral binding force, and should be repealed. And believing that all the evils resulting from unjust legislation now affecting the industrial classes can be removed by the adoption of the principle contained in the following declaration: Therefore,

Resolved, That it is the duty of the Government to establish a just standard of distribution of capital and labor by providing a purely national circulating medium, based on the faith and resources of the nation, issued directly to the people without the intervention of any system of banking corporations, which money shall be legal tender in the payment of all debts, public and private, and interchangeable at the option of the holder for Government bonds bearing a rate of interest not to exceed 3-65 per cent., subject to future legislation by Congress.

2. That the national debt should be paid in good faith, according to the original contract, at the earliest option of the Government, without mortgaging the property of the people or the future exigencies of labor to enrich a few capitalists at home and abroad.

3. That justice demands that the burden of Government should be so adjusted as to bear equally on all classes, and that the exemption from taxation of Government bonds bearing extravagant rates of interest is a violation of all just principles of revenue laws.

4. That the public lands of the United States belong to the people and should not be sold to individuals nor granted to corporations, but should be held as a sacred trust for the benefit of the people, and should be granted to landless settlers only, in amounts not exceeding one hundred and sixty acres of land.

5. That Congress should modify the tariff so as to admit free such articles of common use as we can neither produce nor grow, and lay duties for revenue mainly upon articles of luxury and upon such articles of manufacture as will, we hav-

ing the raw materials, assist in further developing the resources of the country.

6. That the presence in our country of Chinese laborers, imported by capitalists in large numbers for servile use, is an evil, entailing want and its attendant train of misery and crime on all classes of the American people, and should be prohibited by legislation.

7. That we ask for the enactment of a law by which all mechanics and day-laborers employed by or on behalf of the Government, whether directly or indirectly, through persons, firms, or corporations, contracting with the State, shall conform to the reduced standard of eight hours a day, recently adopted by Congress for national employes, and also for an amendment to the acts of incorporation for cities and towns by which all laborers and mechanics employed at their expense shall conform to the same number of hours.

8. That the enlightened spirit of the age demands the abolition of the system of contract labor in our prisons and other reformatory institutions.

9. That the protection of life, liberty, and property are the three cardinal principles of Government, and the first two are more sacred than the latter; therefore money needed for prosecuting wars should, as it is required, be assessed and collected from the wealthy of the country, and not entailed as a burden on posterity.

10. That it is the duty of the Government to exercise its power over railroads and telegraph corporations, that they shall not in any case be privileged to exact such rates of freight, transportation, or charges, by whatever name, as may bear unduly or unequally upon the producer or consumer.

11. That there should be such a reform in the civil service of the national Government as will remove it beyond all partisan influence, and place it in the charge and under the direction of intelligent and competent business men.

12. That as both history and experience teaches us that power ever seeks to perpetuate itself by every and all means, and that its prolonged possession in the hands of one person is always dangerous to the interests of a free people, and believing that the spirit of our organic laws and the stability and safety of our free institutions are best obeyed on the one

hand, and secured on the other, by a regular constitutional change in the chief of the country at each election: therefore, we are in favor of limiting the occupancy of the presidential chair to one term.

13. That we are in favor of granting general amnesty and restoring the Union at once on the basis of equality of rights and privileges to all, the impartial administration of justice being the only true bond of union to bind the States together and restore the Government of the people.

14. That we demand the subjection of the military to the civil authorities, and the confinement of its operations to national purposes alone.

15. That we deem it expedient for Congress to supervise the patent laws, so as to give labor more fully the benefit of its own ideas and inventions.

16. That fitness, and not political or personal considerations, should be the only recommendation to public office, either appointive or elective, and any and all laws looking to the establishment of this principle are heartily approved.

THE BAXTER LIQUOR LAW.

AN ACT to regulate the sale of intoxicating liquors; to provide against evils resulting from any sale thereof; to furnish remedies for damages suffered by any person in consequence of such sale; prescribing penalties; to repeal all laws contravening the provisions of this act, and declaring an emergency.

[APPROVED FEBRUARY 27, 1873.]

SECTION 1. *Be it enacted by the General Assembly of the State of Indiana,* That it shall be unlawful for any person or persons, by himself or agent, to sell, barter, or give away for any purpose of gain, to any person whomsoever, any intoxicating liquors to be drunk in, upon, or about the building or premises where the liquor is sold, bartered, or given away, or in any room, building, or premises adjoining to or connected with the place where the liquor is sold, bartered, or given away for the purpose of gain, until such person or persons shall have obtained a permit therefor from the board of commissioners of the county where he resides, as hereinafter provided.

Sec. 2. Any person desiring a permit to sell intoxicating liquors to be drunk on the premises, shall file in the office of the auditor of the proper county, not less than twenty days before the first day of the term of any regular session of the board of commissioners of such county, a petition in writing, stating therein the building or number, street, ward or township wherein the permission is asked to be granted, praying for such permit, and certifying that the applicant is a resident voter of such county, and a citizen of the State of Indiana, and that he is a proper person to have and receive such permit; which petition shall be signed by the applicant, and also by a majority of the legal voters resident in the ward, if it be in a city or town, if it be in an incorporated town, or township wherein the applicant proposes to sell intoxicating liquors; such petition shall be kept on file by the auditor until the next ensuing regular session of the board of commissioners, when it shall be presented to the board for their action. The board shall examine such petition, and if satisfied the same is in proper form, and that it has been signed as hereinbefore required, shall direct a permit to be issued under the hand and seal of said auditor, and delivered to the person named in such permit, upon his complying with the provisions of this act and paying the costs of filing and recording said petition and costs of issuing said permit.

Sec. 3. Before the granting of a permit by the board of commissioners, the applicant shall cause to be executed and properly acknowledged before an officer authorized to take acknowledgment of deeds, a bond payable to the State of Indiana, in the sum of three thousand dollars, with good freehold security thereon of not less than two persons, to be approved by the board of commissioners, and conditioned for the payment of any and all fines, penalties and forfeitures incurred by reason of the violation of any of the provisions of this act; and conditioned further, that the principal and sureties therein named shall be jointly and severally liable, and shall pay to any person or persons, any and all damages which shall in any manner be suffered by or inflicted upon any such person or persons, either in person or property, or means of support, by reason of any sale or sales of intoxicating liquors to any person, by the person receiving such permit or by any of his agents or employees. Separate suits may be brought on said bond by the person or persons injured, but the aggregate amount recovered thereon shall not exceed the said sum of three thousand dollars, and in case the amount of said bond shall be exhausted by recoveries thereon, a new bond in the same penalty and with like sureties shall be filed within ten days, and in default thereof said permit shall be deemed to be revoked. Such bond, after its approval by the board of commissioners, shall be filed in the office of the auditor of the county, and shall be recorded by such auditor forthwith in a book prepared for that purpose, and shall there remain for the use of the

State of Indiana, and for the use of any person or persons suffering any damage as hereinbefore set forth. Such bond may be sued and recovered upon in any court having civil jurisdiction in the county (except justices' courts) by or for the use of any person or persons, or their legal representatives, who may be injured or damaged by reason of any sale or sales of intoxicating liquors by the person receiving the permit or by any of his agents or employees. The record of the bond or a copy thereof, duly certified by such auditor, shall be admissible in evidence in any suit on such bond, and shall have the same force and effect as the original bond would have if offered in evidence.

Sec. 4. The whole number of votes cast for candidates for Congress at the last preceding Congressional election in the township, and the whole number of votes cast for councilman or trustee in any ward or town, at the last preceding municipal election in any city or town in which the applicant for permit desires to sell said intoxicating liquors, shall be deemed to be the whole number of legal voters of such ward, town or township, a majority of whose names shall be signed to the petition of such applicant; and it is further provided, that any person not a legal voter in said ward, town or township, who shall sign said petition, or any person who signs the name of any person other than himself, without the permission previously obtained of said person to so sign his name, shall be fined not less than fifty nor more than one hundred dollars for each signature so made.

Sec. 5. No permit, as herein provided for, shall be granted for a longer or shorter time than one year. It shall be the duty of the Auditor of the county to furnish the person to whom such permit is granted, a copy of the order of the Commissioners granting the permit, which copy shall show in conspicuous letters the date of the commencement of such permit, and of its expiration; *and it is further provided*, That such copy of the order of the Commissioners, certified by the Auditor, shall be hung up in a conspicuous place in the room where said liquor is sold, where the same may at all times be seen and read by any person desiring so to do. Should any person holding a permit be convicted of a violation of any of the provisions of this act, such conviction shall work a forfeiture of his permit, and of all rights thereunder; and no permit shall thereafter be granted to such person before the expiration of five years from the date of such conviction.

Sec. 6. It shall be unlawful for any person, by himself, or agent, to sell, barter, or give intoxicating liquors to any minor, or to any person intoxicated, or to any person who is in the habit of getting intoxicated.

Sec. 7. All places where intoxicating liquor is sold in violation of this act, shall be taken, held. and declared to be common nuisances; all rooms, taverns, eating-houses, bazaars, restaurants, drug stores, groceries, coffee-houses, cellars, or other places of public resort, where intoxicating liquors are sold in violation of this act, shall be shut up and abated as public nuisances, upon conviction of the keeper thereof, who shall be punished as hereinafter provided.

Sec. 8. Any person or persons who shall by the sale of intoxicating liquor, with or without permit, cause the intoxication, in whole or in part, of any other person, shall be liable for and be compelled to pay a reasonable compensation to any person who may take charge of and provide for such intoxicated person, for every day he or she is so cared for, which sum may be recovered in an action of debt before any court having competent jurisdiction.

Sec. 9. It shall be unlawful for any person to get intoxicated. A person found in a state of intoxication shall upon conviction thereof, be fined in the sum of five dollars. Any person convicted of intoxication shall be required upon the trial to designate the person or persons from whom the liquor in whole or in part was obtained. In default of so designating such person, he or she shall in addition to the fine above mentioned, and as a part of his or her punishment for the offense, be imprisoned in the county jail not less than one day nor more than ten days, at the discretion of the court.

Sec. 10. A permit granted under this act shall not authorize the person so receiving it to sell intoxicating liquors on Sunday, nor upon the day of any State, county, township, or municipal election, in the township, town or city where the same may be held; nor upon Christmas day, nor upon the Fourth of July, nor upon any Thanksgiving day, nor upon any public holiday, nor between nine o clock P. M. and six o'clock

A. M.; and any and all sales made on any such day, or after nine o'clock on any evening, are hereby declared to be unlawful, and upon conviction thereof, the person so selling shall be fined not less than five dollars nor more than twenty-five dollars for each sale made in violation of this section.

Sec. 11. The bartering or giving away of intoxicating liquors, or other shift or device to evade the provisions of this act, by any person or persons keeping liquors for sale, or by his agent or employee, at the place where the same are kept for sale, shall be deemed and held to be an unlawful selling or giving away for the purpose of gain within the provisions of this act.

Sec. 12. In addition to the remedy and right of action provided for in section eight of this act, every husband, wife, child, parent, guardian, employer, or other person who shall be injured in person or property, or means of support, by any intoxicated person, or in consequence of the intoxication, habitual or otherwise, of any person, shall have a right of action in his or her name, severally or jointly, against any person or persons who shall, by selling, bartering, or giving away intoxicating liquors have caused the intoxication, in whole or in part, of such person, and any person or persons owning, renting, leasing or permitting the occupation of any building or premises, and having knowledge that intoxicating liquor is to be sold therein, or having leased the same for other purposes, shall knowingly permit therein the sale of intoxicating liquor, or who having been informed that intoxicating liquor is sold therein that has caused, in whole or in part, the intoxication of any person, who shall not immediately, after being so informed, take legal steps in good faith to dispossess said tenant or lessee, shall be liable jointly with the person selling, bartering or giving away intoxicating liquor as aforesaid, to any person or persons injured, for all damages, and for exemplary damages; *Provided*, however, that execution on any such judgment shall first be levied on the property of the person selling, bartering or giving away such liquor, and in the event of a failure or insufficiency of such property to satisfy the judgment, then of the property of the other defendants. A married woman shall have the same right to bring suit and to control the same, and the ammount recovered as a *femme sole*, and all damages recovered by a minor under this act shall be paid either to such minor or to his or her parent, guardian or next friend, as the court shall direct. The unlawful sale or giving away of intoxicating liquor shall work a forfeiture of all rights of the lessee or tenant under any lease or contract of rent, upon the premises where such unlawful sale, bartering or giving away shall take place. All suits for damages under this act may be by any appropriate action in any of the courts in this State having competent jurisdiction. All judgments recovered under the provisions of this act may be enforced without any relief or benefit from the valuation or appraisement laws.

Sec. 13. In all cases where husband, wife, parent, child or guardian shall have a right of action as provided in section twelve of this act, and shall fail or refuse to prosecute the same, and in all cases where such intoxicated person has neither husband, wife, parent, child or guardian, the township trustee or other officer having charge of the poor of the township where such intoxicated person resides, shall have a right of action as provided in said section twelve, and it is hereby made the duty of such officer to prosecute all such actions in the name of such township. All money collected upon such judgments, after deducting therefrom all costs and charges against such township occasioned thereby, shall be paid by the township trustee, or other officer, into the treasury of the county for the benefit of the poor of such county; provided that the name of any husband, wife, parent, child or guardian, upon proper petition therefore before final judgment, may be substituted for the name of the township, but such person so substituted shall have no power to dismiss such action, or compromise the same in any manner, except by permission of the court.

Sec. 14. For every violation of the provisions of the first and sixth sections of this act, the person so offending shall forfeit and pay a fine of not less than ten dollars nor more than fifty dollars, or be imprisoned in the jail of the county not less than ten nor more than thirty days. For every violation of the provisions of the seventh section of this act, any person convicted as the keeper of any of the places therein declared to be nuisances, shall forfeit and pay a fine of not less than twenty nor more than fifty dollars, and such place or places, so kept by such person so convicted, shall be shut up and abated as a common nuisance by the order of the court before which such conviction may be had as a further punishment, and such order shall be a part of the judgment of conviction.

Sec. 15. For the payment of all fines, costs and damages assessed or adjudged against any person or persons in consequence of the sale of intoxicating liquors as provided for in this act, the real estate and personal property of such person or persons, of every kind, shall be liable, and such fines, costs and damages shall be a lien upon such real estate until paid.

Sec. 16. The penalties and provisions made in the fourteenth section of this act may be enforced by indictment in any court of record having criminal jurisdiction; and all pecuniary fines or penalties provided for in any of the sections of this act, except the eighth and twelfth, may be enforced and prosecuted for before any justice of the peace of the proper county, in an action of debt, in the name of the State of Indiana as plaintiff; and in case of conviction, the offender shall stand committed to the jail of the county until judgment and costs are fully paid, and the magistrate or court in which the conviction is had, shall issue a writ of *capias ad satisfaciendum* therefor. Justices of the peace shall have jurisdiction of all actions arising under the eighth and twelfth sections of this act, when the amount in controversy does not exceed two hundred dollars, such actions to be prosecuted in the name of the party injured or entitled to the debt or damages provided for in said eighth and twelfth sections.

Sec. 17. It shall be unlawful for any person to buy for or furnish to any person who is at the time intoxicated, or in the habit of getting intoxicated, or to buy for or furnish to any minor, to be drunk by such minor, any intoxicating liquor. Any person or persons violating this section shall be fined not less than five dollars nor more than fifty dollars.

Sec. 18. In all prosecutions under this act, by indictment or otherwise, it shall not be necessary to state the kind of liquor sold, or to describe the place where sold, and it shall not be necessary to state the name of the person to whom sold. In all cases, the person or persons to whom intoxicating liquors shall be sold in violation of this act, shall be competent witnesses to prove such facts or any others tending thereto.

Sec. 19. The following form of complaint shall be sufficient in criminal proceedings before justices of the peace or mayors, under this act when applicable, but may be varied to suit the nature of the case, namely:

STATE OF INDIANA, COUNTY, ss. Before me, A. B., a justice of the peace of said county, (or mayor of, &c., as the case may be), personally came C. D., who, being duly sworn according to law, deposeth and saith that on or about the   day of   , in the year   , at the county aforesaid, E. F. did sell intoxicating liquors to one G. H. to be drunk in the place where sold, (or to G. H., a minor, &c.,) or to a person intoxicated, or in the habit of getting intoxicated, as the case may be, where intoxicating liquors are sold in violation of law, and further saith not.

(Signed) C. D.

Sworn to and subscribed before me this   day of   A. D.,

Sec. 20. All laws and parts of laws conflicting with this act, or with any of the provisions of this act, be and the same are hereby repealed; but nothing in this act shall be so construed as to prohibit the common councils of cities and the boards of trustees of incorporated towns, from demanding and enforcing a fee for permit, from all keepers of coffee houses, saloons, or other places where intoxicating liquor is sold and drunk within the limits of their respective corporations.

Sec. 21. It is hereby declared that an emergeny exists for the immediate taking effect of this act, it shall, therefore, be in force from and after its passage, except in so far as relates to those who hold a license under the existing laws of the State. This act shall apply to such as now have license immediately after the expiration thereof.

GEOLOGICAL ITEMS.

"It is not easy to give an accurate and comprehensive definition of the science of geology. It is, indeed, not so much one science, as the application of all the physical sciences to the examination of the structure of the earth, the investigation of the processes concerned in the production of that structure, and the history of their action. That this large view of geology is not only a true but a necessary one, is shown by the fact, that it was not until considerable advances had been made in all the physical sciences which relate directly to the earth, that geology could begin to exist in any worthy form. It was not until the chemist was able to explain the nature of the mineral substances of which rocks are composed; not till the geographer and meteorologist had explored the surface of the earth, and taught us the extent of land and water, and the powers of winds, currents, rains, glaciers, earthquakes and volcanoes; not until the naturalist had classified, named, and described the greater part of existing animals and plants, and explained their anatomical structure, and the laws of their distribution in space;—that the geologist could, with any chance of arriving at sure and definite results, commence his researches into the structure and composition of rocks and the causes which produced them, or utilize his discoveries of the remains of animals and plants that are inclosed in them. He could not until then discriminate with certainty batween igneous and aqueous rocks, between living and extinct animals, and was, therefore, unable to lay down any one of the foundations on which his own science was to rest."--*Encyclopedia Britannica, 8th edition, vol. xv.*

If there is any one fact which the study of geology teaches more unmistakably than another, it is, that the matter composing the crust of the earth, from the time when it was first called into existence by the *fiat* of the Creator to the present, has been subjected to an endless cycle of mutations. There may have been periods of comparative rest and quiescen_e, but none of perfect stagnation and stability; so that the present condition and configuration of the earth's surface may be considered as the last result of a series of cosmical changes, which commenced with the dawn of creation, and are continuing on into the future.

"Had the exterior crust of the earth been subjected to no modifying causes, the world would have presented the same appearance now as at the time of its creation. The distribution of land and sea would have remained the same; there would have been the same surface arrangement of hill, valley and plain, and the same unvarying aspects of animal and vegetable existence. Under such circumstances, geology, instead of striving to present a consecutive history of change and progress, would have been limited to a mere description of permanently enduring appearances. The case. however, is widely different." There is no part of the present land-surface of the globe which has not at some time been covered by the ocean, while much of the present sea bottom has been in turn dry land. Many of the loftiest and most extensive ranges of mountains upon the globe—the Alps, the Andes, and the Himalayas—are of comparatively recent elevation (recent as compared with the White Mountains of New England, or the Appallachian chain of the Atlantic States); while the commencement of the existence of every animal and vegetable species at present found upon the earth was long subsequent to the existence of the myriad organisms, whose remains are now found fossil beneath its surface.

The agencies which have produced, and are still tending to produce, changes in the constitution and structure of our planet, may be classified as follows: 1. Igneous agencies, or such as manifest themselves in connection with some deep-seated source of heat in the interior of the globe. 2. Aqueous, or those arising from the action of the water. 3. Atmospheric, or those operating through the medium of the atmosphere. 4. Organic, or those depending on animal and vegetable growth. 5. Chemical, or those resulting from the chemical action of substances on each other.—*Wells' Illustrated Geology.*

THE TEMPERATURE OF THE EARTH.

The following are some of the observations made most recently on this subject: In England, observations have been made in the vertical shafts of two very deep coal mines, viz., at Monkwearmouth, which is 1800 feet deep, and Dunkinfield, which is upwards of 2000 feet deep, and in both cases the observations were made while the workmen were sinking the shafts, and with every precaution against the influence of any extraneous causes. The former gave an increase of 1 deg. of Fahrenheit for every sixty feet of depth, and the latter 1 deg. for about every seventy feet. The artesian well of Grenelle (Paris), is 1800 feet deep; observations made by Arago, during the boring, showed that the average increase of temperature in this was 1 deg. for sixty feet. At Mordorff, Luxemburg, the depth of the artesian well is 2400 feet, and the increase in temperature 1 deg. for every fifty-seven feet. At the artesian well of New Seltzwork, in Westphalia, the depth is 2100 feet, and the increase 1 deg. for every fifty-five feet. At Louisville, Ky., the depth of an artesian well, finished in 1859, is 2086 feet deep, and the average increase is 1 deg. for every sixty-seven feet below the first ninety feet from the surface. In the silver mine of Guanaxato, Mexico, 1713 feet deep, the increase is 1 deg. for every forty-five feet. In the coal mines of Eastern Virginia, the increase is about 1 deg. for every sixty feet.

VOLCANIC ERUPTIONS.

One or two remarkable instances of volcanic eruptions may be briefly noticed. First, for duration and force we may refer to that which took place in the island of Sumbawa (one of the Sunda Islands lying east of Java), in the year 1815. It commenced on the 5th of April, and did not entirely cease until July. Its influence (*i. e.* shocks, and the noise of the explosions) was perceptible over an area 1,800 miles in diameter, while within the range of its more immediate vicinity, embracing a space of 400 miles, its effects were most terrific. In Java, 300 miles distant, it seemed to be awfully present. The sky was overcast at noon day with clouds of ashes, which the light of the sun was unable to penetrate, and fields, streets, and houses were covered with ashes to the depth of several inches. At Sumbawa itself, immense columns of flame appeared to burst forth from the top of the volcano, Tombora, and in a short time the whole mountain appeared like a mass of liquid fire, which gradually extended in every direction. As the eruption continued, a darkness supervened, so profound as to obscure even the light of the flames; showers of stones and ashes fell continuously over the whole island; the sea rose twelve feet higher than it had ever been known to do before; and finally a whirlwind ensued, which tore up the largest trees, and carried them into the air, together with men, horses, cattle, and whatever else came within its influence. Of 12,000 inhabitants in the vicinity only six are believed to have escaped, and of some entire villages not even a vestige remained.

In 1772, the Papandayang, one of the loftiest volcanic mountains in Java, after a short but severe eruption, suddenly fell in and disappeared in the earth, carrying with it about ninety square miles of territory. Forty villages were engulfed, or covered with ejected matter, at the same time, and nearly 3,000 persons perished.—*Wells' Illustrated Geology.*

DESCRIPTIONS OF AN EARTHQUAKE.

"A powerful eathquake," says Mr. Darwin, "at once destroys the oldest associations; the world, the very emblem of all that is solid, has moved beneath our feet like a crust over a fluid; one second of time has conveyed to the mind a strange idea of insecurity, which hours of reflection would never have created."

"To man," says Humbolt, "the earthquake conveys an idea of some universal and unlimited danger. We may flee from the crater of a volcano in active eruption, or from a locality threatened by the approach of a lava stream; but in an earthquake, direct our flight whithersoever we will, we still feel as though we trod upon the very focus of destruction. Every sound—the faintest motion in the air—arrests our attention, and we no longer trust the ground on which we stand. Animals, especially dogs and swine, participate in the same anxious disquietude; and even crocodiles, in the rivers of South America, which at other times are dumb, have been observed to quit the water and run, with loud cries, into the adjacent forests."

AQUEOUS AND ATMOSPHERIC AGENCIES.

The aqueous and atmospheric agencies most prominently concerned in producing geological changes, are *rains, and the gasses and moisture of the atmosphere, winds, ice, and snow, springs, rivers, waves, tides, and oceanic currents.*

The operation of water, acting mechanically, is, under all circumstances, to wear down the higher portions of the earth's crust, and transport the materials to lower localities—an action which obviously tends to reduce the whole surface to a smooth and uniform level. On the other hand, the operations of igneous agents—volcanoes, earthquakes, etc.—by breaking up and elevating the crust of the earth, tend to counteract the equalizing action of water and to produce that diversity of-surface which is indispensable to variety in both the vegetable and animal kingdoms. These two forces, therefore—the aqueous and the igneous—may be considered as antagonistic to each other, and to them may be ascribed the principal modifications which have taken place, and are still taking place, in the crust of the globe.—*Well's Illustrated Geology*

CORAL REEFS.

"The ocean," says Mr. Darwin, "throwing its breakers on the outer shore, appears an invincible enemy, yet we see it resisted, and even conquered, by means which at first seem weak and inefficient. No periods of repose are granted, and the heavy swell caused by the steady action of the trade wind never ceases. The breakers exceed in violence those of our temperate regions; and it is impossible to behold them without feeling a conviction that rocks of granite or quartz would ultimately be demolished by such irresistable forces. Yet these low coral islands stand and are victorious, for here another power, antagonistic to the former, takes part in the contest. The organic forces separate the atoms of carbonate of lime, one by one, from the foaming breakers, and unite them into a symmetrical structure; myriads of architects are at work day and night, month after month, and we see their soft and gelatinous bodies, through the agency of the vital laws, conquering the great mechanical power of the waves of the ocean, which neither the art of man nor the mechanical works of nature could successfully resist." The animals which produce coral are very simple, and resemble plants both in their figures and colors.

THE FIRST FORMED STRATIFIED ROCKS.

The adoption of the theory, that our earth was once in a state of entire molten fluidity, involves the existence of a subsequent period, when its primeval crust had sufficiently cooled down to allow of the condensation of watery vapor and of the existence of a sea upon its surface. Whenever this happened, the eroding and destructive action of water must have immediately manifested itself, while the particles of the consolidated igneous crust, worn off by the action of waves, tides, and currents, and deposited as sediments, would naturally produce stratified formations.

The internal heat of the earth at that period, however, must have continued to act with great intensity near the surface, and the strata first deposited, consequently, were, in all probability, soon greatly metamorphosed, *i. e.*, remelted down to form igneous rocks, or converted into hard crystalline semi-igneous rocks, that retained, in part, their original lines of stratification.

Whether any of these first formed stratified rocks are in existence, and open to our inspection, it is impossible to affirm. Some geologists incline to the opinion that they were entirely remelted, and are now represented by the older or fundamental granites, which, in some instances, appear to have an obscurely stratified structure.

Be this as it may, it is, however, a matter of fact, that the oldest rocks of which we have any knowledge, which exhibit evidence of a sedimentary origin, appear to have been formed under conditions analogous to those above supposed. Thus, they are all more or less crystalline and indurated; their lines of stratification are indistinct, and often altogether obliterated; and their whole aspect is very different from what is usually ascribed to rocks deposited in water.—*Wells' Illustrated Geology.*

FORMATION OF COAL.

It is now universally admitted by geologists, that coal is a mass of compressed, altered, and mineralized vegetation, just as sandstone is consolidated sand, and the slate and shale consolidated clay or mud.

The evidence upon which the belief is founded may be briefly stated, as follows:

1st. The enormous profusion of fossil plants, in the form of impressions of leaves, trunks, branches, and barks of trees, found in immediate connection with coal seams. 2d. Coal is composed of carbon, hydrogen, and oxygen, the same elements (though differing in proportion) which enter into the composition of plants. 3d. The substance of coal, when examined under the microscope, affords unmistakable evidence of a vegetable (cellular) structure. 4th. All the stages of gradation between perfect wood and perfect coal may be traced with the greatest certainty.

But granting the vegetable origin of coal, the question immediately suggests itself: Under what circumstances could so great an amount of vegetable matter have ever accumulated?—the magnitude of which may be realized in a degree, from the asserted fact "that all the forests of the United States, if gathered into one heap, would fail to furnish the materials of a single coal seam equal to that of Pittsburg, Penn."

Furthermore, coal is found stratified, laminated, and extended, in horizontal beds, which often cover very large areas, with a nearly constant thickness—the great Pittsburg coal seam, above referred to for example, having a nearly uniform thickness of from eight to twelve feet, and is estimated to have once covered a surface of 90,000 square miles. Coal, moreover, is ordinarily encased between beds of shale or sandstone, which bear evident proof of having been slowly deposited in quiet waters. In some coal fields, as many as seventy seams of coal, varying in thickness from a few inches to four, six, eight, ten, twelve, and twenty feet, occur thus interstratified with shales and sandstones; and yet, notwithstanding these frequent alternations of material, the purity of the coal is such, that it rarely contains any considerable admixture of mud, sand, or other foreign mineral substances.

In explanation of these phenomena, various hypotheses have been suggested, but the general opinion of the best geologists of the present day is, that the vegetable matter constituting coal, must, in the main, have grown and accumulated in immense jungles and peat mosses for many years; that the land must have then sunk, and become the basin of a lake or estuary, into which rivers carried mud and sand; these, covering the vegetable matter, gradually consolidated into shales and sandstones, while the vegetable matter itself underwent the process of mineralization, and was converted into coal. This being done, it is supposed that the area of deposit was again elevated, so as to become once more the scene of luxuriant vegetation; then again submerged, and overlaid by new deposits of sandstone and shale; then once more elevated and covered with plants, and again submerged; and these alternations of submergence and elevations are presumed to have taken place as often as there are beds of coal in any particular coal field.—*Well's Illustrated Geology.*

CLIMATIC CONDITIONS OF THE CARBONIFEROUS ERA.

There is one circumstance in connection with the formation of coal which has given rise to a vast amount of ingenious speculation and hypotheses, viz: the apparent sameness of external conditions over such extensive areas of the earth as are now occupied by our known coal fields. Thus, the same gigantic ferns and club-mosses are found alike in the coal fields of America, Europe, Melville Island, Greenland, and Australia—regions widely separated, and at once tropical, temperate, and frigid. To account for this luxuriance and homogeneity of vegetable growth various causes have been suggested, as the earth's central heat, a change in the earth's axis, a larger percentage of carbonic acid in the atmosphere, the planetary system moving through warmer regions of space, and the like; but thus far geologists have arrived at no definite conclusions on the subject.

Deposits of carbonaceous matter have occurred at almost every period of the earth's history, as is evidenced by the fact that thin seams of coal are found in almost all the geological systems; but the coal beds which admit of economical working are almost exclusively confined to the carboniferous system. The only exceptions are a few coal fields belonging to the Oolitic or Jurassic system, which, in Virginia and some other localities, admit of profitable mining. It seems, therefore, certain, that whatever may have been the conditions which allowed of so abundant a terrestrial vegetation at this particular epoch of the earth's history, those conditions ceased about the time when the era of the Carboniferous system terminated. A high temperature was evidently not one of these conditions, for there are evidences of it afterwards; and some authorities incline to the belief that the superabundance of carbonic acid gas, which is supposed to have existed during this era, was expended before its close. "There can be no doubt that the infusion of a large amount of this gas into the atmosphere at the present day would be attended by precisely the same circumstances as in the time of the coal epoch. The higher forms of animal life would not have a place on earth. Vegetation would be enormous; and coal strata would be formed from the vast accumulations of woody matter, which would gather in every favorable locality."

DISTRIBUTION OF COAL.

Coal is very widely distributed over the world, although some countries are more highly favored than others. Available coal fields occur in Great Britain; in Spain, France, Belgium and Middle Europe; in India, China and Japan; in the islands of the Indian Archipelago; in Australia and New Zealand; in South America, Chili and Peru; in Greenland, Melville Island and in British America. But nowhere is the coal formation more extensively displayed than in the United States, and nowhere are its beds of greater thickness, more convenient for working, or of more valuable quality.

The eastern half of the continent of North America exhibits five great coal fields, extending from Newfoundland to Arkansas: 1. The *first*, or most eastern, is that of the British Provinces, Newfoundland, Nova Scotia, and New Brunswick. Its area is probably about 9,000 square miles, though only one tenth of this surface appears to be underlaid by productive coal seams. 2. The *second*, or Great Appalachian coal field, extends from Pennsylvania and Ohio to near Tuscaloosa, in the interior of Alabama. It is about 875 miles long, and is estimated to contain 70,000 square miles. 3. A *third*, and smaller coal field, occupies the center of the State of Michigan; it covers an area of about 15,000 square miles, but is not very productive. 4. A *fourth* great coal field is situated in the States of Kentucky, Indiana and Illionois. Its area is estimated at 50,000 square miles. 5. The *fifth*, and most western, occurs in Iowa, Missouri and Arkansas, and occupies an area of about 57,000 square miles. Besides these great deposits, coal is also found in New England, Kansas, Nebraska, and Texas.

The aggregate space underlaid by the coal fields of North America amounts to at least 200,000 square miles, or to more than twenty times the area which includes all the known coal deposits of Europe.—*Wells' Geology.*

MISCELLANEOUS.

The number of species of animals that now inhabit the globe is about 250,000. The number of fossil species of animals and plants cannot be reliably estimated, but it is safe to say that the number of the different extinct species that have been found in fossil state exceeds many times the number of all the different species now living.

Geologists claim four distinct periods or ages of the earth's history. Beginning at the oldest, they are called or named, First, the Azoic period, or period deficient of the evidence of life; Second, Paleozoic, or period of ancient life; Third, the Mesozoic, or period of middle life; Fourth, or last period, called Cainozoic. This period includes the Post Tertiary, or recent system of rocks or period of recent life.

A picture of the Azoic period has thus been imagined by Hugh Miller. "During the early part of the Azoic period we may imagine," he says, "a dark atmosphere of steam and vapor, which, for age after age conceals the face of the sun, and through which the moon or stars never penetrates; oceans of thermal waters, heated in a thousand centers to the boiling point; low, half molten islands, dim through the fog and scarce more fixed than waves themselves, that heave and tremble under the impulsions of the igneous agencies; roaring geysers that ever and anon throw up their intermittent jets of boiling fluid, vapor and thick steam, from these tremulous lands; and in the dim outskirts of the scene, the red gleam of fire shot forth from yawning cracks and deep chasms. Such would be the probable state of things among the times of the earlier gneiss and mica-chist deposits—times buried deep in that chaotic night which must have continued to exist for, may hap, many ages after that beginning of things in which God created the heavens and the earth."

At length, however, as the earth's surface gradually cooled down and the enveloping waters sunk to a lower temperature, let us suppose during the latter times of the mica-schist and the earlier times of the clay slate, the steam atmosphere would become less dense and thick, and finally the rays of the sun would struggle through it; at first doubtful and diffused, forming a faint twilight, but gradually strengthening, as the later ages of the slate formation passed away, until at the close of the great primary period day and night—the one still dim and grey, the other wrapped in the pall of darkness—would succeed each other as now, as the earth revolved on its axis.

The number of active volcanoes on our globe are about 275. Humboldt suggests the idea that volcanoes are merely vents, located above some far extended subterranean crack or fissure in the crust of the earth, through which the molten matter of the interior escapes to the surface.

The falls of Niagara are 150 feet in height, and the average amount of water passing over each minute is estimated at 670,000 tons. This water, by its abrading power, has undoubtedly excavated for itself the gorge or channel—seven miles long, 200 feet deep, and 1,200 to 2,000 feet wide—which now intervenes between the falls and Lake Ontario. The minimum time required to wear through this space has been estimated by Sir Charles Lyell, at 35,000 years.—*Well's Illustrated Geol.*

STRATIFIED ROCKS.

The stratified rocks of Great Britain have been studied more than any other of the earth, and as the result of these investigations it has been found that the extinct mammalia, found in fossiliferous rocks, is more numerous by half than all the species now existing; and of molluscs, the fossil species nine times as numerous as the living species; the fossil fish five times, the reptiles ten times, and the radiate fourteen times.

The geologist finds no trace of that golden age of the world of which the poets delighted to sing, when all creatures lived together in peace, and wars and bloodshed were unknown. Ever since animal life began on our planet, there existed, in all departments of being, carniverous classes, who could not live but by the death of their neighbors; and who were armed, in consequence, for their destruction, like the butcher with his axe and knife, and the angler with his hook and spear.

In Europe, the caverns or caves that have been discovered, have contained the remains or skeletons of a great many of the different species of animals that now inhabit the earth, and of others that are now extinct. For instance, the bones and skeletons of the mammoth are found in great numbers; also of the mastadon, the epoch of the mastadon, in a geological sense, is very recent. Some think that the mammoths and mastadons did not become entirely extinct in this country until after the advent of man. Sir Charles Lyell is of the opinion that the period of the extinction of the mastadon, although recent, must have been many thousand years ago.

PHILOSOPHY.

No two particles of matter can occupy the same space at the same time.

All bodies weigh heaviest at the earth's surface. A body that weighs 10 pounds at the earth's surface will weigh but $2\frac{1}{2}$ pounds 4,000 miles high.

Take two cog-wheels of the same size; let one stand still put the cogs together and put the other in motion, and when it has made one-half revolution around the standing wheel it will have made a full revolution on its own center, notwithstanding only one-half of the cogs of its own surface has touched the standing wheel.

The atmosphere is the lightest in wet, rainy weather; yet we find people very often who think different. The medium pressure of the atmosphere is about fifteen pounds to the square inch, but this is not always the case. The pressure will vary in the same locality, and sometimes be greater or less. The medium hight that atmospheric pressure will raise water is about 33 feet; but this calculation only holds good at the level of the sea, because as we ascend from the sea level the pressure becomes less; hence, our calculations for raising water by atmospheric pressure must be governed by the pressure that atmosphere has at the hight of the position above the sea level. Illustration: At sea level atmospheric pressure fifteen pounds to the square inch; one mile above sea level, about $12\frac{1}{4}$ pounds; two miles above, 10 pounds; three miles, $7\frac{1}{2}$ pounds; consequently, on an elevation three miles high, water cannot be raised but about $16\frac{1}{2}$ feet by the weight of the air.

The top or upper part of a wagon wheel passes through a greater amount of space in a given time when running than the bottom; or, in other words, runs the fastest.

The piston rod of a steam engine makes two complete stops at every revolution of the crank attached to the end of the pitman.

HORSE POWER.—The average power of a horse is sufficient to raise a weight of about 23,000 pounds one foot per minute, but when calculating the horse power of a steam engine it is estimated at 33,000 pounds. It then follows that a ten horse powers team engine is, in fact, about equal to fourteen average horses.

POWER OF STEAM.—One cubic foot of water converted into steam will raise the enormous weight of three and a half million pounds one foot, or seven hundred pounds one mile high.

All bodies or particles of matter fall to the eath by the attraction of gravity, and their speed is in proportion to their density; but take away the resisting force of the atmosphere, then a cork or feather will fall as fast as a bullet.

Resultant motion may be illustrated by holding a ball or weight in your hand and dropping it from the top of your head while running, you will find that you cannot run fast enough to overtake the ball before it strikes the ground.

A ball may be shot from a cannon from the top of a tower on a horizontal plain, and another dropped from the mouth of the cannon at the same time, and they will both strike the earth at the same time, provided the surface be horizontal with the cannon.

Lever power is almost indispensable, or in other words, without it we could scarcely do anything; yet to take in consideration distance and speed, there is not a particle of power gained by a lever. Illustration: Suppose a lever 20 feet long, the fulcrum 2 feet from one end of the lever, 10 pounds on the long end of the lever is equal to 100 pounds on the short end; but to raise the 100 pounds one foot the ten pounds passes through 10 feet of space, consequently it travels ten times as fast as the 100 pounds, so all that is gained in power is lost in speed and distance; because if both ends of the lever was of the same length while one end of the lever was passing through ten feet of space the other end would pass through the same ten feet; and ten pounds would raise ten pounds ten feet high, or ten times as high as the ten pounds on the long end of the lever would raise the 100 pounds on the short end.

SKETCHES OF ASTRONOMY.

ORIGIN OF THE SOLAR SYSTEM.

Many theories have been propounded at different periods of the history of astronomy, respecting the original formation of our Solar System, as well as all other suns and systems, which it has pleased the GREAT CREATOR OF ALL THINGS to call into existence, but no one has gained so great favor or excited so violent opposition, as the theory first proposed by Sir William Herschel, and afterwards more especially applied by the celebrated La Place to the formation of the solar system.

This theory may be thus stated:—In the beginning all the matter composing the sun, planets, and satellites was diffused through space, in a state of exceedingly minute division, the ultimate particles being held asunder by the repulsion of heat. In process of time, under the action of gravitation, the mass assumed a round or globular shape, and the particles tending to the centre of gravity, a motion of rotation on an axis would commence. The great mass, now gradually cooling and condensing, must increase its rotary motion, thereby increasing the centrifugal force at the equator of the revolving mass, until, finally, a ring of matter is actually detached from the equator, and is left revolving in space by the shrinking away from it, of the interior mass. If now we follow this isolated ring of matter, we find every reason to believe that its particles will gradually coalesce into a globular form, and in turn form satellites, as it was itself formed. It is unnecessary to pursue the reasoning further, for the same laws which produce one planet from the equator of the central revolving mass, may produce many—until finally, the process is ended by a partial solidification of the central mass, so great, that gravity aided by the attraction of cohesion, is more than sufficient to resist the action of the centrifugal force, and no further change occurs.

It has been urged in favor of this theory, that it accounts for the striking peculiarities which are found in the organization of the solar system. That the rings of Saturn are positive proofs of the truth of the theory, they having cooled and condensed without breaking. That the individuals constituting a system thus produced, must revolve and rotate as do the planets and satellites, and in orbits of the precise figure and position, as those occupied by the planets. It accounts for the rotation of the sun on its axis, and presents a solution of the strange appearance connected with the sun called the Zodiacal Light. It goes further and accounts for the formation of single, double, and multiple suns and stars—and by the remains of chaotic matter in the interstics between the stars, and which are finally drawn to some particular sun, whose influence in the end preponderates, accounts for the comets which enter our system from every region in space.

In support of this theory it has been urged that the comets, in their organization, presents us with specimens of this finely divided nebulous or chaotic matter—and that the telescope reveals cloudy patches of light of indefinite extent, scattered throughout space, which give evidence of being yet unformed and chaotic. That many stars are found in which the bright nucleus or centre is surrounded by a halo or haze of nebulous light, and that round nebulous bodies are seen with the telescope, of an extent vastly greater than would fill the entire space encircled by the enormous orbit of the planet La Verrier, or having a diameter greater than 7,000 millions of miles.

Such are a few of the arguments in support of this most extraordinary theory. We now present the objections which have been most strongly insisted on. The retrograde motions of the satellites of Herschel, and their great inclination to the plane of the ecliptic can not be accounted for by this theory. That computation shows that no atmosphere of condensed nebulous matter can extend to so great a distance from the sun, as does the matter composing the Zodiacal Light, and, finally, that the nebulous matter in the heavens will ultimately be resolved into immense congeries and clusters of stars, whose great distance has hitherto defied the power of the best instruments.

In reply to the first objection, the friends of the theory doubt the facts with reference to the satellites of Herschel. They reply that the matter composing the Zodiacal Light being in the nature of cometary matter, is thrown to a greater distance from the sun than gravity would warrant, by that power residing in the sun which is able on the approach of comets to project those enormous trains of light, which sometimes render them so wonderful. As to the last objection, it is urged that although many nebulæ will doubtless be resolved into stars, by using more powerful telescopes, yet that these same telescopes will reveal more new nebulæ which cannot be resolved, than they will resolve—and as to the existence of nebulous matter, it is perfectly demonstrated by the physical organization of comets, and the existence of nebulous stars.

Such was the state of the Astronomical argument, when Lord Rosse's Great Reflector was first applied to the exploration of the distant regions of space. In a religious point of view, this theory had excited no small amount of discussion, in consequence of its supposed Atheistical tendencies. The friends of the theory contend that it was no more Atheistical to admit the formation of the universe by law, than to acknowledge that it is now sustained by laws. Indeed since we must go to the first great cause for matter in its chaotic state, as well as for the laws which govern matter, that this theory gave to us a grander view of the omniscience and omnipotence of God than could be obtained from any other source. In fine, that it harmonized with the declaration of scripture, which tells us that "In the beginning God created the heavens and the earth, and the earth was *without form and void.*" If the earth came into existence in its present condition, then it had *form* and was *not void*. Hence, this first grand declaration of the inspired writer must refer to the formation of the matter of which the heavens and earth were afterwards formed. Some went so far as to trace out dimly a full account of this theory in the order of creation, as laid down in Gensis.

Let us now proceed to the discoveries of Lord Rosse, and their influence on this greatly disputed theory. The space penetrating power of his six feet reflector is much greater than that of Sir William Herschel's great telescope, and it was anticipated that many nebulæ which were unresolved into clusters of stars by Hershel, would yield under the greater power and light of Lord Rosse's telescope. This has proved to be the fact. Very many nebulæ have been removed from their old places, and must hereafter figure among the clusters, while we are informed that many yet remain, even of the old nebulæ, which defy the power of the monster telescope.

The most remarkable object which has been resolved by Lord Rosse, is the great nebula in Orion, one of the most extraordinary objects in the heavens. Its size is enormous, and its figure very extraordinary. In certain parts adjoining the nebula the heavens are *jet black*, either from contrast or by the vacuity of these regions. Two immense spurs of light are seen to project from the principal mass of the nebula, and to extend to a most extraordinary distance. This will be better understood, by remembering that at the distance at which this nebula is removed from us, the entire diameter of the earth's orbit, 190 millions of miles, is an invisable point, less than one second, while this nebula extends to many thousands of times this distance, and more probably to many millions of times.

Several stars have been found, and are visible on the nebula, but have hitherto been regarded as being between the eye of the observer and this remote object. Sir William Herschel was unable to resolve this mysterious body, and yet the nebula gave indications of being of the resolvable kind by its irregular and curdled appearance under high powers. Several years since Dr. J. Lamont, of Munich, after a rigid scrutiny, of this nebula with his great Refractor, pronounced a portion of it to be composed of minute *stellar points*, and predicted its final perfect resolution into stars by greater power. This prediction has been fully verified, for Lord Rosse's great Reflector has solved the mystery, and filled this extraordinary object with the "jewelry of stars."

But the question recurs, what have the defenders of the nebular theory lost, or its enemies gained by this interesting discovery? We are all liable to reach conclusions too hastily, and to join issue on false points. If the nebular theory depended for its existance upon the irresolvability of the nebula in Orion, then indeed has the theory been entirely exploded. But this is not the fact. No one has asserted that the great nebula in Orion was *nebulous matter*, and if it were not, then none existed. Such an issue would have been a false one, had it been made.

The theory has neither lost nor gained by the discoveries

thus far made; what time may develope it is impossible to say. In case certain data can be obtained, which appear to be accessible, then indeed may we demonstrate its truth or falsehood, by mathematical investigation. Until then, the safer plan is neither to adopt nor reject, but investigate until absolute truth shall reward our long continued labor, and reveal the mystery of the organization of that stupendous system, of which our humble planet forms an insignificant part.—*Smith's Astronomy*.

The sun is the center of the solar system, around which all other planets belonging to our universe revolve. The names of all the primary planets that have been discovered that constitute the solar system, are the Sun, Mercury, Venus, the Earth, Mars, Jupiter, Saturn, Herschel, Uranus, Neptune, and twenty-three asteroids, or small planets. The approximate distance each of the large planets travel in making one revolution around the sun is about as follows:

Mercury, number of miles	220,000,000
Venus, " " "	408,000,000
Earth, " " "	570,000,000
Mars, " " "	852,000,000
Jupiter, " " "	2,910,000,000
Saturn, " " "	5,340,000,000
Herschel, " " "	10,800,000,000
La Verrier " " "	17,100,000,000

COMETS.

Very little is known of the physical nature of comets. They are thought by some astronomers to be about as dense as smoke. They are bodies that revolve around the sun in very elongated orbits, and some astronomers think that the greater number visit our system but once, and then fly off in nearly straight lines, and go to revolve around other suns in the far-off distant heavens. The length of the tail of a comet, as measured by astronomers, seem almost incredible.

Comet of 1680, length of the tail	123,000,000	miles.
Do. 1744, " "	35,000,000	"
Do. 1769, " "	48,000,000	"
Do. 1811, " "	130,000,000	"
Do. 1843, " "	130,000,000	"

The sun is 1,384,472 times as large as the earth; Jupiter is 1,280 times larger than the earth, and Saturn 1,000 times.

DIRECTIONS FOR FINDING THE NORTH STAR, AT ANY TIME.

Every pupil should be instructed in the manner of pointing out the North Star at any time of the night. If they are enabled to do this at any time, it will assist them in making other important observations, as well as being of use on many occasions which occur in the life of every man. Many persons have been lost in a *prairie* or other unfrequented places, when if they had been able to have told the points of the compass they could have extricated themselves from their lost situation. This may be done in a very easy manner. There is hardly a child of ten years of age who cannot at any time of night point out the stars in the Great Bear which form what is called the *Great Dipper*. Now if an imaginary line be drawn through the two stars which form the front edge of the Dipper, from the bottom towards the top, and continued about 20 degrees, it will pass very near the North Star—so near that it cannot be mistaken, there being no other stars of that magnitude near it. It should be borne in mind that this rule holds good in whatever position the Dipper may be at the time.—*Smith's Illustrated Astronomy.*

ECLIPSES.

Eclipses are among the most interesting phenomena presented to us by the heavenly bodies. In all ages, when an eclipse has taken place, it has excited the profound attention of the learned, and the fears and superstitions of the ignorant. The causes of eclipses before the seventeenth century were known only to a few, and they generally took advantage of this knowledge to impose upon the credulity of the ignorant by pretending that they were inspired by the Gods. Among the ancient nations, the Chaldeans were the foremost in their observations of the phenomena of the heavens; perhaps this was owing in some measure to their occupation; they being shepherds were obliged to watch their flocks by night to protect them from the wild beasts which were at that time numerous. Men under such circumstances would naturally be led to watch closely the movements of the heavenly bodies, and more especially so, for in the earlier periods of the world they had no correct mode of reckoning time in order to determine the seasons or the proper seed time and harvest.

Eclipses attracted the particular attention of the Chaldeans, and by a series of observations extended through several centuries, they discovered a very important fact relating to eclipses, although they did not understand the cause.

By comparing the records which had been made for a great length of time, they found that a certain period of time elapsed between eclipses of the same kind and magnitude; that is, if 18 years, 11 days, 7 hours and 43 minutes, were added to the time of the happening of any eclipse, it would show the time of the return of the same eclipse; the only differences would be that it would not happen at the same time in the day and it would be a little greater or less than the previous eclipse—thus they were able to predict eclipses with sufficient accuracy to answer their designs upon the ignorant without understanding the laws by which these periodical returns were produced.

To explain this briefly, it must be remembered that the moon's orbit makes an angle with the plane of the earth's orbit of $5\frac{1}{3}$ deg.; these two points where the moon's orbit cuts the plane of the earth's orbit, are called nodes. Now we will suppose that on any day at noon it is new moon, and the moon is just 16 deg. from her descending node, the shadow of the moon would just *touch* the earth at the north pole; in 223 lunations, or 18 years, 11 days, 7 hours, 43 minutes thereafter, the moon would come nearly to the same position as it was at the beginning, consequently there would be another small eclipse of the sun, and at the expiration af every 223 lunations it would return, and at each return the moon's shadow would pass across the earth a little more to the south until the eclipse had appeared about 77 times, when it would pass off at the south pole, occupying a period of 1,388 years: The same period would not commence again until the expiration of 12,492 years. Each eclipse which takes place during any year, belongs to a separate and similar period. Those periods of eclipses which come in at the moon's ascending node, first come on to the earth at the south pole, and at each return the moon's shadow passes across the earth more to the north, and after appearing about 77 times, they finally leave the earth at the north pole.—*Smith's Astronomy.*

IMMENSITY OF SPACE.

Great is the immensity of space. Light travels at the rate of one hundred and ninety-two thousand miles per second, and yet at this great speed it would take it over thirty million years to come from some of the far off nebulas to the earth. Some ideas of the immensity of space may be gathered by the calculation of the distance that light would travel in thirty millions of years, and then supposing that the distance ascertained by the calculation, was to the remaining distance as one drop of water is to the ocean. In all probability the most powerful telescope has only brought to view a small portion of creation.

The nearest fixed stars, according to the best astronomical calculation, 20,000,000,000,000 of miles from the earth. To assist the mind of the reader to get some idea of the immensity of this distance, I have taken the pains to make the following calculation: Suppose that when the Lord past sentence upon Cain for killing his brother, that he had banished him to the nearest fixed star, and had caused a whirlwind or some other power to have taken him at the rate of one thousand miles an hour day and night from that time till now, counting the time past six thousand years, at 360 days travel to the year, he would have traveled at the end of the six thousand years only one 3.80th part of the distance, and at the same rate of speed at the end of two million years from this time he would not reach his destination, but would yet be one trillion three hundred and eighty-two billion four hundred million miles from his future home, or place of banishment. So you see that after two million and six thousand years travel at the enormous speed of one thousand miles an hour, leaves a distance yet untraveled equal to about fifty-five million times the distance of Cook's voyage around the earth.

PAY OF GOVERNMENT OFFICERS.

President of the United States	per annum,	$50,000	00
Vice-President	" "	8,000	00
Cabinet Officers each	" "	8,000	00
Speaker of the House of Representatives	" "	8,000	00
Members of Congress	" "	5,000	00
Chief Justice of the United States	" "	6,500	00
Associate Justices	" "	6,000	00

MINISTERS TO FOREIGN COUNTIES.

In Great Britain or France	per annum	17,500	00
In Russia, Spain, Prussia, Austria, Italy, China, Mexico or Brazil	" "	12,000	00
In Chili or Peru	" "	10,000	00
In Nicaragua	" "	7,000	00
In Portugal, Belgium, Netherlands, Denmark, Sweden, Switzerland, Hawaiian Islands, Ecuador, Argentine Confederation, Venezuela and all other foreign countries	" "	7,500	00

WAR DEPARTMENT.

Lieutenant-General	per month	720	00
Major-General	" "	445	00
Brigadier-General	" "	299	50
Adjutant General	" annum	3,950	00
Surgeon-General	" "	3,594	00
Paymaster General	" "	2,740	00
Commissary-General	" "	2,552	00
Surgeon-General	" month	299	50

OFFICERS OF INFANTRY AND ARTILLERY.

Colonel	per month	194	00
Lieutenant-Colonel	" "	170	00
Major	" "	151	00
Captain	" "	118	50
First Lieutenant	" "	108	50
Second Lieutenant	" "	103	50
Brevet Second Lieutenant	" "	103	50

ORDNANCE AND TOPOGRAPHICAL DEPARTMENT.

Chief of Ordnance	per month	407	50
Colonel	" "	221	00
Lieutenant-Colonel	" "	211	00
Major	" "	187	00
Captain	" "	129	00
First Lieutenant	" "	112	83
Second Lieut	" "	112	83
Brevet Second Lieutenant	" "	112	83

RELIGIOUS.

The number of Protestants of the world, according to the statistics of all nations, is about as follows:

United States	33,000,000
Great Britain and Ireland	25,000,000
Asia and Armenia	5,000,000
British America and West Indies	4,000,000
France, Belgium and Holland	5,000,000
South America	1,500,000
Sweden, Norway and Denmark	7,600,000
The German Empire	25,000,000
Throughout the rest of the world	13,000,000
Total	121,000,000

Or about one in every fourteen of the inhabitants of the world are Protestants. Of this number there is about one in every four identified with or members of the different Protestant churches of the world. It then follows that the entire membership of all the Protestant churches of the world amounts to one in fifty-six of the inhabitants.

The number of Roman Catholics (approximately correct) is as follows:

United States	3,500,000
Great Britain and Ireland	6,000,000
Russia	7,200,000
South America	21,000,000
France	36,000,000
Austria and Venetia	28,000,000
Spain	17,000,000
Other parts of the world	60,000,000
Total	200,900,000

Pagans, or those who worshipped idols, or created things or beings, they number near three-fourths of the entire inhabitants of the earth. They number at present about 1,000,000,000. This includes the Mohammedans, the Buddhists and the Mormons, or Latter Day Saints. Of this number there is to be found in the United States, of Mormons, 75,000. And strange as it may seem, we have about 60,000 Heathen idol worshippers, who have began erecting their temples on American soil. There is one in San Francisco, California, and I understand one is being erected at Denver City, Colorado.

The number of church edifices and value of church property of the principal religious organizations in the United States, are as follows:

NAME.	CHURCHES.	VALUE.
Baptist (regular)	12,857	$39,229,221
Baptist (other)	1,105	2,378,977
Christian	2,822	6,425,137
Congregational	2,715	25,069,698
Episcopal	2,601	36,514,549
Evangelical Association	641	2,301,650
Friends	662	3,939,560
Jews	152	5,155,234
Lutheran	2,776	14,917,747
Methodist	21,337	69,854,121
Moravian	67	709,100
Mormon	171	656,750
Swedenborgian	61	869,700
Presbyterian (regular)	5,683	47,828,732
Presbyterian (other)	1,388	5,436,524
Dutch Reform	468	10,359,255
Late German Reform	1,145	5,775,215
Roman Catholic	3,806	60,985,566
Second Advent	140	306,240
Shakers	18	86,900
Spiritualist	22	100,150
Unitarian	310	6,282,675
United Brethren	937	1,819,810
Universalist	602	5,692,325
Unknown (union)	552	965,295
Unknown Local Missions	27	687,800
Total	63,082	$354,483,581

STATISTICAL.

POPULATION OF EACH STATE.

Alabama	996,992	Missouri	1,721,295
Arkansas	484,471	Nebraska	122,993
California	560,247	Nevada	42,491
Connecticut	537,454	New Hampshire	318,300
Delaware	125,015	New Jersey	906,095
Florida	187,748	New York	4,382,759
Georgia	1,184,109	North Carolina	1,071,361
Illinois	2,539,891	Ohio	2,665,260
Indiana	1,680,637	Oregon	90,923
Iowa	1,194,020	Pennsylvania	3,521,951
Kansas	364,399	Rhode Island	217,353
Kentucky	1,321,011	South Carolina	705,606
Louisiana	726,915	Tennessee	1,258,520
Maine	626,915	Texas	818,579
Maryland	780,894	Vermont	330,551
Massachusetts	1,457,351	Virginia	1,225,163
Michigan	1,184,059	West Virginia	442,014
Minnesota	459,706	Wisconsin	1,054,670
Mississippi	827,922		
		Total	38,115,641

POPULATION OF THE TERRITORIES.

Arizona	9,658	New Mexico	91,874
Colorado	39,864	Utah	86,786
Dakota	14,181	Washington	29,955
District of Columbia	131,700	Wyoming	9,118
Idaho	14,999		
Montana	20,595	Total	442,730

POPULATION OF THE PRINCIPAL CITIES.

New York, N. Y	942,292	Charleston, S. C	48,956
Philadelphia, Pa	674,022	Indianapolis, Ind	48,244
Brooklyn, N. Y	396,099	Troy, N. Y	40,465
St. Louis, Mo	310,864	Syracuse, N. Y	43,051

STATISTICAL.

POPULATION OF THE PRINCIPAL CITIES—CONTINUED:

City	Population	City	Population
Chicago, Ill.	298,977	Worcester, Mass.	41,105
Baltimore, Md.	267,354	Lowell, Mass.	40,928
Boston, Mass.	250,526	Memphis, Tenn.	40,226
Cincinnati, Ohio	216,239	Cambridge, Mass.	39,634
New Orleans, La.	191,418	Hartford, Conn.	37,180
San Francisco, Cal.	149,473	Scranton, Pa.	35,092
Buffalo, N. Y.	117,714	Reading, Pa.	33,630
Washington, D. C.	109,199	Patterson, N. J.	33,579
Newark, N. J.	105,059	Kansas City, Mo.	32,260
Louisville, Ky.	100,753	Mobile, Ala.	32,034
Cleveland, Ohio	92,829	Toledo, Ohio	31,584
Pittsburgh, Pa.	86,076	Portland, Me.	31,413
Jersey City, N. J.	82,546	Columbus, Ohio	31,274
Detroit, Mich.	79,577	Wilmington, Del.	30,841
Milwaukee, Wis.	71,440	Dayton, Ohio	30,473
Albany, N. Y.	69,422	Lawrence, Mass.	28,921
Providence, R. I.	68,904	Utica, N. Y.	28,804
Rochester, N. Y.	62,386	Charlestown, Mass.	28,323
Allegheny, Pa.	53,180	Savannah, Ga.	28,235
Richmond, Va.	51,038	Lynn, Mass.	28,233
New Haven, Conn.	50,840	Fall River, Mass.	26,766

THE NUMBER of all the male citizens over the age of twenty-one years in the United States and Territories, as shown by the statistics of the last Census:

State	Number	State	Number
Alabama	202,046	Missouri	380,235
Arizona	3,397	Montana	11,523
Arkansas	100,043	Nebraska	36,169
California	145,802	Nevada	18,652
Colorado	15,515	New Hampshire	83,361
Connecticut	127,499	New Jersey	194,109
Dakota	5,234	New Mexico	22,442
Delaware	28,207	New York	981,587
District of Columbia	31,622	North Carolina	214,224
Florida	38,854	Ohio	592,350
Georgia	234,919	Oregon	24,608
Idaho	5,557	Pennsylvania	776,345
Illinois	542,843	Rhode Island	43,996
Indiana	376,780	South Carolina	146,614
Iowa	255,802	Tennessee	259,016
Kansas	99,065	Texas	169,215
Kentucky	282,305	Utah	10,147
Louisiana	159,201	Vermont	74,867
Maine	153,160	Virginia	266,680
Maryland	169,845	Washington	7,902

NUMBER MALE CITIZENS, etc.—COTINUED:

Massachusetts	312,770	West Virginia	93,435
Michigan	274,459	Wisconsin	203,077
Minnesota	75,274	Wyoming	5,297
Mississippi	169,737		
		Total,	8,425,941

By the above the full amount of the vote of each State is shown, and as the vote for President in 1872 was not a strict party vote, we will give the vote for President in 1868, as polled for Grant and Seymour, as we think this more satisfactory.

VOTE OF EACH STATE OF THE UNION.

	Rep.	Dem.
Alabama	76,366	72,086
Arkansas	22,152	19,078
California	54,592	54,078
Connecticut	50,996	47,951
Delaware	7,623	10,980
Florida (By Legislature.)		
Georgia	57,134	102,822
Illinois	250,293	199,143
Indiana	176,552	166,980
Iowa	120,399	74,040
Kansas	31,046	14,019
Kentucky	39,569	115,889
Louisiana	33,263	80,225
Maine	70,426	42,396
Maryland	30,438	62,357
Massachusetts	136,437	59,408
Michigan	128,550	97,069
Minnesota	43,542	28,072
Mississippi (No vote.)		
Missouri	85,671	59,878
Nebraska	9,729	5,439
Nevada	6,480	5,218
New Hampshire	38,191	31,224
New Jersey	80,121	83,001
New York	419,883	429,883
North Carolina	96,226	84,090
Ohio	280,828	238,700
Oregon	10,961	11,125
Pennsylvania	342,280	313,382
Rhode Island	12,903	6,548
South Carolina	62,301	45,237
Tennessee	56,757	26,311
Texas (No vote.)		

VOTE OF EACH STATE OF THE UNION—CONTINUED.

Vermont	44,167	12,045
Virginia (No vote.)		
West Virginia	29,025	20,306
Wisconsin	108,857	84,710
Total	3,012,188	2,703,590

POPULATION OF INDIANA BY COUNTIES, 1870.

Adams	11,382	Madison	22,770
Allen	43,494	Marion	71,939
Bartholomew	21,131	Marshal	20,211
Benton	5,615	Martin	11,103
Blackford	6,272	Miami	21,052
Boone	22,593	Monroe	14,168
Brown	8,681	Montgomery	23,765
Carroll	16,152	Morgan	17,528
Cass	24,193	Newton	5,829
Clarke	24,770	Noble	20,389
Clay	19,084	Ohio	5,837
Clinton	17,330	Orange	13,497
Crawford	9,851	Owen	16,137
Daviess	16,747	Park	18,166
Dearborn	24,116	Perry	14,801
Decatur	19,053	Pike	13,779
DeKalb	17,167	Porter	13,942
Delaware	19,030	Posey	19,185
Dubois	12,597	Pulaski	7,801
Elkhart	26,026	Putnam	21,514
Fayette	10,476	Randolph	22,862
Floyd	23,300	Ripley	20,977
Fountain	16,389	Rush	17,626
Franklin	20,223	Scott	7,823
Fulton	12,726	Shelby	21,892
Gibson	17,371	Spencer	17,998
Grant	18,487	Starke	3,888
Greene	19,514	Steuben	12,854
Hamilton	20,882	St. Joseph	25,322
Hancock	15,123	Sullivan	18,453
Harrison	19,913	Switzerland	12,134
Hendricks	20,277	Tippecanoe	33,515
Henry	22,986	Tipton	11,953
Howard	15,847	Union	6,341
Huntington	12,036	Vanderburg	33,145
Jackson	18,974	Vermillion	10,840
Jasper	6,354	Vigo	33,549

STATISTICAL.

POPULATION OF INDIANA BY COUNTIES—CONTINUED.

Jay	15,000	Wabash	21,305
Jefferson	29,741	Warren	10,204
Jennings	16,218	Warrick	17,653
Johnson	18,366	Washington	18,495
Knox	21,562	Wayne	34,048
Kosciusko	23,531	Wells	13,585
LaGrange	14,148	White	10,554
Lake	12,339	Whitley	14,399
LaPorte	27,062		
Lawrence	14,628	Total	1,680,637

INDIANA TOWNS THAT HAVE 500, OR OVER, INHABITANTS.

Decatur, Adams county	858
New Haven, Allen county	912
Ft. Wayne, Allen county	17,718
Monroeville, Allen county	630
Columbus, Bartholomew county	3,359
Hope, Bartholomew county	765
Oxford, Benton county	519
Hartford, Blackford county	878
Lebanon, Boone county	1,572
Zionsville, Boone county	956
Jamestown, Boone county	603
Thorntown, Boone county	1,526
Delphi, Carroll county	1,614
Browntown, Cass county	903
Logansport, Cass county	8,950
West Logan, Cass county	978
Charleston, Clarke county	2,204
Jeffersonville, Clarke county	7,254
Brazil, Clay county	2,186
Staunton, Clay county	587
Knightsville, Clay county	1,071
Harmony, Clay county	597
Bowling Green, Clay county	606
Frankfort, Clinton county	1,300
Leavenworth, Crawford county	567
Washington, Daviess county	2,901
Aurora, Dearborn county	3,304
Cochran, Dearborn county	675
Lawrenceburg, Dearborn county	3,159
Moore's Hill, Dearborn county	617
Waterloo, DeKalb county	1,259
Auburn, DeKalb county	677
Muncie, Delaware county	2,992

INDIANA TOWNS, ETC.—CONTINUED.

Jasper, Dubois county	547
Elkhart, Elkhart county	3.265
Goshen, Elkhart county	3,133
Bristol, Elkhart county	681
Connersville, Fayette county	2,496
New Albany, Floyd county	15,396
Attica, Fountain county	2,273
Covington, Fountain county	1,888
Laurel, Franklin county	741
Rochester, Fulton county	1,528
Owensville, Gibson county	522
Princeton, Gibson county	1,847
Patoka, Gibson county	844
Marion, Grant county	1,658
Jonesboro, Grant county	581
Bloomfield, Green county	656
Westfield, Hamilton county	608
Noblesville, Hamilton county	1,435
Greenfield, Hancock county	1,203
Corydon, Harrison county	747
Danville, Hendricks county	1,080
Plainfield, Hendricks county	795
Brownsburg, Hendricks county	551
Middletown, Henry county	711
Knightstown, Henry county	1,528
Kokomo, Howard county	2,177
Roanoke, Huntington county	627
Brownstown, Jackson county	572
Seymour, Jackson county	2,372
Rensselaer, Jasper county	617
Hanover, Jefferson county	564
North Madison, Jefferson county	1,007
Madison, Jefferson county	10,709
North Vernon, Jennings county	1,758
Vernon, Jennings county	673
Edinburg, Johnson county	1,799
Franklin City	2,707
Vincennes, Knox county	5,440
Pierceton, Kosciusko county	1,063
LaGrange, LaGrange county	1,038
LaPorte, LaPorte county	6,581
Michigan City, LaPorte county	3,985
Westville City, LaPor e county	640
Mitchell, Lawrence county	1,087

INDIANA TOWNS, ETC.—CONTINUED.

Anderson, Madison county	3,126
Pendleton, Madison county	675
Bourborn, Marshall county	874
Plymouth, Marshall county	2,482
Shoals, Martin county	512
Loogootee, Martin county	748
Peru, Miami county	3,617
Bloomington, Monroe county	1,030
Ladoga, Montgomery county	878
Crawfordsville, Montgomery county	3,701
Mooresville, Morgan county	1.229
Martinsville, Morgan county	1,131
Kentland, Newton county	802
Kendallville, Noble county	2,164
Ligonier, Noble county	1,514
Rising Sun, Ohio county	1,760
Orleans, Orange county	905
Paoli, Orange county	628
Spencer, Owen county	971
Gosport, Owen county	860
Rockville, Park county	1,187
Montezuma, Park, county	624
Cannelton, Perry county	2,481
Tell City, Perry county	1,660
Petersburg, Pike county	923
Valparaiso, Porter county	2,765
Mount Vernon, Posey county	2,880
New Harmony, Posey county	836
Winnamack, Pulaski county	906
Greencastle, Putnam county	3,227
Ridgeville, Randolph county	716
Farmland, Randolph county	532
Union City, Randolph county	1,439
Winchester, Randolph county	1,456
Versails, Ripley county	500
Rushville, Rush county	1,096
Shelbyville, Shelby county	2,731
Rockport, Spencer county	1,720
Angola, Steuben county	1,072
Mishawaka, St. Joseph county	2,617
South Bend, St. Joseph county	7,206
Sullivan, Sullivan county	1,396
Lafayette, Tippecanoe county	13,516
Tipton, Tipton county	892

INDIANA TOWNS, ETC.—CONTINUED.

Liberty, Union county	700
Evansville, Vanderburgh county	21,830
Clinton, Vermillion county	564
Perrysville, Vermillion county	690
Terre Haute, Vigo county	16,103
Lagro, Wabash county	519
Wabash City, Wabash county	2,881
Williamsport, Warren county	988
Booneville, Warrick county	1,039
Newburg, Warrick county	1,464
Salem, Washington county	1,294
Centreville, Wayne county	1,077
East Germantown, Wayne county	536
Hagerstown, Wayne county	833
Richmond, Wayne county	9,445
Milton, Wayne county	823
Blufftown, Wells county	1,138
Monticello, White county	887
Columbia, Whitley county	1,633

SABBATH SCHOOLS.

The first Sabbath School that we have been able to find a record of, was established in the year 1769 in the town of Wycumbe, England, by a young Methodist lady by the name of Hannah Ball. A few years after this another young lady who afterwards became the wife of Samuel Bradburn, suggested the idea of Sabbath Schools to Robert Rakes. He being a man of quick perception and great energy saw at once the advantages to be gained by schools of this kind. He immediately set to work and organized a school in the city of Gloucester, England, and through his labors and influence other cities of that country were induced to establish Sabbath Schools and work for the Sunday School interest.

The first Sabbath School established in the United States was organized by Bishop Asbury, in the year 1786, in Hanover County, Va., at the house of Mr. Thomas Cranshaw. The progress of Sabbath Schools in the United States until about the year 1830, was rather slow, as but few of the Christian denominations up to that time had become interested in the Sunday School cause. But one by one, the different organizations of Christians have gradually adopted the institution of Sabbath Schools, till now, the popular method of all churches for the religious training of the young is the Sunday School. Now, in every land and nation, where Christian people reside, the Sabbath School cause is advancing.

>The organization of Sabbath Schools,
> Remember one and all,
>Was first established in Wycumbe,
> By Miss Hannah Ball.

>After this Miss Bradburn
> Suggested to Robert Rakes
>To organize a Sabbath School,
> And helped him set the stakes.

They organized in Gloucester,
  The banner they unfurled,
The fame and name of which has spread,
  Almost throughout the world.

The honor due to Robert Rakes,
  Miss Bradburn and Miss Ball.
Should not be given to Robert Rakes,
  But given to them all.

For the institution of Sabbath Schools,
  The honor is due Miss Ball.
To her for lighting up the lamp,
  We give the honor all.

Miss Bradburn she is worthy of
  Our honor, love, and praise,
For her suggestions, and her work,
  In keeping up the blaze.

And to Robert Rakes is due
  The honor of school extension,
For adding fuel to the light,
  And widening its dimension.

VALUABLE RECIPES.

For Cleaning Silverware, and for Silvering Copper.—One-fourth ounce crystal nitrate of silver, one-half ounce cream of tartar, one-fourth ounce of common salt; pulverize all to a fine powder together, bottle it up and it is ready for use. Apply with a woolen rag, wetting the rag so as the powder will stick to it.

For Distemper in Horses.—Ground ginger, two ounces; flour of sulphur, two ounces; copperas, two ounces; Spanish brown, two ounces; saltpeter, one-half ounce; mix thoroughly. Give a tablespoonful once a day in bran mash. Keep the animal warm and dry, with light exercise.

Whitewash for Out Doors.—Take good white unslacked lime, one peck; salt, one quart; two pounds Spanish whiting; one gallon good flour paste; first slack the lime in hot water; be sure to put enough on to keep the lime from burning; then add while warm the salt and Spanish white, and then the paste; let stand over night. It is better to have it warm while applying it.

For Removing Paint From Glass.—Baking soda and warm water.

Antidote for Poison.—Give sweet oil in large doses.

For Worms in Children.—Santenine, nine grains; calomel, six grains; white sugar, eighteen grains; mix well; make in six powders for a child two years old, and give one before each meal for two days; work off with oil.

For Removing Grease Spots From Cloth.—Soda, two drachms; borax, one drachm; dissolve it together in one ounce of hot water, then add one ounce of alcohol. Shake it well and apply with woolen rag or brush, rubbing briskly.

To Get Rid of Little Ants.—Use salt and water freely where they infest.

Washing Fluid.—Borax, one pound; soda, one pound; dissolve in two gallons of hot water. Put the clothes in the tub, cover them with water containing a half gallon of the fluid, and let stand over night.

For Toothache, Headache, Neuralgia, and Rheumatic Pains.—Make a liniment of the following preparations: One ounce of tincture of Amonia, one ounce tincture of camphor, one ounce oil of organum, one-half ounce oil of cedar, one ounce oil of hemlock, and one quart linseed oil; mix all together, put it in a bottle and shake well. Directions for using. Apply the liniment freely to the affected parts, and rub and bathe it as often as three or four times daily. For the toothache, put a little on a piece of cotton, and put it in the tooth, and rub it on the jaw of the patient. I have found this to be one of the best liniments in use.

For Cuts and Bruises on Man or Beast.—Take two ounces tincture of camphor, two ounces linseed oil, one ounce of turpentine; mix all together, and apply to the affected parts.

For Pickling Beef.—To 100 pounds of beef take one gallon of salt, three-fourths of a pound of sugar, three ounces black pepper ground; add together, put all in a kettle containing three gallons of water; boil slowly, and skim occasionally. Pack the beef in tight tubs, and cover with the brine.

DIRECTORY

OF

MORGAN COUNTY

FOR 1874.

PREFACE.

The subscribers for this work will remember that the agents who solicited for their subscription promised that it should contain a historical sketch of Morgan county. Therefore, we pen the following pages after a careful examination of the records and a personal interview with the pioneer settlers of the county; and we hope that our patrons will be satisfied with our efforts to fulfill our promise.

The facts that we have collected in reference to the early history and growth of this county are somewhat limited, yet we feel that they are of sufficient worth for presentation, as such information is constantly becoming more difficult to obtain, as the old pioneers of the county are swiftly passing away, and in a few more years they will have all passed away to an unknown world, and it is to be hoped that our efforts in collecting statistics and historical information in reference to the county may have the effect to stimulate some one who is more competent to write a more complete and better history of Morgan county, and preserve the memory of those who first settled this county, who withstood the hardships and privations of a pioneer life, and through whose patient endurance and hardships the present citizens enjoy the fruits of their labor and so many of the blessings of life.

For the items of information and statistics that will be found recorded in this historical sketch, I take pleasure in acknowledging my obligations to the present gentlemanly county officials who so kindly assisted me to obtain the needed information. Also, I take pleasure in thanking the old pioneer settlers of the county for the information that I have received from them, hoping that when they are called to leave this mundane sphere, these homes and beautiful fields, that they may receive the pleasures of a new world, minus the privations and toils that it has been their lot to endure here.

P. S. Mr. John Lesley, who made the canvass of a portion of this county, requests of me to return his thanks to the citizens whom he visted for their gentlemanly treatment and liberal patronage.

PREFACE.

The subscribers for this work will remember that the agents who solicited for their subscription promised that it should contain a historical sketch of Morgan county. Therefore, we pen the following pages after a careful examination of the records and a personal interview with the pioneer settlers of the county; and we hope that our patrons will be satisfied with our efforts to fulfill our promise.

The facts that we have collected in reference to the early history and growth of this county are somewhat limited, yet we feel that they are of sufficient worth for presentation, as such information is constantly becoming more difficult to obtain, as the old pioneers of the county are swiftly passing away, and in a few more years they will have all passed away to an unknown world, and it is to be hoped that our efforts in collecting statistics and historical information in reference to the county may have the effect to stimulate some one who is more competent to write a more complete and better history of Morgan county, and preserve the memory of those who first settled this county, who withstood the hardships and privations of a pioneer life, and through whose patient endurance and hardships the present citizens enjoy the fruits of their labor and so many of the blessings of life.

For the items of information and statistics that will be found recorded in this historical sketch, I take pleasure in acknowledging my obligations to the present gentlemanly county officials who so kindly assisted me to obtain the needed information. Also, I take pleasure in thanking the old pioneer settlers of the county for the information that I have received from them, hoping that when they are called to leave this mundane sphere, these homes and beautiful fields, that they may receive the pleasures of a new world, minus the privations and toils that it has been their lot to endure here.

P. S. Mr. John Lesley, who made the canvass of a portion of this county, requests of me to return his thanks to the citizens whom he visted for their gentlemanly treatment and liberal patronage.

HISTORICAL SKETCH

OF

MORGAN COUNTY.

MORGAN COUNTY, Indiana, is centrally located in the State, and is bounded on the north by Hendricks and Marion counties, on the east by Johnson, on the south by Brown and Monroe, and on the west by Owen and Putnam, and contains an area of about 450 square miles, or 291,800 acres of land; and is watered by White River, White Lick Creek, Mud Creek, Big Indian Creek, Stotts's Creek, Clear Creek, Burnett's Creek, Rhodes's Creek, Mill Creek, and their tributaries.

There is a considerable portion of this county that is rough and broken, especially the bluffs of White River, which is not very profitable for grain growing, but can be made the most profitable part of the county for the production of fruits, such as apples, peaches, pears; and, in fact, all kinds of fruits grown in this climate do well here, and the horticulturist is sure to receive a profitable return for his labor. There is about one-third of this county that is bottom lands; the soil of this portion of the county is a sandy loam, and very rich and productive. Grain and vegetables of all kinds can be profitably cultivated here, and especially Indian corn, which is grown in great quantities, and is the principal product of the county.

The timber of the county is hardly surpassed in the State, both for quantity and quality, consisting of poplar, walnut, white oak, hickory, beech, sugar-tree, and other varieties. There is also to be found in this county some mineral wealth. The amount is yet untold, but those monstrous hills are not rolled up there for nothing, but surely contain a mint of wealth. Already some of them have been visited by exploring parties prospecting for gold, and some explorers have been bountifully paid for their labor by washing the dirt along the streams.

ORGANIZATION.

By an act of the Legislature in 1823, the boundaries of the county were established, and the county was organized and named in honor of Gen. Daniel Morgan. The regular county officials being duly installed, she commenced business as an independent county, subject only to the State of Indiana. Her first County Commissioners were Benjamin Huffman, Jonathan Williams, and Larken Reynolds.

The first county election that was held in the county was held in a log house that was built by Mr. Stotts. The house was built in the year 1819, and still stands, one and one-half miles west of Waverly, on the gravel road running from Brooklyn to Indianapolis. This house is claimed by some to be the first house built in the county.

The first Clerk of the county was George H. Beeler, succeeded by George A. Phelps, H. R. Stevens, James Jackson, O. R. Dougherty, J. K. Scott, J. J. Wright, J. J. Johnson, John Hardwick, J. H. Piercy by appointment, and Willis Record, the present incumbent of the office.

The office of Recorder was not called into existence in the county as a separate office until about the year 1840; the business prior to this time was done by the Clerk of the county. The first Recorder that was elected to act as Recorder of the county, independent of the Clerk's office, was Stephen Mc-

Cracken, who was succeeded by Hiram T. Craig, A. J. Whitesett, Stephen McCracken, etc.

The first Sheriff of the county was Benjamin Cutberth.

The first school taught in the county was taught by Hiram T. Craig, in a small log school-house located in what is now called Harrison Township, one and one-half miles west of Waverly; and as Uncle Hiram is still living in the county, we presume he has lived to see some wonderful changes in the public school property and the manner of teaching schools.

The first dry goods merchant in the county was Samuel Moore, the founder of the town of Mooresville. He came to the county in the year 1823, and laid out the town of Mooresville, and has lived in the place ever since.

The first gristmill that was built in the county was located on White Lick Creek, near the town of Brooklyn, and was built and run by Benjamin Cutberth.

The first couple that were joined in marriage in the county were Reuben Claypool and Mattie Russel.

The first white child born in the county was a son of James A. Laughlen.

The first paper published in the county was the *Mooresville Chronicle*, owned and edited by Thomas J. Worth.

The first purchase of land in the county was made by Philip Hodges, in the year 1818, but said land was not surveyed until the year 1819.

The first woolen factory in the county was owned by Wm. C. Cline, and was run by a tread-wheel; at that time there was not a steam engine in the State.

FIRST SETTLERS.

With rations short and home-spun dress,
For many years in this wilderness
  They struggled with their lot.
They killed the beasts that there did roam,
And made a paradise of home
  From many a rugged spot.

The first settlers of which any reliable information has been obtained, came to this county between the years 1817 and 1819. Upon this point there seems to be some little difference of opinion. Mr. Philip Hodges claims to have purchased land in this county in the year 1818, and to have settled in the county the same year. Mrs. Rebecca Douglass claims to have come to the county in the year 1817, and settled among the Indians. Mr. Hiram T. Craig, one of the first settlers of the county, and an old citizen that is possessed of a great memory, is of the opinion that the first colony of emigrants to this county arrived here on the third day of March, 1819, and among whom were Robert C. Stotts, James A. Laughlen, James Stotts, Nathan Laughlen, W. M. Offield, and himself, and settled in what is now called Harrison Township. I would be pleased to have the space and information, so that I could give the names of all the first settlers of this county, especially those whose date of settlement is not given in the Directory part of this work; but as the names of almost all of the old settlers that are still living will be shown up in the Township sketches or Directory, I will only mention the names of a few that should be held in remembrance by the rising generation. Among those are the six families that have already been mentioned as forming the first colony, also the families of Hodges, Samuel Moore, Judge Hiram Mathews, Benjamin Huffman, Jonathan Williams, Larken Reynolds, George H. Beeler, G. A. Phelps, the family of McCrackens, Benjamin Cutberth, Reuben Claypool, Alexander and Thomas J. Worth, Daniel Thornberg, Jack Record, John Bray, Madison Hadley, Richard Hadley, Benjamin Stafford, and Rebecca Blunk. She is now a citizen of Clay Township. She was one of the first settlers, and is the oldest person in the county, and perhaps the oldest lady in the State. She was born in Richmond, Va., in the year 1768, and is now one hundred and six years old. She was one of a party that emigrated to

Kentucky, and was piloted to the State by Daniel Boone, as he, Boone, returned to the State of Kentucky after paying a visit to the State of Virginia, his old native State. She afterwards removed to Morgan county, Ind., in the year 1819. She is an old pioneer that has withstood the privations and labor that were necessary to be endured by the old settlers of the States of Kentucky and Indiana.

THE PAST AND PRESENT.

In the year 1799 Indiana Territory was not known as a separate territory, but was embraced in what was called the Northwestern Territory, comprising what is now the States of Illinois, Indiana, Michigan, Wisconsin, and a part of the State of Minnesota. In the year 1800 Indiana was carved out as a separate territory, with a population (according to the census report) of 5330 inhabitants, and was divided into three counties, namely, Knox, Dearborn and Clark. From 1800 to 1813 the seat of government was at Vincennes. In the year 1813 it was removed to Corydon. In the year 1816 Indiana was admitted into the Union as an independent State, and was divided into eighteen counties. At this time more than three-fourths of the State was in possession of the Indians. A law of Congress forbade the private purchase of the Indian lands; but by a treaty with the Indians, which was negotiated at St. Mary's in the year 1818, by Gov. Jennings, Gov. Cass, and Judge Parke, Commissioners on the part of the United States, the Indians gave up all claim and title to the lands southeast of the Wabash River, except a few small reservations. By this treaty central Indiana was made accessible to the whites, and the settlement of this county began soon after. The survey of lands was not made until the years 1819 and 1820. Prior to the year 1818 no white man had ever settled on this soil, felled a tree or built a cabin in this county. In the year 1819 a few settlements were made, and gradually the tide of emigration to the county increased, until the year 1823, the county had increased to a sufficient population to form the county organization.

After the organization the increase in the population was more rapid. In 1830 she had increased in population to 5,593; in 1840 to 10,741; in 1850 to 14,576; in 1860 to 16,110, and in 1870 to 17,528, and since 1870 her population has been gradually on the increase. Here vote has increased at the same rate of her population, and now she has a voting population of over 4,000. The vote at the last State election was just 4,000. Her increase in wealth, improvement and enterprise have surpassed her increase of numbers. She now has 14 civil townships, namely: Washington, Jackson, Green, Harrison, Madison, Brown, Clay, Monroe, Gregg, Adams, Ray, Jefferson, Baker and Ashland. The county, past and present, seems to have been very well supplied with towns and villages. At present she has 16, namely: Martinsville, the county seat, located near the center of the county in Washington township, has a population of about 1700 inhabitants, and is the most central trading point in the county. The citizens in this place are alive to business, clever and social. Hastings, a small town on the railroad, is also located in Washington township. Cross Roads, a small trading point located in Green township. Waverly is a nice little village, and perhaps the oldest town in the county, situated close to White River in Harrison township. Monrovia, a town of some four hundred inhabitants, is a nice enterprising business place, located near the north line of the county in Monroe township. Hall, Pine City and Lincoln are all villages of respectability, situated in Gregg township. Eminence, a town of three hundred citizens, is located near the west line of the county, in Adams township. Brooklyn and Centerton are places of considerable note in Clay township, and both are on the railroad. Centerton once received the vote of the county to make it the county seat, but for some cause the removal was not made. Hynd's Station is a small railroad village in Jefferson township. Morgantown, located in the southeast corner of the county in Jackson township, is a nice railroad trading point of considerable business. Maheleysville is also located in Jackson township. Alaska, the post-office of Ashland township, and Lewisville, one half mile east of Alaska, in the same township. Atlanta, a small village located in the southeast part of Green township. Paragon, located in Ray township, is a railroad village and quite a trading point for the southwestern portion of the county. Matthew's Station, a station on the railroad, three and one half miles south of Mooresville, in Brown township. Last but not least is Mooresville, located in the northeast corner of the county in Brown township, and has a population of about 1600 inhabitants. In point of business enterprise and wealth, Mooresville is hardly surpassed in the county. The founder of this place, who is well known to the citizens of the county, is still one of its most influential citizens.

CHURCHES AND SCHOOLS.

The county is well supplied in most parts with good churches and schools. There have been in the last few years great improvements made in the way of fine school houses and neat and costly churches. The old log school houses and churches are things of the past, and at almost every cross-road we now see beautiful frame or brick building supplying their places.

The public improvements of the county will compare favorable with other counties of the State, and the citizens of most parts of the county are favorable to the expenditures of money that are constantly being made by the present County Commissioners for public improvements, and if the same spirit of enterprise continues to exist in the minds of the County Commissioners and the tax-payers, this county ere long will rank high in the scale of public improvement.

Morality and education are likewise on the advance, both marching forward to greater perfection, and leaving behind superstition, ignorance and rowdyism, that existed in this county in former years.

MANUFACTURING ESTABLISHMENTS.

For many years after the organization the only manufacturing establishment of the county was the old-fashioned horse mill for cracking corn, where every man furnished the horse power for grinding his own grist of corn, and now and then a small water or tread wheel for the same purpose. But gradually the spirit of improvement for manufacturing moved the people to attach machinery for carding wool, sawing lumber, threshing wheat, etc.

One by one different manufacturing establishments have been erected to supply the demands of the people, until now in this age of improvement the county has 164 manufacturing establishments, consisting of woolen mills, grist mills, saw mills, planing mills, sash and door factories, stave factories, furniture and other establishments too tedious to mention. She has 43 steam engines and 9 water wheels. Said establishments consume about $500,000 worth of raw material annually, and give employment to near 700 hands, and produce annually near $1,000,000 worth of manufactured articles.

HER AGRICULTURAL RESOURCES.

The agricultural resources of the county have been in proportion to the number of acres of improved land and the facility for cultivating the same; consequently for the first few years after the settlement of the county the agricultural products were very limited, and the old pioneer could not depend altogether on the proceeds of his lands for support, but had to resort to the rifle and the tomahawk to supply his clapboard table with the necessaries to feed his patient wife and hungry children.

> Day after day his table was spread,
> His wife would call him to eat;
> Very often minus the bread,
> But *never* minus the meat.

But the clearing of the lands has given a gradual and steady increase to the products of the county until she now has 133,-615 acres of improved land, producing annually 330,000 bushels of winter wheat, 6,500 bushels of rye, 1,190,000 bushels of Indian corn, 65,000 bushels of oats, from 200 to 1500 bushels of barley, 50,000 bushels of potatoes, 229,355 pounds of butter, near 10,000 tons of hay, and over 60,000 pounds of wool, besides thousands of dollars worth of vegetables. The value of the improved land in the county, according to the statistics of 1872, was $8,565,565.

LIVE STOCK.

The domesticated animals of the county have been greatly improved, both in numbers and quality. Stock raising has become profitable, and now some of the best stock raisers of the State are citizens of Morgan county. The total estimated value of all her live stock for the year 1872 is $1,250,651. The number of horses in the county is 6142; mules and asses, 550; milch cows, 4375; work oxen, 184; sheep, 21,000, and about 35,000 head of swine.

ROADS AND MARKETS.

For several years the first settlers of this county kept track of the roads by blazing the timber as a guide for the direction they wished to travel. In that day the travel was generally done on foot, except the milling, and in this case the settler would take his horse, if he had any, because it was necessary that he should be used as the power for propelling the mill to grind his corn. Wheat bread was then out of the question. The only market they had much need of then was the fur trader, who bought their furs and gave them in exchange a few of the necessaries of life. But gradually as their field expanded they began to produce a surplus of wheat and Indian corn. Consequently better roads to a more distant market had to be made and put in condition to travel with wagons. Then for several years their markets were Madison, Lawrenceburg and Cincinnati; but the steady growth of the State and the rapid increase of the population of Indianapolis, soon gave them a market closer to home; and now in this age of railroads and steam power, every farmer in the county has a market at home for his surplus.

The county now has some very fine turnpike and gravel roads, and near fifty miles of railroad; the Indianapolis & Vincennes R. R. spanning the entire county from its northeast to its southwest corner, and the Martinsville & Cincinnati R. R. traversing the county from Martinsville to the southeast corner. Instead of the old-fashioned way of traveling by ox-teams in the mud at the rate of one or two miles per hour, we now travel by steam on the railroad at the rate of twenty or thirty miles per hour. Instead of waiting six or eight days to get an answer to a letter from Indianapolis, we now get an answer the same evening; and if we are in a hurry, we communicate by telegraph at lightning speed.

TAXATION.

The total assessed value of all real estate and personal property of the county, according to the statistics of 1872, is $8,320,400; the true value will reach at least $13,000,000. The true amount of all the taxes that were paid into the treasury the same year, the National tax not included, was $128,558; of this amount $36,396 were for State purposes, $53,532 for county, and $38,630 for township purposes.

THE PUBLIC DEBT.

The entire public debt of the county is a very small affair, considering the public improvements of the county. In examining the statistics for the year 1872, I find that the debt of the county at that time only amounted to $30,000; and at the present time I am unable to tell what the actual amount is, but it is to be hoped that it is considerable less.

MORGAN COUNTY, ITS SETTLERS AND ITS BLESSINGS.

> Only fifty-five years ago,
> This was a wilderness of woe,
> The red men wandered to and fro,
>   A roving band.
> The forests then were thick with deer,
> Wild beasts in number everywhere;
> The howling wolf and bear were here.
>   All o'er this land.
>
> The forest oak grew thick and tall,
> No woodsman here to make her fall,
> Untouched by settlers' ax or maul
>   She proud did stand.
> The panther basked within her shade,
> The wildcat on her branches played,
> While at her root the serpent laid
>   In this wild land.
>
> A chaperal of underbrush,
> The bramble and the water rush,
> Grew thick with thorns and hazel brush
>   On every hand.
> The streams ran sluggishly and slow,
> The drift-wood caused their overflow,
> And green ponds made a horrid show,
>   A doleful land.

But, hark! I hear the settler's tread,
He marches onward, looks ahead;
He brings his powder, brings his lead,
      His dog and gun.
He comes to settle in the west,
To clear the land, remove the pest
That did this county then infest;
      More work than fun.

He marches forth with ax in hand,
He takes possession, makes a stand,
He builds his cabin, clears his land,
      And settles down.
His brawny arm is never still,
His energy and iron will,
Will clear this land of every ill
      That here is found.

Serpents and beasts they make retreat,
His dog and gun they fear to meet,
The red man takes a wandering beat
      Still further west.
Onward, still onward, is the settler's tread,
Making improvements, pushing a-head;
His blessings on this people shed
      Till they are blessed.

Blessed with homes, blessed with land,
Life's blessings are at their command,
Blessed with the PEOPLE'S GUIDE in hand,
      Blessed with wealth.
Blessed with the spirit of enterprise,
Blessed with energy to bring supplies;
Forward, onward, upward rise
      To greater wealth.   WM. CLINE, JR.

VOTE OF THE COUNTY BY TOWNSHIPS.

The vote of the county by townships, according to the statistics of the tally-sheet of the last State election, is as follows:

Washington township—Rep., 401; Dem., 386; total, 788; Rep. majority, 18.

Jackson township—Rep., 191; Dem., 186; total, 379; Rep. majority, 8.

Brown township—Rep., 240; Dem., 136; total, 386; Rep. majority, 104.

Clay township—Rep., 196; Dem., 87; total, 285; Rep. majority, 109.

Monroe township.—Rep., 306; Dem., 51; total, 357; Rep. majority, 256.

Gregg township—Rep., 161; Dem., 66; total, 229; Rep. majority, 95.

Ray township—Rep., 115; Dem., 95; total, 214; Rep. majority, 19.

Baker township—Rep., 43; Dem., 41; total, 85; Rep. majority, 2.

Jefferson township—Rep., 153; Dem., 77; total, 223; Rep. majority, 76.

Adams township—[The vote of this township at the last election was not a full one]. Rep., 115; Dem., 150; total, 265; Dem. majority, 35.

Ashland township—Rep., 86; Dem., 137; total, 223; Dem. majority, 51.

Green township—Rep., 38; Dem., 219; total, 263; Dem. majority, 181.

Harrison township—Rep., 36; Dem., 38; total, 74; Dem. majority, 2.

Madison township—Rep., 59; Dem., 155; total, 216; Dem. majority, 61.

The total vote of this county was 4,000 at the last State election; Republican majority, 318.

ADAMS TOWNSHIP.

ADAMS TOWNSHIP is located in the northwest corner of the county, and contains about 30 square miles. It is bounded on the north by Hendricks county, on the west by Putnam county, on the south by Ashland township, and on the east by Monroe and Gregg townships. The most of this township is a low and rich bottom, and is watered by Mud Creek, which runs through this township from the northeast to the southwest corner, emptying into Mill Creek, which is the west line of the county adjoining Putnam county. There is also a low wet scope of country, clear across the township, generally known as the lake. There are several hundred acres of the best land in the county that is covered with water about two-thirds of the time, but when cleared and well ditched will be the most productive part of the township, equal nearly to the bottoms of White River. The citizens of this township are generally industrious and intelligent. The church and school privileges are as good as any in the county.

Eminence, a little village of 250 inhabitants and the only town in the township, is situated on the Stilesville and Gosport road, 10 miles south of Stilesville and on the extreme south of the township. There are 3 dry goods stores in the town, 2 drug stores, 1 picture gallery, 1 saddle and harness shop, and it is one of the best points for trade of all kinds in the surrounding country, there being all the conveniences any small town could wish. Her business men are energetic and clever, and improvements are good.

CHURCH, LODGE AND SCHOOL STATISTICS.

M. Baptist Church, Eminence; pastor, Rev. G. W. Terry; membership, 80; Sabbath school superintendent, N. N. Patrick; average attendance of Sabbath school, 80; value of church property, $1,000.

Christian Church, Eminence; pastor, Rev. J. H. Bauserman; Sabbath school superintendent, W. C. Banta; average attendance of Sabbath school, 60; value of church property, $2,000; membership, 80.

M. E. Church, Eminence; pastor, Rev. J. H. Hamilton; membership, 60; Sabbath school superintendent, not elected; average attendance of Sabbath school, 80; value of church property, $1200.

Christian Church, Mt. Tabor, 5 miles southeast of Stilesville; membership, 130; pastor, Rev. Eli Prunt; value of church property, $1200.

Christian Church, Oak Grove, 4 miles south of Stilesville; pastor, Wm. Runion; membership, 100; Sabbath school superintendent, Samuel Wilson; average Sabbath school attendance, 50; value of property, $1,000.

M. E. Church, Lake Valley, 5 miles southeast of Stilesville; pastor, Rev. Pruitt; membership, 75; Sabbath school superintendent, Wesley McClellan; average Sabbath school attendance, 50; value of church property, $2500.

Eminence Lodge of Free Masons, No. 440; membership, 54; value of Lodge Property, $75.

Eminence Lodge of Odd Fellows, No. 317; membership, 58; value of property, $900.

Eminence Patrons of Husbandry, No. 1091; membership, 50; master, John Rhea; treasurer, W. A. Ryan; secretary, Hiram Staley.

ADAMS TOWNSHIP. 149

Oak Grove Grange, No. 1464, 4 miles south of Stilesville; membership, 28; Henry Bourn, master; Harrison Gentry, secretary.

Township trustee, Solomon Dorsett; number of school houses, 8; value of property, $5,000.

DIRECTORY OF ADAMS TOWNSHIP.

Adams, W. E.; farmer; 4¼ m w Monrovia. Born in Ky. 1842; settled in M. C. 1865. Dem. Christian.

Alley, Thomas; farmer; 7 miles s e Stilesville. Born in N. C. 1845; settled in M. C. ——. Rep. Methodist.

Alexander, John; farmer; 2½ miles n e Eminence. Born in Ind. 18—. Dem. Protestant.

Arnold, Jacob; Proprietor of Eminence House; Eminence. Born in Ind. 1825; settled in M. C. 1840. Rep. Protest.

Bland, William; farmer and carpenter; 5 miles s Stilesville. Born in Ind. 1811; settled in M. C. 1871. Rep. M. Bap.

Bourn, J. M.; farmer; ¼ mile w Eminence. Born in 1847; settled in M. C. 1873. Rep. Baptist.

BRAY, JOHN W.; farmer; 3½ miles s e Stilesville. Born in Ohio 1833; settled in M. C. 1865. Rep. Christian.

Bray, Calvin; farmer; 5 miles s e Stilesville. Born in M. C. 1838. Rep. Christian.

Bray, Atlas; farmer; 6 miles s e Stilesville. Born in N. C. 1826; settled in M. C. 1844. Rep. Methodist.

Bradley, Henry; farmer; 4 miles s e Stilesville. Born in N. C. 1818; settled in M. C. 1821. Dem. Protestant.

Blunk, Joseph; farmer; 2½ miles n w Hall. Born in M. C. 1841. Dem. Protestant.

Baldon, A. J.; farmer; 3 m n w Hall. Born in M. C. 1841. Dem. M. Baptist.

Brasier, Gideon; carpenter; Eminence. Born in Ky. 1814; settled in M. C. 1863. Dem. Baptist.

Brewer, Jesse; farmer; Littlepoint. Born in M. C. 1846. Protestant.

Bourn, Henry; farmer; 3 miles n Eminence. Born in M. C. 1837. Rep. Christian.

Brasier, J. R.; blacksmith; Eminence. Born in Ind. 1836; settled in M. C. 1858. Rep. Protestant.

Brasier, M. W.; saddle and harness maker; Eminence. Born in Ind. 1831; settled in M. C. 1865. Rep. Christian.

Banta, W. C.; physician; Eminence. Born in Ind. 1839; settled in M. C. 1870. Rep. Christian.

Brick, J. A.; druggist; Eminence. Born in Ind. 1844. Rep. Methodist.

Brasier, T. T.; medical student; Eminence. Born in Ind. 1853; settled in M. C. 1865. M. Baptist.

Brasier, P. S.; carpenter and saddler; Eminence. Born in Ind. 1851; settled in M. C. 1860. Rep. Methodist.

Curtis, Peter S.; farmer; 3 miles n w Hall. Born in M. C. 1837. Dem. Christian.

Curtis, Emeziah; farmer; 3 miles n w Hall. Born in M. C. 1839. Dem. Christian.

Curtis, D. A.; farmer; 3½ miles n w Hall. Born in N. C. 1806; settled in M. C. 1837. Dem. Christian.

Curtis, Wesley; farmer; 3 miles n w Hall. Born in N. C. 1831; settled in M. C. 1837. Dem. Christian.

Curtis, Calvin; farmer; 3 miles n w Hall. Born in N. C. 1827; settled in M. C, 1837. Dem. Christian.

Costin, Wm.; farmer; 2½ miles e Eminence. Born in Ky. 1840; settled in M. C. ——. Dem. Protestant.

Chenoweth, S. H.; blacksmith; Littlepoint. Born in M. C. 1837. Christian.

Chenoweth, Jas. E.; mechanic; Littlepoint. Born in M. C. 1846. Neutral. Protestant.

Chenoweth, Ephraim B.; farmer; ¼ mile e Littlepoint. Born in Va. 1805; settled in M. C. 1834. Rep. Christian.

Costin, M. H.; farmer and teacher; 3 miles e Eminence. Born in Ky. 1837; settled in M. C. 1844. Dem. Protestant.

COLLINSWORTH, NATHANIEL; farmer; 4 miles s Stilesville. Born in M. C. 1849. Dem. Protestant.

Collinsworth, Thomas; farmer; 4 miles s Stilesville. Born in M. C. 1844. Dem. Church of God.

Collinsworth, Russel; farmer; 4 miles s Stilesville. Gone from home.

Dorsett, M. R.; farmer; 6 m s e Stilesville. Born in N. C. 1839; settled in M. C. 1861. Dem. Christian.

Donaldson, Jacob; farmer; ½ m e Eminence. Born in Ky. 1826; settled in M. C. 1834. Rep. Protestant.

Donaldson, J. H.; farmer; ½ m e Eminence. Born in M. C. 1853. Rep. Protestant.

Donaldson, Joseph; farmer; ½ m e Eminence. Born in Ky. 1822; settled in M. C. 1834. Rep. Protestant.

Donaldson, Marion; farmer; ½ m e Eminence. Born in M. C. 1847. Rep. M. Baptist.

Donaldson, John; farmer; ½ m e Eminence. Born in M. C. 1853. Rep. M. Baptist.

DORSETT, SOLOMON; farmer and Tp. trustee; Eminence. Born in N.C. 1832; settled in M.C. 1840. Lib. Dem. Christ.

Demott, Abraham; fruit distillery; Eminence. Born in Ohio 1831; settled in M. C. 1850. Dem. Protestant.

Estes, James; carpenter; 2½ m n w Hall. Born in N. C. 1817; settled in M. C. 1851. Dem. Protestant.

Estes, Henry; farmer; 2½ m n w. Hall. Born in N. C. 1839; settled in M. C. 1851. Dem. Christian.

Gentry, Elerson; farmer and mechanic; 6 m n e Eminence. Born in Ind. 1833; settled in M.C. 1855. Dem. Christian.

Gash, S. G.; farmer; 2 m e Eminence. Born in Ky. 1828; settled in M. C. 1853. Dem. Methodist.

Green, Cornelius; farmer; 1¼ m n e Eminence. Born in N.C. 1826; settled in M. C. 1868. Rep. Methodist.

Gray, Wm. G.; farmer; 2¼ m n e Eminence. Born in M. C. 1831. Rep. Christian.

Gray, Alonzo B.; farmer; 1½ m n e Eminence. Born in M.C. 1835. Rep. Methodist.

Garrison, J. E.; blacksmith; Eminence. Born in Ind. 1839; settled in M. C. 1866. Protestant.

Gum, Anderson; dealer in dry goods and notions, and silversmith; Eminence. Born in M. C. 1842. Rep. Meth.

Gum, Berry; farmer; 1 m n Eminence. Born in Ky. 1822; settled in M. C. 1836. Methodist.

Glasco, Richard; farmer; ¼ m w Littlepoint. Born in Ky. 1827; settled in M. C. 1853. Dem. Protestant.

Greenaway, W. H; tinner; Eminence. Born in Ky. 1841; settled in M. C. 1866. Christian.

Gray, Wm. G.; justice of the peace; 2¼ m n e Eminence. Born in M. C. 1831. Rep. Christian.

Gentry, Harrison; farmer; 4 m s Stilesville. Born in Ind. 1846; settled in M. C. 1848. Christian.

Hazlett, W. J.; farmer; 5 m s Stilesville. Born in M. C. 1855. Protestant.

Hazlett, Samuel; retired farmer; 4 m s e Stilesville. Born in Ky. 1790; settled in M. C. 1847. Rep. Christian.

Hubbard, E. H.; farmer; 5 m s e Stilesville. Born in N. C. 1813; settled in M. C. 18—. Rep. Prot.

Hurt, Rob. B.; farmer; 5 m s e Stilesville. Born in Ky. 1848; settled in M. C. 1858. Dem. Christian.

Holmes, D. N.; farmer and blacksmith; 1½ m n e Eminence. Born in Ind. 1831; settled in M.C. 1856. Rep. M. Bap.

HURST, M. M.; dealer in dry goods and groceries; Eminence. Born in Ind. 1845; settled in M. C. 1873. Dem. Prot.

HURST & PATRICK; Eminence; dealers in dry goods, groceries, notions and farming implements.

Hulse, J. H.; dealer in dry goods, farming and trading; Eminence. Born in M. C. 1840. Dem. Christian.

Hulse, J. T.; formerly merchant; Eminence.

Hurst, Jefferson; trader; Eminence. Born in Ind. 1843; settled in M. C. 1867. Rep. Protestant.

Holbert, John; artist; Eminence. Born in Ky. 1840; settled in M. C, 1873. Dem. Protestant.

Hubbel, Sarah; farming; 4 m s Stilesville. Born in Va. 1810; settled in M. C. 1854. Christian.

Hodge, Morgan; farmer; 4 m s Stilesville. Born in Ind. 1855; settled in M. C. 1871. Dem. Protestant.

HOLLOWAY, JAMES; farmer; 5 m s w Stilesville. Born in E. Tenn. 1835; settled in M. C. 1869. Dem. Christian.

Hubbel, Peleg; farmer; 4½ m s w Stilesville. Born in Ky. 1831; settled in M. C. 1854. Rep. Christian.

Horner, J. W.; farmer and carpenter; 3 m s e Stilesville. Born in Ind. 1824; settled in M. C. 1840. Dem. Christian. Was never out of the State.

Horner, T. T.; farmer; 3 m s e Stilesville. Born in Ind. 1838; settled in M. C. 1840. Dem. Christian.

Johnson, D. S.; farmer; 5 miles s e Stilesville. Born in N. C. 1821; settled in M. C. 1833. Rep. Protestant.

Johnson, Brooks S.; farmer; 4½ miles s e Stilesville. Born in N. C. 1799; settled in M. C. 1834. Rep. Methodist.

Johnson, W. H.; merchant; 5 miles s e Stilesville. Born in M. C. 1835. Rep. Methodist.

Johnson, J. P.; farmer; 5 miles s e Stilesville. Born in M. C. 184-. Rep. Methodist.

Johnson, J. B.; farmer; 5 miles s e Stilesville. Born in M. C. 1838. Rep. Christian.

Johnson, J. M.; farmer; 5 miles s e Stilesville. Born in N. C. 1801; settled in M. C. 1832. Rep. Methodist.

Johnson, Morgan; farmer; 6 miles s e Stilesville. Born in N. C. 1807; settled in M. C. 1834. Rep. Methodist.

Kivett, C. H.; farmer; 5 m s e Stilesville. Born in Ind. 1834; settled in M. C. 1849. Dem. Methodist.

Kirkham, George; wagonmaker; Eminence. Born in Ohio 1826; settled in M. C. 1843. Rep. Methodist.

Kirkham, O.; carpenter; Eminence. Born 1853; settled in M. C. 1860. Rep. Methodist.

LITTLE, MILO D.; farmer; 1¼ m s e Eminence. Born in Ind. 1816; settled in M. C. 1851. Christian.

Little, Milo T.; farmer; 1½ m n e Eminence. Born in Ind. 1840; settled in M. C. 1859. Rep. Protestant.

Leonard, J. M.; clerk for H. A. Patrick; Eminence. Born in Ind. 1846; settled in M. C. 1871. Dem. Protestant.

Lacy, Wm. C.; farmer; 4 m n w Hall. Born in Ind. 1850; settled in M. C. 1870. Protestant.

Lambert, J. T.; farmer; 4 m s e Stilesville. Born in M. C. 1840. Dem. Protestant.

McCOLLUM, CLARK; farmer; 4½ m s Stilesville. Born in N. C. 1823; settled in M. C. 1834. Dem. Protestant.

McCollum, Hugh; farmer; 4¾ m n e Eminence. Born in N. C. 1832; settled in M. C. 1834. Dem. Protestant.

McCOLLUM, SAMUEL; farmer; 4 m s e Stilesville. Born in M. C. 1850. Dem. Protestant.

McCollum, Allen; farmer; 5½ m s e Stilesville. Born in Ind. 1853; settled in M. C. 1862. Dem. Protestant.

McCLELLAN, WESLEY; farmer and carpenter; 4½ m s e Stilesville. Born in Ky. 1836; settled in M. C. 1839. Rep. Methodist.

McGINNIS, J. D.; farmer; 3 m n e Eminence. Born in M. C. 1847. Rep. M. Baptist.

McGinnis, John; farmer; 1 m s e Eminence. Born in Ky. 1818; settled in M. C. 1837. Rep. M. Baptist.

McGinnis, J. C.; farmer; 2½ m n e Eminence. Born in M. C. 1842. Protestant.

McCollum, Horace; farmer; 2½ m n e Eminence. Born in N. C. 1824; settled in M. C. 1835. Dem. Christian.

McCollum, James; farmer; 2½ m n e Eminence. Born in M. C. 1852. Dem. Protestant.

McCollum, T. J.; farmer; ½ m n Littlepoint. Born in M. C. 1850.

MILLS, THOS.; farmer; 2½ m n Eminence. Born in Ohio 1838; settled in M. C. 1865. Rep. Protestant.

McCollum, John; farmer; Eminence. Born in N. C. 1821; settled in M. C. 1834. Rep. Methodist

Modrell, A. H.; carpenter; Eminence. Born in Ind. 1829; settled in M. C. 1865. Rep. Protestant.

Marker, E. H.; flouring and custom milling; Eminence. Born in Va. 1838; settled in M. C. 1852. Protestant.

Miller, M. E.; saw milling; Eminence. Born in Va. 1824; settled in M. C. 1871. Dem. Protestant.

Miller, L. J. Miss; milliner; Eminence. Born in M. C. 1851. Christian.

Meazel, Elizabeth; 4 m s Stilesville. Born in Ky. 1834; settled in M. C. 1854. Christian.

McFadden, John; farmer; 3 m s e Stilesville. Born in Ohio 1842; settled in M. C. 1846. Dem. Protestant.

Meazel, Levi H.; farmer; 4 m s Stilesville. Born in Ky. 1847; settled in M. C. 1856. Christian.

Nichols, C. E.; dealer in dry goods and notions; Eminence. Born in M. C. 1836. Temperance and honesty. Prot.

Nichols, H. H. Mrs.; milliner and dress maker; Eminence. Born in Va. 1831; settled in M. C. 1854. Methodist.

Ogles, Levi; farmer; 1½ m w Eminence. Born in M. C. 1844. Liberal. Methodist.

Ogles, Ira; farmer; 1¼ m w Eminence. Born in Ky. 1824; settled in M. C. 1834. Rep. Methodist.

Odell, Linza; farmer; 3 m s e Stilesville. Born in M. C. 1839. Dem. Protestant.

Odell, Isaac; farmer and coon hunter; 4 m s Stilesville. Born in N. C. 1802; settled in M. C. 1832. Dem. Protestant.

Odell, Lydia; farmer; 4 m s e Stilesville. Born in Va. 1824; settled in M. C. 1832. Christian.

Pratt, James; farmer; 5 m s e Stilesville. Born in Ind. 1842; settled in M. C. 1867. Rep. Protestant.

Pruitt, J. M.; farmer; 4½ m w Monrovia. Born in M. C. 1844. Dem. Christian.

PRUITT, ELI; farmer and minister; 4¼ m w Monrovia. Born in Ky. 1820; settled in M. C. 1832. Christian.

Pruitt, E. J.; farmer; 6 m s e Stilesville. Born in M. C. 1844. Rep. Methodist.

Patrick, N. N.; farmer; 1¾ m n e Eminence. Born in Ind. 1835; settled in M. C. 1847. Dem. M. Baptist.

PATRICK, E. A.; deale in dry goods and groceries; Eminence. Born in Ind. in 1837; settled in M. C. 1847. Dem. M. Baptist.

Poynter, J. A.; blacksmith; Eminence. Born in Ind. 1848; settled in M. C. 1860. Rep. Protestant.

Pottorff, R. F.; sawmilling; Eminence. Born in Ky. 1831; settled in M. C. 1864. Neutral. Methodist.

Pottorff, W. A.; physician; Eminence. Born in Ky. 1839; settled in M. C. 1870. Protestant.

Pattan, E. J. Mrs.; farmer; ¾ m s e Littlepoint. Born in Ky. 1822: settled in M. C. 1856.

PRUITT, E. R.; farmer; 5 m s Stilesville. Born in M. C. 1851. Dem. Christian.

Pruitt, B. A.; farmer; 4 m s Stilesville. Born in Ky. 1835; settled in M. C. 1835. Christian.

PRITCHETT, F. M.; farmer; 5 m s Stilesville. Born in M. C. 1837. Rep. Methodist.

Pike, John; farmer and carpenter. Not at home.

Rike, Silas; blacksmith; 5 m w Monrovia. Born in N. C. 1834; settled in M. C, 1866. Rep. Protestant.

Rushton, G. H.; farmer; 3½ m s e Stilesville. Born in M. C. 1843. Protestant.

Richard, Amos; farmer; 4 m s w Hall. Born 1834; settled in M. C. 18—. Protestant.

Ryan, J. E.; farmer; 3 m s e Eminence. Born in Tenn. 1831; settled in M. C. 1841. Rep. M. Baptist.

RUSHTON, ALLEN; farmer; ¾ m s e Eminence. Born in M. C. 1834. Rep. Protestant.

Ryan, W. A., farmer; 2½ m n e Eminence. Born in Tenn. 1825; settled in M. C. 1841. M. Baptist.

Ratliff, R. W.; farmer and granger; ½ m e Littlepoint. Born in Ind. 1835; settled in M. C. 1836. Rep. Friend.

Rhea, J. W.; farmer and school-teacher; ½ m e Eminence. Born in Va. 1825; settled in M. C. 1852. Dem. Protest.

Ryan, J. G.; farmer; ½ m n Eminence. Born in Ky. 1836; settled in N. C. 1849. Rep. Protestant.

Ratliff, David; farmer; 3¼ m n Eminence. Born in Ohio 1824; settled in M. C. 1831. Rep. Friend.

Ratliff, Sicily; farmer; ½ m e Littlepoint. Born in N. C. 1800; settled in M. C. 1829. Friend.

Rhea, J. C.; teacher, mechanic, county com.; Eminence. Born in Va. 1838; settled in M. C. 1861. Rep. Protestant.

RYAN, WM. A.; farmer and cattle dealer; 2 m n e Eminence. Born in E. Tenn. 1825; settled in M. C. 1847. Rep. Bapt.

Rhea, Jno. L.; farmer and carpenter; 1 m w Eminence. Born in Va. 1836; settled in M. C. 1854. Granger Rep. Meth.

Smith, J. J.; farmer; 5 m s Stilesville. Born in N. C. 1818;- settled in M. C. 18—. Rep. Friend.

Smith, E. R.; farmer; 5 m s e Stilesville. Born in N. C. 1834; settled in M. C. 1858. Rep. Christian.

Shields, David, Jr.; farmer; 5 m s e Stilesville. Born in N. C. 1799; settled in M. C. 18—. Rep. Christian.

Shields, David, Sr.; farmer; 5 m s e Stilesville. Born in M. C. 1846. Rep. Protestant.

Shumaker, John; farmer; 5 m s e Stilesville. Born in Ky. 1794; settled in M. C. ——. Rep. Protestant.

Shake, Jacob; farmer; 2 m e Eminence. Born in Ky. 1812; settled in M. C. 1835. Dem. Methodist.

Shake, Alexander; farmer; 1½ m e Eminence. Born in Ky. 1835; settled in M. C. 1835. Rep. Methodist.

SHUMAKER, THOS. J.; farmer; 1½ m e Eminence. Born in M. C. 1844. Rep. Protestant.

Summers, G. G.; farmer; 3 m n e Eminence. Born in Ky. 1819; settled in M. C. 1851. Dem. Protestant.

Summers, J. A.; farmer; 3 m n e Eminence. Born in Ky. 1849; settled in M. C. 1851. Dem. Protestant.

Summers, W. E.; farmer; 3 m n e Eminence. Born in M. C. 1852. Dem. Protestant.

SHAW, L. B.; farmer and trader; 5 m s Littlepoint. Born in Ohio 1832; settled in M. C. 1855. Protestant.

SMITH, A. M.; school teacher and farmer; Littlepoint; Born in M. C. 1852. Protestant.

Shake, A. R.; farmer; 1¼ m e Eminence. Born in Ky. 1821; settled in M. C. 1835. Rep. Christian.

Surber, Jacob; farmer; Eminence. Born in Ky. 1812; settled in M. C. 1830. Rep. M. Baptist.

Shoppell, Peter; wagon maker; Eminence. Born in Ind. 1845; settled in M. C. 1871. Dem. Christian.

Summers, J. S.; farmer; Eminence. Born in Ky. 1845; settled in M. C. 1851. Dem. Protestant.

SLIGAR, W. E.; carp'ter, engineer and sch'l teacher; Eminence. Born in Ky. 1844; settled in M.C. 1859. Dem. Protest.

Sligar, E.; farmer and mechanic; ¼ m n e Eminence. Born in Ky. 1822; settled in M. C. 1844. Dem. Meth.

Smith, W. H. Sr.; farmer; ¾ m s e Littlepoint. Born in Ind. 1843; settled in M. C. 1847. Rep. Christian.

Smith, J. H.; farmer; 1 m e Littlepoint. Born in M. C. 1845. Rep. Christian.

Scott, Hardin M.; farmer and carpenter; 2½ m s Stilesville. Born in Ind. 1830; settled in M. C. 1861. Rep. M. Baptist.

Scott, W. W.; druggist; Eminence. Born in Ind. 1833; settled in M. C. 1873. M. Baptist.

Stringer, Richard; 3 m s Stilesville. Gone from home.

Terrell, Alfred; farmer; 6 m s e Stilesville. Born in N. C. 1831; settled in M. C. ——. Dem. Protestant.

Taylor, David; farmer; ¾ m n w Eminence. Born in Ky. 1831; settled in M. C. 1869. Dem. Protestant,

TWOMEY, JOHN H.; sawmilling; Eminence. Born in Ind. 1848; settled in M. C. 1868. Dem. Protestant.

Terrell, J. A.; farmer; 5 m s Stilesville. Born in N. C. 1843; settled in M. C. 1866. Dem. Protestant.

Warmoth, Geo.; farmer; 5 m s e Stilesville. Born in Ky. Dem. Christian.

Whitlow, Pleasant; farmer; 5 m s e Stilesville. Born in Ind. 1829; settled in M. C. ——. Rep. Christian.

Wilhite, L. B.; farmer; 4½ m w Monrovia. Born in M. C. 1846. Rep. Methodist.

Wilhite, J. S.; farmer; 4 m w Hall. Born in M. C. 1853. Rep. Protestant.

WOODEN, R. S.; farmer; 3 m s w Hall. Born in Ky. 1845; settled in M. C. 1851. Dem. Christian.

Wooden, Joshua; farmer; 3¼ m s w Hall. Born in Ky. 1822; settled in M. C. 1851. Dem. Protestant.

Whitaker, L. P.; farmer; 2½ m n e Eminence. Born in Ky. 1819; settled in M. C. 1827. Rep. Protestant.

Whitaker, Orville; farmer; 2½ m n e Eminence. Born in M. C. 1828. Rep. Protestant.

Wood, W. H.; farmer and Granger; ½ m e Littlepoint. Born in M. C. 1849. Dem. Christian.

Whitehead, Riley; laborer; Littlepoint. Born in M. C. 1847; Protestant.

Watson, E. N.; mechanic; Eminence. Born in M. C. 1837. Protestant.

Watson, J. M.; painter and paper hanger; Eminence. Born in M. C. 1838. Dem. M. Baptist.

Watters, N. J.; farmer. 1½ m w Eminence. Born in Ind. 1835; settled in M. C. 1858. Rep. Protestant.

Watson, Alfred; blacksmith; Eminence. Born in M. C. 1842. Dem. M. Baptist.

Walters, McDonald; farmer and druggist; Eminence. Born in Ind. 1833; settled in M. C. 1854. Rep. Methodist.

Watson, John; painter and paper hanger; Eminence. Born in M. C. 1842. Dem. Protestant.

Wheeler, J. S.; dealer in dry goods and notions; Littlepoint. Born in M. C. 1842. Neutral. Christian.

Wright, A.; farmer; Eminence. Born in M. C. 1852. Dem. Protestant.

Wooden, John L.; farmer and teacher; 4½ m n e Eminence. Born in Ky. 1848; settled in M. C. 1850. Dem. Christ.

Wilson, S. A.; farmer; 5 m s Stilesville. Born in N. C. 1834; settled in M. C. 1874. Christian.

Wilson, A. B.; farmer; 5 m s Stilesville. Born in N. C. 1854; settled in M. C. 1874. Protestant.

Wheeler, Allen; farmer; 3 m s e Stilesville. Born in Ky. 1800; settled in M. C. 1834. Dem. Christian.

Wallace, James; farmer; 4½ m s w Stilesville. Born in M. C. 1837. Dem. Protestant.

Warmoth, J. W.; farmer; 4 m s e Stilesville. Born in Ky. 1840; settled in M. C. 1856. Dem. Christian.

Wheeler, Allen, Jr.; farmer; 4 m s e Stilesville. Not at home.

Wheeler, Pruitt; farmer and broom maker; 4 m s e Stilesville.

ASHLAND TOWNSHIP.

ASHLAND TOWNSHIP is located in the southwest part of the county, and contains about 32 square miles. It is bounded on the north by Adams township, on the east by Gregg and Jefferson, on the south by Ray township and Owen county, and on the west by Putnam county. The surface of this township is somewhat rolling, with some breaks along the creeks. It is watered by Rhodes' Creek and its tributaries. Rhodes' Creek runs across the township angling. The soil is generally good and produces well, and is generally well timbered with poplar, oak, ash, hickory and some sycamore. It is well adapted to raising stock, &c. Her citizens are lively and jovial and obliging.

Alaska, a small village 3 miles east of the Putnam county line, and right on the line of Owen county, is well represented by kind and respectable citizens. Dr. Kieper and Dr. McCallister are well prepared with pills and emetics to cure all their ills. Both these gentlemen are kind and affable. A part of the village is in Owen county. The school and church privileges are moderately good. The Christian Church of Alaska has a good list of enrolled members, and all are working together in harmony, with John Brown as pastor. There is no store in Alaska, but just east, at Lewisville, Messrs. Hodson & Stillwell keep a very nice little country store, surrounded by all conveniences necessary, and the citizens are very generous and enterprising.

CHURCH, LODGE AND SCHOOL STATISTICS.

M. Baptist Church, 3½ miles southeast of Alaska; membership, 79; value of church property, $1500.

Christian Church, Mount Olive; 5½ miles north of Paragon; membership, 35; value of church property, $500.

Christian Church, Alaska; Elder John Brown, pastor; membership, 135; superintendent of Sabbath school, David M. Gray; average attendance of Sabbath school, 40; value of church property, $2,000.

Beach Grove Grange, No. 1293, of the P. of H., organized February 3, 1874; membership, 43; P. O., Alaska, 3 miles west of grange; E. N. Voshel, Master; M. L. Marsh, Sec'y.

Grange No. 863; membership, 31; Master, G. D. Ryan; Secretary, Wm. C. Mannan,; Treasurer, Wm. R. Wilson.

DIRECTORY OF ASHLAND TOWNSHIP.

Asher, Henry; farmer; 5 m s Hall. Born in Ind. 1830; settled in M. C. 1858. Rep. Protestant.

Anders, F. C.; farmer; 1½ m n e Alaska. Born in Ky. 1844; settled in M. C. 1862. Dem. Christian.

Awbrey, Phillip; farmer; 4 m s e Eminence. Born in Ky. 1818; settled in M. C. 1873. Dem. Protestant.

BROWN, W. A., farmer; ½ m n Alaska. Born in Ind, 1848; settled in M. C. 1868. Rep. Protestant.

Bressmahan, Jeremiah; farmer; 3 m n e Alaska. Born in Ind. 1840; settled in M. C. 1867. Protestant.

Bowman, Abel; farmer; 4 m s e Eminence. Born in N. C.; settled in M. C. ———. Dem. Protestant.

Boyd, F. W.; farmer; 1¾ m s w Eminence. Born in Ky. 1840; settled in M. C. 1870. Dem. Methodist.

BROWN, JOHN, Elder; farmer; ¼ m n e Alaska. Born in N. C. 1804; settled in M. C. 1870. Rep. Christian.

Costin, Granville; farmer; 3½ m e Alaska. Born in Ind. 1841. Dem. Protestant.

Costin, Lewis; farmer; 1 m s w Herbemont. Born in Ky. 1814; settled in M. C. 18—. Dem. Methodist.

Costin, R. H.; farmer; 1 m s w Herbemont. Born in Ind. 1850. Dem. Protestant.

Caldwell, Phillip; farmer; 2½ m e Alaska. Born in Ireland 1814; settled in M. C. 1856. Dem.

Cummings, Abigail; farmer, 2½ m n e Quincy. Born in N. Y. 1804; settled in M. C. 1835. Methodist.

CUMMINGS, OLIVER; farmer; 2½ m n e Quincy. Born in M. C. 1849. Dem. Protestant.

Cummings, W. L.; farmer; 3 m n e Quincy. Gone from home.

Cummings, Wm. E.; farmer; 3 m n e Quincy. Born in M. C. 1855. Protestant.

Cornwell, Benjamin; blacksmith; Alaska. Born in Ky. 1844; settled in M. C. 1864. Dem. Protestant.

Chenoweth, G. W.; farmer; 1½ m n Alaska. Born in M. C. 1839. Rep. Christian.

Dow, D. B.; farmer; 3 m s e Alaska. Born in Ind. 1831; settled in M. C. 1837. Rep. Christian.

Dunnagan, John; farmer; 4½ m s e Eminence. Born in Ky. 1830; settled in M. C. 1831. Dem. Christian.

Edwards, Jesse; farmer; 3 m s e Eminence. Born in Ind. 1836; settled in M. C. 1838. Rep. Christian.

Foxworthy, H. C.; school and music teacher and P. M.; Alaska. Born in M. C. 1849. Rep. Christian.

Foxworthy, Philip A.; farmer; Alaska. Born in Va. 1797; settled in M. C. 1828. Rep. Christian.

Finchum, Rob't; farmer; weight, 340; 1½ m s e Eminence. Born in E. Tenn. 1815; settled in M. C. 1829. Dem. Prot.

Finchum, R. J.; farmer; 1½ m s e Eminence. Born in M. C. 1850. Dem. Protestant.

Ground, H. A.; farmer; 3½ m e Alaska. Born in Ind. 1846. Dem. Protestant.

Guy, A. D.; farmer; 3½ e Alaska. Born ——. Dem. Protestant.

GRAY, DAVID W.; farmer; ½ m w Alaska. Born in Ind. Territory 1815; settled in M. C. 1835. Rep. Christian.

Gray, Catharine B.; farmer; 1¼ m e Alaska. Born in Ky. 1807; settled in M. C. 1835. Christian.

Hedrick, Wiley; farmer; 6 m n Paragon. Born in Ind. 1836. Dem. Protestant.

Hancock, John; farmer; 6 m n w Hinesdale. Born in Ind. 1827. Rep. Protestant.

Hedrick, Alexander; farmer; 6 m n Paragon. Born in Ind. 1844. Protestant.

Hancock, W. B.; farmer and engineer; 1¼ m w Herbemont. Born in Ky. 1826; settled in M. C. 1853. Rep. Protest.

Holmes, J. M.; farmer; 5 m s w Hall. Born in Ind. 1848; settled in M. C. 1859. Rep. Protestant.

Herdel, Lewis; farmer; 4 m s e Eminence. Born in Ky. 1836; settled in M. C. 1872. Rep. Methodist.

HODSON, MILES J. Rev., of the firm of Hodson & Stillwell; dealers in dry goods, groceries and general merchandise; ½ m e Alaska. Born in Ohio 1846; settled in M. C. 1873. Rep. Christian.

Kanoy, Philip; farmer; 3 m e Alaska. Born in Ind. 1830. Dem. Christian.

Kanoy, Jacob; farmer; 1½ m s Herbemont. Born in Ind. 1838. Dem. Protestant.

Kanoy, Elias; farmer; 1½ m s Herbemont. Born in Ind. 1835. Dem. Protestant.

Kanoy, Daniel; farmer; 6 m n Paragon. Born in Ind. 1844. Dem. Protestant.

Kanoy, David; farmer; 6 m n Paragon. Born in Ind. 1846. Dem. Protestant.

Kanoy, John; farmer; 6 m n Paragon. Born in N. C. 1801; settled in M. C. 1830. Dem. Lutheran.

KIRKHAM, JOHN; farmer and stock raiser; 4 m s Hall. Born in Ohio 1819; settled in M. C. 1847. Rep. Protest.

Kanoy, K.; farmer; ¾ m s Herbemont. Born in Ind. 1845. Dem. Protestant.

Keiper, Geo. F.; physician and surgeon; Alaska. Born in Pa. 1836; settled in M. C. 1856. Dem. Protestant.

Little, Isaac; country merchant; 3½ m e Alaska. Born in Ind. 1811. Rep. Christian.

Lambert, Jesse; brick mason; Alaska. Born in M. C. 1846. Dem. Protestant.

Lewis, Henry; saw milling; ½ m e Alaska. Born in N. J. 1832; settled in M. C. 1862. Rep. Christian.

Lewis, A. J.; farmer; 1 m n Alaska. Born in M. C. 1838. Dem. Protestant.

LACY, JOHN R.; farmer; 1 m n e Alaska. Born in M. C. 1843. Rep. Christian.

Marsh, M. L.; farmer; 3 m e Alaska. Born in Ind. 1839. Rep. Christian.

Myers, D. C.; farmer; 3 m s e Alaska. Born in Ind. 1848. Dem. Protestant.

Mosier, Tobias; farmer; 1½ m n w Herbemont. Born in Ind. 1853. Dem. Protestant.

Murphy, T. C.; farmer; 5 m s Hall. Born in Ind. 1851. Rep. Protestant.

MURPHY, EDGAR; farmer; 5 m s Hall. Born in Ind. 1841; settled in M. C. 1843. Rep. Protestant.

McGinnis, Samuel; farmer; 2 m s e Eminence. Born in Ky. 1822; settled in M. C. 1845. Rep. Protestant.

McGinnis, J. M.; farmer; 2 m s e Eminence. Born in M. C. 1850. Rep. Protestant.

Michael, A.; farmer; 3 m s w Eminence. Born in Va. 1830; settled in M. C. 1853. Granger.

Mannan, W. R.; farmer; 3 m n e Quincy. Born in Va. 1810; settled in M. C. about 1830. Rep. M. Baptist.

McAllister, Alexander; physician; Alaska. Born in Ind. 1826; settled in M. C. 1880. Rep. Christian.

Nichols, Zeph; farmer; 3 m s e Eminence. Born in Ind. 1843. Rep. Protestant.

Ogles, Joel; farmer; 2½ m s w Eminence. Born in M. C. Mixed. Mixed.

Pottorff, W. A.; farmer; 5 m s e Eminence. Born in Ky. 1817; settled in M. C. 1864. Rep. Methodist.

POTTORFF, G. S.; farmer and carpenter; 5 m s e Eminence. Born in Ky. 1852; settled in M. C. 1864. Rep. Meth.

ASHLAND TOWNSHIP.

RATTS, F. G.; farmer; 5 m n Paragon. Born in Ind. 1847. Dem. Christian.

Ratts, P. P.; farmer; 5 m n Paragon. Born in Ind. 1849. Dem. Protestant.

Ratts, Henry; farmer; 5½ m n Paragon. Born in Ind. 1839. Dem. Christian.

Ratts, Ephraim; farmer; 5½ m n Paragon. Born in Ind. 1817; settled in M. C. 1827. Dem. Christian.

Ratts, Ephraim, Sr.; farmer; 5½ m n Paragon. Born in Ind. 1851. Dem. Christian.

RATTS, RINEHART; farmer; 6 m n Paragon. Born in Ind. 1830. Dem. Christian.

Ratts, G. M.; farmer; 4 m e Alaska. Born in Ind. 1833. Dem. Protestant.

Ratts, Obadiah; farmer; 8 m w Martinsville. Born in Ind. 1821. Dem. Protestant.

Reed, Thomas; farmer; 4 m s e Eminence. Born in Ky. 1841; settled in M. C. 1853. Dem. Methodist.

Risinger; J. S.; farmer; ½ m s Eminence. Born in M. C. 1850.

REID, NEWTON; farmer; ¾ m n w Alaska. Born in Ky. 1835; settled in M. C. 1854. Dem. Methodist.

Ray, Wm. H.; farmer; 3½ m s e Eminence. Born in Tenn. 1846; settled in M. C. 1873. Dem. Protestant.

REID, MILTON; farmer; 1 m e Alaska. Born in Ky. 1836; settled in M. C. 1854. Dem. Methodist.

Reid, Wm.; farmer; 1 m e Alaska. Born in Ky. 1801; settled in M. C. 1854. Dem. Methodist.

Reid, James C.; farmer; 1 m e Alaska. Born in Ky. 1846; settled in M. C. 1854. Dem. Protestant.

Shuler, Mary Ann, farmer; 4 m n e Paragon. Born in N. C. 1829; settled in M. C. 1829.

Stierwalte, Hamilton; farmer; 2½ m e Alaska. Born in Ind. 1830; settled in M. C. 1852. Rep. Christian.

Shuler, J. K.; farmer; 4 m e Alaska. Born in Ind 1844. Dem. Christian.

Shuler, D. K.; farmer; 3¼ m e Alaska. Born in Ind. 1850. Dem. Christian.

SHULER, EPHRAIM; farmer; 6 m n w Hinesdale. Born in Ind. 1837. Dem. Protestant.

Secrest, Thomas; farmer; 4½ n w Paragon. Born in Ind. 1837. Dem. Protestant.

Sandy, Wm. H.; farmer; 3 m s e Alaska. Born in N.C. 1805; settled in M. C. 18—. Dem. M. Baptist.

Stierwalt, Michael; farmer; 3 m s e Alaska. Born in Ind. 1821; settled in M.C. 1852. Dem. M. Baptist.

Stierwalt, J. F.; farmer; 3 m s e Alaska. Born in Ind. 1834; settled in M. C. 1853. Dem. M. Baptist.

Stierwalt, J. M.; farmer: 3 m s e Alaska. Born in Ind. 1846;
settled in M. C. 1852. Dem. M. Baptist.

STOCKWELL, JAMES; farmer; 1 m s w Herbemont. Born
in Ind. 1823. Rep. Protestant.

Shumaker, Wm. H.; farmer; 4 m s e Eminence. Born in Ind.
1834. Rep. Christian.

Stierwalt, J. H.; farmer and blacksmith; 3½ m s e Eminence.
Born in Ind. 1833. Dem. M. Baptist.

Stierwalt, T. S.; farmer; 4 m s e Eminence. Born in Ind.
1835. Dem. M. Baptist.

Schwomeyer, Wm.; cooper; 3 m s w Eminence. Born in Germany 1835; settled in M. C. 1871. Granger. Lutheran.

Smith, B. C.; laborer; 2½ m s w Eminence. Born in N. C.
1851; settled in M. C. 1870. Rep. Protestant.

SPEERS, ALEXANDER; farmer; 1 m n w Alaska. Born in
N. C. 1847; settled in M. C. 1868. Dem. Protestant.

Stillwell, F. C.; of the firm of Hodson & Stillwell, dealer in dry
goods, groceries and general merchandize; ½ m e Alaska.
Born in Ind. 1843; settled in M. C. 1873. Dem. Christian.

Stephens, John H.; farmer; 1½ m n e Alaska. Born in E.
Tenn. 1833; settled in M. C. 1867. Dem. Christian.

Shumaker, Jesse; farmer; 2 m n e Alaska. Born in Ind. 1824;
settled in M. C. 1826. Rep. M. Baptist.

SHIELDS, WM. H.; farmer; 1½ m e Alaska. Born in N. C.
1824; settled in M. C. 1830. Rep. Christian.

Spain, T. D.; farmer; 3 m s e Eminence. Born in Ky. 1802;
settled in M. C. 1834. Christian.

Taylor, J. W.; farmer; 3 m s e Eminence. Born in Ind. 1836; settled in M. C. 18—. Rep. Protestant.

Voshel, E. N.; farmer; 2 m s w Herbemont. Born in Ind. 1836. Dem. M. Baptist.

Whitaker, Wm. K.; farmer; 1½ m n w Alaska. Born in M. C. 1829. Dem. Protestant.

Wigal, J. W.; saw milling; ½ m e Alaska. Born in M. C. 1840. Methodist.

Whitaker, Newton J.; farmer and carpenter; ½ m e Alaska. Born in M. C. 1833. Rep. M. Baptist.

Whitaker, L. B.; farmer; 1½ m s e Eminence. Born in M. C. 1828. Dem. M. Baptist.

Warthen, Wm. A.; soldier of 1812, and still drawing pension; 3½ m n Paragon. Born in N. C. 1795. Dem. Christian.

Wingler, John; proprietor of brickyard; Alaska. Born in Ind. 1842 Dem. Protestant.

Whitson, John; farmer; 6 m n w Hinesdale. Born in Ky. 1820; settled in M. C. 1823. Methodist.

Wakeland, P. D.; farmer; 5 m n w Hinesdale. Born in Ohio 1830; settled in M. C. 1856. Rep. Protestant.

Whitson, Nathan; farmer; 6 m n w Paragon. Born in Va. 1793. Dem. Protestant.

Whitlow, Eli; farmer; 3 m s e Eminence. Born in M. C. 1847. Rep. Protestant.

ASHLAND TOWNSHIP.

White, J. J.; farmer; 4 m s e Eminence. Born in Ind. 1840; settled in M. C. 1861. Dem. Christian.

Watson, A. J.; school teacher; 1¼ m s w Eminence. Born in M. C. 1845. Dem. Protestant.

Wilson, Wm. R.; farmer; 2½ m s w Eminence. Born in Ind. 1841; settled in M. C. 1869. Dem. Protestant.

Wheeler, Henry; 2½ m s w Eminence. Born in Ky. 1835; settled in M. C. 1855. Granger. Christian.

Whicker, G. W.; painter; 3 m s w Eminence. Born in N. C. 1836; settled in M. C. 1869. Dem. Protestant.

Watson, B. C.; farmer and teacher; 1¼ m s w Eminence. Born in M. C. 1852. Dem. Baptist.

Watson, J. S.; plasterer; 1¼ m s w Eminence Born in M. C. 1850. Dem. Baptist views.

Wantland, Jos.; farmer; 2 m s w Eminence. Born in Ohio 1811; settled in M. C. 1862. Rep. Methodist.

BAKER TOWNSHIP.

BAKER TOWNSHIP is located in the southwest corner of the county, and is bounded as follows: On the north and west by White River, on the east by Washington township, and on the south by Monroe county, and contains about 14 square miles. This is the smallest township in the county. There are some portions of it that are very broken, especially in the southern part, although there is some very fine farming land in this township. The bottoms are very rich and productive. It is very sparsely settled, large bodies of land being owned by parties living outside of the township. The church and school privileges are very good. Among the first settlers of this township were the family of Lafavers.

CHURCH, LODGE AND SCHOOL STATISTICS.

M. Baptist Church, New Salem, Union Church, 8 miles southwest of Martinsville; James M. Barrow, pastor; membership, 130; value of church property, $1,000.

Christian Church, Union Meeting House, 8 miles southwest of Martinsville; —— Johnson, pastor; membership, 43; value of church property, $1,000.

M. E. Church, Mt. Zion, 3 miles south of Paragon; —— Burge, Pastor; membership, 24; value of church property, $1500.

Good Hope Grange, No. 1626; Master, H. W. Miller; Secretary, W. N. Hodges; No. of members, 40; P. O. address, Martinsville.

DIRECTORY OF BAKER TOWNSHIP.

BAKER, HARDEN M.; farmer; 10 m s w Martinsville. Born in M. C. 1843. Rep. M. Baptist.

Burton, S. G.; farmer; 2½ m s Paragon. Born in M. C. 1840. Rep. Methodist.

Buskirk, J. V.; farmer; 4½ m e Gosport. Born in Ind. 1847; settled in M. C. 1871. Rep. Methodist.

Buskirk, Bennett V.; farmer; 4 m e Gosport. Born in Ind. 1837; settled in M. C. 1849. Rep. Protestant.

COLIER, JOHN farmer; 10 m s w Martinsville. Born in Ky. 1821; settled in M. C. 1869. Rep. R. P. Baptist.

Denney, Dorsey; farmer; 3 m s e Paragon. Born in Ind. 1839; settled in M. C. 1873. Rep. Protestant.

FARR, NATHAN; farmer; 3 m s w Paragon. Born in Ind. 1824; settled in M. C. 1843. Rep. Christian.

Farr, J. B.; farmer; 11 m s w Martinsville. Born in M. C. 1840. Rep. M. Baptist.

Farr, Jefferson; farmer; 9 m s w Martinsville. Born in Ky. 1812; settled in M. C. 1825. Rep. M. Baptist.

Guy, Martin V.; farmer; 2½ m s e Paragon. Born in M. C. 1834. Lib. M. Baptist.

Hodges, Perry; farmer; 9 m s w Martinsville. Born in M. C. 1850. Lib. M. Baptist.

Hodges, J. M.; farmer; 8 m s w Martinsville. Born in Ind. 1845; settled in M. C. 1845. Ind. Protestant.

Johnson, Presly; 7 m s w Martinsville. Born in Ind. 1835; settled in M. C. 1859. Dem. Christian.

Johnson, Asa; farmer; 3 m s e Paragon. Born in M.C. 1837. Rep. Protestant.

LAFAVERS, SAMUEL; farmer; 6 m e Gosport. Born in M. C. 1835. Rep. Methodist.

Lafavers, Rev. J. B.; farmer; 6¼ m e Gosport. Born in Ky. 1805; settled in M. C. 1824. Rep. Methodist.

Lafavers, Isaac; farmer; 6½ m e Gosport. Born in Ky. 1801; settled in M. C. 1824. Dem. Methodist.

LAFAVERS, ISAAC J.; farmer; 2 m s Paragon. Born in M. C. 1846. Dem. Methodist.

Lafavers, Jacob C.; farmer; 3 m s Paragon. Born in M. C. 1833. Rep. Methodist.

Miller, H. W.; farmer; 8 m s w Martinsville. Born in N. C. 1836; settled in M. C. 1839. Lib. M. Baptist.

Miller, J. D.; farmer; 9 m s w Martinsville. Born in Ind. 1830; settled in M. C. 1835. Rep. Protestant.

Payton, L. R.; farmer; 3 m n Windricksburg. Born in Ky. 1820; settled in M. C. 1838. Dem. Christian.

Payton, Losson; farmer; 3 m n Windricksburg. Born in M. C. 1853. Dem. Christian.

Thomas, John H.; farmer; 4 m e Gosport. Born in Ind. 1839; settled in M. C. 1855. Rep. Methodist.

Thomas, Wm.; farmer; 4½ m e Gosport. Born in Ind. 1838; settled in M. C. 1867. Protestant.

WILLIAMS, JOEL; farmer; Born in N. C. 1826; settled in M. C. 1851. Dem. M. Baptist.

BROWN TOWNSHIP.

Brown Township is located in the north part of the county, about six miles west of the Johnson county line. It contains about 26 square miles, and is bounded on the north by Hendricks county, on the east by Madison township, on the south by Clay, and on the west by Monroe. The surface of the township is slightly rolling, and somewhat broken along the creeks that flow through it, White Lick being the largest stream. It is a beautiful stream of clear, crystal water, running a southeast direction, and affording never-failing stock water for the citizens who live along its bottoms. The soil is generally of a sandy nature, mixed with some clay, and is very productive for wheat, oats, corn and grass. The supply of gravel for making good roads is almost inexhaustible, and the citizens are generally using it, as is seen in traveling upon her roads.

Some of the first settlers of this township were as follows: Harris Bray, Benjamin Thornburgh, Jesse Tansey, Nathan Carter, J. D. Carter, Joseph Newby and Samuel Moore.

CHURCH, LODGE AND SCHOOL STATISTICS.

M. E. Church, Mooresville; membership, 300; pastor, Rev. I. N. Thompson; Sabbath school superintendent, J. H. Thornburgh; average attendance, 200; value of church property, $2500.

Christian Church, Mooresville; membership, 18; Sabbath school superintendent, —— White; average attendance of Sabbath school, —; value of church property, $800.

Friends Church, Mooresville; membership, 160; Sabbath school superintendent, J. R. Hunt; average attendance, 60; value of church property, $6,000.

Friends Church, White Lick, 1 mile west of Mooresville; membership, 114; Sabbath school superintendent, P. M. Hadley; average attendance, 35; value of church property, $1,000.

Friends Church, Bethel; 2½ miles southwest of Mooresville; membership, 100; Sabbath school superintendent, Calvin Harvey; average attendance, 50; value of church property, $1350.

M. E. Church, White Lick, 3 miles southeast of Mooresville; membership, 53; pastor, Rev. J. Wall; Sabbath school superintendent, S. M. Rooker; average attendance, 40; value of church property, $2500.

Morgan Lodge, No. 211, I. O. O. F.; membership, 100; value of Lodge property, $7,000.

Mooresville Encampment, No. 74, I. O. O. F.; membership, 40; value of Lodge property, $500.

Mooresville Lodge, No. 78, F. and A. M.; average membership, 40; value of Lodge property, $5,000.

Mooresville Lodge, No. 274, I. O. G. T.; membership, 108; James Carter, Worthy Chief.

Mooresville Grange, No. 79, organized March 25, 1873; membership, 53; Master, J. F. Hadley; Secretary, Allen Hadley.

John M. Snoddy, township trustee; No. of school houses, 6; value of property, $3800.

DIRECTORY OF BROWN TOWNSHIP.

Acton, H. S.; carpenter; Mooresville. Born in Ind. 1849; settled in M. C. 1867. Rep. Methodist.

Arnold, R.; wagon maker; Mooresville. Born in N. C. 1801; settled in M. C. 1856. Rep. Friend.

BUCKER, JOHN; marble business; Mooresville. Born in Germany 1815; settled in M. C. 1867. Rep. Methodist.

Bucker, Wm.; marble business; Mooresville. Born in Ohio 1851; settled in M. C. 1869. Rep. Methodist.

Burke, J. H.; printer and publisher; Mooresville. Born in Mass. 1846; settled in M. C. 1872. Methodist.

Bundle, W. W.; engineer; Mooresville. Born in Ky. 1821; settled in M. C. 1847. Rep. Methodist.

Butner, J. A.; cabinet maker; Mooresville. Born in Ind. 1833; settled in M. C. 1839. Rep. Protestant.

Butner, Christian; retired farmer; Mooresville. Born in N. C. 1790; settled in M. C. 18—. Rep. Methodist.

BALLARD, C. W.; blacksmith; Mooresville. Born in Ind. 1836; settled in M. C. 1845. Rep. Protestant.

BEASON, W. S.; farmer; 1 m e Mooresville. Born in Ohio 1825; settled in M. C. 1826. Rep. Friend.

Benbow, A. T.; hotel keeper; Mooresviile. Born in N. C. 1828; settled in M. C. 1832. Rep. Methodist.

Bray, Harris; farmer; 1 m e Mooresville. Born in N. C, 1798; settled in M. C. 1821. Dem. Methodist.

Bray, Riley; miller; 1 m s e Mooresville. Born in Ind. 1832. Dem. Protestant.

Boman, Madison; farmer; 2½ m w Mooresville. Born in N. C. 1833; settled in M. C. 1871. Methodist.

Burns, Caleb: constable; Mooresville. Born 1822; settled in M. C. 18—. Rep. Methodist.

Beason, C. T.; farmer; Mooresville. Born in Ohio 1818; settled in M. C. 1826. Rep. Methodist.

Butler, B. F.; county surveyor and minister; Mooresville. Born in Ohio 1827; settled in M. C, 1862. Rep. M. Baptist.

Calvert, J. P.; photographer; Mooresville. Born in N. Y. 1842; settled in M. C. 1868. Rep. Methodist.

CARTER, THOS.; farmer; Mooresville. Born in Ind. 1831. Rep. Friend.

Callahan, W.; huckster; Mooresville. Born in Ind. 1832. Rep. Methodist.

Craton, G. W.; brick maker; Mooresville. Born in Ind. 1842; settled in M. C. 1853. Dem. Protestant.

Crayton, John; brick maker; Mooresville. Born in Ind. 1834; settled in M. C. 1873. Rep. M. Baptist.

Carter, Nathaniel; farmer; 1 m e Mooresville. Born in Ind. 1815; settled in M. C. 1822. Rep. Friend.

Carter, J. R.; farmer; 1 m e Mooresville. Born in Ind. 1838. Rep. Friend.

Carter, John D.; farmer; 1½ m s e Mooresville. Born in N. C. 1811; settled in M. C. 1822. Rep. Friend.

CARTER, NAT.; farmer; 1½ m s e Mooresville. Born in Ind. 1848. Rep. Friend.

Carter, B. L.; farmer; 1½ m s e Mooresville. Born in Ind. 1851. Rep. Friend.

Cox, Paul; farmer; 3 m s e Mooresville. Born in Pa. 1808; settled in M. C. 1824. Dem. Christian.

Carlies, W. H.; farmer; 1 m s w Mooresville. Born in N. C. 1840; settled in M. C. 1870. Methodist.

COOK, THOMAS; insurance agent; Mooresville. Born in Ill. 1833. Rep. Methodist.

Compton, A. J.; tailor; Mooresville. Born in Va. 1813; settled in M. C. 1854. Dem. Methodist.

Clapp, J. C.; dentist; Mooresville. Born in N. C. 1841; settled in M. C. 1870. Dem. German Reform.

Conduitt, H. C.; firm of Conduitt & Co.; Mooresville. Born in Ind. 1844. Dem. Protestant.

Conduitt, A. W.; firm of Conduitt & Co.; Mooresville. Born in Ind. 1849. Dem. Methodist.

Carlisle, C. C.; farmer. Born in Ind. 1852. Rep. Protestant.

Comer, J. L.; teamster; Mooresville. Born in Ind. 1842; settled in M. C. 1864. Rep. Methodist.

CARLISLE, WM.; blacksmith; Mooresville. Born in N. C. 1805; settled in M. C. 1833. Rep. Methodist.

Crayton, J. M.; boot and shoe maker; Mooresville. Born in Ind. 1836; settled in M. C. 1854. Dem. Protestant.

Callett, T. A.; carriage painter; Mooresville. Born in N. C. 1857; settled in M. C. 1871. Rep. Protestant.

Cummins, Joseph; marshall; Mooresville. Born in N. C. 1820; settled in M. C. 1856. Dem. Methodist.

COMER, JOSEPH; retired farmer; Mooresville. Born in S. C. 1802; settled in M. C. 1862. Rep. Friend.

Cope, Hiram; farmer; Mooresville. Born in Ohio 1821; settled in M. C. 1864. Methodist.

Comer, Matthew; saw mill and lumber; Mooresville. Born in Ind. 1826; settled in M. C. 1865. Rep. Methodist.

Deckerson, A. R.; harness maker; Mooresville. Born in Ind. 1848; settled in M. C. 1872. Rep. Protestant.

Dakin, S. H.; farmer; Mooresville. Born in Ohio 1831; settled in M. C. 1833. Rep. Friend.

Day, J. P.; farmer; Mooresville. Born in N. C. 1825. Rep. Methodist.

Davis, J. M.; farmer; Mooresville. Born in Ind. 1832; settled in M. C. 1869. Dem. Methodist.

DAY, NATHAN; farmer; ½ m e Mooresville. Born in Ind. 1843. Rep. Friend.

Davison, Jeptha; carpenter; Mooresville. Born in Ind. 1834. Rep. Protestant.

Dewees, Wm.; farmer; 1 m w Mooresville. Born in Ohio 1837; settled in M. C. 1856. Dem. Friend.

Dryden, W. H.; farmer; 3½ m s Mooresville. Born in Ohio 1840; settled in M. C. 1853. Rep. Methodist.

Edwards, J. H.; farmer; 3 m s w Mooresville. Born in Va. 1833; settled in M. C. 1856. Rep. Friend.

Edmonds, R. H.; farmer and stock trader; Mooresville. Born in Ind. 1832; settled in M. C. 1845. Ind. Methodist.

ELLIOTT, JOHN; laborer; Mooresville. Born in N. C. 1821; settled in M. C. 1858. Protestant.

Elmore, Thos.; farmer; 2 m s Mooresville. Born in Ill. 1839; settled in M. C. 1850. Rep. Friend.

FOGLEMAN, WM. M.; farmer; 3 m s w Mooresville. Born in Ind. 1837; settled in M. C. 1865. Rep. Methodist.

Forest, A. J.; farmer; 1 m w Mooresville. Born in N. C. 1841; settled in M. C. 1866. Dem. Protestant.

Fansler, George; retired farmer; Mooresville. Born in N. C. 1801; settled in M. C. 1864. Rep. Methodist.

Feazel, Jacob; boot and shoemaker; Mooresville. Born in Va. 1803; settled in M. C. 1844. Dem. Protestant.

Fogleman, D.; farmer and stock trader; Mooresville. Born in N. C. 1828; settled in M. C. 1833. Rep. Methodist.

Fogleman, John; butcher; Mooresville. Born in N. C. 1827; settled in M. C. 1848. Dem. Methodist.

FANSLER, DAVID; wagonmaker; Mooresville. Born in N. C. 1823; settled in M. C. 1849. Rep. Methodist.

Fuson, J. F.; farmer; Mooresville. Born in Ohio 1819; settled in M. C. 1866. Ind. Protestant.

Farmer, Geo.; farmer; 3 m s e Mooresville. Born in N. C. 1821; settled in M. C. 1824. Rep. Methodist.

Farmer, D. D.; harness maker and farmer; 3½ m e Mooresville Born in Ind. 1834. Rep. Protestant.

Farmer, Peter; farmer; 3½ m s w Mooresville. Born in N. C. 1798. Rep. Methodist.

Greeson, J. B.; carpenter; Mooresville. Born in Ind. 1851. Rep. Protestant.

Gregory, W. H.; merchant; Mooresville. Born in Ind. 1847. Rep. Methodist.

Gregory, A. B.; firm of A. B. & W. H. Gregory; Mooresville. Born in Ind 1844. Rep. Methodist.

Greeson, Peter; retired farmer; Mooresville. Born in N. C. 1807; settled in M. C. 1833. Rep. Methodist.

GRAY, FRANK; farmer; Mooresville. Born in Ireland 1840; settled in M. C. 1868. Dem. R. Catholic.

Glardan, J. E.; farmer; 2¼ m s e Mooresville. Born in Ind. 1833; settled in M. C. ——. Dem. Methodist.

Grave, Jesse; carpenter; 1 m n Brooklyn. Born in Ind. 1836; settled in M. C. 1854. Rep. Friend.

Gilbert, Nathan; farmer; 4 m s Mooresville. Born in Va. 1801; settled in M. C. 1853. Rep. Methodist.

Hadley, S. M.; druggist; firm of Pruitt & Hadley; Mooresville. Born in Ind. 1838. Rep. Friend.

Harris, Reuben; firm of Harris & Woodard; Mooresville. Born in N. C. 1815; settled in M. C. 1837. Dem. Methodist.

Hobbs, J. M.; farmer; Mooresville. Born in N. C. 1821; settled in M. C. 1847. Rep. Methodist.

Hobbs, J. E.; boot and shoe maker; Mooresville. Born in N. C. 1836; settled in M. C. 1868. Methodist.

Hinson, J. W.; postmaster; Mooresville. Born in Ind. 1842; settled in M. C.—. Rep. Methodist.

Hinson, H. J.; cabinet maker; Mooreville. Born in Ind. 1848. Rep. Protestant.

Hadley, Thomas M.; farmer; Mooresville. Born in N. C. 1810; settled in M. C. 1824. Rep. Friend.

Harryman, S. F.; attorney; Mooresville. Born in Ind. 1826; settled in M. C. 1837. Rep. Methodist.

Hadley, Wm. M.; principal teacher in High School; Mooresville. Born in Ind. 1845. Rep. Friend.

HILL, J. M.; blacksmith; Mooresville. Born in Ohio 1839; settled in M. C. 1871. Rep. Christian.

Hunt, J. R.; farmer and school teacher; Mooresville. Born in Ohio 1843; settled in M. C. 1861. Rep. Friend.

HARVEY, CHANDLER; saw-milling; Mooresville. Born in Ind. 1826; settled in M. C. 1858. Rep. Friend.

Harvey, Elam; school teacher; Mooresville. Born in Ind. 1846. Rep. Methodist.

HADLEY, ALLEN; farmer; Mooresville. Born in Ind. 1828. Rep. Friend.

HADLEY, W. F.; telegrapher and agent; Mooresville. Born in Ind. 1855. Rep. Friend.

Hercog, John; farmer; Mooresville. Born in Germany 1821; settled in M. C. 1857. Protestant.

Harryman, Sam'l; soldier of 1812; mustered out 1815. Born in Va. 1795; settled in M. C 1837. Rep. Christian.

Harris, J. H.; carpenter; Mooresville. Born in Ind. 1849. Dem. Methodist.

Hadley, Albert M.; farmer; ¾ m n w Mooresville. Born in Ind. 1842; settled in M. C. 1872. Rep. Friend.

Hadley, Abner; farmer; ½ m n w Mooresville. Born in Ind. 1828; settled in M. C. 1863. Rep. Friend.

HOUSE, HENRY; farmer; 2½ m s e Mooresville. Born in Va. 1823; settled in M. C. 1836. Dem. Methodist.

HADLEY, M. S.; farmer; 1½ m n w Mooresville. Born in Ind. 1828; settled in M. C. 1863. Rep. Friend.

HADLEY, J. F.; farmer; 1½ m w Mooresville. Born in Ind. 1840. Rep. Friend.

Hadley, A. L.; farmer; 1¾ m w Mooresville. Born in Ind. 1835. Rep. Friend.

HADLEY, P. M.; farmer; 1 m w Mooresville. Born in Ind. 1845. Rep. Friend.

Hadley, Evan; farmer; 1 m w Mooresville. Born in Ind. 1854; settled in M. C. 1872. Rep. Friend.

Hadley, L. S.; farmer; ¾ m w Mooresville. Born 1822; settled in M. C. 1822. Rep. Friend.

Hadley, A. W.; farmer; 1½ m w Mooresville. Born in Ind. 1846; settled in M. C, 1874. Rep. Friend.

Harvey, William; farmer; 2½ m s w Mooresville. Born in Ohio 1830; settled in M. C. 1830. Rep. Friend.

HADLEY, NEWTON; farmer; 2½ m s w Mooresville. Born in Ind. 1832. Rep. Friend.

Hadley, Eli; farmer; 2 m s Mooresville. Born in Ind. 1841. Rep. Friend.

Hutton, J. P.; toll keeper Monrovia & Mooresville pike. Born in N. C. 1839; settled in M. C. 1869. Dem. Protestant.

HARVEY, DAVID; farmer; 3 m s w Mooresville. Born in Ohio 1817; settled in M. C. 1830. Rep. Friend.

HARVEY, ELI; farmer; 2¼ m s w Mooresville. Born in 1819; settled in M. C. 1827. Rep. Friend.

Hornaday, I. M.; farmer; 4½ m s e Mooresville. Born in N. C. 1830; settled in M. C. 1838. Rep. Methodist.

Harvey, E. H.; farmer; 3 m s w Mooresville. Born in Ind. 1837; settled in M. C. 1869. Rep. Friend.

Harvey, ——; farmer; 3½ m s w Mooresville. Born in Ohio 1811; settled in M. C. 1834. Rep. Friend.

HARVEY, CALVIN; farmer; 3½ m s w Mooresville. Born in Ind. 1848. Rep. Friend.

Hadley, J. N.; farmer; 1½ m s Mooresville. Born in Ind. 1846. Rep. Friend.

Hinson, J. A.; drayman; Mooresville. Born in Ind. 1844. Rep. Protestant.

Hobson, Nathan; farmer; 3½ m s w Mooresville. Born in N. C. 1821; settled in M. C. 1825. Rep. Methodist.

Jones, B. F.; saddler and harness maker; Mooresville. Born in Ohio 1846. Rep. Protestant.

JOHNSON, H.; merchant; Mooresville. Born in Ky. 1817; settled in M. C. 1847. Dem. Methodist.

Johnson, J. F.; carriage trimmer; Mooresville. Born in N. C. 1822; settled in M. C. 1862. Rep. Methodist.

Jackson, H. Livery; feed and sale stable; Mooresville. Born in Ind. 1834; settled in M. C. 1870. Rep. Protestant.

Jackson, G. A.; farmer; 2½ m s e Mooresville. Born in N. C. 1842; settled in M. C. 1866. Dem. Protestant.

Jones, Isaac; school teacher; Mooresville. Born in Ohio. 1824; settled in M. C. 1870. Rep. Friend.

Keller, Fred.; farmer; 2 m s w Mooresville. Born in Germany 1826; settled in M. C. 1848. Dem. Friend.

KELLER, DAVID W.; farmer; 2 m s w Mooresville. Born in Ind. 1851. Rep. Methodist.

Lubbie, H.; engineer at flour mill; Mooresville. Born in Prussia 1826; settled in M. C. 1873. Presbyterian.

Linens, D. M.; farmer; 1 m e Mooresville. Born in N. C. 1843; settled in M. C. 1873. Dem. Protestant.

Love, Silas; farmer; 1 m e Mooresville. Born in Ind. 1848; settled in M. C. 1873. Protestant.

LEATHERS, J. M.; farmer; 3½ m s e Mooresviile. Born in Ky. 1814; settled in M. C. 1829. Dem. Christian.

Lawrence, Thomas E.; farmer; 3 m s w Mooresville. Born in Ind. 1852; settled in M. C. 1867. Rep. Friend.

Lashley, John; farmer; 3½ m s w Mooresville. Born in N. C.; settled in M. C. 1851. Rep. Protestant.

Lashley, James; farmer; 3¼ m s w Mooresville. Born in N. C. 1794; settled in M. C. 1858. Rep. Protestant.

Lashley, Benjamin; farmer; 3¼ m s w Mooresville. Born in N. C. 1846; settled in M. C. 1851. Rep. Protestant.

Lash, Henry; railroader; Mooresville. Born in Ill. 1842; settled in M. C. 1851. Dem. Protestant.

MARTIN, E.; miller; Mooresville. Born in Ky. 1847; settled in M. C. 1873. Dem. M. Baptist.

MACY, P. T.; firm of Macy & Burke; Mooresville. Born in Ind. 1825; settled in M. C. 1856. Rep. Friend.

MILLS, J. M.; farmer; 1 m n Mooresville. Born in Ohio 1840; settled in M. C. 1860. Rep. Methodist.

Mendenhall, H. B.; farmer; ¾ m n e Mooresville. Born in Ind. 1847. Protestant.

McPherson, O. H.; carpenter; 2½ m s e Mooresville. Born in N. C. 1820; settled in M. C. 1826. Rep. Methodist.

NcNeff, P. C.; farmer; 4 m s e Mooresville. Born in Ind. 1836. Dem. Methodist.

Macy, Wm. M.; farmer; 1 m s w Mooresville. Born in Tenn. 1820; settled in M. C. 1856. Rep. Friend.

Moon, Wm. R.; farmer; 3 m s w Mooresville. Born in Ohio 1825; settled in M. C. 1828. Rep. Friend.

MOON, ELI S.; farmer; 3 m s w Mooresville. Born in Ohio 1822; settled in M. C. 1846. Rep. Methodist.

Moon, Milo H.; farmer; 3 m s w Mooresville. Born in Ind. 1842. Rep. Methodist.

Moon, A. R.; farmer; 2¾ m s w Mooresville. Born in Ind. 1830. Rep, Friend.

Moon, Simeon; retired farmer; 2¾ m s w Mooresville. Born in N. C. 1786; settled in M. C. 1828. Rep. Friend.

Marley, Abel; farmer; 3½ m s w Mooresville. Born in N. C. 1819; settled in M. C. 1839. Rep. Methodist.

Moon, L. D.; farmer; 1½ n Brooklyn. Born in Ohio 1817; settled in M. C. 1828. Rep. Methodist.

Matthews, Calvin; farmer; 1½ m n Brooklyn. Born in Ind. 1828. Rep. Protestant.

Manical, J. M.; farmer; 1 m n Brooklyn. Born in Ind. 1827. Rep. Methodist.

Matthews, Fletcher; farmer; 3 m s Mooresville. Born in Ind. 1850. Rep. Methodist.

Matthews, Hiram; soldier of 1812; 3 m s Mooresville. Born in N. C. 1797; settled in M. C. 18—. Rep.

Matthews, Seth; farmer; 3 m s Mooresville. Born in Ind. 1832. Rep. Protestant.

May, J. W.; farmer; 2½ m s Mooresville. Born in N.C. 1838; settled in M. C. 1870. Dem. Methodist.

Medley, J. A.; farmer; 1½ m n w Brooklyn. Born in Ohio 1817; settled in M. C. 1842. Dem.

Moore, Samuel; retired merchant; Mooresville. Born in N.C. 1799. Rep.

Moore, W. S.; farmer and stock trader; Mooresville. Born in Ind. 1845; settled in M. C. 1853. Rep. Protestant.

MITCHELL, G. B.; physician and surgeon; Mooresville. Born in Ind. 1822; settled in M. C. 1833. Dem. Methodist.

Macy, J. C.; catarrh doctor; Mooresville. Born in Ind. 1828; settled in M. C. 1856. Rep. Friend.

Mills, J. H.; carriage maker; Mooresville. Born in Ind. 1843; settled in M. C. 1869. Rep. Friend.

Mills, C. H.; firm of Mills Brothers; Mooresville. Born in Ind. 1848; settled in M. C. 1873. Rep. Friend.

Merrill, C. J.; real estate agent; Mooresville. Born in N. Y. 1832; settled in M. C. 1872. Rep. Methodist.

Moon, Wm.; farmer; Mooresville. Born in Ind. 1832. Rep. Protestant.

Manker, A. F.; carpenter; Mooresville. Born in Ohio 1827; settled in M. C. 1844. Protestant.

McMeff, T. W.; carpenter; Mooresville. Born in Ind. 1834. Dem. Methodist.

McCracken, J. W.; farmer; Mooresville. Born in N. C. 1831; settled in M. C. 1833. Rep. Friend.

McNABB, P.; physician and surgeon; Mooresville. Born in Ind. 1833; settled in M. C. 1868. Rep. Christian.

McCracken, Wm.; retired merchant; Mooresville. Born in N. C. 1800; settled in M. C. 1833. Rep. Friend.

MARINE, J. A.; carpenter and builder; Mooresville. Born in N. C. 1826; settled in M. C. 1849. Dem. Methodist.

NEWMAN, J. A.; groceries, firm of Sellers & Newman; Mooresville. Born in N. C. 1849; settled in M. C. 1871. Dem. Protestant.

Newby, Milton; farmer; Mooresville. Born in Ind. 1835; settled in M. C. 1849. Rep. Friend.

Newby, Wm.; farmer; Mooresville. Born in Ind. 1837; settled in M. C. 1849. Rep. Friend.

Nelson, W.; farmer; 1 m e Mooresville. Born in N. C. 184–; settled in M. C. 1871. Rep. Protestant.

Newby, Joseph; farmer; 2½ m s Mooresville. Born in Ind. 1822; settled in M. C. 1825. Rep. Methodist.

Newby, F. A.; farmer; 1 m n w Brooklin. Born in M. C. 1848. Rep. Protestant.

NEWBY, J. F.; farmer; 1 m n w Brooklyn. Born in M. C. 1854. Rep. Protestant.

NEWBY, RIX; farmer and carpenter; 1 m n Brooklyn. Born in Ind. 1817; settled in M. C. 1826. Rep. Methodist.

OZMENT, JESSIE; farmer; 1½ m w Mooresville. Born in Tenn. 1837; settled in M. C. 1871. Rep. Protestant.

OVERMAN, ALPHEUS; farmer; 1 m s e Mooresville. Born in Ind. 1839; settled in M.C. 1857. Rep. Friend.

PERCE, B. H.; physician and surgeon; Mooresville. Born in Mich. 1838; settled in M. C. 1859. Rep. Methodist.

BROWN TOWNSHIP.

Pool, Soseph; druggist; Mooresville. Born in Ind. 1835; settled in M. C. 1852. Rep. Friend.

Pruitt, ——; firm of Pruitt & Hadley, druggists; Mooresville.

Pierson, S. D.; tailor; Mooresville. Born in Ohio 1827; settled in M. C. 1873.

Pruitt, George; firm of Pruitt & Hadley; Mooresville. Born in M. C. 1850. Dem. Protestant.

Poe, J. J.; farmer; Mooresville. Born in Ky. 1835; settled in M. C. 1860. Dem. Christian.

Pierce, Henry; boot and shoe maker; Mooresville. Born in N. C. 1821; settled in M. C. 1864. Rep. Protestant.

Pennington, Dixon; farmer; 4 m s e Mooresville. Born in Ky. 1798; settled in M. C. 1831. Rep. Protestant.

REAGAN, A. W.; physician and surgeon; Mooresville. Born in Ind. 1826; settled in M. C. 1839. Rep. Methodist.

Richardson, T. A.; stoves and tin ware; Mooresville. Born in Ind. 1837; settled in M. C. 18—. Dem. Methodist.

RUSIE, JACOB; butcher and horse farrier; Mooresville. Born in Va. 1831; settled in M. C. 1836. Dem. Protestant.

Ray, Wm. H.; lawyer and harness maker; Mooresville. Born in Ind. 1818; settled in M. C. 1852. Lib. Dem. Prot.

Ray, Wm.; farm laborer; Mooresville. Born in Ohio 1848; settled in M. C. 1852. Dem. Protestant.

ROSSIER, HENRY; silversmith and watch maker; Mooresville. Born in Switzerland 1839; settled in M. C. 1867. Rep. Protestant.

Rooker, S. S.; painter; Mooresville. Born in Tenn. 1800; settled in M. C. 1866. Dem. Methodist.

Rusie, J. H.; firm of Rusie & Richardson; Mooresville. Born in Va. 1834; settled in M. C. 1837. Dem. Methodist.

Reed, J. W.; barber; Mooresville. Born in Va. 1851; settled in M. C. 1874. Rep. Methodist.

Rushton, C. C.; farmer; 1 m n w Mooresville. Born in Ind. 1844. Rep. Friend.

Rushton, Joshua; farmer; 1 m n w Mooresville. Born in N. C. 1809; settled in M. C. 1835. Rep. Friend.

ROOKER, T. B.; farmer; 1½ m s e Mooresville. Born in Ind. 1841. Dem. Methodist.

Rooker, J. W.; farmer; 1½ m s e Mooresville. Born in Ind. 1839. Dem. Methodist.

Rushton, J. C.; farmer; 1 m n w Mooresville. Born in Ind. 1842. Rep. Friend.

RENCH, E. H.; farmer; 3 m s w Mooresville. Born in Ind. 1840; settled in M. C. 1873. Dem. Protestant.

RANDOLPH, G. B.; farmer; 3 m' s w Mooresville. Born in Ind. 1848. Dem. Protestant.

Rightman, Gideon; farmer; 3 m n w Brooklyn. Born in N.C. 1821; settled in M. C. 1828. Rep. Protestant.

Robbins, Lewis; farmer; 1½ m s Mooresville. Born in Ohio 1833; settled in M. C. 18—. Dem. Friend.

Rusie, Alex; carpenter; Mooresville. Born in Va. 1822; settled in M. C. 1836. Rep. M. E.

Rooker, Capt.; miller; Mooresville.

Snoddy, J. M.; physician and surgeon; Mooresville. Born in Ind. 1834. Rep. Christian.

SELLERS, PETER; grocery, firm of Sellers & Newman; Mooresville. Born in N. C. 1834; settled in M. C. 1873. Rep. Friend.

Shanafelt, Miss Mary; milliner; Mooresville. Born in Ind. 1824; settled in M. C. 1850. Methodist.

SHANAFELT, L. A.; painter; Mooresville. Born in Ind. 1854; settled in M. C. 1859. Methodist.

Sheets, D. P.; harness maker; Mooresville. Born in Va. 1833; settled in M. C. 1836. Methodist.

Scott, B. D.; boot and shoe maker; Mooresville. Born in Va. 1822; settled in M. C. 1844. Dem. Protestant.

Sheets, Daniel; firm of Sheets Brothers; Mooresville. Born in Va. 1825; settled in M. C. 1836. Rep. Methodist.

Sheets, Fred; firm of Sheets Brothers; Mooresville. Born in Va. 1823; settled in M. C. 1836. Rep. Methodist.

Scott, R. R.; merchant; Mooresville. Born in Ind. 1833; settled in M. C. 1857. Rep. Methodist.

Spoon, John W.; farmer; Mooresville. Born in M. C. 1840. Dem. Protestant.

SHELLEY, ISAAC; confectioner; Mooresville.. Born in Ind. 1844; settled in M. C. 1865. Dem. Methodist.

Springer, David; retired wagon maker; Mooresville. Born in Ohio 1824; settled in M. C. 1874. Protestant.

Spoon, Peter; farmer and shoemaker; Mooresville. Born in N. C. 1802; settled in M. C. 1828. Dem. Protestant.

Sumner, Eli J.; banker; Mooresville. Born in Ohio 1812; settled in M. C. 1835. Rep. Friend.

Stone, Eli; farmer and stock trader; Mooresville. Born in Ky. 1830; settled in M. C. 1834. Dem. Protestant.

Spoon, Burl; farmer; Mooresville. Born in N. C. 1835; settled in M. C. 1844. Rep. Protestant.

SHEETS, HARVEY; manufacturer and lumber dealer; Mooresville. Born in Ind. 1844; settled in M. C. 1868. Rep. Friend.

Sheets, John; farmer; ½ m e Mooresville. Born in Va. 1821; settled in M. C. 18—. Rep. Methodist.

Sheets, George; carpenter; Mooresville. Born in Germany 1786; settled in M. C 1838. Rep. Lutheran.

Sheets, Fred.; farmer and merchant; Mooresville. Born in Va. 1823; settled in M.C. 1838. Rep. Methodist.

Stephenson, Wm. S.; brick maker; Mooresville. Born in Ind. 1835; settled in M. C. 1869. Rep. M. Baptist.

SMITH, J. N.; farmer; 4½ m s e Mooresville. Born in N. C. 1852; settled in M. C. 1852. Dem. Protestant.

Staley, Monroe; farmer; 1½ m n w Mooresville. Born in N. C. 1839; settled in M. C. 1848. Dem. Protestant.

Staley, Hiram; farmer; 1½ m n w Mooresville. Born in N.C. 1804; settled in M. C. 1848. Dem. Protestant.

Sumner, W. P.; farmer; ½ m w Mooresville. Born in Ind. 1840. Rep. Friend.

Shepherd, W. J.; brick mason; Mooresville. Born in Ky. 1841; settled in M. C. 1869. Rep. Protestant.

SUMNER, T. C.; farmer; 1½ m s w Mooresville. Born in Ind. 1837; settled in M. C. 1854. Rep. Friend.

Stevens, C. R.; farmer; 3½ m s w Mooresville. Born in N. C. 1849; settled in M. C. 1867. Rep. Protestant.

Sellers & Newman; groceries, hardware and queensware. Call and see them.

Summers, M.; general purpose; 1¼ m n w Brooklyn. Born in Ky. 1810; settled in M. C. 1834. Dem.

Summers, Sanford; engineer; 1¼ m n w Brooklyn. Born in M. C. 1839. Dem.

Small, John; harness maker; 1½ m n w Brooklyn. Born in Ind. 1838; settled in M. C. 1842. Dem. Methodist.

Smothers, Wm. R.; farmer; 4 m s e Mooresville. Born in Tenn. 1825; settled in M. C. 1863. Dem. Methodist.

Thornburgh, J. H.; merchant and farmer. Born in Ind. 1821; settled in M. C. 1822. Rep. Methodist.

Tansey, Hiram; mail carrier; Mooresville. Born in Tenn. 1802; settled in M. C. 18—. Rep. Methodist.

Thompson, J. H.; firm of Woodward & Co.; Mooresville. Born in N. C. 1816; settled in M. C. 1845. Rep. Methodist.

Thompson, J. O.; firm of Woodward & Thompson; Mooresville. Born in N. C. 1839; settled in M. C. 1845. Rep. Meth.

Thompson, J. N.; pastor M. E. church; Mooresville. Born in Tenn. 1823; settled in M. C. 1869. Rep. Methodist.

TREMBLE, ALLEN; blacksmith; Mooresville. Born in Ohio 1831; settled in M. C. 1856. Rep. Methodist.

Taylor, Thomas J.; wagon maker; Mooresville. Born in Ohio 1815; settled in M. C. 1869. Rep. Protestant.

Taylor, Robert; wagon maker; Mooresville. Born in Ind. 1847; settled in M. C. 1874. Rep. Protestant.

Tansey, Jesse; farmer; Mooresville. Born in N. C. 1812; settled in M. C. 1822. Rep. Methodist.

THOMPSON, J. A.; farmer; 1¼ m s w Mooresville. Born in Ind. 1844. Rep. Protestant.

Thompson, G. P.; farmer; 2 m s w Mooresville. Born in N. C. 1814.; settled in M. C. 1833. Dem. Christian.

Thornburgh, Amos; farmer; 1½ m n Brooklyn. Born in Ind. 1827. Rep. Methodist.

Thornburgh, Benj.; retired farmer; 3½ m s Mooresville. Born in Ky. 1796; settled in M. C. 1822. Rep. Methodist.

Woodward, H. L.; firm of Harris & Woodward, Mooresville. Born in Ind. 1843; settled in M. C. 1861. Rep. Protest.

Woodward, W. H. P.; firm of Woodward & Thompson, Mooresville. Born in Va. 1816; settled in M. C. 1835. Rep. Methodist.

White, W. F.; carriage smith; Mooresville. Born in Ind. 1843; settled in M. C. 1873. Rep. Methodist.

WORTH, ALEXANDER; cash. First National Bank, Mooresville. Born in N. Y. 1803; settled in M. C. 1826. Rep. Methodist.

Welman, G W.; hack driver, Mooresville and Monrovia line. Born in Ky. 1821; settled in M. C. 1845. Rep. Christ'n.

Williams, N. C.; farmer; 1 m n Mooresville. Born in Ind. 1844. Rep. Protestant.

White, Elwood; farmer; ½ m n Mooresville. Born in Ind. 1834. Rep. Friend.

Williams, Isaac; farmer; 1 m n Mooresville. Born in N. C. 1801; settled in M. C. 1826. Rep. Friend.

Williams, Wm.; farmer; 2 m n e Mooresville. Born in Ind. 1819; settled in M. C. 1850. Dem. Christian.

Wright, Griffith; farmer; 2½ m s w Mooresville. Born in Ohio 1833; settled in M. C. 1841. Rep. Friend.

Whitehead, W. H. H.; farmer; 1½ m s w Mooresville. Born in Ind. 1840; settled in M. C. 1872. Rep. Protestant.

Wilson, M. M.; farmer; 1½ m s w Mooresville. Born in N. C. 1838; settled in M. C. 1865. Dem. Methodist.

Whitehead, Jacob; farmer; 3½ m s w Mooresville. Born in N. C. 1825; settled in M. C. 1850. Rep. Methodist.

CLAY TOWNSHIP.

CLAY TOWNSHIP, located in the central part of the county, contains thirty-two square miles, and is bounded on the north by Brown, east by Madison, west by Gregg, and south by Washington townships, White River being the line between Clay and Washington. The eastern part is moderately rolling and very fertile. The western part is very broken and barren; timber and stone abound in quantities in this part of the township; gold has been found and mined to some extent. Brooklyn, a pleasantly situated village of three hundred inhabitants, is located on the I. & V. R. R., in the northeast part of the township. It contains two dry good stores, two grocery stores, one drug store, two churches, Odd Fellow, Masonic, Good Templar and Grange Lodges. More grain is shipped from this place than any other in the county. Clay township was one of the first settled of Morgan county, it being settled in 1819. George and Joel Matthews, Isaiah Drury and John Butterfield being among the first.

Centerton, a small town on the I. & V. R. R., about three miles south of Brooklyn, is represented by an honest and respectable class of citizens, and is a point for trade, accommodating the citizens of the surrounding country.

CHURCHES AND LODGES.

M. E. Church; Zion Chapel, 2½ miles southeast of Brooklyn; James Wall, pastor; membership, 65; value of church property, $2000; superintendent Sabbath school, J. W. Rinker; average attendance of Sabbath school, 60.

M. E. Church, Dryland Grove school house; Sabbath school superintendent, Joseph Hobson; average attendance, 30; Jacob White, head leader.

M. E. Church, Brooklyn; James Wall, pastor; membership, 200; Sabbath school superintendent, Clark Robbins; average attendance, 100.

Christian Church, Brooklyn; H. A. Kerr, pastor; membership, 100; value of church property, $3000; Sabbath school superintendent, Miss Hattie Cox; average attendance, 60.

Willow Grove Class Membership; pastor, W. H. Fisher; superintendent Sabbath school, W. Dofford; average attendance, 60.

Freemasons: Brooklyn Lodge, U. D.; membership, 25.

Odd Fellows: Brooklyn Lodge, No. 303; membership, 60; value of Lodge property, $900.

Patrons of Husbandry: Brooklyn Grange, No. 1246; John W. Furgason, Master; Scott W. Stafford, Secretary; number of members, 30.

Centerton Grange, No. 1564; membership, 30; Charles Record, Master; Wm. Hatwell, Secretary.

Number of school houses, 8; valuation, $2800.

Population of township, 900. Wm. Black, Trustee.

DIRECTORY OF CLAY TOWNSHIP.

Albertson, J. C.; farmer; 2½ m w Centerton. Born in N. C. 1850; settled in M. C. 1851. Rep.

Albertson, Jacob; farmer and carpenter; 3 m w Centerton. Born in Ind. 1833. Rep. M. Baptist.

ALLEN, JOSEPH; farmer; 3½ m w Centerton. Born in Ind. 1821; settled in M. C. 1829. Dem. Methodist.

Allen, B. F.; farmer; 3½ m w Centerton. Born in Ind. 1846. Dem. Methodist.

Albertson, John, Sen.; farmer and milling; 2 m w Centerton. Born in N. C. 1804; settled in M. C. 1834. Rep. Honesty.

ADAMS, WM. E.; farmer; 4½ m s e Monrovia. Born in N. C. 1802; settled in M. C. 1848. Rep. M. Baptist.

Albertson, J. B.; farmer; 2 m n w Centerton. Born in N. C. 1823; settled in M. C. 1850. Rep. Methodist.

ANDERSON, J. W.; section foreman; Brooklyn. Born in Ind. 1841; settled in M. C. 1874. Rep. Methodist.

Blunk, Aaron; farmer, stock and fruit grower; Centerton. Born in Ind. 1820. Rep. R. Baptist.

Blunk, Rebecca, the oldest person living in M. C. Born in V a 1768; came to Ind. 1790; settled in M. C. 1819.

Bayliff, Daniel; farmer; 3½ m s e Monrovia. Born in Va. 1799; settled in M. C. 1844. Rep. Friend.

BAYLIFF, J. M.; farmer; 2 m e Wilber. Born in Ohio, 1833; settled in M. C. 1844. Rep.

BLACKBORN, P. C.; day laborer; 2½ m w Centerton. Born in Ind. 1851; settled in M. C. 1861. Rep.

Burch, George; wagon maker and blacksmith; 2 m w Centerton. Born in Ky. 1813; settled in M. C. 1846. Rep. M. Baptist.

BREEDLOVE, E. M.; farmer; ½ m s e Centerton. Born in Ohio, 1834; settled in M. C. 1843. Rep. Christian.

Baber, Levi; farmer; Centerton. Born in Ind. 1838; settled in M. C. 1840. Rep. Protestant.

Bradford, John; farmer; 2 m s w Centerton. Born in Ohio, 1828; settled M. C. 1867. Rep. Protestant.

BATTE, T. H.; farmer; 1½ s w Centerton. Born in Miss. 1848; settled in M. C. 1871. Dem. Protestant.

BLUNK, WM. A.; farmer; ½ m w Centerton. Born in Ind. 1848. Rep. Protestant.

Black, William; carpenter; Brooklyn. Born in Ind. 1836. Rep. Christian.

Breedlove, William; farmer; Brooklyn. Born in N. C. 1818; settled in M. C. 1867. Rep. Methodist.

BROWN, ISAIAH; shoe and boot maker; Brooklyn. Born in Ind. 1836; settled in M. C. 1870. Rep. Christian.

BROWN, WM.; contractor and stone mason; Brooklyn. Born in N. C. 1833; settled in M. C. 1859. Dem. Methodist.

BREEDLOVE, R. L.; farmer; 2 m s e Brooklyn. Born in Ind. 1844. Rep. Christian.

Breedlove, A. W.; farmer; 2½ m s e Brooklyn. Born in Ohio 1830; settled in M. C. 1843. Rep. Protestant.

Bryant, Henry; farmer; 2 m e Centerton. Born in Ind. 1840; settled in M. C. 1874. Rep. Protestant.

Blunk, Jas. M.; farmer; 1½ m s e Centerton. Born in Ind. 1856. Rep. Protestant.

BREEDLOVE, ROBERT; farmer; 3 m s e Brooklyn. Born in Va. 1803; settled in M. C. 1842. Rep. Protestant.

Butterfield, Amanda; farmer; 3 m s e Brooklyn. Born in Ky. 1818; settled in M. C. 1856. Rep. Protestant.

Bird, J. B.; farmer; 2½ m e Brooklyn. Born in Ky. 1843; settled in M. C. 1873. Rep. Protestant.

Butterfield, T. P.; fancy groceries and boarding; Brooklyn. Born in Ind. 1834. Rep. Christian.

Butterfield, V.; farmer and millwright; Brooklyn. Born in N. Y. 1805; settled in M. C. 1825. Rep. Christian.

Butterfield, L. K.; professional school teacher; Brooklyn. Born in Ind. 1851; settled in M. C. 1874. Rep. Methodist.

CUMMINS, THOMAS; farmer; 4 m s e Monrovia. Born in Mo. 1847; settled in M. C. 1850. Rep.

CUMMINS, ALEXANDER; farmer; 4¼ m s e Monrovia. Born in Mo. 1850; settled in M. C. 1862. Rep.

Collins, David; farmer; 3 m w Centerton. Born in N. C. 1800; settled in M. C. 1830. Rep. M. Baptist.

CORNWELL, C. C.; farmer; 5 m n Martinsville. Born in N. C. 1846; settled in M. C. 1862. Rep.

Collins, John; farmer; 2½ m s w Centerton. Born in Ind. 1838. Rep.

CARLYLE, JONATHAN; cooper and basket maker; 2 m n Brooklyn. Born in Va. 1812; settled in M. C. 1872. Dem. Methodist.

Clark, Lewis; farmer; 1 m e Centerton. Born in Ind. 1836 Dem. Protestant.

Clark, John; farmer; 1 m e Centerton. Born in Md. 1798; settled in M. C. 1834. Dem. Christian.

Clark, George; farmer; 1 m e Centerton. Born in Ind. 1838. Dem. Christian.

Clark, George; farmer; 2 m w Centerton. Born in England 1847; settled in M. C. 1871. Rep. Protestant.

Cox, G. W.; drugs and patent medicines; Brooklyn. Born in Ind. 1851. Rep.

COBLE, JOHN; carpenter; Brooklyn. Born in N. C. 1837; settled in M. C. 1868. Rep. Methodist.

COMPTON, WM.; farmer; Brooklyn. Born in Ind. 1853. Rep. Christian.

Currey, Solomon; farmer; Brooklyn. Born in N. C. 1850; settled in M. C. 1874. Dem.

Cramer, John S.; farmer; 2 m s w Brooklyn. Born in N. J. 1844; settled in M. C. 1859. Rep. Methodist.

COX, ANN, Mrs.; farmer; ½ m n Centerton. Born in Ohio 1820; settled in M. C. 1830. Christian.

CLAY TOWNSHIP. 213

Clark, Milton; farmer; Centerton. Born in Ohio 1833; settled in M. C. 1835. Dem. Christian.

Cawsey, Thomas; blacksmith; Brooklyn, Born in N.C. 1829; settled in M. C. 1873. Protestant.

Cramer, ——; farmer; 2½ m s e Brooklyn. Born in N. J. 1842; settled in M. C. 1857. Rep. Methodist.

DAILEY, FRANCIS M.; farmer; 3 m w Centerton. Born in Ind. 1839; settled in M. C. 1860. Dem. Methodist.

Dooley, M. H.; farmer; 4 m s e Monrovia. Born in Ind. 1852. Rep.

Dooley, Hiram; farmer; 4½ m s e Monrovia. Born in Ohio 1816; settled in M. C. 1842. Rep. R. Baptist.

Dyke, J. D.; farmer; Centerton. Born in Ky. 1852; settled in M. C. 1863. Rep. Protestant.

DYKE, WM.; blacksmith and farmer; Centerton. Born in Tenn. 1825 settled in M. C. 1868. Granger. Protestant.

Dill, Erasmus; farmer; 2 m s Brooklyn. Born in Ohio 1831; settled in M. C. 1840. Dem. Christian.

Ewgers, Wm.; farmer; 2½ m s e Centerton. Born in Ind. 1840. Rep.

ELY, CALVIN; farmer; Brooklyn. Born in Ind. 1851. Rep. Christian.

Evans, John; farmer; 3 m s e Brooklyn. Born in Ky. 1820; settled in M. C. 1871. Rep. Christian.

Evans, I. L.; farmer; 3 m s e Brooklyn. Born in Ind. 1852; settled in M. C. 1871. Rep. Christian.

Forbis, Nathaniel; farmer; Centerton. Born in N. C. 1850; settled in M. C. 1868. Rep. Christian.

Ferguson, John S.; wagonmaker; Brooklyn. Born in Ind. 1836; settled in M. C. 1870. Rep. Methodist.

Fogleson, Christian; day laborer; Centerton. Born in Ohio 1801; settled in M. C. 1868. Dem. Protestant.

Fultz, G. W.; farmer and trader; 3 m s w Centerton. Born in Ind. 1836; settled in M. C. 1846. Rep.

Fair, Robt. C.; farmer; 4½ m s w Centerton. Born in Ind. 1833; settled in M. C. 1871. Rep.

Fair, Robt. C., Sen.; farmer and blacksmith; 3½ m n w Centerton. Born in N. C. 1800; settled in M. C. 1872. Rep. M. Baptist.

Fair, Wm.; farmer and blacksmith; 2 m w Centerton. Born in Ind. 1835; settled in M. C. 1862. Rep.

Fields, A. J.; farmer; 1 m s e Brooklyn. Born in Ind. 1830. Dem. Christian.

(FURGASON, J. W.; farmer; 2 m s e Brooklyn. Born in Ky. 1814; settled in M. C. 1853. Rep. Christian.)

Griggs, Hiram ; farmer ; 4 m s e Monrovia. Born in Va. 1804 ; settled in M. C. 1850. Liberal. United Brethren.

Greeson, J. T.; farmer ; 4 m w Brooklyn. Born in Ind. 1849. Rep. Methodist.

Greeson, Daniel ; farmer and trader; 3 m n w Brooklyn. Born in N. C. 1817 ; settled in M. C. 1855. Rep.

Greeson, William; Centerton. Born in Ind. 1844. Rep. Christian.

GOOCH, WM.; Jr.; farmer ; 1 m s w Centerton. Born in Ind. 1854. Dem. Protestant.

Gooch, Dalney ; farmer; 1 m s w Centerton. Born in Ky. 1810; settled in M. C. 1831. Dem. Protestant.

Gooch, Henry; farmer; 1 m s w Centerton. Born in Ind. 1847. Dem. Protestant.

Gregory, B. L.; firm of Gregory & Son ; Brooklyn. Born in Ind. 1850. Rep. Christian.

GRIGGS, ABRAHAM; farmer; ¼ m w Brooklyn. Born in N. J. 1807; settled in M. C. 1829. Rep. Christian.

GARRETT, H. W.; druggist; Centerton. Born in Ohio 1845 ; settled in M. C. 1871. Rep. Protestant.

Gooch, Wm.; merchant; Centerton. Born in Ind. 1841. Dem. Protestant.

GREEN, B. R.; farmer; Brooklyn. Born in Ky. 1834; settled in M. C. 1856. Rep. Christian.

Griggs, Clark; farmer and trader; 1½ m s Brooklyn. Born in Ohio 1829; settled in M. C. 1829. Rep. Christian.

Gregory, J. H.; farmer; 2¾ m s e Brooklyn. Born in Ind. 1842. Rep. Methodist.

Gamble, L.; saw milling; 1½ m n e Brooklyn. Born in N. C. 1847; settled in M. C. 18—. Dem. Protestant.

Gregory, Stephen; farmer; 1½ m n e Brooklyn. Born in Ind. 1829. Rep. Christian.

Hammack, George; farmer; 3 m s e Monrovia. Born in Tenn. 1807; settled in M. C. 1853. Lib. Methodist.

Hobson, J. W.; farmer; 2½ m n w Brooklyn. Born in N. C. 1824; settled in M. C. 1827. Rep. Methodist.

Hobson, William; farmer; 3 m s w Brooklyn. Born in Ind. 1833. Rep. Protestant.

Henderson, Elijah; farmer; 1 m n w Brooklyn. Born in Ky. 1799; settled in M. C. 1829. Rep. Christian.

Horaday, W. W.; farmer; Brooklyn. Born in Ind. 1844. Rep. Methodist.

Hardwick, Wm.; farmer; Centerton. Born in Tenn. 1807; settled in M. C. 1823. Rep. Protestant.

Hayes, W. H.; firm of Stipp & Hayes; Brooklyn. Born in N. C. 1848; settled in M. C. 1859. Rep. Protestant.

Howe, Adam; blacksmith; Brooklyn. Born in Mass. 1835; settled in M. C. 1856. Rep.

HARDWICK, ALEXANDER; school teaccher; Brooklyn. Born in Ind. 1842. Rep. Friend and Methodist.

HARPER, ALFRED; engineer; Brooklyn. Born in Ky. 1835; settled in M. C. 1873. Rep. Christian.

Harper, L. A.; milliner; Brooklyn. Born in Ind. 1846; settled in M. C. 1873. Christian.

HOUSAND, IRA; farmer and carpenter; ½ m n w Brooklyn. Born in Va. 1818; settled in M. C. 1827. Dem. Christian.

Hienstand, H. H.; farmer; 1¼ m n w Centerton. Born in Ind. 1834; settled in M. C. 1868. Rep. Methodist.

Hadley, Calvin; farmer and shoe maker; 3 m s e Monrovia. Born in Ind. 1825. Rep. Friend.

Hess, J. W.; farmer; 1¼ m e Centerton Born in Ind. 1842. Dem. Protestant.

Hand, Henry; farmer; 2½ m s e Brooklyn. Born in Ind. 1835; settled in M. C. 1872. Dem. Methodist.

Hix, Isaac; farmer; 2 m s e Centerton. Born in Ky. 1839; settled in M. C. 1873. Dem. Protestant.

Hendrix, John J.; farmer; 3 m s e Brooklyn. Born in Ind. 1845; settled in M. C. 1848. Rep. Protestant.

Helton, J. L.; day laborer; 2½ m e Brooklyn. Born in Ky. 1850; settled in M. C. 1863. Dem. Protestant.

Johnson, Aleck; farmer; 4 m s e Monrovia. Born in N. J. 1822; settled in M. C. 1862. Rep. Methodist.

Jackson, James; farmer; 4 m n e Centerton. Born in Ind. 1844. Dem.

Julian, Wm. E.; farmer; 4 m s e Monrovia. Born in Ind. 1846. Rep. Methodist.

Johnson, J. H.; farmer; 2 m w Centerton. Born in Ind. 1846; settled in M. C. 1863. Rep. Methodist.

Johnson, Elijah; farmer; 2½ m n w Centerton. Born in Ind. 1853; settled in M. C. 1862. Rep. Protestant.

JORDON, W. H.; farmer; 1 m s Centerton. Born in N. C. 1840; settled in M. C. 1870. Rep. Protestant.

Kiser, John; farmer; 4 m w Centerton. Born in Ind. 1829; settled in M. C. 1855. Rep. R. Babtist.

Kirkendoll, Elizabeth; farmer; 3 m w Centerton. Born in Tenn. 1827; settled in M. C. 1830. M. Baptist.

King, Wm. H.; farmer; 4 m w Centerton. Born in Ind. 1842. Rep.

Kiser, Jacob; farmer; 3½ m s w Centerton. Born in Ky. 1815; settled in M. C. 1816. Rep.

Kitchen, Calvin; farmer; 1 m s Centerton. Born in Ind. 1844. Dem. Protestant.

King, George L.; Carpenter; Brooklyn. Born in Ky. 1833; settled in M. C. 1870. Dem.

KOONS, THOS. H.; dry goods and groceries, Centerton. Born in Ind. 1851. Rep. Christian.

KALE, CHARLES; engineer; Centerton. Born in N. C. in 1852; settled in M. C. 1868. Dem. Protestant.

Knox, Catharine; farmer; 2¾ m s e Brooklyn. Born in Va. 1801; settled in M. C. 1840. Methodist.

Kays, Geo. W.; farmer; 2 m e Brooklyn. Born in Ky. 1847; settled in M. C. 1865. Rep. Christian.

Kays, Mason; farmer; 2 m e Brooklyn. Born in Ky. 1822; settled in M. C. 1863. Dem. Protestant.

KAYS, G. H.; farmer; ½ m n e Brooklyn. Born in Ky. 1848; settled in M. C. 1862. Dem. Christian.

Leer, G. W.; farmer; ½ m s e Centerton. Born in Ind. 1849. Dem. Protestant.

Lacefield, George; farmer; 1½ m s w Centerton. Born in Ky. 1812; settled in M. C. 1829. Rep. Christian.

Line, Samuel; farmer; Brooklyn. Born in Pa. 1798; settled in M. C. 1848. Dem. R. Baptist.

Line, George W.; railroader; Brooklyn.

Larsh, Wm.; day laborer; Brooklyn. Born in Ill. 1845; settled in M. C. 1847. Dem.

Leon, J. J.; shoe and boot maker; Centerton. Born in Mass.; settled in M. C. 1873. Rep. Protestant.

Long, William M.; engineer; Brooklyn. Born in Ind. 1855. Dem. Christian.

Lang, Dennis; farmer; 2 m s Brooklyn.   Born in Ind. 1851. Dem. Christian.

Lamb, Joseph; farmer; 3 m s Brooklyn.   Born in Ind. 1844 Rep. Protestant.

LAMB, JOHN; farmer; 3 m s Brooklyn.   Born in Ind. 1833. Rep. Protestant.

Lindley, C. M.; physician and surgeon; Brooklyn. Born in Ill. 1833; settled in M. C. 1856. Rep. Methodist.

McNICHOLS, JOHN; farmer and fruit grower; 2½ m s e Monrovia. Born in Ohio 1827; settled in M. C. 1861. Rep. Friend.

McKinley, Jeremiah; farmer; 3½ m n w Centerton. Born in Ind. 1846. Rep. Methodist.

MAXWELL, HENRY C.; farmer; 3 m n w Centerton. Born in Ind. 1828. Rep. Methodist.

McCANDLESS, E. P.; farmer; Centerton. Born in Pa. 1839; settled in M. C. 1872. Rep. Protestant.

Mills, George W.; farmer; 2 m s w Centerton. Born in Ky. 1834; settled in M. C. 1871. Rep. Protestant.

Maxwell, George W.; farmer; ½ m w Centerton. Born in Ind. 1838. Rep. Protestant.

Maxwell, Wm. P.; farmer and school teacher; ½ m n w Centerton. Born in Ind. 1842. Rep. Protestant.

McNeff, Wm. A.; merchant; Brooklyn. Born in Ind, 1838. Presbyterian.

Morris, Salem; blacksmith; Brooklyn. Born in Ohio 1836;
settled in M. C. 1868. Rep. Methodist.

Morris, Michael; blacksmith; Brooklyn. Born in Ohio 1832;
settled in M. C. 1868. Rep. Methodist.

McDANIEL, JOHN; prop'r flouring mill; Brooklyn. Born
in N. C. 1805; settled in M. C. 1836. Rep. Methodist.

Maxwell, J. B.; freight agent; Centerton. Born in Ky. 1804;
settled in M. C. 1827. Rep. Christian.

McNEFF, P. S. & BRO.; dry goods and general merchants,
and dealers in grain, &c.; Brooklyn. Born in Ind. 1832.

Moser, Charles; farmer; 3½ m s e Brooklyn. Born in Ind. 1848.
Dem. Christian.

MOSS, HENRY; farmer; 3 m s e Brooklyn. Born in M. C.
1847. Dem. Methodist.

Morgan, Wm. A.; farmer; 1½ m n e Brooklyn. Born in Ind.
1853. Dem. Protestant.

Morgan, Thomas; farmer; 1½ m n e Brooklyn. Born in Tenn.
1810; settled in M. C. 1823. Dem. Christian.

Miller, Ileviao; farmer; 3 m s e Brooklyn. Born in Va. 1847;
settled in M. C. 1863. Rep. Protestant.

Overton, Benj.; farmer; 3 m s w Centerton. Born in Tenn.
1816; settled in M. C. 18—. Rep.

Parson, Edmond; farmer; 2½ m w Centerton. Born in N. C.
1851; settled in M. C. 1856. Rep. Methodist.

Parson, J. H.; farmer; 3 m w Centerton. Born in N. C. 1849; settled in M. C. 1866. Rep.

Parker, Wm.; farmer; 6 m n Martinsville. Born in N. C. 1800; settled in M. C. 1824. Rep. Christian.

Parker, Joseph; farmer; 4½ m s w Centerton. Born in Ind. 1827. Rep. Methodist.

Phillips, John; farmer; 2½ m w Centerton. Born in N. C. 1822; settled in M. C. 1841. Rep. Methodist.

PATRUM, M. A.; farmer; 3 m w Brooklyn. Born in Ind. 1844. Methodist.

Pearcy, J. W.; farmer; 1½ m s w Centerton. Born in Ind. 1851. Dem. Christian.

Parker, W. H.; farmer; 2 m s w Centerton. Born in Ind. 1830; settled in M. C. 1831.

Padrick, G. W.; saw milling; Centerton. Born in Ind. 1837; settled in M. C. 1867. Dem. Protestant.

Phillips, J. A.; day laborer; Centerton. Born in Ind. 1850. Dem. Protestant.

Provinee, D. H.; school teacher; Brooklyn. Born in Ky. 1849; settled in M. C. 1867. Dem. Protestant.

PARSONS, WM.; farmer, 1½ m s Brooklyn. Born in N. C. 1838; settled in M. C. 1866. Rep. Christian.

Petty, Jonathan; farmer; 2½ m s e Centerton. Born in N. C. 1819; settled in M. C. 1862. Rep. Protestant.

Pointer, B. F.; farmer; 2 m s Brooklyn. Born in Ind. 1835. Rep. Christian.

ROBBINS, Clark; physician and surgeon; Brooklyn. Born in Ind. 1836. Rep. Methodist.

RECORD, CHARLES; farmer; Centerton. Born in Ind. 1838. Rep. Christian.

Rothrock, John H.; farmer; 2 m s Brooklyn. Born in N. C. 1847; settled in M. C. 1866. Dem. Protestant.

RINKER, GEO.; farmer and saw milling; 3 m s e Brooklyn. Born in Ind. 1821; settled in M. C. 1829. Rep. Meth.

RINKER, JOHN W.; farmer and machininist; 3 m s e Brooklyn. Born in Ind. 1846. Rep. Methodist.

RINKER, GEO. L.; farmer and engineer; 3 m s e Brooklyn. Born in Ind. 1853. Rep. Methodist.

Rinker, Wm.; farmer; 2 m s e Brooklyn. Born 1816; settled in M. C. 1830. Dem. Methodist.

RINKER, N. R.; farmer; 1 m s e Brooklyn. Born in Ind. 1820; settled in M. C. 1832. Dem. Methodist.

Rinker, A. D.; farmer; 1 m s e Brooklyn. Born in Ind. 1858. Dem. Methodist.

Rinker, John; farmer; 2 m s e Brooklyn. Born in Ind. 1846. Dem. Protestant.

Roe, A. J.; farmer; 2½ m n e Brooklyn. Born in Ind. 1844. Dem. Protestant.

Robbins, James; brick mason and contractor; 3 m n e Brooklyn. Born in Ind. 1839. Dem. Christian.

RICHARDS, JOSHUA; farmer; 4 m s e Monrovia. Born in Tenn. 1825; settled in M. C. 1865. Rep. Christian.

RUSSELL, J. T.; farmer and small fruits; 1½ m n w Brooklyn. Born in Ind. 1821; settled in M. C. 1871. Rep. Methodist.

RECORD, JACKSON; farmer; Centerton. Born in Ky. 1815; settled in M. C. 1833. Rep. Protestant.

RINKER, C. C.; farmer; 1 m e Brooklyn. Born in Ind. 1853. Dem. Methodist.

REYNOLDS, CHAS. O.; ¾ m s Centerton. Born in Ind. 1836; settled in M. C. 1872. Rep. Methodist.

RECORD, PERRY; farmer and trader; ¾ m s Centerton. Born in Ind. 1846. Rep. Christian.

RECORD, A. R.; ½ m w Centerton. Born in Ind. 1852. Rep. Protestant.

Reisner, J. W.; clerk in store; Brooklyn. Born in Ohio 1849; settled in M. C. 1873. Rep. C. Presbyterian.

Stanton, Hiram J.; farmer and carpenter; 3½ m s e Monrovia. Born in Ohio 1831; settled in M. C. Rep. Friend.

Smallwood, Evoline; farmer; 3½ m w Centerton. Born in Ky. 1822; settled in M. C. 1859. M. Baptist.

STAFFORD, BENJ.; farmer; 2¼ m s. w Centerton. Born in Ohio 1810; settled in M. C. 1820. Rep. Methodist.

Stafford, F. M.; farmer; 4 m s e Monrovia. Born in Ind. 1839. Rep. Methodist.

Stafford, J. K.; farmer; 3 m n w Centerton. Born in Ind. 1837. Rep. Methodist.

Spoon, Adam; farmer; 5 m s e Monrovia. Born in N. C. 1811; settled in M. C. 1839. Rep. Methodist.

Sanders, E. H.; farmer and carpenter; 2½ m n w Brooklyn. Born in N. C. 1826; settled in M. C. 1874. Rep. Protest.

Stayton, Thos.; farmer and trader; 2½ m n w Centerton. Born in Ohio 1845; settled in M. C. 1868. Rep. Methodist.

Spencer, E. E.; engineer; Centerton. Born in Pa. 1845; settled in M. C. 1871. Dem. Protestant.

Stipp, J. A.; school teacher; Centerton. Born in Va. 1810; settled in M. C. 1821. Rep. Christian.

Strader, George; farmer and blacksmith; Centerton. Born in Ohio 1825; settled in M. C. 1834. Rep. Christian.

Stipp, K. H.; farmer; Centerton. Born in Ind. 1844. Rep. Protestant.

Swisher, S. M.; farmer; Centerton. Born in Ohio 1840; settled in M. C. 1871. Dem. Christian.

Stafford, B. B.; farmer; ½ m s e Centerton. Born in Ind. 1846. Rep. Protestant.

STILLWAGGON, M.; farmer; 1½ m n w Centerton. Born in Pa. 1841; settled in M. C. 1871. Rep. Christian.

SAILORS, A. C.; saddle and harness maker, and Justice of Peace; Brooklyn. Born in Ind. 1836; settled in M. C. 1838. Rep. Christian.

Stipp, Abraham, of the firm of Hayes; Brooklyn. Born in Ohio 1815; settled in M. C. 1820. Rep. Protestant.

Scowt, Wm., farmer; 1 m n w Brooklyn. Born in Ky. 1847; settled in M. C. 1860. Rep.

Shelley, B. R.; farmer; Brooklyn. Born in Ind. 1840; settled in M. C. 1870. Dem. Methodist.

Shepherd, Lafayette; railroader; Brooklyn. Born in N. C. 1841; settled in M. C. 1868. Dem. Protestant.

Swisher, Wm. H.; wagonmaker; Centerton. Born in Va. 1832; settled in M. C. 1861. Dem. Christian.

Swisher, David; wagonmaker; Centerton. Born in Va. 1804; settled in M. C. 1873. Dem. Christian.

Smith, W. D.; day laborer; 1½ m s e Centerton. Born in Ky. 1851; settled in M. C. 1862. Rep. Protestant.

Smith, M. M.; sawmilling; Brooklyn. Born in N. C. 1827; settled in M. C. 1860. Dem. Methodist.

Smith, Lewis; wagonmaker; Brooklyn. Born in N. C. 1830; settled in M. C. 1866. Rep. Protestant.

Stafford, Scott; farmer; 2 m s e Brooklyn. Born in Ind. 1857. Rep. Presbyterian.

Stafford, A. B.; farmer; 2 m s Brooklyn. Born in Ind. 1841. Rep. Christian.

Steward, Wm. M.; farmer; 2 m s e Brooklyn. Born in Ohio 1821; settled in M. C. 1841. Dem. Methodist.

SHELLEY, WM.; farmer; Brooklyn. Born in Ind. 1836; settled in M. C. 1857. Dem. Protestant.

STAPLETON, T. W.; veterinary surgeon and general purpose man. Born in Ill. 1823; settled in M.C. 1873. Dem. Prot.

THURMON, J. P.; farmer; Centerton. Born in Ky. 1848; settled in M. C. 1870. Dem. Protestant.

THOMPSON, JAMES; farmer; 1 m s Centerton. Born in Ind. 1840. Rep. Protestant.

TROWBRIDGE, J. W.; farmer; Brooklyn. Born in Ky. 1845; settled in M. C. 1870. Dem. Christian.

Thompson, Willis; farmer; Centerton. Born in Ind. 1835. Rep. Protestant.

Tierce, Henry; farmer; 2½ m s e Brooklyn. Born in S. C. 1836; settled in M. C. 1865. Rep. Protestant.

Underwood, James; farmer; 1 m s w Centerton. Born in N. C. 1807; settled in M. C. 1867. Dem. Protestant.

Underwood, W. K., farmer; 1 m s w Centerton. Born in N. C. 1832; settled in M. C. 1859. Dem. Methodist.

Vaughn, J. M.; farmer; 3 m n w Brooklyn. Born in Ohio 1825; settled in M. C. 1872. Rep. M. Baptist.

VANCIL, WM. J.; blacksmith; Brooklyn. Born in Va. 1843; settled in M. C. 1873. Rep. Protestant.

Vogus, Frank; farmer; 1¼ m e Centerton. Born in Ind. 1849. Dem. Protestant.

Vogus, Jacob; farmer; 1½ m s e Centerton. Born in Ind. 1845. Rep. Protestant.

Wilson, Thomas; farmer; 3 m s e Monrovia. Born in N. C. 1804; settled in M. C. 1850. Rep. Methodist.

Wilson, James; farmer; 4 m w Centerton. Born in Va. 1812; settled in M. C. 1832. Rep.

Wall, William; farmer; 2 m w Centerton. Born in Ky. 1795; settled in M. C. 1824. Rep. Christian.

WILLIAMS, PHILIP T.; farmer and harness maker; 4 m w Brooklyn. Born in Ind. 1833; settled in M.C. 1874. Rep.

WOODYARD, J. A.; farmer; ¾ m s w Centerton. Born in N. C. 1842; settled in M. C. 1867. Rep. Christian.

WALL, B. M.; farmer; ¾ m s w Centerton. Born in Ind. 1830. Rep. Protestant.

Wyatt, Wm.; farmer; 1¼ m n w Centerton. Born in Ky. 1826; settled in M. C. 1844. Dem. M. Baptist.

WORTHINGTON, J. M.; farmer; ¾ m n w Brooklyn. Born Mo. 1817; settled in M. C. 1835. Rep. C. Presbyterian.

Woodard, C. W.; farmer; Brooklyn. Born in Ky. 1825; settled in M. C. 1828. Dem. Methodist.

Williamson, George; day laborer; Centerton. Born in Ind. 1855; seettled in M. C. 1874. Rep. Methodist.

Welty, Walter W.; farmer; 1¼ m e Brooklyn. Born in Pa. 1841; settled in M. C. 1850. Dem. Protestant.

Young, H. H; farmer; 2 m e Brooklyn. Born in Va. 1821; settled in M. C. 1848. Dem. Protestant.

Young, Wm. A.. farmer; 2 m e Brooklyn. Born in Ind. 1853. Dem. Protestant.

GREGG TOWNSHIP.

GREGG TOWNSHIP is located about the center of the county, west of White river, and contains about twenty-six square miles. It is bounded on the north by Monroe township, on the east by Clay, on the south by Jefferson and Ashland, and on the west by Adams. The surface of this township is somewhat broken, especially on the south; it is well watered by small streams, which flow through the township and afford never failing water. The soil of this township is generally productive. Hall, a small village situated in the northeast part of the township, is well furnished with gentlemanly merchants and mechanics who are clever and affable; churches and school houses show to the traveler that they are not behind in church and school privileges. There are also two other villages, viz: Wilber and Herbemont, which supply the citizens with all kinds of merchandise. There is also a post office in each one of these villages.

CHURCH, LODGE AND SCHOOL STATISTICS.

M. Baptist Church; one-fourth mile w of Wilber, at Burn's Creek; pastor, Rev. Wm. Christy; membership 22; Sabbath school superintendent, Miles Howell; average attendance 20.

Christian Church; Hall; pastor, Rev. S. C. Pruitt; Sabbath school superintendent, Wm. H. Elmore; elder, J. B. Johnson; average attendance of Sabbath school 80; value of church property $3,000; membership, 165.

M. E. Church; Hall; pastor, Rev. James F. Fish; Sabbath school superintendent, Wm. Wilhite; average attendance of

Sabbath school 40; membership, 82; value of church property, $1000.

M. E. Church; Wilber; pastor, Rev. Fish; membership, 69; average attendance of Sabbath school, 50; value of church property, $1000.

The Methodist Church at Wilber called Harmony; pastor, Rev. Wm. H. Fisher; membership, 33; average attendance of Sabbath school, 35; value of property, $600.

Friends Church; Highland; two miles south Monrovia; Prisselar Lawrence, minister; membership, 51; superintendent Sabbath school, Samuel Henley; average attendance of Sabbath school, 45; value of property, $1000.

Mt. Gilead Class; membership, 11; pastor, Rev. W. H. Fisher.

Union Sabbath school ¾ mile northwest of Herbemont; superintendent Sabbath school, Levi Fowler; average attendance of school, 60.

Herbemont Grange, No. 1292; Master, Robert Wooden; membership, 32; Secretary, Thos. Dixon; organized Feb. 1874.

Ferguson School House Grange, No. —; membership, 32.

DIRECTORY OF GREGG TOWNSHIP.

Adkins, Herod; farmer; 2¼ m n w Wilber. Born in Ind. 1844; settled in M. C. 1850. Dem.

Applegate, B. N.; farmer and mechanic; ½ m n Wilber. Born in Ind. 1830; settled in M. C. 1868. Rep. Methodist.

Albertson, Jasper; carpenter; 2½ m w Wilber. Born in M. C. 1837. Rep. Methodist.

Albertson, Elijah; farmer; 1 m s Hall. Born in Ky. 1808. settled in M. C. 1832. Rep. Christian.

Bray, James W.; farmer; ¾ m n e Wilber. Born in Tenn. 1810; settled in M. C. 1824. Rep. Methodist.

Brown, R. E.; farmer; 1½ m s w Hall. Born in Ky. 1819; settled in M. C. 1834. Dem. Christian.

Brown, James H.; merchant; Hall. Born in M. C. 1842. Rep. Christian.

Black, Wm. H.; blacksmith; Hall. Born in Md. 1833; settled in M. C. 1872.

BODENHAMER, JAMES; minister and blacksmith; Wilber. Born in N. C. 1822; settled in M. C. 1839. Dem. P. Meth.

Brown, John A.; farmer; Wilber. Born in N. C. 1818; settled in M. C. 1871. Granger. Methodist

Brown, R. M.; shoemaker and saw milling; Wilber. Born in N. C. 1846; settled in M. C. 1866. Rep. Methodist.

Bryant, J. S.; farming; 2 m s w Wilber. Born in Ohio 1815; settled in M. C. 1852. Rep. Methodist.

Baron, S. W.; farmer; ½ m s Hall. Born in N. C. 1804; settled in M. C. 1869. Dem. Protestant.

Bucker, Henry; blacksmith; 2½ m s Monrovia. Born in Ohio 1854; settled in M. C. 1867.

Bradley, Eli; farmer; 1½ m n w Wilber. Born in M. C. 1829. Dem. Protestant.

Bradley, Jesse; farmer and blacksmith; ½ m n w Wilber. Born in N. C. 1788; settled in M. C. 1827. Dem. Prot.

Brown, Thomas, farmer; ½ m s e Hall. Born in Ky. 1822; settled in M. C. 1838. Christian.

Brown, Wm.; saw milling; Herbemont. Born in M. C. 1853. Rep. Protestant.

Brown, P. N.; farmer; 1 m n Wilber. Born in M. C. 1855. Rep. Protestant.

Brown, A. J.; farmer; 3 m s w Hall. Born in M. C. 1842. Dem. Christian.

Costin, M. A.; farmer; 3 m s w Hall. Born in Ky. 1836; settled in M. C. 1842. Dem. Protestant.

Carer, Wm.; farmer; 1¼ m e Wilber. Born in N. C. 1818; settled in M. C. 1867. Dem. Protestant.

Dane, T. J.; Township Trustee; Hall. Born in Ind. 1839; settled in M. C. 1858. Rep. Christian.

Dawson, S. C.; farmer; 2½ m s e Hall. Born in Ky. 1830; settled in M. C. 1844. Rep. Methodist.

Dawson, N. M.; farmer; 1 m s w Herbemont. Born in Ky. 1835; settled in M. C. 1848. Dem. Methodist.

Dixon, T. H.; lumber dealer; ½ m n e Herbemont. Born in M. C. 1840. Rep. Methodist.

Elmore, W. H.; boot and shoemaker; Hall. Born in Ky. 1840; settled in M. C. 1866. Rep. Christian.

Felkins, Thomas; farmer; 2½ m n w Hall. Born in Ky. 1825; settled in M. C. 1844. Dem. Christian.

Felkins, J. R.; farmer; 2½ m w Hall. Born in M. C. 1850. Dem. Granger.

Furgison, Tobias; farmer; Wilber. Born in N. C. 1806; settled in M. C. 1842. Rep. Meth. Ant. Granger.

Fultz, Sol.; saw milling; Wilber. Born in M. C. 1841. Dem. Protestant.

Ferguson, S.; farmer; 4 m s Hall. Born in M. C. Protestant. Granger.

Ferguson, H.; farmer and carpenter; 2 m w Wilber. Born in N. C. 1824; settled in M. C. 1843. Dem. Granger.

FREET, GEO. W.; general purpose, and dealer in walnut knots and veneering; 2½ m s Monrovia. Born in Ohio 1846; settled in M. C. 1873. Rep. Protestant.

Fowler, Elvis; of the firm of Fowler & Bro., merchants; Herbemont. Born in N. C. 1831; settled in M. C. 1831. Rep. Methodist.

Fowler, L. V.; of the firm of Fowler & Bro., merchants; Herbemont. Born in M. C. 1837. Rep. Methodist.

Garrison, Franklin; carpenter; 1½ m n w Hall. Born in Ky. 1816; settled in M. C. 1843. Liberal. Christian.

Garrison, Robert; farmer and teacher; 1½ m n e Hall. Born in M. C. 1849. Lib. Rep. Christian.

GREGG TOWNSHIP. 235

Garrison, Bradford; farmer; 1½ m n e Hall. Born in Ky. 1823; settled in M. C. 1834. Rep. Christian.

Garrison, William; farmer; ½ m s e Wilber. Born in Ky. 1821; settled in M. C. 1840. Rep. Methodist.

Hunt, Asa; farmer; 3 m s e Monrovia. Born in Ohio 1831; settled in M. C. 1861. Rep. Friend.

Hunt, Thos.; farmer; 3 m s e Monrovia. Born in Va. 1806; settled in M. C. 1861. Rep. Friend.

Hinshaw, Jesse; farmer; 3 m s e Monrovia. Born in N. C. 1848; settled in M. C. 1863. Rep. Protestant.

HOCKETT, THOS. L.; farmer; 3½ m s Monrovia. Born in Ohio 1849; settled in M. C. 1860. Rep. Friend.

Hockett, Alvah; farmer; 3½ m s Monrovia. Born in Ohio 1828; settled in M. C. 1860. Rep. Friend.

HUNT, JABEZ H.; farmer; 3 m s Monrovia. Born in Ohio 1841; settled in M. C. 1861. Rep. Friend.

Henley, Samuel H.; farmer; 2 m s e Monrovia. Born in N. C. 1845; settled in M. C. 1851. Rep. Friend.

Hancock, Alonzo; farmer; 1 m n w Herbemont. Born in Ind. 1850; settled in M. C. 1874. Rep. Protestant.

Holman, C. C.; physician and farmer; 1 m e Hall. Born in Ky. 1820; settled in M. C. 1855. Protestant.

Howel, Miller; farmer and mechanic; ½ m s w Wilber. Born in N. C. 1808; settled in M. C. 1836. Rep. M. Baptist.

Harper, Samuel; farmer; 1½ m s Hall. Born in N. C. 1798; settled in M. C. 1833. Dem. Christian.

Hicks, Jonathan; farmer and trader; 2 m s w Herbemont. Born in Ind. 1837; settled in M. C. 1844. Dem. Meth.

Hardy, J. D.; carpenter; Hall. Born in Ky. 1834; settled in M. C. 1854. Rep. Christian.

HOWELL, MICHAEL; farmer; ½ m s w Wilber. Born in M. C. 1855. Protestant.

Johnson, J. B.; farmer and minister; Hall. Born in M. C. 1837. Rep. Christian.

Jordon, Wm. M.; farmer; 1¾ m s w Hall. Born in Va. 1822; settled in M. C. 1838. Rep. Christian.

Kenworthy, Isaac; farmer; 4 m s w Monrovia. Born in Ohio 1810; settled in M. C. 1852. Rep. Protestant.

Kirkham, James; farmer; ½ m n Wilber. Born in Ind. 1834; settled in M. C. 1842. Rep. Methodist.

Labertew, Smith; farmer; 1 m w Hall. Born in Ind. 1841; settled in M. C. 1867. Rep. Christian.

Lacy, Jesse; farmer; 3 m s w Hall. Born in M. C. 1846. Rep. Protestant.

Leaton, A. R.; retired farmer; Hall. Born in Ky. 1808; settled in M. C. 1832. Rep. Christian.

Ludlow, J. M.; farmer; 1 m n e Hall. Born in Ind.; settled in M. C. 1830. Rep. Christian.

Ludlow, G. W.; farmer; 1 m n e Hall. Born in M. C. 1839. Rep. Christian.

Lambert, A. L.; farmer and carpenter; 2 m n w Hall. Born in N. C. 1830; settled in M. C. 1836. Dem. Protestant.

McNichols, Rebecca; farmer; 2½ m s e Monrovia. Born in Ohio 1818; settled in M. C. 1863. Friend.

Miller, Harrison; farmer; 1 m e Wilber. Born in Ky. 1838; settled in M. C. 1871. Rep. Methodist.

Mason, John; farmer; 3½ m s Monrovia. Born in Ind. 1836; settled in M. C. 1873. Rep. Methodist.

Mason, Moses; farmer; 2 m s Monrovia. Born in M. C. 1849. Rep. Protestant.

Mosier, John T.; farmer; 2½ m s w Hall. Born in M. C. 1851. Dem. Granger.

Mannan, E. W.; farmer; 2½ m s w Hall. Born in M. C. 1839. Rep. Protestant.

McDANIEL, J. C.; farmer; ¼ m n w Hall. Born in M. C. 1840. Rep. Granger. Methodist.

Meredith, G. W.; farmer; 2 m s e Hall. Born in Ind. 1825; settled in M. C. 1834. Dem. Methodist.

Meredith, W. W.; farmer; 2 m w Hall. Born in M. C. 1851. Rep. Protestant.

Minter, J. W.; retail dealer in dry goods, groceries and general merchandise and P. M.; Wilber. Rep. Methodist.

Minter, Thos.; dealer in lumber and milling; Wilber. Born in Tenn. 1846; settled in M. C. 1853. Rep. Methodist.

McNawght, R. W.; harness maker and Justice of Peace; Wilber. Born in M. C. 1837. Rep. Protestant.

McClellan, David; saw milling; Wilber. Born in M. C. 1839. Rep. Protestant.

Minton, E.; retired farmer; 2¼ m w Wilber. Born in Va. 1800; settled in M. C. 1851. Rep. Methodist.

Marley, Jesse B.; farmer; 2 m s Monrovia. Born in N. C. 1834; settled in M. C. 1851. Rep. Protestant.

Marley, Wm.; farmer; 2 m s Monrovia. Born in N. C. 1804; settled in M. C. 1851. Dem. R. Baptist.

Mason, James; farmer; 2 m s Monrovia. Born in Va. 1809; settled in M. C. 1849. Rep. Methodist.

Meredith, Joshua; 3 m s Monrovia. Born in M. C. 1862. Protestant.

McClellan, Wm.; farmer and milling; Wilber. Born in Ky. 1831; settled in M. C. 1858. Rep. Protestant.

McDANIEL, MARY; farmer; ½ m n Wilber. Born in Ohio 1832; settled in M. C. 1842. Methodist.

Nicholas, Nathan; farmer; 1½ m s w Hall. Born in Ky. 1804; settled in M. C. 1830. Rep. Methodist.

Ogborn, Joseph; farmer; 3 m s w Monrovia. Born in Ohio 1833; settled in M. C. 1874. Dem. Protestant.

Orwick, John; farmer; 1½ m n Hall. Born in Va. 1825; settled in M. C. 1873. Rep. Protestant.

PAGE, JOSEPH T.; farmer; 2¼ m s Monrovia. Born in M. C. 1848. Dem. Protestant.

Pruitt, S. E. Rev.; merchant, teacher and minister; Hall. Born in Ky. 1834; settled in M. C. 1834. Rep. Christian.

Phillips, W. F.; merchant; Hall. Born in Ind. 1838. Rep. Christian.

Phillips, H. C.; farmer; Hall. Born in Ind. 1853. Protestant.

Portis, G. W.; farmer and broom maker; 2 m n Wilber. Born in N. C. 1849; settled in M. C. 1864. Rep. Protestant.

Pearce, J. C.; blacksmith and wagonmaker; Wilber. Born in M. C. 1850. Rep. Protestant.

Phillips, J. A.; farmer; 1 m n e Hall. Born in M. C. 1844. Rep. Protestant.

Powell, M. M.; farmer; 2 m s w Monrovia. Born in Ky. 1826; settled in M. C. 1874. Dem. Protestant.

Phillips, David; farmer and brickmason 3 m s Monrovia. Born in Ind. 1830; settled in M. C. 1863. Rep. Protestant.

Plain, M. A. H.; farmer; 3 m s w Monrovia. Born in Germany 1835; settled in M. C. 1872. Rep. Methodist.

Purvis, Gideon S.; farmer; Wilber. Born in Ind. 1852; settled in M. C. 1869. Dem. Methodist.

Quillen, Armsterd; farmer; ½ m w Wilber. Born in N. C. 1811; settled in M. C. 1862. Lib. Protest. Granger.

Riggan, Joel; farmer; ¾ m n e Wilber. Born in Ohio 1852; settled in M. C. 1874. Dem. Protestant.

Riggan, Jacob; farmer; ¾ m n e Wilber. Born in N. C. 1844; settled in M. C. 1874. Dem. Protestant.

Riggan, James; farmer; ¾ m n e Wilber. Born in N. C. 1821; settled in M. C. 1874. Dem. Protestant.

RIDGEWAY, JOS.; farmer, brick maker and brick mason; 2 m s Monrovia. Born in Ohio 1828; settled in M. C. 1847. Rep. Friend.

Rankin, R. P.; farmer and carpenter; 1¼ m w Hall. Born in Ky. 1825; settled in M. C. 1855. Rep. Christian.

Rankin, T. F.; carpenter; 1¼ m w Hall. Born in Ky. 1827; settled in M. C. 1856. Rep. Christian.

Ragan, W. H.; boot and shoe maker; Hall. Born in Ind. 1833. Dem. Spiritualist.

Reaves, S. A.; farmer; 1½ m s Wilber. Born in M. C. 1852. Rep. Protestant.

Stafford, Grant; farmer and huckster; 1¼ m e Wilber. Born in M. C. 1848. Rep. Protestant.

Smith Elijah; farmer; 1¼ m s w Hall. Born in M. C. 1829. Dem. Christian.

Staley, J. B.; farmer and stock trader; 1 m w Hall. Born in N. C. 1821; settled in M. C. 1832. Dem. Christian.

Shake, E. P.; farmer; 2 m s w Hall. Born in M. C. 1841. Dem. Granger. Christian.

Smith, Daniel; farmer; ½ m s w Hall. Born in Ky. 1796; settled in M. C. 1828. Dem. Christian.

Scrimsher, J. W.; druggist; Hall. Born in Ky. 1846; settled in M. C. 1853. Dem. Christian.

Scrimsher, T. J.; mechanic; Hall. Born in Ky. 1800; settled in M. C. 1853. Dem. Christian.

Shake, G. W.; farmer; 1½ m s w Hall. Born in Ky. 1818; settled in M. C. 1835. Dem. Christian.

Stout, W. C.; brick mason and attorney; Wilber. Born in N. C. 1828; settled in M. C. 1831. Rep. Ant.Grang. Meth.

Smith, W. H.; farmer and huckster; 1½ s Hall. Born in M. C. 1846. Dem. Christian.

Shake, J. H.; farmer; ½ m s Hall. Born in M. C. 1849. Dem. Granger. Christian.

Seaton, J. P.; farmer; 1 m n w Hall. Born in Ky. 1831; settled in M. C. 1832. Rep. Protestant.

Seaton, James P.; farmer; 2 m n w Hall. Born in M. C. 1841. Rep. Protestant.

Seaton, George W.; farmer; 2¼ m n w Hall. Born in M. C. 1833. Rep. Protestant.

Seaton, Grafton W.; physician; Hall. Born in M. C. 1846. Rep. Christian.

Summers, Geo. T.; farmer; ½ m w Herbemont. Born in Ky. 1844; settled in M. C. 1852. Dem. Protestant.

Shake, William A.; farmer; 2½ m s w Hall. Born in M. C. 1841. Christian.

Thatcher, Wm.; huckster; 2¾ m s w Monrovia. Born in Ky. 1818; settled in M. C. 1868. Dem. Newlight.

WARD, ISAAC; cooper and miller; 3 m s e Monrovia. Born in N. C. 1814; settled in M. C. 1823. Rep. Protestant.

Watson, John R.; farmer; ½ m s e Wilber. Born in England 1811; settled in M. C. 1853. Methodist.

Wilhite, Wm.; ½ m n w Hall. Born in Old Va. 1822; settled in M. C. 1839. Rep. Methodist.

Wilhite, Aaron B.; farmer and trader; 1¼ m n w Hall. Born in Ky. 1820; settled in M. C. 1834. Rep. Christian.

WOODEN, JEFFERSON; farmer; ¼ m n w Hall. Born in Ky. 1820; settled in M. C. 1865. Rep. M. Baptist.

Wooden, J. R.; farmer; ¼ m n w Hall. Born in Ind. 1855; settled in M. C. 1865.

Wilson, Jeremiah; farmer; 2½ m s w Hall. Born in Ind. 1836; settled in M. C. 1863. Rep. Protestant.

Wilhite, Michael; farmer; 2½ m s w Hall. Born in Ky. 1826; settled in M. C. 1834. Rep. Christian.

Wilhite, T. J.; mechanic; Hall. Born in M. C. 1840. Rep. Christian.

Wilhite, G. W.; farmer; 1½ m s w Wilber. Born in M. C. 1834. Rep. Methodist.

Wilhite, J. R. S.; farmer; 3 m s w Hall. Born in M. C. 1851. Rep. Methodist.

Wilhite, A. L.; farmer and teacher; 1 m n Hall. Born in M. C. 1848. Lib. Rep. Protestant.

Wilhite, A. P.; farmer; 1 m n Hall. Born in Ky. 1824; settled in M. C. 1836. Rep. Methodist.

WILLIAMS, JOHN; farmer; 2½ m n e Hall. Born in Ky. 1801; settled in M. C. 1830.

Wilson, John A.; farmer; 2½ m e Hall. Born in M. C. 1843. Rep. Christian.

Wilson, A. H.; farmer; 2½ m e Hall. Born in M. C. 1849. Rep. Christian.

WILHITE, JACOB; farmer; ½ m w Herbemont. Born in M. C. 1849. Rep. Protestant.

Wilhite, Elijah; farmer; 2½ m s w Hall. Born in Ky. 1825; settled in M. C. 1836. Rep. Methodist.

Wilhite, Joshua; farmer; 2½ m s w Hall. Born in Ky. 1825; settled in M. C. 1836. Rep. Methodist.

Wilhite, J. W.; farmer and teamster; 1 m w Wilber. Born in M. C. 1836. Lib. Methodist.

Wilhite, E. L.; farmer; 3 m s w Hall. Born in Ky. 1825; settled in M. C. 1835. Rep. Christian.

Wilhite, John R.; farmer; 3 m s w Hall. Born in M. C. 1851. Rep. Methodist.

Yager, H. F.; farmer; 4 m s w Hall. Born in Ky. ——; settled in M. C. ——. Methodist.

Yager, Jas. D.; farmer; 3 m s w Hall. Born in Ky. 1842; settled in M. C. 1853. Dem. Methodist.

Yager, W. W.; farmer; 4½ m s w Hall. Born in Ky. 1814; settled in M. C. 1846. Dem. Granger. Methodist.

Yager, John T.; farmer and teacher; 4 m s Hall. Born in Ky. 1844: settled in M. C. 1853. Dem. Methodist.

GREEN TOWNSHIP.

GREEN TOWNSHIP is located on the east side of the county and is bounded on the north by White river and Harrison township, on the east by Johnson county, on the south by Jackson township, and on the west by Washington, and is watered by White river, Stotts' creek, Clear creek, and numerous spring branches. This is one of the best watered townships in the county, thereby making it a desirable place for the stock raiser. The soil is of very good quality, while the surface is generally rolling, and, in many places, broken. The timber of this township is rather better than an average of the county, and the gravel beds along the streams are almost inexhaustible. The citizens are industrious and enterprising, while her church and school privileges will compare very favorably with other parts of the county. Among the first settlers were John Williams, Samuel Carrell, Jesse Warton, Joseph Johnson and the families of Badgleys and Ennises.

CHURCH, LODGE AND SCHOOL STATISTICS.

M. E. Church, Union Chapel; 2 miles east Cope; Rev. H. Boyer, pastor; membership, 80; Sunday school superintendent W. T. Miller; average attendance of Sunday school, 35; value of Church property, $2,500.

M. E. Church, Mt. Olivet; 7½ miles northeast Martinsville; Gideon Heavenridge, Pastor; membership, 16; Sunday school superintendent, William Cain; average attendance of Sunday school, 30; value of Church property, $1,000.

Prot. M. E. Church, Bethel; Absalom Parris, Pastor; membership, 45; Sunday school superintendent, Geo. Baker; average attendance of Sunday school, 50.

Green township Grange, No. 999, 8 miles east Martinsville; John E. Greer, Master. Address, Martinsville.

Number of school houses in the township, 10; value of the same, $3,000; vote of township, 285.

DIRECTORY OF GREEN TOWNSHIP.

Abraham, Wm.; farmer; 4 m e Cope. Born in England 1815; settled in M. C. 1845. Dem. Christian.

Abraham, J. A.; farmer; 4 m n e Cope. Born in M. C. 1850. Dem. Christian.

Badgley, B. F.; farmer; 1½ m n w Cope. Born in Ind. 1819; settled in M. C. 1827. Dem. Christian.

Badgley, G. W.; farmer; 1½ m n w Cope. Born in M. C. 1852. Dem. Protestant.

Balay, H. W.; farmer; 1 m s Cope. Born in M. C. 1832. Dem. Methodist.

Bates, Alfred; farmer; 4 m s w Waverly. Born in Tenn. 1818; settled in M. C. 1822. Dem. Protestant.

BRADFORD, MARTHA E.; farmer; 6 m n e Martinsville. Born in Ohio 1825; settled in M. C. 1858. Methodist.

Brunnemer, Jeremiah; carpenter; 4 m s w Waverly. Born in Va. 1816; settled in M. C. 1866. Dem. Protestant.

Brickert, Samuel; farmer; 2½ m n e Cope. Born in Pa. 1834; settled in M. C. 1850. Protestant.

Baker, John M.; farmer and blacksmith; 3½ m e Cope. Born in Ind. 1836; settled in M. C. 1869. Methodist.

BRADLEY, ELIJAH; farmer and shingle maker; 4 m e Cope. Born in Ky. 1829; settled in M. C. 1871. Dem. Protest.

Bailey, B. C.; farmer; 4 m s e Waverly. Born in Ky. ——. Protestant.

Bailey, M. H.; farmer; 5 m s Waverly. Born in M. C. 1847. Dem. Protestant.

Bailey, George; farmer; 5 m s Waverly. Born in Tenn. 1800; settled in M. C. 1841. Dem. Methodist.

BROON, JOSEPH W.; farmer; 5 m s Waverly. Born in Va. 1824; settled in M. C. 1844. Dem. Protestant.

Brunnemer, W. M.; farmer and carpenter; 4½ m s Waverly. Born in Va. 1826; settled in M. C. 1849. Dem. Protest.

Brunnemer, J. L.; farmer; 4¼ m s Waverly. Born in Ind. 1850; settled in M. C. 1858. Dem. Protestant.

Carroll, G. W.; farmer; 1 m n w Cope. Born in M. C. 1852. Dem. Christian.

Caldwell, L. L.; farmer; 1½ m n e Cope. Born in M. C. 1838. Dem. Christian.

Carrell, Samuel, farmer; 2 m n e Cope. Born in Ky. 1813; settled in M. C. 1822. Dem. Methodist.

Cain, Wm.; farmer and blacksmith 6 m s w Waverly. Born in Ky. 1820; settled in M. C. 1843. Dem. Methodist.

Caldwell; Alexander; 4 m s w Waverly. Born in Tenn. 1826; settled in M. C. 1833. Dem. Christian.

Coonfield, Isaac; farmer and blacksmith; 5 m s e Waverly. Born in Ind. 1827; settled in M. C. 1844. Dem. P. Meth.

Coonfield, Wm.; farmer; 5 m s Waverly. Born in Ind. 1836; settled in M. C. 1855. Dem. Protestant.

Caldwell, John W.; farmer; 8 m n e Martinsville. Born in M. C. 1853. Dem. Christian.

Doty, J. M.; farmer; 1 m n w Cope. Born in Ind. 1852; settled in M. C. 1873. Dem. Christian.

DENT, JOHN C.; farmer; 4½ m s w Waverly. Born in Ind. 1838; settled in M. C. 1852. Dem. M. Baptist.

Duke, John; farmer; 5 m s w Waverly. Born in Va. 1799; settled in M. C. 1852. Dem. Protestant.

Drake, Amos; farmer; 3 m n e Cope. Born in Ind. 1828; settled in M. C. 1848. Dem. Protestant.

Doty, W. A.; farmer and carpenter; 3¼ m e Cope. Born in Ind. 1844; settled in M. C. 1864. Christian.

Duke, Wm.; farmer; 4 m s Waverly. Born in Va. 1802; settled in M. C. 1832. Dem. Protestant.

Dresslar, Arch; farmer; 3 m s Waverly. Born in Va. 1829; settled in M. C. 1853. Rep. Methodist.

Douglass, Rebecca; farmer; claims to be the oldest settler in the county. Settled in M. C. 1817.

GREEN TOWNSHIP. 249

Egbert, Joseph; farmer; 2 m n w Cope. Born in Ohio' 1835; settled in M. C. 1838. Dem. Christian.

Egeert, J. W.; farmer; 7 m e Martinsville. Born in M. C. 1840. Dem. Christian.

ENNIS, J. M.; farmer; ¾ m e Cope. Born in M. C. 1829. Dem. Protestant.

Elkins, James; farmer; 2 m n e Cope. Born in M. C. 1846. Dem. Methodist.

Elkins, J. H.; farmer; 3 m e Cope. Born in M. C. 1846. Dem. Methodist.

ELKINS, JOSEPH; farmer; 3 m e Cope. Born in Ky. 1817; settled in M. C. 1830. Dem. Protestant.

Elkins, Henry; farmer; 2½ m e Cope. Born in Ky. 1819; settled in M. C. 1830. Dem. Methodist.

ENNIS, WM. K. Dr.; proprietor of the Instant Pain Eradicator; 2½ m e Cope. Born in M. C. 1841. Dem. Prot.

Ennis, A.; farmer; 3 m e Cope. Born in Ky. 1819; settled in M. C. 1829. Dem. Methodist.

ENNIS, HUGH; farmer; 3 m e Cope. Born in M. C. 1841. Dem. Methodist.

Ennis, Emery; farmer; 3 m e Cope. Born in M. C. 1829. Dem. Methodist.

ENNIS, W. N.; farmer; 3½ m e Cope. Born in M. C. 1841; Dem. Methodist.

Franklin, Sarah; farmer; 3½ m n e Cope. Born in Ky. 1811; settled in M. C. 1854. Christian.

Flake, G. W.; farmer; 3 m n e Cope. Born in Ind. 1838; settled in M. C. 1854. Dem. Christian.

Gardner, D. P.; house and sign painter; Cope. Born in Ohio 1844; settled in M. C. 1872. Rep. Methodist.

Guthridge, Lem.; farmer, merchant and P. M.; Cope. Born in Ohio 1826; settled in M. C. 1847. Dem. Protestant.

Greer, J. M.; farmer; 8 m n e Martinsville. Born in Ky. 1826; settled in M. C. 1836. Dem. Protestant.

Greer, John M.; farmer; 8 m n e Martinsville. Born in M. C. 1849. Dem. Protestant.

Greer, B. F.; farmer; 8 m n e Martinsville. Born in M. C. 1851. Dem. Protestant.

Greer, L. M.; farmer; 2 m n Cope. Born in Ky. 1831; settled in M. C. 1838. Rep. Protestant.

Greer, A. C.; farmer; 2½ m n Cope. Born in M. C. 1841. Granger. Protestant.

Garrett, T. O. W.; prop'r Atlanta flour mill; 2½ m e Cope. Born in Ky. 1811; settled in M. C. 1870. Rep. Methodist.

Glasgo, Presley; farmer; 6 m s Waverly. Born in Pa. 1813; settled in M. C. 1858. Dem. Protestant.

Hoglan, J. H.; farmer; 1 m n Cope. Born in M. C. 1847. Dem. Christian.

Harper, John; farmer; 4½ m s w Waverly. Born in Ind. 1833; settled in M. C. 1837. Dem. Protestant.

Hawkins, Sylvester; farmer; 3 m e Cope. Born in Ohio 1822; settled in M. C. 1846. Dem. Methodist.

Hofmann, Jacob; farmer; 3 m s Waverly. Born in Germany 1829; settled in M. C. 1858. Dem. Protestant.

INGOLD, HIRAM; farmer; 5 m s w Waverly. Born in N. C. 1835; settled in M. C. 1854. Rep. Methodist.

Johnson, Joseph; farmer; Cope. Born in Ohio 1810; settled in M. C. 1829. Dem. Protestant.

Jones, Robert; farmer; 9 m e Martinsville. Born in M. C. 1850. Dem. Protestant.

KELLY, JOSEPH; farmer; 8 m n e Martinsville. Born in Pa. 1850; settled in M. C. 1863. Rep. R. Catholic.

Kidwell, J. N.; farmer; 3½ m s e Waverly. Born in Ky. 1844; settled in M. C. 1865. Rep. Methodist.

Leckman, James; farmer; 4 m s Waverly. Born in Ind. 1837; settled in M. C. 1864. Dem. Protestant.

Musgrave, J. E.; farmer; 1¼ m n e Cope. Born in M. C. 1852. Dem. Christian.

Musgrave, E. F.; farmer; 1 m n Cope. Born in Ind. 1831; settled in M. C. 1841. Dem. Christian.

Maples, B. F.; farmer; 2½ m n w Cope. Born in Ohio 1832 settled in M. C. 1865. Dem. Protestant.

OHORROW, HENRY; farmer; 2½ m n e Cope. Born in Ind. 1837; settled in M. C. 1854. Rep. Protestant.

Perry, Richard; farmer; 3 m n w Cope. Born in M. C. 1847. Dem. Methodist.

POOR, JOHN T.; farmer; 9 m n e Martinsville. Born in N. C. 1831; settled in M. C. 1851. Granger. Protestant.

Perry, Richard; farmer; 6 m n e Martinsville. Born in M. C. 1847. Dem. Methodist.

Paxson, William; farmer; 4¾ m s w Waverly. Born in Va. 1812; settled in M. C. 1856. Dem. Protestant.

Pierce, Jacob; farmer; 3½ m e Cope. Born in M. C. 1832. Protestant.

Perry, Peter C.; farmer; 4 m s Waverly. Born in M. C. 1844. Dem. Protestant.

Persinger, Barbary; 4 m s e Waverly; daughter of Henry and Catharine Trusler. Born in Va. 1792; settled in M. C. 1844. Methodist.

SKAGGS, JOHN S.; farmer and stock raiser; Cope. Born in M. C. 1831. Dem. Protestant.

SHIRLEY, J. T.; physician and surgeon; Cope. Born in Ky. 1843; settled in M. C. 1869. Dem. M. Baptist.

Slogis, Geo.; blacksmith; Cope. Born in Baden, Germany, 1852; settled in M. C. 1870. Lutheran.

Scaggs, ———; farmer and stock raiser; ½ m n Cope. Born in Ind. 1828; settled in M. C. 1829. Dem. Protestant.

St. John, Aaron; farmer; 7 m e Martinsville. Born in Ohio 1821; settled in M. C. 1851. Rep. Protestant.

Stephenson, W. H.; farmer; 6 m e Martinsville. Born in Ky. 1836; settled in M. C. 1846. Dem. Christian.

Skaggs, Edny, Mrs.; farmer; 1 m s e Cope. Born in Ky. 1800. Dem. P. Methodist.

SKAGGS, MADISON; farmer; 1 m s Cope. Born in M. C. 1844. Dem. P. Methodist.

St. John, J. W.; farmer; 6½ m n e Martinsville. Born in Ohio 1846; settled in M. C. 1852. Granger. Protestant.

Skaggs, J. W.; farmer; 2 m e Cope. Born in M. C. 1836. Dem. Protestant.

SHELTMIRE, CHARLES; farmer; 4 m e Cope. Born in Germany 1836; settled in M. C. 1847. Dem. Protest.

Sheltmire, Henry; farmer; 4 m n e Cope. Born in Germany 1834; settled in M. C. 1848. Dem. Protestant.

Smith, Berryman; farmer; 5 m s e Waverly. Born in Ky. 1821; settled in M. C. 1874. Dem. M. Baptist.

Taylor, E. S.; farmer; 7 m n e Martinsville. Born in Ky. 1807; settled in M. C. 1850. Granger. R. Baptist.

THOMPSON, FRANCIS A.; farmer; 8 m n e Martinsville. Born in Va. 1847; settled in M. C. 1870. Rep. Prot.

Trent, Margaret; farmer; 8 m n e Martinsville. Born in Ky. 1803; settled in M. C. 1831. Christian.

Thompson, J. J.; farmer; 2 m n Cope. Born in Ind. 1847; settled in M. C. 1874. Dem. Christian.

Thompson, J. W.; farmer; 3 m e Cope. Born in Ky. 1819; settled in M. C. 1834. Methodist.

Tresslar, H. A.; farmer; 6 m s w Bluff Creek. Born in Ind. 1849; settled in M. C. 1874. Rep. Christian.

Underwood, C. W.; farmer; 1¼ m e Cope. Born in Ind. 1837; settled in M. C. 1863. Indpt. Methodist.

Wemer, Fred; blacksmith; Cope. Born in Wertemberg, Germany, 1844; settled in M. C. 1853. Rep. Lutheran.

WILLIAMS, JOHN; farmer; 2½ m n w Cope. Born in Ind. 1819; settled in M. C. 1820. Rep. Protestant.

WAGAMAN, J. N.; carpenter and sawmilling; Cope. Born in Ind. 1845; settled in M. C. 1860. Dem. Methodist.

Williams, W. R.; farmer; 8 m e Martinsville. Born in M. C. 1852. Dem. Protestant.

WILLIAMS, JONATHAN; farmer; 7 m e Martinsville. Born in M. C. 1847. Rep. Protestant.

Wagaman, Charles; carpenter; Cope. Born in Ind. 1853; settled in M. C. 1860. Dem. Protestant.

Wagman, J. L.; engineer; 1½ m n e Cope. Born in Ind. 1842; settled in M. C. 1860. Dem. Lutheran.

Wharton, J. H.; farmer; 4 m s w Waverly. Born in M. C. 1847. Rep. Protestant.

Williams, David; farmer; 6 m e Martinsville. Born in M. C. 1827. Dem. Protestant.

WHITE, WESLEY; physician; 7 m n e Martinsville. Born in N. C. 1805; settled in M. C. 1842. Dem. Methodist.

WILLIAMS, ELIZA; farmer; 2½ m n Cope. Born in E. Tenn. 1820; settled in M. C. 1833. Prot.

WARTON, JESSE; farmer; 4 m s w Waverly. Born in Ky. 1811; settled in M. C. 1826. Rep. Protestant.

Wagaman, J. M.; farmer; 3½ m n e Cope. Born in Ind. 1847; settled in M. C. 1873. Dem. Protestant.

Wemer, Geo.; farmer; 3½ m e Cope. Born in Wodenberry, Germany, 1837.

HARRISON TOWNSHIP.

HARRISON TOWNSHIP is located on the east side of the county, and only contains about 10 square miles. It is bounded on the north and west by White River, on the east by Johnson county, and on the south by Green township. The surface of this township is generally tillable, but there are some broken lands which are good pasture lands. A greater part of this township is in the bottoms of White River, and contains some of the best lands in the county.

Waverly, a little village just on the north side of the township, on the banks of White River, is a small town of some 80 inhabitants. It has 1 dry goods store and 2 doctor shops. The citizens are a generous, intelligent and enterprising people. The church and school privileges are good. It is the smallest township in the county.

CHURCH, LODGE AND SCHOOL STATISTICS.

M. E. Church, Shiloh, 2 miles south of Waverly; pastor, Rev. Gideon Heavenridge; Sabbath school superintendent, H. B. Taylor; average attendance of Sabbath school, 50; value of church property, $800.

M. E. Church, Waverly; Rev. Gideon Heavenridge, pastor; membership, 35; Sabbath school superintendent, D. Evans; average attendance of Sabbath school, 30; value of church property, $1200.

Waverly Lodge, No. 318, I. O. O. F.; membership, 62; value of Lodge property, $300; instituted Feb. 29, 1869.

Waverly Grange, No. 608; membership, 45; Master, John A. Shafflebarger; Secretary, Thos. C. W. Perry.

DIRECTORY OF HARRISON TOWNSHIP.

ALDRICH, REUBEN S.; farmer; 1½ m s w Waverly. Born in Ind. 1824; settled in M. C. 1825. Rep. Protestant.

ADAMS, G. W.; clerk in store; Waverly. Born in Tenn. 1843; settled in M. C. 1856. Dem. M. Baptist.

Adams, T. J.; wagonmaker; Waverly. Born in N. C. 1807; settled in M. C. 1856. Dem. M. Baptist.

ADAMS, ANDREW J.; farmer; ½ m s Waverly. Born in E. Tenn. 1833; settled in M. C. 1854. Dem. M. Baptist.

Adams, J. M.; teamster; Waverly. Born in E. Tenn. 1836; settled in M. C. 1856. Dem. M. Baptist.

Aldrich, Barlow; farmer; 1 m s w Waverly. Born in Ind. 1841. Rep. Protestant.

Arms, Moses; farmer; ½ m s e Waverly. Born in N. C. 1816; settled in M. C. 1863. Dem. Protestant.

Armstrong, Henry; farmer; 2 m s e Waverly. Born in Va. 1806; settled in M. C. 1847. Dem. Protestant.

CRAIG, JOHN T.; blacksmith, Waverly. Born in Va. 1814; settled in M. C. 1852. Rep. Protestant.

COSAND, GABRIEL J.; shoe and boot maker, Waverly. Born in N. C. 1822; settled in M. C. 1862. Dem. M. Baptist.

CARRELL, WM.; farmer; 3 m s w Waverly. Born in Ind. 1837. Dem. Protestant.

Dresslar, G. A.; farmer; 2½ m s w Waverly. Born in Ind. 1841; settled in M. C. 1866. Rep. Methodist.

Dresslar, J. H.; farmer; 2¼ m s w Waverly. Born in Va. 1829; settled in M. C. 1859. Rep. Methodist.

Dresslar, J. B.; farmer; 1¼ m s Waverly. Born in Ind. 1843; settled in M. C. 1864. Rep. Methodist.

ETTER, WM. H.; farmer; 3 m s w Waverly. Born in Ind. 1849. Dem. Protestant.

FIELDS, F. M.; merchant; Waverly. Born in Ind. 1836. Dem. Protestant.

FITZPATRICK, H. L.; shoe and boot maker; Waverly. Born in Ind. 1839; settled in M. C. 1866. Dem. Protestant.

Graves, John; merchant; Waverly. Born in Ind. 1820; settled in M. C. 1828. Rep. Methodist.

HARELL, WILLIAM; farmer; Waverly. Born in Ind. 1816; settled in M. C. 1833. Dem. Protestant.

HARELL, ELIAS; farmer; ½ m s w Waverly. Born in Ind. 1827; settled in M. C. 1835. Dem. Protestant.

Harell, James; farmer; ½ m s w Waverly. Born in Ind. 1853. Dem. Methodist.

Heavenridge, Rev. Gideon; Waverly. Born in Ind. 1836; settled in M. C. 1854. Rep. Methodist.

KEPHART, MESLESSA, farmer; 3 m s w Waverly. Born
in Ind. 1827; settled in M. C. 1857. Methodist.

Mitchel, T. H.; cabinet maker; 2 m s w Waverly. Born in
E. Tenn. 1799; settled in M. C. 1830. Rep. Methodist.

Musser, John; farmer; 3 m s w Waverly. Born in Ind. 1849.
Rep. Protestant.

Musser, Samuel; farmer; 3 m s w Waverly. Born in Va. 1808;
settled in M. C. 1844. Rep. M. Baptist.

MUSSER, JOSEPH H.; farmer; 3 m s w Waverly. Born in
Va. 1844; settled in M. C. 1864. Dem. Protestant.

MURRAY, THOMAS; farmer; 3 m s w Waverly. Born in
N. C. 1827; settled in M. C. 1849. Rep. Protestant.

Morningstar, Peter; farmer; 2 m s w Waverly. Born in Ohio
1826; settled in M. C. 1861. Rep. Protestant.

MORGAN, WM. D.; farmer; 2 m s Waverly. Born in Ind.
1849. Dem. Protestant.

PAUL, PHILIP; farmer; ¾ m s Waverly. Born in Va.
1817; settled in M. C. 1822. Dem. Universalist.

Persinger, Samuel; farmer; 3½ s e Waverly. Born in Ind.
1842; settled in M. C. 1848. Rep. Methodist.

PAUL, FRANCIS; farmer; 2 m s w Waverly. Born in Ind.
1859. Rep. Protestant.

Paul, George; farmer and trader; 2 m s Waverly. Born in Va. 1814; settled in M. C. 1822. Rep. Protestant.

Paul, Jacob; farmer; 2½ m s Waverly. Born in Ind. 1854. Rep. Protestant.

Paul, John; farmer; 2 m s Waverly. Born in Ind. 1844. Rep. Methodist.

Perry, S. C. M.; teacher; Waverly. Born in Ohio 1847; settled in M. C. 1849. Dem. Protestant.

ROBISON, C. W.; carpenter; Waverly. Born in Ky. 1836; settled in M. C. 1860. Dem. Protestant.

Smith, B. F.; farmer; 2 m s w Waverly. Born in Ind. 1827. settled in M. C. 1864. Dem. Methodist.

Sedam, Uriah S.; blacksmith; Waverly. Born in Ind. 1848; settled in M. C. 1869. Rep. Methodist.

Stotts, J. A.; farmer; 2 m s Waverly. Born in Ill. 1834; settled in M. C. 1855. Dem. Protestant.

SWEARENGIN, A. W.; merchant and trader; Waverly. Born in Ind. 1845. Rep. Christian.

SMITH, ROBERT; farmer and trader; ½ m s Waverly. Born in Ohio 1817; settled in M. C. 1827. Rep.

TRUSTY, JOHNATHAN; farmer; Waverly. Born in 1820; settled in M. C. 1838. Dem. Protestant.

Trusty, Frank; farmer; 3 m s Waverly. Born in Ky. 1835; settled in M. C. 1845. Dem. Protestant.

Thompson, William; farmer; Waverly. Born in Ind. 1831. Dem. Protestant.

Tackitt, Morgan; farmer and teamster; Waverly. Born in Va. 1831; settled in M. C. 1844. Rep. Protestant.

Taylor, A. K.; farmer; 3 m s e Waverly. Born in Va. 1822; settled in M. C. 1870. Rep. Methodist.

TACKETT, MANZA J.; farmer; 3 m s w Waverly. Born in Va. 1817; settled in M. C. 1840. Methodist.

UNDERWOOD, Z. T.; farmer; 2 m s e Waverly. Born in Ind. 1849; settled in M. C. 1871. Dem. Methodist.

Vincent, Jeremiah; physician and surgeon; Waverly. Born in Ind. 1831; settled in M. C. 1837. Rep. Protest.

Wheaton, C. C.; farmer; Waverly. Born in Ind. 1829; set- settled in M. C. 1869. Dem. Christian.

Wiley, Aaron T.; farmer; 2 m s Waverly. Born in Ky. 1823 settled in M. C. 1844. Rep. Methodist.

Wright, Mary S.; milliner and dressmaker; Waverly. Born in Ind. 1842. Methodist.

Wiley, V. T.; school teacher; 2 m s w Waverly. Born in Ind. 1848. Rep. Methodist.

Wiley, R. T.; school teacher; 2 m s w Waverly. Born in Ind. 1851. Rep. Methodist.

WOOD, JAMES; farmer; ¾ m s Waverly. Born in Ohio 1832; settled in M. C. 1864. Dem. Protestant.

Wright, Henry; proprietor boarding house; Waverly. Born in Ind. 1850. Rep. Protestant.

JACKSON TOWNSHIP.

JACKSON TOWNSHIP is located in the southeast corner of the county, and is bounded as follows: On the north by Green township, on the east by Johnson county, on the south by Brown county, and on the west by Washington township, and contains thirty-six square miles. This is the only square township in the county. The surface of the township is generally broken; the soil is of a red cast on the breaks, but is rather sandy and produces well. The creek bottoms are rich and black. The voting precinct of this township is Morgantown. This place is quite an enterprising town, located on the Cincinnati and Martinsville Railroad. This township is watered by Big Indian Creek. This creek takes its rise in Johnson county, and runs through the south part of this township from east to west. The church and school privileges are good, and the citizens enterprising.

CHURCH, LODGE AND SCHOOL STATISTICS.

Missionary Baptist Church; Morgantown; elder, John W. Ragsdale; membership, 63; Sabbath school superintendent, Miss Charity Fesler; average attendance of Sabbath school, 75; value of property, $2500.

Pleasant Grove separate Baptist Church; membership, 13; value of property, $200; church five miles northwest of Morgantown.

Protestant Methodist Church; Mahalasville; pastor, A. Parris; Membership, 28; Sabbath school superintendent, Wm. Hadley;

average attendance of Sabbath school, 50; value of property, $400.

Christian Church, Morgantown; Gilbert L. Harney, minister in charge; membership, 54; Sabbath school superintendent, Wm. Robertson; average attendance of Sabbath school, 74; value of property, $3600.

M. E. Church, Morgantown; membership, 122; superintendent Sabbath school, J. W. King; average attendance of Sabbath school, 75; Miles Woods, pastor; value of property, $2500.

M. E. Church, Hamilton Chapel, 2 miles west of Morgantown; Miles Woods, pastor; membership, 70; Sabbath school superintendent, T. S. Benson; average attendance of Sabbath school, 30; value of church property, $300.

M. E. Church, Nast Chapel, 4 miles northwest of Morgantown; Miles Woods, pastor; membership, 22; superintendent of Sabbath school, John Afflerbach; average attendance of Sabbath school, 20; value of church property, $300.

M. E. Church, Mt. Nebo, 5½ miles west of Morgantown; Miles Woods, pastor; membership, 50; Sabbath school superintendent, A. Able; average attendance of Sabbath school, 30; value of church property, $1500.

M. E. Church, Mahalasville; Miles Woods, pastor; membership, 60; Sabbath school superintendent, E. Fergeson; average attendance of Sabbath school, 60; value of church property, $800.

Morgantown Lodge, No. 358, F. and A. M.; membership, 54; value of Lodge property and fixtures, $1000.

Morgantown Lodge, No. 196, I. O. O. F.; membership, 54; value of Lodge property and equipments, $500; organized July 8, 1872.

Morgan Grange, No. 799; membership, 31; Secretary, Peter Fesler; organized December, 1873.

Mahalasville Grange; membership, 45; Secretary, David Gibbs; organized February 10, 1874.

No. of school houses, 10; value of same, $9,000; school house at Morgantown, graded school, $9,000; township trustee, H. R. Butler.

DIRECTORY OF JACKSON TOWNSHIP.

Adams, W. R.; farmer; Morgantown. Born in Ind. 1844. Dem. Protestant.

Alexander, G. H.; plasterer; Morgantown. Born in Ohio 1832; settled in M. C. 1873. Indpt. Protestant.

Adams, John; farmer; ½ m w Morgantown. Born in M. C. 1834. Dem. Protestant.

Adams, Henry; farmer; 1 m n Morgantown. Born in Ky. 1814; settled in M. C. 1829. Dem. Protestant.

Adams, Samuel; farmer; 2 m n Morgantown. Born in M. C. 1848 Dem. Protestant.

ADAMS, JACOB; farmer; 3 m n Morgantown. Born in M. C. 1829. Dem. Protestant.

Adams, G. W.; farmer; 2½ m n Morgantown. Born in M. C. 1839. Dem. Protestant.

AFFLERBACH, JOHN; farmer; 3¾ m n w Morgantown. Born in Prussia 1814; settled in M. C. 1852. Rep. Meth.

Adams, Wm.; farmer; 2 m n Morgantown. Born in M. C. 1844. Dem. Protestant.

Adams, Jacob; farmer and stock trader; ½ m n Morgantown. Born in Ky. 1813; settled in M. C. 1834. Dem. Prot.

Adams, Hugh; farmer; 4 m n w Morgantown. Born in Ky. 1808; settled in M. C. 1832. Dem. Protestant.

Abel, Alfred; farmer; 4 m n w Morgantown. Born in Tenn. 1812; settled in M. C. 1844. Rep. Methodist.

ABEL, W. G.; engineer; 3 m n Mahalasville. Born in Ind. 1837; settled in M. C. 1844. Rep. Methodist.

Adams, C. H.; farmer; 3½ m n w Morgantown. Born in M. C. 1840. Dem. S. Baptist.

Adams, David; farmer; 3½ m w Morgantown. Born in Ky. 1830; settled in M. C. 1832. Dem. Methodist.

Adams, W., Colonel; retired merchant; Mahalasville. Born in Tenn. 1839; settled in M. C. 1866. Rep. Methodist.

Alexander, G. H.; plasterer; Morgantown. Born in Ohio 1837; settled in M. C. 1873. Dem. Protestant.

BUCKNER, T. J.; of firm of Buckner & Long; Morgantown. Born in Ind. 1850; settled in M. C. 1853. Rep. Protest.

BUTLER, H. R.; general merchandise; Morgantown. Born in Ohio 1840; settled in M. C. 1866. Radical. Protest.

Butler, D. F.; carpenter; Morgantown. Born in Ohio. 1849; settled in M. C. 1871. Dem. Protestant.

Barnes, J. A.; farmer; ½ m s Morgantown. Born in Ohio 1842; settled in M. C. 1873. Dem. Protestant.

Bahding, Daniel; farmer; 2½ m s e Cope. Born in Prussia 1808; settled in M. C. 1847. Dem. Lutheran.

Brown, Commodore; farmer; 4½ m n w Morgantown. Born in Tenn. 1850; settled in M. C. 18—. Dem. Protestant.

Burns, A. J.; farmer; 4½ m e Martinsville. Born in N. C. 1818; settled in M. C. 18—. Dem. Protestant.

Baxter, J. S.; farmer; 3 m n e Mahalasville. Born in Ohio 1827; settled in M. C. 1849. Rep. Methodist.

Briggs, E. H.; farmer; 4 m n w Morgantown. Born in Mass. 1824; settled in M. C. 1864. Rep. Protestant.

Beechem, John; farmer; 1½ m n e Mahalasville.

Beckenbaugh, H. J.; wagon maker; Mahalasville.

Coleman, J. S.; dealer in hardware and tinware; Morgantown. Born in Conn. 1848; settled in M. C. 1866. Rep. Prot.

Coleman, J. O.; insurance agent; Morgantown. Born in Conn. 1820; settled in M. C. 1866. Rep. Protestant.

Campbell, Mrs. S. M.; dress maker; Morgantown. Born in Ind. 1835; settled in M. C. 1870. Rep. Methodist.

Canatsey, A. J.; livery and sale stable; Morgantown. Born in Ind. 1846. Rep. Protestant.

COFFMAN, J. R.; farmer and stock trader; ¼ m e Morgantown. Born in Ind. 1837. Rep. Protestant.

Coleman, W. S.; flouring mill; Morgantown. Born in Ind. 1847; settled in M. C. 1858. Rep. Protestant.

Christy, John; farmer; Morgantown. Born in N. Y. 1827; settled in M. C. 1860. Rep, Episcopalian.

COLLETT, J. P.; farmer; ¼ m e Morgantown. Born in Ind. 1853; settled in M. C. 1873. Dem. Protestant.

CANATSEY, C. M.; farmer; ¼ m e Morgantown. Born in Ind. 1856. Rep. Protestant.

Campbell, R. L.; harness maker; Morgantown. Born in Ind. 1832; settled in M. C. 1869. Rep. Methodist.

Collett, J. M.; farmer, and breeder and shipper of fine stock; Morgantown. Born in Ky. 1818; settled in M. C. 1833. Rep. Methodist.

Canatsey, G. R.; farmer; ¾ m s e Morgantown. Born in Ky. 1821; settled in M. C. 1827. M. Baptist.

Canatsey, Mary A.; farmer; ¾ m s e Morgantown. Born in Tenn. 1827; settled in M. C. 1844. Methodist.

Canatsey, J. K.; farmer; ½ m s e Morgantown. Born in Ind. 1856. Rep. Protestant.

Cranford, J. W.; firm of Coleman flour mill; Morgantown. Born in Ohio 1832; settled in M. C. 1853. Rep. Prot.

Castner, John; farmer; 3¼ m n w Morgantown. Born in Prussia 1845; settled in M. C. 1851. Rep. Protestant.

Castner, Julius; farmer; 2 m n Morgantown. Born in Prussia 1849; settled in M. C. 1850. Rep. M. Baptist.

Castner, John; farmer; 2 m n Morgantown. Born in Prussia 1792; settled in M. C. 1850. Rep. Lutheran.

JACKSON TOWNSHIP.

Chipps, Morris; farmer; 4 m e Martinsville. Born in N. J. 1790; settled in M. C. 1848. Dem. Protestant.

Chipps, G. W.; farmer; 4 m e Martinsville. Born in N. J. 1843; settled in M. C. 1848. Dem. C. Presbyterian.

CLODFELDER, GEO.; farmer; 3½ m e Martinsville. Born in Ind. 1840; settled in M. C. 1846. Dem. C. Presby'n.

Coffey, Moses; farmer; 1½ m e Mahalasville. Born in M. C. 1831. Dem. Protestant.

Cain, Jesse; miller; Mahalasville. Born in Ohio 1831; settled in M. C. 1868. Dem. Protestant.

Colaer, J. T.; merchant and lumber dealer; Mahalasville.

Coleman, Harvey; farmer; Morgantown. Born in Ohio 1811; settled in M. C. 1838. Dem. Christian.

Dill, R. M.; proprietor flouring mill; Morgantown. Born in Ohio 1833; settled in M. C. 1840. Dem. Protestant.

DUTY, G. E.; barber and hair dresser; Morgantown. Born in Ind. 1849; settled in M. C. 1870. Rep. Christian.

Duty, J. F.; barber and hair dresser; Morgantown. Born in Ind. 1856; settled in M. C. 1874. Rep. Protestant.

DILL, W. P.; engineer; Morgantown. Born in Ind. 1856. Dem. Protestant.

Dill, Theo.; merchant with Butler; Morgantown. Born in Ind. 1854; settled in M. C. 1857. Dem. Protestant.

Donelson, John; farmer; 1½ m w Morgantown. Born in Ireland 1816; settled in M. C. 1864. Rep. Methodist.

Dill, F. M.; farmer; 4 m n Morgantown. Born in Me. 1841. Dem. Protestant.

Davee, John; farmer; 5 m n w Morgantown. Born in M. C. 1829. Rep. Protestant.

DODSON, D. S.; firm of Dodson & Bros., general merchants; Mahalasville. Born in Ky. 1836; settled in M. C. 1860. Dem. Protestant.

Dodson, J. H.; firm of Dodson & Bros., general merchants; Mahalasville. Born in Ky. 1840; settled in M. C. 1866. Dem. Methodist.

DAVIS, MARK; physician; Mahalasville. Born in Ohio 1814; settled in M. C. 1871. Rep. Methodist.

Davidson, Samuel; painter; ¾ m n Mahalasville.

Eliassen, Edward; groceries and provisions; Morgantown. Born in Norway 1803; settled in M. C. 1871. Dem. R. Baptist.

Egbert, James W.; farmer; Morgantown. Born in Ind. 1848. Dem. Christian.

Eves, W. D.; sewing machine agent; Morgantown. Born in Ill. 1844; settled in M. C. 1871. Rep. Methodist.

Elgin, Hugh; farmer; 2 m e Mahalasville. Born in M. C. 1843. Protestant.

Egbert, Israel; farmer; ¼ m w Morgantown. Born in Ohio 1831; settled in M. C. 1838. Dem. Christian.

Egbert, J. W.; farmer; Morgantown. Born in M. C. 1848. Dem. Christian.

Egbert, T. J.; farmer; Morgantown. Born in M. C. 1851. Dem. Protestant.

Fesler, Oliver; carpenter; Morgantown. Born in Ind. 1852. Rep. Methodist.

Fesler, Mrs. M. A.; farmer; Morgantown. Born in Ireland 1834; settled in M. C. 1857. Methodist.

FUGATE, J. W.; carpenter and contractor; Morgantown. Born in Ind. 1837; settled in M. C. 1860. Rep. Meth-

Fesler, Fremont; clerk in store; Morgantown. Born in Ind. 1856; settled in M. C. 1861. Rep. Methodist.

Fesler, Peter; farmer; Morgantown. Born in Va. 1836; settled in M. C. 1838. Rep. Methodist.

Ferguson, Edward; farmer; 2½ m n w Morgantown. Born in Ireland 1810; settled in M. C. 1840. Dem. Meth.

Fugate, E. L.; farmer and fur dealer; 3½ m n w Morgantown. Born in Ind. 1841; settled in M. C. 1846. Rep. Meth.

Fletcher, J. O.; farmer and school teacher; 2 m s e Cope. Born in Canada 1837; settled in M. C. 1841. Dem. Protest.

Ferguson, John; farmer; 4½ m n w Morgantown. Born in Pa. 1844; settled in M. C. 1846. Dem. Methodist.

Fletcher, E. D.; farmer; 6 m e Martinsville. Born in Ky. 1847; settled in M. C. 1870. Rep. Protestant.

Foster, P. A.; farmer; Morgantown. Born in Ind. 1847; settled in M. C. 1871. Rep. Protestant.

Fergeson, Wm.; farmer; 1½ m n Mahalasville. Born in Ohio 1838; settled in M. C. 1846. Dem. Methodist.

GRIFFITT, R. C.; physician and surgeon; Morgantown. Born in Ind. 1845. Rep. Protestant.

Gerholdt, Fred; farmer; 3½ m n w Morgantown. Born in Prussia 1822; settled in M. C. 1837. Dem. Lutheran.

Gross, John W.; farmer; 3 m n w Morgantown. Born in Ky. 1815; settled in M. C. 1827. Dem. M. Baptist.

Griner, C. F.; farmer; 4 m n w Morgantown. Born in Prussia 1816; settled in M. C. 1844. Dem. S. Baptist.

Green, John; farmer and lumber dealer; Morgantown. Born in Ind. 1821; settled in M. C. 1870. Rep. Christian.

Gerholdt, ——; farmer; 3½ m n w Morgantown. Born in Ind. 1840; settled in M. C. 1840. Dem. Lutheran.

Hamilton, R. A.; surgeon and dentist; Morgantown. Born in Ky. 1837; settled in M. C. 1873. Rep. Methodist.

Hilton, E. B.; carpenter and undertaker; Morgantown. Born in Ind. 1823; settled in M. C. 1850. Rep. Protestant.

Haggard, Harvey; farmer and cooper; 2 m s Morgantown. Born in Ind. 1829; settled in M. C. 1839. Dem. Baptist.

Harney, G. G.; minister; Morgantown. Born in Ind. 1851; settled in M. C. 1873. No politics. Christian.

HICKEY, J. K.; farmer; ½ m s Morgantown. Born in Tenn. 1840; settled in M. C. 1842. Rep. Methodist.

Hickey, John; retired farmer; ½ m s Morgantown. Born in Tenn. 1799; settled in M. C. 1842. Rep. Methodist.

Hamilton, John; farmer; 2½ m s w Morgantown. Born in Ky. 1820; settled in M. C. 1827. Rep. Methodist.

HAMILTON, J. F.; farmer; 2 m w Morgantown. Born in Ind. 1833. Dem. Methodist.

Hickman, J. H.; farmer; 2 m w Morgantown. Born in Ind. 1833; settled in M. C. 1834. Rep. Methodist.

HAMILTON, WM.; farmer; 2½ m w Morgantown. Born in Ky. 1811; settled in M. C. 1827. Dem. Methodist.

Hamilton, James; farmer; 2 m w Morgantown. Born in Ky. 1816; settled in M. C. 1827. Rep. Methodist.

Hickey, James; general trader; Morgantown. Born in Tenn. 1824; settled in M. C. 1843. Indp. Methodist.

Hogeland, Isaac; farmer; 3½ m n Morgantown. Born in Ky. 1825; settled in M. C. 1852. Dem. M. Baptist.

Hine, J. S.; farmer; 5½ m e Martinsville. Born in N. C. 1836; settled in M. C. 1837. Dem. Protestant.

Hine, J. G.; farmer; 4½ m e Martinsville. Born in N. C. 1806; settled in M. C. 1836. Dem. Lutheran.

Hine, T. W.; farmer; 4¼ m e Martinsville. Born in M. C. 1852. Dem. Protestant.

Hart, A. B.; farmer; 4¼ m e Martinsville. Born in N. J. 1819; settled in M. C. 1841. Dem. Prot.

Hart, Aaron; farmer; 4¼ m e Martinsville. Born in M. C. 1849. Dem. Protestant.

Haase, Michael; farmer; 5 m s e Martinsville. Born in M. C. 1833. Dem. Protestant.

Haase, Jefferson; farmer; 5 m s e Martinsville. Born in M. C. 1851. Dem. Protestant.

Hine, Henry; farmer; 4½ m e Martinsville. Born in N. C. 1814; settled in M. C. 1836. Dem. Lutheran.

Howell, David; farmer; 4½ m e Martinsville. Born in Ky. 1830; settled in M. C. 1840. Rep. Methodist.

Haase, Noah; farmer; 4 m e Martinsville. Born in N. C. 1820; settled in M. C. 1838. Dem. Protestant.

Haase, Ephraim; farmer; 2 m n e Mahalasville. Born in N. C. 1818; settled in M. C. 1838. Dem. Protestant.

Howell, J. W.; farmer; 5½ m e Martinsville. Born in M. C. 1843. Rep. Methodist.

Howell, Emery; farmer; 4 m n w Morgantown. Born in M. C. 1837. Rep. Protestant.

Hickman, John; farmer; 3½ m w Morgantown. Born in M. C. 1852. Rep. Methodist.

Hickman, C. H.; farmer; 3½ m w Morgantown. Born in Ky 1827; settled in M. C. 1830. Rep. Methodist.

Hickman, J. H.; farmer; 3½ m w Morgantown. Born in M. C. 1848. Rep. Methodist.

HELTON, J. B.; farmer and saw milling; 1 m e Mahalasville. Born in Ky. 1828; settled in M. C. 1828. Dem. Meth.

Helton, W. W.; farmer and saw milling; Mahalasville. Born in Tenn. 1807; settled in M. C. 1828. Dem. Methodist.

Haase, David, Sr.; farmer; 3 m w Morgantown. Born in N. C. 1801; settled in M.C. 1828. Dem. Protestant.

Haase, Wm.; farmer; 3 m w Morgantown. Born in M. C. 1852. Dem. Protestant.

Haase, David, Jr.; farmer; 3½ m w Morgantown. Born in M. C. 1840. Dem. Protestant.

Haase, Isaac; farmer; 3¼ m w Morgantown.

Hulen, Wm.; farmer; 2 m s e Mahalasville.

Helton, J. W.; farmer and groceries; Mahalasville. Born in M. C. 1848. Dem. Protestant.

Howell, William; farmer; Morgantown. Born in Ky. Meth.

Jones, G. W.; blacksmith and wagon maker; Morgantown. Born in Ind. 1840; settled in M. C. 1859. Rep. Meth.

Johnson, James; farmer; 2 m e Mahalasville. Born in M. C. 1852. Dem. Protestant.

Jones, Lewis; carpenter; Mahalasville.

Jodson, G. W.; blacksmith; Mahalasville. Born in Ind. 1850; settled in M. C. 1867. Dem. Protestant.

Karst, G. L.; boot and shoe maker; Morgantown. Born in Germany 1831; settled in M. C. 1869. Dem. Lutheran.

Kain, J. G.; miller; Morgantown. Born in Pa. 1816; settled in M. C. 1839. Rep. Methodist.

Kelso, J. S,; carpenter; Morgantown. Born in Ind. 1849. Rep. Methodist.

KNIGHT, ISAAC; farmer; Morgantown. Born in Va. 1830; settled in M. C. 1852. Rep. Christian.

King, J. W.; blacksmith; Morgantown. Born in Ind. 1838; settled in M. C. 1849. Rep. Methodist.

Kemp, J. M.; farmer; 1½ m s Morgantown. Born in Ky. 1815; settled in M. C. 1823. Dem. Protestant.

Kemp, Peter; farmer; 1½ m s Morgantown. Born in Ind. 1841. Rep. Protestant.

Kelso, J. J.; farmer; 2¼ m s w Morgantown. Born in Tenn. 1811; settled in M. C. 1832. Dem. Protestant.

Kelso, J. J.; farmer; 1 m n e Morgantown. Born in Ind. 1832. Dem. Protestant.

Kephart, Robert; farmer; 3 m n Morgantown. Born in M. C. 1850. Dem. Protestant.

Kephart, James; farmer; 3 m n Morgantown. Born in Ky. 1823; settled in M. C. 1848. Dem. Protestant.

Kemp, Albert; farmer; 4¾ m n w Morgantown. Born in M. C. 1834. Dem. Methodist.

Kelso, Jamison; farmer; 3¾ m w Morgantown. Born in M. C. 1845. Rep. Protestant.

Kelso, J. P.; carpenter; 1 m e Mahalasville. Born in Ind. 1844; settled in M. C. 1859. Rep. Methodist.

Kingsberry, Thos.; farmer; 1 m n Mahalasville. Born in Ohio 1832; settled in M. C. 1854. Rep. Protestant.

Kingsberry, Wm.; farmer; 1 m n Mahalasville. Born in Ireland 1814; settled in M. C. 1854. Rep. Methodist.

Kemp, G. W.; farmer; 3½ m w Morgantown. Born in M. C. 1849. Dem. Protestant.

Kemp, James; farmer; 3½ m w Morgantown. Born in Tenn. 1814; settled in M. C. 1844. Dem. S. Baptist.

Kelso, John; farmer; 3¾ m w Morgantown. Born in M. C. 1851. Rep. Protestant.

Kemp, Wm.; farmer; 1¼ m e Mahalasville. Born in M. C. 1841. Dem. Protestant.

Kinney, Geo.; farmer; 1¼ m e Mahalasville.

Kemp, Riley; farmer; 1¾ m s e Mahalasville. Born in M.C. 1852. Dem. Protestant.

Karst, Thereris; milliner and dressmaker; Morgantown. Born in Bohemia 1831; settled in M. C. 1869. Catholic.

Lang, B. B.; physician and druggist; Morgantown. Born in Ind. 1852; settled in M. C. 1867. Rep. Protestant.

LONG, K. E.; firm of Buckner & Long, druggists; Morgantown. Born in Ind. 1859. Rep. Protestant.

Lake, L.; livery, feed and sale stable; Morgantown. Born in Va. 1818; settled in M. C. 1836. Rep. Universalist.

LONG, PETER; saloon and billiards; Morgantown. Born in Pa. 1839; settled in M. C. 1870. Dem. Lutheran.

Lake, W. C.; carpenter; Morgantown. Born in Ind. 1843; settled in M. C. 1853. Rep. Protestant.

Lake, James; farmer; 3 m w Morgantown. Born in Tenn. 1831; settled in M. C. 1831. Dem. Protestant.

LEE, ISAAC H.; farmer; 1½ m w Morgantown. Born in N. J. 1856; settled in M. C. 1864. Rep. Methodist.

Lloyd, Owen; farmer; 1¼ m w Morgantown. Born in Ireland 1807; settled in M. C. 1840. Dem. Protestant.

LAMBERT, G. W.; farmer; ¾ m s w Morgantown. Born in Ky. 1815; settled in M. C. 1848. Dem. Protestant.

Lambert, John; farmer; 2½ m n Morgantown. Born in M. C. 1851. Dem. Methodist.

Lawrence, Simon; farmer; 4½ m n w Morgantown. Born in Canada East 1836; settled in M. C. 1838. Rep. Protest.

Lake, Wm.; farmer; 3 m n w Morgantown. Born in Va. 1826; settled in M. C. 1838. Dem. Protestant.

Lake, Martin; farmer; 4 m n w Morgantown. Born in M. C. 1840. Dem. Protestant.

Lack, F. M.; farmer; 4 m n w Morgantown. Born in Ind. 1841; settled in M. C. 1854. Dem. Methodist.

LAWRENCE, AMOS; farmer; 4½ m n w Morgantown. Born in Mass. 1809; settled in M. C. 1837. Rep. Universalist.

Lawrence, Amos, Jr.; farmer; 4½ m n w Morgantown. Born in M. C. 1850. Rep. Protestant.

Leonard, Geo.; farmer; 5 m e Martinsville. Born in M. C. 1848. Dem. Protestant.

Leonard, Henry; farmer; 5 m e Martinsville. Born in M. C. 1850. Dem. Protestant.

LAKE, GEO.; farmer; 3½ m w Morgantown. Born in M.C. 1851. Dem. Methodist.

Lloyd, Owen, Jr.; farmer; 3½ m n w Morgantown. Born in M. C. 1842. Dem. Protestant.

Lemon, J. P.; farmer; 1½ m s e Mahalasville. Born in Ind. 1832; settled in M. C. 1859. Dem. Sep. Baptist.

Lemon, Isaac; farmer; 2 m s e Mahalasville.

Lemon, S. L.; farmer; 2¾ m s e Mahalasville. Born in Ind. 1830; settled in M. C. 1855. Dem. Sep. Baptist.

McJlhenny, J. R.; clerk and salesman; Morgantown. Born in Ind. 1840; settled in M. C. 1866. Rep. Protestant.

MONTGOMERY, EDWARD; harness maker; Morgantown. Born in Ohio 1844; settled in M. C. 1873. Rep. Meth.

Melton, Robert; farmer; 1 m s Morgantown. Born in Ind. 1840; settled in M. C. 1850. Rep. Protestant.

Minner, Ernst; farmer; 1½ m s w Morgantawn. Born in Germany 1825; settled in M. C. 1870. Indpt. Methodist.

Miller, Christian; farmer; 1½ m s w Morgantown. Born in Prussia 1832; settled in M. C. 1852. Indpt. Methodist.

Miller, Henry; farmer; 1½ m s w Morgantown. Born in Prussia 1824; settled in M. C. 1852. Rep. Protestant.

Merriman, Sophia, Mrs.; farmer; 2 m s w Morgantown. Born in Ind. 1840. Dem. Methodist.

Merriman, T. F.; farmer; 2¼ m s w Morgantown. Born in Tenn. 1828; settled in M. C. 1828. Dem. Protestant.

McDaniel, Harvey; butcher; Morgantown. Born in Ind. 1837; settled in M. C. 1873. Rep. Methodist.

Miller, Daniel; farmer; 3 m n w Morgantown. Born in Prussia 1822; settled in M. C. 1856. Rep. Methodist.

Miller, A.; farmer; 3 m n w Morgantown. Born in Prussia 1819; settled in M. C. 1847. Rep. Methodist.

Miller, Fred.; farmer; 3½ m n w Morgantown. Born in Prussia 1814; settled in M. C. 1840. Rep. Methodist.

Moore, David; farmer; 5 m n w Morgantown. Born in Ky. 1823; settled in M. C. 1835. Dem. Methodist.

Moore, Hugh; farmer; 5 m n w Morgantown. Born in Ky. Methodist.

Moore, Samuel; farmer; 4½ m n w Morgantown. Born in M. C. 1848. Dem. Methodist.

McGowen, Thos.; farmer; ½ m e Mahalasville. Born in M. C. 1835. Dem. Protestant.

McFarland, Harrison; farmer; 2 m s e Mahalasville.

McShane, F. M.; farmer and school teacher; 2 m e Mahalasville. Born in Ind. 1841; settled in M. C. 1867. Rep. Protestant.

NICHOLS, T. C.; firm of Nichols & Bro., painters; Morgantown. Born in Ind. 1842; settled in M. C. 1870. Dem. Protestant.

Nichols, J. S; painter; Morgantown. Born in Ind. 18—; settled in M. C. 1873. Dem. Methodist.

Neely, J. M.; postmaster; Morgantown. Born in Ind. 1840; settled in M. C. 1868. Rep. Protestant.

Norman, J. H.; farmer; 3 m w Morgantown. Born in M. C. 1839. Dem. Methodist.

JACKSON TOWNSHIP.

Norman, Hiram; farmer; 1½ m e Mahalasville. Born in Ky. 1818; settled in M. C. 18—. Rep. Methodist.

Norman, W. W.; farmer; 1½ m e Mahalasville. Born in M. C. 1839. Rep. Protestant.

Norman, Francis; farmer; 1½ m e Mahalasville. Born in M. C. 1842. Rep. Protestant.

Norman, J. J.; farmer; 3¾ m w Morgantown. Born in M. C. 1849. Rep. Protestant.

Norman, J. T.; farmer; 4 m w Morgantown. Born in Tenn. 1822; settled in M. C. 1829. Rep. Protestant.

Norman, F. P.; 4 m w Morgantown. Born in M. C. 1852. Rep. Protestant.

Norman, W. H.; farmer; 1 m s e Mahalasville. Born in Tenn. 1814; settled in M. C. 1829. Dem. Protestant.

Obenshain, T. L.; mechanic; Morgantown. Born in Va. 1818; settled in M. C. 1837. Rep. Protestant.

Obenshain, George; groceries, boots and shoes; Morgantown. Born in Va. 1822; settled in M. C. 1846. Rep. M. Baptist.

Owen, Thomas; farmer; 1¾ s Morgantown. Born in Wales 1809; settled in M. C. 1837. Rep. M. Baptist.

Obenshain, C. H.; merchant salesman; Morgantown. Born in Va. 1849; settled in M. C. 1871. Dem. M. Baptist.

Patterson, M. J.; merchant; Morgantown. Born in Pa. 1811; settled in M. C. 1868. Rep. Methodist.

Pangborn, S.; dealer in furniture; Morgantown. Born in Ohio 1834; settled in M. C. 1872. Rep. Methodist.

PERKINS, B. F.; farmer; 1¼ m s Morgantown. Born in Ky. 1835; settled in M. C. 1849. Rep. Methodist.

Pratt, James H.; farmer; 1 m n w Morgantown. Born in Va. 1810; settled in M. C. 1838. Rep. Methodist.

Prior, Wm.; farmer; 5½ m e Martinsville. Born in Ohio 1842; settled in M. C. 1866. Protestant.

Pate, Samuel; farmer; 3¼ m w Morgantown. Born in Geo. 1839; settled in M. C. 1864. Dem. Protestant.

PRATHER, ——; engineer; Mahalasville. Born in M. C. 1851. Dem. Protestant.

Prather, John; sawyer; Mahalasville. Born in M. C. 1849. Dem. Protestant.

Robertson, W. S.; physician; Morgantown. Born in Ind. 1839; settled in M. C. 1872. Rep. Protestant.

Reeder, W. C.; farmer; 2½ m s w Morgantown. Born in Tenn. 1820; settled in M. C. 1840. Protestant.

Redwine, J. W.; farmer; 1 m w Morgantown. Born in Ind. 1832; settled in M. C. 1873. Dem. M. Baptist.

RAGSDALE, J. W.; minister; Morgantown. Born in Ky. 1811; settled in M. C. 1854. M. Baptist.

Reeder, W. A.; blacksmith; 5 m e Martinsville. Born in M.C. 1851. Rep. Protestant.

Raper, A. J.; farmer; 3 m n e Mahalasville. Born in Ind. 1828; settled in M. C. 1868. Dem. Methodist.

Renner, Henry, of firm of Hoover & Renner, flouring mill; Mahalasville. Born in Ohio 1828; settled in M. C. 1840. Dem. Protestant.

Reeder, Joseph; farmer; 2 m s w Morgantown. Born in Tenn.; settled in M. C. 1828. Dem. S. Baptist.

Roberts, Hiram; farmer; ½ m s e Mahalasville. Born in M. C. 1847. Dem. Protestant.

Renner, Enoch; blacksmith; Mahalasville. Born in M. C. 1845. Dem. Protestant.

Saltcorn, Chas.; prop'r Sherman House; Morgantown. Born in Germany 1831; settled in M. C. 1859. Rep. Pretest.

SPARKS, T. A.; physician and surgeon; Morgantown. Born in Ky. 1822; settled in M. C. 1856. Dem. Protestant.

SHANK, J. H.; carpenter; Morgantown. Born in Ind. 1854; settled in M. C. 1856. Rep. Protestant.

SKINNER, G. W.; farmer; ½ m s w Morgantown. Born in Ohio 1825; settled in M. C. 1843. Rep. M. Baptist.

Satterwhite, Owen; farmer; 2 m n Morgantown. Born in Ky. 1833; settled in M. C. 1842. Dem. Protestant.

Sichling, Fred; farmer; 4 m n w Morgantown. Born in Prussia 1838; settled in M. C. 1847. Rep. Lutheran.

Sanders, E. C.; farmer; 3 m n w Morgantown. Born in Prussia 1845; settled in M. C. 1847. Rep. Methodist.

Sanders, C. J.; farmer; 3 m n Morgantown. Born in Prussia 1836; settled in M. C. 1848. Rep. Lutheran.

Sander, Julius; farmer and shoemaker; 2¼ m n Morgantown. Born in Prussia 1810; settled in M. C. 1847. Rep. Luth.

Sprague, James W.; farmer; 2 m n w Morgantown. Born in Ohio 1840; settled in M. C. 1869. Rep. Methodist.

Sprague, S. J.; farmer; 2½ m n w Morgantown. Born in Ohio 1846; settled in M. C. 1873. Rep. Methodist.

Snyder, Wm.; farmer; 5 m e Martinsville. Born in Baden 1836; settled in M. C. 1864. Dem. C. Presbyterian.

Stack, Samuel; farmer; 1¼ m s e Mahalasville.

Scaggs, John; farmer; 1½ m s e Mahalasville.

Simmons, William; farmer; 1½ m s e Mahalasville.

Slack, C. D.; farmer; 2½ m s e Martinsville. Born in Ohio 1819; settled in M. C. 1853. Dem. Protestant.

Scaggs, Charles; farmer; 2½ s e Mahalasville.

Smith, James; farmer; ½ m w Mahalasville.

Slack, R. W.; physician and surgeon; Mahalasville. Born in Ind. 1840; settled in M. C. 1873. Dem. Universalist.

Shank, John; wagonmaker; Morgantown. Born in Ohio 1828; settled in M. C. 1858. Rep. Methodist.

Traxel, A. S.; farmer; 6 m e Martinsville. Born in Tenn. 1823; settled in M. C. 1827. Rep. Methodist.

VARBLE, HENRY; farmer; 1¼ m s e Morgantown. Born in Ky. 1843; settled in M. C. 1851. Rep. Methodist.

Vandergrift, David; farmer; 2¾ m w Morgantown. Born in M. C. 1849. Rep. Protestant.

Vandergrift, Elijah; farmer; 3 m w Morgantown. Born in Ky. 1825; settled in M. C. 1830. Rep. Methodist.

Vandergrift, Samuel; farmer; 4½ m n w Morgantown. Born in Ky. 1817; settled in M. C. 1840. Dem. Protestant.

Vandergrift, Elijah; farmer; 4½ m n w Morgantown. Born in Ind. 1842. Dem. Protestant.

Voyls, S. E.; farmer; 5 m e Martinsville. Born in N. C. 1808; settled in M. C. 1832. Dem. Protestant.

Voyls, C. M.; farmer; 5 m e Martinsville. Born in M. C. 1842. Dem. Protestant.

Voyls, A. B.; farmer; 5½ m e Martinsville. Born in M. C. 1852. Dem. Protestant.

Voyls, Joseph; farmer; 5 m e Martinsville. Born in Ind. 1811; settled in M. C. 1833. Dem. Protestant.

Vansickel, G. W.; farmer; Mahalasville. Born in M. C. 1847. Rep. Methodist.

Vansickel, Andrew; farmer; Mahalasville. Born in M. C. 1842. Rep. Methodist.

Wharton, R. T.; firm of Wharton & Co.; dry goods and groceries; Morgantown. Born in Ky. 1832; settled in M. C. 1872. Rep. Methodist.

Walker, Louisa Miss; milliner and dressmaker; Morgantown. Born in Ind. 1827; settled in M. C. 1857. Rep. Meth.

Walker, James; miller and engineer; Morgantown. Born in in Ky. 1828; settled in M. C. 1857. Dem. Protestant.

Whetstine, Alfred; constable; Morgantown. Born in Ohio 1820; settled in M. C. 1837. Rep. Methodist.

WHARTON, E. A.; clerk in store; Morgantown. Born in Ind. 1854; settled in M. C. 1872. Rep. Protestant.

Woods, Miles; minister; Morgantown. Born in Ind. 1836; settled in M. C. 1873. Rep. Methodist.

Weimer, Fred; blacksmith; Morgantown. Born in Wertenburg, Germany, 1840; settled in M. C. 1866. Rep. Luth.

Wershing, John; farmer; 1½ m s Morgantown. Born in Ohio 1864 settled in M. C. 1852. Dem. Protestant.

Whitaker, C. T.; farmer; ¾ m s Morgantown. Born in Ind. 1847. Dem. Methodist.

Whitaker, J. J.; farmer; 1 m s Morgantown. Born in Ind. 1855. Dem. Methodist.

Whitaker, J. H.; farmer; 1 m s Morgantown. Born in Ky. 1820; settled in M. C. 1834. Dem. Methodist.

WILLIAMS, WM.; farmer; 2½ m w Morgantown. Born in N. C. 1797; settled in M. C. 1831. Rep. Methodist.

Williams, David; farmer; 3 m w Morgantown. Born in Ind. 1844. Indp't. Protestant.

Williams, Fred.; farmer; 3¼ m w Morgantown. Born in N.C. 1828; settled in M. C. 1831. Dem. Protestant.

JACKSON TOWNSHIP.

Williams, Henry; farmer; 2½ m w Morgantown. Born in M. C. 1834. Rep. Protestant.

Williams, Jacob; farmer; 3 m w Morgantown. Born in N. C. 1825; settled in M. C. 1831. Rep. Methodist.

Woalfar, J. C.; farmer; 2 m n Morgantown. Born in Prussia 1804; settled in M. C. 1854. Dem. Lutheran.

Williams, Monroe; farmer; 4½ m e Martinsville. Born in N. C. 1824; settled in M. C. 1838. Rep. Methodist.

Whetstine, Mathias; farmer; 5 m e Martinsville. Born in N. C. 1808; settled in M. C. 1827. Rep. Methodist.

Whetstine, J. F.; farmer; 4 m n w Morgantown. Born in N. C. 1813; settled in M. C. 1827. Rep. Methodist.

Whitaker, Joshua; carpenter; Morgantown.

Williams, Noah; farmer; 1½ m n Mahalasville. Born in N. C. 1829; settled in M. C. 1839. Rep. Methodist.

Williams, James; farmer; 6 m s e Martinsville. Born in N. C. 1833; settled in M. C. 1839. Rep. Methodist.

Yager, Joseph; clothing; Morgantown. Born in Exeter, England. Conservative.

JEFFERSON TOWNSHIP.

JEFFERSON TOWNSHIP is located near the center of the county on the west side of White River, and is bounded on the north by Gregg and Clay townships, on the east and south by White River and Washington township, and on the west by Ashland and Ray, and contains about 40 square miles. It is generally broken or undulating, and next to White River is very broken, although along the bottoms of the river and other smaller streams there are some very fine farms. It is well timbered, and saw mills are in operation at different points along the bottoms of the small streams that course their way through the township.

Hyndsdale, a small station on the I. and V. Railroad, about 3 miles southwest of Martinsville, is the only town in the township of any business note. Stout & Richards have a very nice stock of dry goods, groceries, notions, etc.; also keep the post office. There is some shipping done from this point. They have nice roads, and the appearance of the wheat fields seen along the bottoms indicates a rich harvest. The church and school privileges are very good.

CHURCH, LODGE AND SCHOOL STATISTICS.

Mt. Gilead Baptist Church, 1½ miles west of Hyndsdale; no pastor in charge; Sunday school superintendent, Joseph Morrison; membership, 36; average attendance of school, 30.

Mt. Olive M. E. Church, Pastor, Eld. Fisher; membership, 60; class leader, Wm. Harris; Sunday school superintendent,

JEFFERSON TOWNSHIP.

Brice Howell; average attendance of school, 60; value of property, $2,000.

Presbyterian church, ½ mile west of Hyndsdale; Pastor, W. T. Ferguson; Sunday school superintendent, H. Shepler; membership, 30; average attendance of school, 45; value of property, $2,500.

Bethlehem Grange, Patrons of Husbandry, No. 1746; membership, 33; Jerry Mosier, Master; J. B. Stiles, Secretary.

Mt. Olive Grange, No. 1369; Master, Wm. Bradley; Secretary, Wm. Dilley; membership, 37; situate 3 miles southeast of Wilber.

DIRECTORY OF JEFFERSON TOWNSHIP.

Anderson, C. M.; farmer; 2 m n w Hynsdale. Born in Ind. 1848. Rep. Methodist.

Allen, J. W.; carpenter; 2½ m n Hynsdale. Born in Ind. 1852. Indpt. Protestant.

Brown, G. M.; farmer; 1½ m e Paragon. Born in Ind. 1837; settled in M. C. 1859. Dem. M. Baptist.

Bunting, Wm.; 6 m n w Martinsville. Born in N. C. 1840; settled in M. C. 183–. Rep. Methodist.

Bragg, W. J.; farmer; 1½ m w Martinsville. Born in Tenn. 1813; settled in M. C. 1827.

Bane, Bethsheba; farmer; 2 m w Martinsville. Born in Ind. 1835; settled in M. C. 1851. Presbyterian.

Bane, Wm. G.; farmer; Hynsdale. Born in Ind. 1848. Rep. Granger.

Brown, Dr. G.; farmer; 1½ m s w Hynsdale. Born in Ind. 1847; settled in M. C. 1857. Dem. Baptist.

Buckhart, Alex; farmer and teamster; 4 m s w Paragon. Born in M. C. 1850. Rep. Protestant.

BUNTEN, JOS.; farmer; 3 m n Hynsdale. Born in —— 1852; settled in M. C. 1861. Rep. Methodist.

Best, Wm.; farmer; 7 m n w Martinsville. Born in Ohio 1814; settled in M. C. 1852. Rep. Methodist.

Bothwell, David; farmer; 6 m n w Martinsville. Born in Ireland 1816; settled in M. C. 1852. Straight Dem. Presb.

Bradley, Dr.; physician; 2 m s Wilber. Gone from home.

Bradley, William; 2 m s Wilber. Master of Mt. Olive Grange, No. 1369.

Curtis, W. C.; teamster; 1½ m n w Hindsdale. Born in M.C. 1848. Rep. Methodist.

Cunningham, Wm.; farmer; ½ m s Hyndsdale. Born in Ky. 1807; settled in M. C. 1832. Rep. Christian.

CURTIS, W. B.; sawyer; 1½ m w Hyndsdale. Born in Ind. 1848. Granger. Protestant.

Collins, Abraham; farmer and cooper; 1 m w Hyndsdale. Born in N. C. 1804; settled in M. C. 1832. Rep. Meth.

Clark, B. F.; farmer; 3 m n w Martinsville. Born in Ind. 1829; settled in M. C. 1834. Rep. Christian.

Carpenter, Wiatt; horse doctor; 4 m n w Martinsville. Born in Ky. 1811; settled in M. C. 1852. Dem. Baptist.

Cox, John W.; farmer and miller; w Martinsville. Born in Ind. 1848. Rep. Granger. Protestant.

Crutchfield, Philip; Hyndsdale. Born in Ky. 1835; settled in M. C. 18—.

Cunningham, W. A.; farmer; 1 m w Hyndsdale. Born in Ind. 1847. Rep. Protestant.

Crone, Henry; farmer; 4 m w Hyndsdale. Born in Ireland 1823; settled in M. C. 1858. Rep. Methodist.

Duckworth, Wm.; farmer; 1¼ m s w Hyndsdale. Born in Ind. 1830. Dem. Granger. Protestant.

Duckworth, J. H. A.; farmer; 5½ m w Martinsville. Born in M. C. 1858. Dem. Protestant.

Duckworth, James; farmer; 3 m w Hyndsdale. Born in M. C. 1833. Dem. Granger. Protestant.

Dixon, John; farmer; 6 m n w Martinsville. Born in Ireland 1799; settled in M. C. 1839. Methodist.

Dixon, Wm. H.; farmer; 4½ m n w Martinsville. Born in M. C. 1844. Granger. Methodist.

Dilley, A. M.; farmer and carpenter; 2½ m s Wilber. Born in Ohio 1814; settled in M. C. 1840. Methodist.

Dilley, J. W.; farmer and carpenter; 2½ m Wilber. Born in M. C. 1847. Methodist.

Dane, D. C.; farmer and carpenter; 5 m n w Wilber. Born in Vermont 1815; settled in M. C. 1848. Rep. Methodist.

Dilley, Wm. A.; farmer and carpenter; 4 m n w Martinsville. Born in Ohio 1840. Rep. Methodist.

EGGERS, J. E.; farmer; ¼ m s Hyndsdale. Born in Ind. ——; settled in M. C. 1871. Dem.

EDWARDS, NEWTON; farmer; 4½ m n w Martinsville. Born in M. C. 1842. Rep. Granger. Methodist.

Elmore, James; farmer; 2 m s Wilber. Born in Ohio 1845; settled in M. C. 1873. Dem. Methodist.

Elmore, Wm.; gone from home.

FISHER, NATHANIEL; farmer and saw miller, Hyndsdale. Born in Ohio 1834; settled in M. C. 1848. Dem. M. Baptist.

Fletcher, A. J.; blacksmith; ½ m w Hyndsdale. Born in —; settled in M. C. 1849. Rep. Christian.

Fowler, W. W.; farmer and miller; 5 m n w Martinsville. Born in M. C. 1834. Rep. Granger. Methodist.

Foster, Robert; farmer; 5 m n w Martinsville. Born in Ireland 1810; settled in M. C. 1839. Neutral. Methodist.

Griffin, J. P.; farmer; ½ m s w Hynsdale. Born in Ind.; settled in M. C. 1850. Dem. Protestant.

Griffin, Greenberry; farmer. Born in Ind. 1840; settled in M. C. 1856. Dem. Protestant.

Green, Thomas; 5½ m n w Martinsville. Born in N. C. 1787; settled in M. C. about 1851.

GLOVER, J. W.; carpenter; 4 m n w Martinsville. Born in Tenn. 1839; settled in M. C. 1863. Rep. Presbyterian.

Green, Alvin; farmer; 4½ m n w Martinsville. Born in N. C. 1831; settled in M. C. 1854. Granger. Methodist.

Haase, C.; sawmilling; 2 m e Paragon. Born in Ind. 1844. Dem. Protestant.

Hall, Thos.; teamster and farmer; 2 m n Hyndsdale. Born in Ind. 1849; settled in M. C. 1872. Rep. Pres.

Hancock, Lewis; farmer; 1 m n Hyndsdale. Born in Ky. 1825; settled in M. C. 1848. P. Methodist.

Hynds, Wm.; farmer and trader; Hyndsdale. Born in Ireland 1822; settled in M. C. 18—. Granger.

Harrison, O. H.; sawmilling; Hyndsdale. Born in Ky. 1838; settled in M. C. 1853. Granger.

Hynds, W. P.; farmer; 1¼ m n w Hyndsdale. Born in Ind. 1848. Rep. Granger.

Hale, A. L.; farmer; 1 m w Hyndsdale. Born in Ind. 1859. Rep. Granger.

Hyndman, Nancy; farmer. Born in Ind. 1825; settled in M. C. 1850. Christian.

Haase, James L.; farmer; 3 m w Hyndsdale. Born in Ky. 1847; settled in M. C. 1871. Protestant.

Howard, Tilman; farmer; 1½ m n w Hyndsdale. Born in M. C. 1849. Rep. Methodist.

Hand, Uriah; farmer; 1½ m n w Hyndsdale. Born in Ky. 1824; settled in M. C. 1849. Methodist.

Hinson, J. J.; farmer; 5 m n w Martinsville. Born in N. C. 1838; settled in M. C. 1851. Rep. Methodist.

Harigan, Wm.; teamster; 4 m n w Hyndsdale. Born in Ohio 1842; settled in M. C. 1849. Rep. Protestant.

Hegans, John N.; farmer; 1½ m s Wilber. Born in Ky. 1795; settled in M. C. 1837. Christian.

Howell, Brice M.; farmer and saw milling; 4 m n w Martinsville. Born in M. C. 1846. Rep. Granger. Methodist.

Isenhower, D. E.; 1½ m s w Hynsdale. Born in Ind. 1836. Dem. Protestant.

JONES, ISAAC; saw milling; Hynsdale. Born in Ind. 1846. Dem. Protestant.

Jordon, John W.; farmer; 2 m s Wilber. Born in M. C. 1851. Rep. Christian.

Jordon, O. T.; farmer; 2 m s Wilber. Born in Ind. 1856.

Kennedy, L. C.; farmer; 1½ m s w Hynsdale. Born in Ky. 1804; settled in M. C. 1830. Rep. Presbyterian.

Kennedy, B. D.; farmer; 1½ m s w Hynsdale. Born in Ind. 1840. Rep. Granger. Protestant.

Kirby, John; farmer; 1 m e Paragon. Born in Ky. 1826; settled in M. C. 1834. Rep. Protestant.

Kivett, J. S.; farmer; 3 m e Herbemont. Born in M. C. 1838. Dem. Granger. Protestant.

Louis, Henry; 2½ m n w Martinsville. Born in Ind. 1852. Rep. Protestant.

Loper, Wm. L.; saw milling and merchant; 2 m n Hynsdale. Born in Ind. 1834; settled in M. C. 1856.

Mosier, J.; farmer; ½ m n Hyndsdale. Born in N. C. 1801; settled in M. C. 1834. Dem.

McCLISTER, JOHN A.; engineer; Hyndsdale. Born in Ky. 1847; settled in M. C. 18—. Dem.

Morrison, Joseph; farmer; 1 m e Paragon, Ray tp. Born in Tenn. 1827; settled in M. C. 1862. Dem. M. Baptist.

Morrison, J. W.; 1 m e Paragon, Ray tp. Born in Ind. 1849; settled in M. C. 1862. Dem.

Morgan, D. W.; farmer; 2 m n w Hyndsdale. Born in S. C. 1833; settled in M. C. 1869. Rep. Christian.

Mosier, Jerry; farmer; 4 m n w Hyndsdale. Born in Ind. 1819; settled in M. C. 1835. Dem. Christian.

More, J. B.; farmer; 4½ m n w Hyndsdale. Born in Ind. 1821; settled in M. C. 1826. Dem. Granger. Christian.

More, Ira; farmer; 4½ m n w Hyndsdale. Born in M. C. 1844. Rep. Granger. Christian.

McKee, Hiram; farmer; 2½ m s e Wilber. Born in Ind. 1834; settled in M. C. 1865. Rep. Protestant.

Miller, ——; 2½ m e Herbemont. Age about 69 years.

Majors, R. B.; farmer and lumber dealer; 2½ m n w Martinsville. Born in Ind. Territory, 1813, in a block house; settled in M. C. 1841. Rep. Methodist.

OLIVER, JOHN J.; farmer; 1½ m n e Paragon. Born in E. Tenn. 1827; settled in M. C. 1840. Rep. Protestant.

O'Neal, John; 4 m n Hyndsdale. Born in Tenn. 1798; settled in M. C. 1826. Christian. Has been blind six years.

Powls, N.; farmer; 1 m w Hyndsdale. Born in Ohio 1849; settled in M. C. 1871. Dem. Baptist.

PHELPS, E. T.; farmer; 4 m n w Martinsville. Born in 1826; settled in M. C. 1826. Rep. Presbyterian.

RICHARD, D. G.; general merchandise; Hyndsdale. Born in Ind. 1837. Rep. Protestant.

Robertson, J.; farmer; 2 m e Paragon. Born in E. Tenn. 1844; settled in M. C. 1869. Dem. Protestant.

Rogers, James; farmer; 6 m n w Martinsville. Born in Ind. 1852. Granger. Christian.

Robertson, D.; farmer; 2 m n e Paragon. Born in Ind. 1825; settled in M. C. 1870. Dem. M. Baptist.

Robertson, Eli; farmer; 1½ m n w Hyndsdale. Born in Ind. 185–. Christian.

Rutan, Isaac; farmer and carpenter; Hyndsdale. Born in N. J. 1838; settled in M. C. 1862. Protestant.

Stout, John D.; farmer and merchant; Hyndsdale. Born in Ind. 1813; settled in M. C. 1836. Dem. Protestant.

SULLIVAN, WM.; saw milling; 2 m e Paragon. Born in Ind. 1853. Rep. Protestant.

Shular, Charlton; farmer and stock dealer; 4 m e Paragon. Born in W. Va. 1829; settled in M. C. 1831. Rep. Christ.

Steles, J. B.; farmer; 2½ m n Hyndsdale. Born in Ind. 1827. Christian.

Shepler, Henry; farmer; 1¼ m e Paragon. Born in Ohio 1829; settled in M. C. 1854. Pres. Granger.

Spires, Valentine; farmer; 2 m w Hyndsdale. Born in Ind. 1842; settled in M. C. 1873. Rep.

Stine, Joseph; farmer; 4½ m n w Hyndsdale. Born in N. C. 1811; settled in M. C. 1864. Christian.

Shirrell, Leonard; farmer; 1 m s Wilber. Born in Ind. 1837; settled in M. C. 1866. M. Baptist.

Shipley, Tolbert; farmer; 6 m n w Martinsville. Born in Tenn. 1803; settled in M. C. 1819. Protestant.

SHIPLEY, JACOB A.; farmer and saw milling, Born in M. C. 1845. Rep. Methodist. Granger.

Wall, Wm.; wagonmaker; ½ m w Hyndsdale. Born in Ind. 1845; settled in M. C. 1871. Dem.

WELTY, ADAM; farmer and tanner; 4½ m n w Martinsville. Good Templar. Rep. Methodist. Has a farm for sale in Clay township. Born in Pa. 1819; settled in M. C. 1850.

Warthen, W.; farmer; 3 m w Martinsville. Born in Ind. 1846. Rep. Protestant.

Williamson, Wilson; farmer; Hyndsdale. Born in Ireland 1836: settled in M. C. 1860. Rep. Episcopalian.

Welty, L. F.; farmer; 4 m n w Martinsville. Born in Ind. 1852. Rep. Methodist.

MADISON TOWNSHIP.

MADISON TOWNSHIP is located in the northeast corner of the county, and is bounded on the north by Hendricks and Marion counties, on the east by Johnson county, on the south by White river, and on the west by Clay and Brown townships. The surface of this township, except the breaks of White river, is generally rolling. The soil is of good quality, and timber in abundance for all needful purposes. There is plenty of gravel, and, in most cases, good roads. This township is watered by White river and spring branches. The church and school privileges of this township will compare favorably with other portions of the county, while her citizens are energetic, intelligent and enterprising.

CHURCH STATISTICS.

Christian Church; Friendship; ¾ mile northeast of Landersdale; Rev. Cheer, pastor; membership, 86; value of church property, $3000; Sabbath school superintendent, John Trowbridge; average attendance, 40.

M. E. Church; Siloam; 1¼ m s e Friendswood; pastor, Rev. James Wall; average attendance of Sabbath school, 30; membership, 30; value of church property, $1200.

M. E. Church; Centennary; 3½ m e Brooklyn; pastor, Rev. James Wall; Sabbath school superintendent, Peter Farmer; average attendance of Sabbath school, 45; membership, 40; value of church property, $1,000.

Christian Church; Mt. Gilead; 3½ m s e Mooresville; membership, 46; Sabbath school superintendent, James Carter; average attendance, 60; value of church property, $1400.

M. E. Church; Mt. Olive; ¾ miles southwest of Landersdale; pastor, Rev. Gideon Heavenridge; membership, 40; value of church property, $1200.

DIRECTORY OF MADISON TOWNSHIP.

Bishop, Alfred; farmer; 3 m n e Brooklyn. Born in N. C. 1850; settled in M. C. 1850. Dem. Protestant.

Bragg, Wm. P.; farmer; 3½ m e Brooklyn. Born in Ky. 1844; settled in M. C. 1862. Dem. Protestant.

Bates, Thomas M.; farmer; 1 m w Red House. Born in Ky. 1835; settled in M. C. 1867. Dem. Protestant.

Beasley, John; farmer; 4½ m s e Mooresville. Born in N. C. 1828; settled in M. C. 1832. Dem. Protestant.

Boyd, Hugh; farmer; 3 m s e Mooresville. Born in E. Tenn. 1806; settled in M. C. 1830. Rep. Methodist.

Boyd, J. W.; farmer; 3 m s e Mooresville. Born in Ind. 1853. Dem. Protestant.

Britton, L.; farmer; 3 m e Brooklyn. Born in Ky. 1849; settled in M. C. 1864. Dem. Methodist.

Broon, Penecy; farmer; 2½ m s w Landersdale. Born in Ind. 1817; settled in M. C. 1826. Protestant.

Broon, Wesley; farmer; Landersdale. Born in Ind. 1840; settled in M. C. 1843. Dem. Methodist.

BOGGS, ALVIS; farmer; Landersdale. Born in N. C. 1833; settled in M. C. 1869. Rep. Protestant.

Baker, J. A.; school teacher; Maywood. Born in Ind. 1850. Methodist.

BAKER, WM. J.; farmer; 2½ m w Landersdale. Born in Ind. 1849. Rep. Methodist.

BELL, ELI; farmer; ½ m w Landersdale. Born in Ohio 1836; settled in M. C. 1853. Rep. Methodist.

BOYD, ALEXANDER; farmer; ¾ m s w Landersdale. Born in Ind. 1835; settled in M. C. 1845. Rep. Methodist.

BARLOW, CASWELL; shingle maker; 4 m e Mooresville. Born in N.C. 1825; settled in M. C. 1869. Dem. Meth.

Bishop, Geo. M.; day laborer; 1¼ m s e Friendswood. Born in N. C. 1818; settled in M. C. 1872. Rep. Methodist.

BEASLEY, ISUM; farmer; 2 m s w Landersdale. Born in N. C. 1826; settled in M. C. 1836. Dem. Protestant.

Brees, Robert; farmer; 1 m n e Waverly. Born in Ind. 1840. Rep. Protestant.

Carpenter, Robert; farmer; 3¼ m e Brooklyn. Born in Ind. 1845. Dem. Protestant.

COOK, GEO.; blacksmith; 2½ m s w Red House. Born in Md. 1828; settled in M. C. 1856. Rep. Methodist.

Carpenter, Eli; farmer; 1 m s w Red House. Born in Ind. 1854. Dem. Protestant.

Carpenter, F. J.; farmer; 1 m w Red House. Born in Ky. 1821; settled in M. C. 1826. Dem. Protestant.

CARPENTER AMANDA A.; tailoress, 1 m s w Red House. Born in Ind. 1856. Methodist.

Copeland, J. B.; farmer; 3 m s e Mooresville. Born in Ind. 1841; settled in M. C. 1857. Rep. Christian.

Clapp, Alison; farmer; 3 m e Brooklyn. Born in N. C. 1849; settled in M. C. 1870. Rep. Protestant.

Clark, Wm. H.; farmer; 3½ m e Brooklyn. Born in Va. 1822; settled in M. C. 1859. Dem. Protestant.

Carter, James A.; farmer; 3 m e Mooresville. Born in Ky. 1826; settled in M. C. 1836. Rep. Christian.

Carter, Alonzo B.; farmer; 3 m e Mooresville. Born in Ind. 1851. Rep. Protestant.

Cox, Meshach; farmer; 2½ m s w Landersdale. Born in Ind. 1833. Dem. Methodist.

CARPENTER, C. A.; farmer; 2 m s w Landersdale. Born in Ind. 1854. Dem. Protestant.

Carpenter, Madison; farmer; 1¾ m s w Landersdale. Born in Ky. 1818; settled in M. C. 1827. Dem. Christian.

Coster, Wm.; farmer; 3 m n w Red House. Born in Ohio 1850; settled in M. C. 1856. Rep. Protestant.

Coster, J. H.; farmer; 3 m n w Red House. Born in Ohio 1847; settled in M. C. 1856. Rep. Protestant.

Coble, Ranken; farmer; ½ m s w Landersdale; Born in N. C. 1851; settled in M. C. 1871. Dem. Protestant.

CLAPP, PRESLEY; farmer; 1 m s Landersdale. Born in N. C. 1848; settled in M. C. 1867. Dem. Protestant.

COPELAND, J. M.; farmer; 2 m s w Landersdale. Born in Ind. 1839; settled in M. C. 1856. Rep. Christian.

MADISON TOWNSHIP. 303

Craig, C. C.; farmer; 2 m n e Red House. Born in Ky. 1844; settled in M. C. 18—. Rep. Protestant.

Dollarhide, Elijah; farmer; ¼ m e Landersdale. Born in N. C. 1815; settled in M. C. 1873. Rep. Methodist.

Edwards, Nathan; merchant; Red House. Born in N. C. 1811; settled in M. C. 1838. Rep. Christian.

Ely, Thomas; farmer; 3 m e Brooklyn. Born in Va. 1825; settled in M. C. 1847. Dem. Protestant.

FIELDS, ALFRED; farmer; 2½ m n e Brooklyn. Born in Ind, 1834. Dem. R. Baptist.

Farmer, Wm. A.; farmer; 3 m e Brooklyn. Born in Ind. 1848. Dem. R. Baptist.

Farmer, W. A.; carpenter; 2 m n e Brooklyn. Born in N. C. 1845; settled in M. C. 1866. Dem. Protestant.

Fields, Allen; farmer; 2½ m e Brooklyn. Born in N. C. 1789; settled in M. C. 1826. Dem. R. Baptist 40 years.

Farmer, Peter; farmer; 3 m n e Brooklyn. Born in N. C. 1822; settled in M. C. 1845. Dem. Methodist.

FIELDS, H. N.; farmer; 2½ m e Brooklyn. Born in N. C. 1822; settled in M. C. 1829. Dem. Protestant.

Fleener, J. M. V.; farmer; 3 m e Brooklyn. Born in Ind. 1841; settled in M. C. 1868. Dem. Protestant.

Francis, John H.; farmer; ½ m s w Landersdale. Born in N. C. 1828; settled in M. C. 1834. Dem. Methodist.

Fisher, S. M.; farmer; 1 m s Friendswood. Born in Ky. 1825; settled in M. C. 1874. Rep. Christian.

Francis, Coleman; farmer; 3 m n e Mooresville. Born in N. C. 1815; settled in M. C. 1844. Protestant.

FARMER, D. M.; farmer; 3 m e Mooresville. Born in Ind. 1847. Dem. Methodist.

FOSTER, WM.; farmer; 1 m s w Landersdale. Born in N.C. 1848; settled in M. C. 1871. Dem. Protestant.

Foster, Asa; farmer; 1 m s w Landersdale. Born in N. C. 1816; settled in M. C. 1873. Rep. Protestant.

FOSTER, B.; farmer; 1 m s w Landersdale. Born in N. C. 1846; settled in M. C. 1873. Dem. Protestant.

Fitzjerl, Thomas; farmer; 2 m n e Red House. Born in Ind. 1832; settled in M. C. 1874. Rep. Methodist.

GRISOM, WM.; farmer; 3 m n e Brooklyn. Born in Ind. 1823; settled in M. C. 1824. Dem. Methodist.

Grisom, J. N.; farmer; 3 m n e Brooklyn. Born in Ind. 1857; Dem. Methodist.

GOODPASTER, S. M.; farmer; 1½ m s Landersdale. Born in Ky. 1828; settled in M. C. 1839. Dem. Christian.

Goodpaster, M. W.; farmer; 1½ m s Landersdale. Born in Ind. 1852. Dem. Christian.

Gray, Wm. A.; farmer; 4 m e Mooresville. Born in N. C. 1834; settled in M. C. 1866. Rep. Methodist.

GRAY, WM.; farmer; 2½ m s e Friendsood. Born in N. C. 1801; settled in M. C. 1871. Rep. Methodist.

Hiatt, H. H.; farmer; 2¾ m e Brooklyn. Born in Ind. 1837. Rep. Methodist.

HALE, WM. A.; farmer; 2¾ m e Brooklyn. Born in Ind. 1839. Rep. Protestant.

HAYS, J. R.; farmer; 3 m e Brooklyn. Born in N. C. 1847; settled in M. C. 1870. Rep. Protestant.

Hale, James; farmer; 3 m s Red House. Born in Ind. 1823. Rep. Protestant.

House, John; farmer; 3 m s e Mooresville. Born in Baden, Germany, 1793; settled in M. C. 1837. Dem. Meth.

Hiser, L. H.; farmer; 3 m n e Brooklyn. Born in Ky. 1834; settled in M. C. 1865. Dem. Protestant.

Hale, George; day laborer; 3 m e Brooklyn. Born in Ind. 1851. Dem. Protestant.

Hale, John; farmer; 2¾ m s e Brooklyn. Born in Tenn. 1811; settled in M. C. 1829. Rep. Methodist.

HENDRIX, WM.; blacksmith; Landersdale. Born in Va. 1822; settled in M. C. 1873. Soldier of 1862. Rep. Prot.

Harrah, Sam'l H.; farmer; 1 m w Landersdale. Born in Ky. 1831; settled in M. C. 1837. Dem. Protestant.

Harrah, Thos. C.; farmer; ¾ m w Landersdale. Born in Ky. 1795; settled in M. C. 1833. Dem. Protestant.

Horton, Jacob; farmer; 2½ m s w Newton. Born in Ind. 1825; settled in M. C. 1864. Rep. Friend.

Harrah, Wm. M.; farmer; 2 m w Landersdale. Born in Ky. 1829; settled in M. C. 1833. Dem. Protestant.

Hagee, S. P.; farmer; 3 m e Mooresville. Born in N. C. 1831; settled in M. C. 1851. Dem. Methodist.

HODGES, J. T.; farmer; 2 m n e Red House. Born in Ky. 1850; settled in M. C. 1863. Rep. Christian.

Hodges, Theodore; farmer; 2½ m n e Red House. Born in Ind. 1853; settled in M. C. 1863. Rep Christian.

Hodges, J. W.; farmer; 2 m n w Red House. Born in Ind. 1855; settled in M. C. 1864. Rep. Christian.

Howe, B. F.; farmer; 1 m n Waverly. Born in Ind. 1837. Dem. Protestant.

Johnson, Wm. T.; farmer; 3 m e Brooklyn. Born in Ky. 1837; settled in M. C. 1856. Dem. Protestant.

JACKSON, ELI; farmer and trader; 1¼ m w Landersdale. Born in Ind. 1834; settled in M. C. 1847. Dem. Chris.

Jessup, Oswold; farmer; 1½ m n Red House. Born in Ind. 1851; settled in M. C. 1873. Rep. Friend.

Kitchen, John; farmer; 2 m Red House. Born in Ind. 1850. Dem. Christian.

King, Lewis; farmer; 3 m s e Mooresville. Born in Baden, Germany, 1835; settled in M. C. 1860. Dem. Prot.

KINNEY, WM. A.; farmerm; 3 m s e Mooresville. Born in Ind. 1853. Dem. Methodist.

King, Wm. T.; farmer; 3 m n e Brooklyn. Born in Ky. 1849; settled in M. C. 1861. Dem. Protestant.

Kays, Alfred; farmer; 2 m e Brooklyn. Born in Ky. 1851; settled in M. C. 1863. Dem. Protestant.

Kays, John H.; farmer; 3 m e Brooklyn. Born in Ky. 1849; settled in M. C. 1863. Dem. Protestant.

Kinney, Moses; farmer; 3 m e Mooresville. Born in Ind. 1827; settled in M. C. 1850. Methodist.

Leathers, J. M.; farmer; 1½ m n w Red House. Born in Ind. 1833. Dem. Christian.

Leathers, S. A.; farmer; 1 m w Red House. Born in Ind. 1845. Dem. Protestant.

Leathers, J. J.; farmer; 1 m w Red House. Born in Ky. 1806; settled in M. C. 1827. Rep. Christian.

Leathers, C. S.; farmer; 2 m s e Red House. Born in Ind. 1838. Dem. Christian.

Low, G. W.; farmer; 3½ m s e Mooresville. Born in N. C. 1832; settled in M. C. 1833. Dem. Methodist.

Low, Absalom; farmer; 3 m s e Mooresville. Born in N. C. 1801; settled in M. C. 1834. Dem. Methodist.

Lee, J. A.; farmer; 3 m s e Brooklyn. Born in Va. 1846; settled in M. C. 1872. Dem. Protestant.

Mendenhall, Benj.; farmer and notary public; 2½ m e Mooresville. Born in Ind. 1828. Rep. Friend.

Miller, Daniel J.; farmer; 2¾ m s e Brooklyn. Born in Ohio 1828; settled in M. C. 1870. Rep. Methodist.

Martin, Jas. W.; farmer; 3 m n e Brooklyn. Born in Ind. 1811; settled in M. C. 1823. Dem. Methodist.

Martin, John W.; farmer; 3 m n e Brooklyn. Born in Ind. 1834. Dem. Protestant.

Martin, Lamertine; farmer; 3 m w Brooklyn. Born in Ind. 1849. Dem. Protestant.

MENDENHALL, JOEL; farmer; 2 m n e Red House. Born in Ind. 1851. Rep. Friend.

Mann, Wm. H.; farmer; ½ m n Landersdale. Born in Mo. 1840; settled in M. C. 1849. Dem. Methodist.

Myers, D. W.; farmer; ¾ m n w Landersdale. Born in N. C. 1850; settled in M. C. 1873. Dem. Christian.

Mendenhall, John; farmer; 2 m s w West Newton. Born in Ohio 1825; settled in M. C. 1825. Rep. Friend.

McNab, Rebecca; farmer; 1 m w Landersdale. Born in Ky. 1808; settled in M. C. 1832. Methodist.

McNab, Andrew; farmer; ½ m w Landersdale. Born in Ind. 1839. Dem. Protestant.

McCrary, W. F.; farmer; 1 m w Landersdale. Born in N. C. 1840; settled in M. C. 1868. Dem. Protestant.

Mendenhall, Anderson; farmer; 2 m s w West Newton. Born in Ind. 1848. Rep. Friend.

MILLER, A. N.; farmer; 2 m s w Landersdale. Born in Md. 1808; settled in M. C. 1860. Rep. Methodist.

Mendenhall, Albert; farmer; 2½ m s w Newton. Born in Ind. 1832. Rep. Friend.

MILLER, C. N.; farmer; ¼ m e Red House. Born in Va. 1849; settled in M. C. 1862. M. Baptist.

Murray, Joseph; farmer; ¼ m n Red House. Born in N. C. 1793; settled in M. C. 1870. Rep. Protestant.

Murray, Wm. G.; farmer; ¼ m n Red House. Born in Ind. 1844; settled in M. C. 1861. Rep. Protestant.

NEESE, J. R.; carpenter; 2½ m n Red House. Born in N. C. 1836; settled in M. C. 1859. Dem. Christian.

OLDS, WM. A.; farmer; 3 m e Brooklyn. Born in Ind. 1852. Dem. Protestant.

OLLEMAN, E. A. Jr.; farmer; 2 m n Red House. Born in Ind. 1850. Rep. Protestant.

PAUL, J. W.; farmer; 3 m n Red House. Born in Ind. 1847. Rep. Protestant.

Park, Wm. P.; farmer; 1 m w Red House. Born in Ind. 1842. Dem. Christian.

Passmore, G. W.; farmer; 2 m e Mooresville. Born in Ky. 1833; settled in M. C. 1850. Dem. Methodist.

Poore, Wm. T.; farmer; 3 m s w Landersdale. Born in Ind. 1843; settled in M. C. 1868. Rep. Methodist.

Purkeypile, John; farmer; 4½ m s e Mooresville. Born in Ind. 1832. Rep. Protestant.

Purkeypile, George; farmer; 4½ m s e Mooresville. Born in Va. 1814; settled in M. C. 1826. Dem. Protestant.

Park, S. R.; farmer; 1¼ m n Red House. Born in Ky. 1824; settled in M. C. 1840. Dem. Protestant.

Park, Henrietta S.; farmer; 1¼ m n Red House. Born in Ky. 1799; settled in M. C. 1840. Christian.

PFAFF, JOEL; blacksmith; Landersdale. Born in Ind. 1850; settled in M. C. 1874. Rep. Methodist.

Perry, E. D. Jr.; farmer; ½ m n w Landersdale. Born in Ind. 1852. Dem. Protestant.

Plummer, Wm.; farmer; 3 m e Mooresville. Born in Ind. 1843. Dem. Methodist.

Perry, E. D., Sen.; farmer; 1 m n w Landersdale. Born in N. C. 1823; settled in M. C. 1864. Dem. Protestant.

PARK, B. P.; farmer; 1¼ m n Red House. Born in Ky. 1828; settled in M. C. 1840. Dem. Protestant.

Randolph, Joseph; farmer; 2 m n e Red House. Born in Ky. 1849; settled in M. C. 1870. Dem. Protestant.

Rays, G. W.; farmer; ½ m n e Brooklyn. Born in Ky. 1816; settled in M. C. 1863. Dem. Christian.

ROZIER, JESSE ; farmer ; 3 m n e Brooklyn. Born in Ind. 1841. Dem. Protestant.

Rooker, C. F.; farmer ; 3 m e Brooklyn. Born in Ind. 1830. Dem. Methodist.

Rinker, B. F.; farmer; 3 m s e Brooklyn. Born in Ind. 1853. Dem. Methodist.

Rinker, J. B.; farmer; 3 m e Brooklyn. Born in Ind. 1825 ; settled in M. C. 1832. Dem. Methodist.

Rinker, Silas; farmer; 3 m s e Brooklyn. Born in Ind. 1835. Dem. Methodist.

Rinker, Oliver; farmer ; 3½ m e Brooklyn. Born in Ind. 1855. Dem. Methodist.

Rains, Ishmael; farmer; 3 m e Mooresville. Born in Tenn. 1806; settled in M. C. 1857. Rep. Protestant.

REES, SHEDLOCK ; farmer and stock trader; Red House. Born in Penn. 1829; settled in M. C. 1853. Rep. Meth.

Ritchey, J. W.; farmer; ¾ m n e Waverly. Born in Ind. 1833; settled in M. C. 1856. Dem. Protestant.

SLAUGHTER, PETER ; farmer; 3 m e Brooklyn. Born in Ind. 1838. Dem. Protestant.

SMITH, SYLVESTER ; farmer; 3¼ m e Brooklyn. Born in Ind. 1850; settled in M. C. 1865. Dem. Protestant.

SISSON, VALENTINE ; farmer and carpenter; ¼ m w Red House. Born in Ky. 1833; settled in M. C. 1852. Rep. Protestant.

Swearengin, H. T.; farmer; ¼ m w Red House. Born in N. C. 1819; settled in M. C. 1836. Rep. Christian.

Steel, A. J.; farmer; 1 m s w Red House. Born in Ind. 1852. Dem. Protestant.

SCHOOLEY, WM.; laborer; 4 m s e Mooresville. Born in Ohio 1844; settled in M. C. 1873. Rep. Christian.

Swope, Samuel; farmer; 3½ m e Mooresville. Born in Md. 1814; settled in M. C. 1840. Dem. Protestant.

Swope, Anderson T.; farmer; 3½ m Mooresville. Born in Ind. 1848. Dem. Protestant.

Squires, C. Y.; farmer; ¾ m n e Landersdale. Born in N. C. 1829; settled in M. C. 1848. Dem. Methodist.

Stephenson, Zena; farmer; ¾ m n e Landersdale. Born in N. C. 1827; settled in M. C. 1837. Dem. Methodist.

Sears, Geo. G. M.; farmer; ⅔ m n w Landersdale. Born in Ind. 1843; settled in M. C. 1874. Rep. Protestant.

STONE, AMELIA; 1½ m s e Friendswood. Born in Ky. 1821; settled in M. C. 1839. Protestant.

Sheperd, D. R.; farmer; 1½ m s e Friendswood. Born in N. C. 1847; settled in M. C. 1872. Rep. Methodist.

SMITH, RUFUS B.; farmer and trader; 3½ n Waverly. Born in Ind. 1845. Rep. Protestant.

Sawyers, John; farmer; 1¾ n e Red House. Born in N. C. 1809; settled in M. C. 1864. Dem. Protestant.

Simmons, Thos.; farmer; 1¾ m n e Red House. Born in N. C. 1797; settled in M. C. 1864. Protestant.

STOKESBERRY, J. M.; farmer; 1¾ m s e Friendswood. Born in Ohio 1820; settled in M. C. 1830. Dem. Methodist.

Stokesberry, J. H.; farmer; 1½ m s e Friendswood. Born in Ind. 1848. Dem. Protestant.

Thornberry, Milt A.; farmer and carpenter; 3½ m e Brooklyn. Born in Va. 1829; settled in M. C. 1840. Dem. Prot.

Thornberry, Daniel; farmer; 4 m s e Mooresville. Born in Va. 1794; settled in M. C. 1839. Dem. Was drafted in the war of 1812, and was honorably discharged.

Thornberry, Daniel, Jr.; farmer; 4 m s e Mooresville. Born in Ind. 1847. Dem. Protestant.

THORNBERRY, P. H.; farmer; 3 m n e Brooklyn. Born in Va. 1835; settled in M. C. 1839. Dem. Methodist.

Taylor, John; farmer; 3 m e Brooklyn. Born in Ind. 1852; settled in M. C. 1873. Rep. Protestant.

Thompson, John A.; farmer; 3 m e Brooklyn. Born in N. C. 1834; settled in M. C. 1874. Dem. Protestant.

Thomas, E. K.; school teacher; ¼ m n Red House. Born in Ky. 1840; settled in M. C. 1871. Dem. Protestant.

Thompson, S. D.; ½ m s e Landersdale. Born in N. C. 1845; settled in M. C. 1866. Dem. Protestant.

Turley, A. J.; farmer and trader; 1½ m s w Landersdale. Born in Ind. 1849. Dem. M. Baptist.

TURLEY, D. H.; farmer; 1½ m s w Landersdale. Born in Ind. 1850. Dem. Protestant.

THACKER, JAMES L.; farmer; ½ m s e Red House. Born in Ky. 1843; settled in M. C. 1855. Dem. Protestant.

THURMAN, PLEASANT; farmer and trader; 3½ m e Mooresville. Born in Ind. 1840. Rep. Protestant.

Watson, Cicero; farmer; ¼ m s Red House. Born in Ind. 1833. Dem. Protestant.

Watson, Benj. R.; farmer; 4 m e Brooklyn. Born in Ind. 1838. Dem. Protestant.

Watson, C. A.; farmer; 1½ m s w Red House. Born in Ind. 1829. Jackson Dem. Protestant.

Wright, J. A.; farmer; 2½ m n e Brooklyn. Born in Ind. 1852. Methodist.

WATSON, ALFRED; farmer; 3 m n e Brooklyn. Born in Ind. 1831. Dem. Protestant.

Wright, Andrew; farmer; 2½ m n e Brooklyn. Born in Ind. 1808; settled in M. C. 1840. Rep. Methodist.

Whetzell, J. W.; farmer; 1¼ m n Red House. Born in Tenn. 1841; settled in M. C. 1864. Rep. Methodist.

Whitehead, Murphy; groceryman; Landersdale. Born in N. C. 1822; settled in M. C. 1857. Dem. Christian.

Williams, Vinson ; farmer ; 2 m s e Friendswood. Born in Ind. 1846; settled in M. C. 1850. Dem. Christian.

Wells, Richard ; farmer ; 2 m n Waverly. Born in Ky. 1813; settled in M. C. 1874. Dem. Protestant.

WHITE, GRANT; farmer ; 1 m e Red House. Born in Tenn. 1855; settled in M. C. 1869. Dem. Protestant.

MONROE TOWNSHIP.

MONROE TOWNSHIP is located in the northwest part of Morgan county, and contains 27 square miles. It is bounded on the north by Hendricks county, on the west by Adams township, on the south by Gregg and Clay, and on the east by Brown. The surface of this township is slightly rolling, with bluffs along the creeks. It is well watered by Sycamore creek and its branches. The soil of the township is more or less of a dark rich loam, mixed with sand, and produces well. There is plenty of gravel in this township to make turnpike, and the citizens are making use of it for that purpose. The township is third in population and second in wealth. Some of the first settlers of this township were Robert McCracken, Henry Brewer, Zimri Allen, James Demoss, Lot M. Hadley, James D. Hadley, T. E. Hadley, Philip Johnson, John H. Bray (94 years), Samuel Hadley, Wm. Weasner, Woodson Lewallen, James Marley, John S. Hubbard, Daniel Ferree, Jonathan Doan, Benjamin Woodard, Hiram Hadley, Amos Marker, Evan Hadley, Mary Myrick (widow of Charles Myrick), Mary Sanborn (widow of A. Sanborn), Sarah Grishan (widow of Thomas Grishan), Thomas Nichols, Joseph Pray, Thomas A. Johnson, Wm. B. Thompson and Wm. Bray.

Monrovia is located about the centre of the township, and contains 460 inhabitants. The present township trustee is John A. Taylor. The board of trustees of the corporation is W. R. McCracken, Dr. Jesse Reagan, J. H. Osborn, Wm. H. Mull and Philip J. Pray.

The school and church privileges of this township are as good as can be found in the State. Her citizens are kind, affable and intelligent. Morality, education and temperance go hand in hand here, thereby making Monrovia the resort for those who wish to educate, and the resort for the retired Israelites. Her business men are energetic and clever, and her improvements are good.

Gasburg is situated in Monroe township, on the gravel road midway between the towns of Monrovia and Mooresville, and contains about 40 inhabitants. It has 1 store, 1 shoe shop, 1 blacksmith shop, steam saw mill, and post office.

CHURCH, LODGE AND SCHOOL STATISTICS.

Christian Church; Monrovia; membership, 35; average attendance of Sunday school, 80; superintendent, J. H. Osborn; value of church property, $3,000.

Antioch M. E. Church, 2 miles east of Monrovia; Pastor, W. H. Fisher; membership, 68; average attendance of Sunday school, 35; superintendent, Alfred Allen; value of church property, $800.

M. E. Church, Monrovia; Pastor, ——— Fish; membership, 200; Sunday school superintendent, W. H. Mull; average attendance of Sunday school, 125; value of property, $1,000.

M. E. Church, Bethesda, 3½ miles east of Monrovia; W. W. Puitt, Pastor; membership, 40; Sunday school superintendent, M. Hornaday; average attendance of Sunday school, 80; value of property, $500.

Friends' Church, West Union, 1 mile east of Monrovia; Ruth Ann Stanton and Enoch Moon, Ministers; membership, 325; Sunday school superintendent, John A. Taylor; average attendance of Sunday school, 120; value of property, $6,000.

M. E. Church, Antioch, 2 miles east Monrovia; Pastor, Rev.

W. H. Fisher; membership, 68; Sunday school superintendent, Alfred Allen; average attendance of Sunday school, 35; value of property, $800.

Freemasons' Monrovia Lodge, No. 261; membership, 70; value of Lodge property, $2,000.

I. O. O. F., Monrovia Lodge, No. 354; membership, 45; value of property, $1,000.

West Union Lodge, Good Templars, No. 664; membership, 37.

North Branch Grange, No. 361; membership, 32; J. M. Cook, Secretary; post office, Mooresville.

Monrovia Grange, No. 89; organized, March, 1873; number of members, 60; Wm. B. Thompson, Master; W. H. Hubbard, Secretary.

J. S. Elliott, Trustee of corporation of Monrovia; school property, $1,000; population of town, 460.

DIRECTORY OF MONROE TOWNSHIP.

Ayers, Jidtham; blacksmith; 2½ m n e Monrovia. Born in N. C. 1824; settled in M. C. 1861. Rep. Methodist.

Allen, John D.; tinner; Monrovia. Born in Ind. 1806; settled in M. C. 1866. Rep. Friend.

Allen, Wm.; Post Master and Justice of Peace; Monrovia. Born in N. C. 1827; settled in M. C. 1859. Rep. Friend.

Allen, Newton; boot and shoe maker; Monrovia. Born in Ind. 1834; settled in M. C. 1837. Rep. Methodist.

ALLEN, ZIMRI; farmer; 1 m e Monrovia. Born in N. C. 1800; settled in M. C. 1826. Rep. Friend.

ALLEN, SARAH; farmer; 1½ m n e Monrovia. Born in N. C. 1818; settled in M. C. 1828. Friend.

ALLRED, WM. R., farmer; 1 m s Gasburg. Born in N. C. 1838; settled in M. C. 1868. Rep. Methodist.

Ayers, Wm.; blacksmith; ¾ m n Gasburg. Born in N. C. 1831; settled in M. C. 1866. Rep. Methodist.

Allen, Enos; farmer; 4½ m n w Monrovia. Born in Ind. 1838. Rep. Methodist.

ACRE, WM.; farmer; 3 m w Monrovia. Born in Ky. 1811; settled in M. C. 1856. Dem. Christian.

Bray, Asa; farmer; 2½ m w Mooresville. Born in Ind. 1827. Rep. Friend.

Bray, John H.; farmer; 2½ m w Mooresville. Born in N. C. 1780; settled in M. C. 1823. Rep. Friend.

BRAY, SIMON H.; farmer; 3 m w Mooresville. Born in Ind. 1847; settled in M. C. 1860. Rep. Methodist.

BREEDLOVE, WESLEY; farmer; 3½ m e Center Valley. Born in N. C. 1812; settled in M. C. 1868. Rep. Meth.

BRAY, E. W.; farmer and inventor of guide and stop for looms; 3 m w Mooresville. Born in Ind. 1820; settled in M. C. 1823. Rep. Methodist.

Bray, Wm. J.; farmer; 3 m w Mooresville. Born in Ind. 1846. Rep. Methodist.

Bray, T. W.; farmer; 3 m w Mooresville. Born in Ind. 1849. Rep. Protestant.

BREWER, JOHN W.; farmer; 2 m n e Monrovia. Born in Ind. 1854. Rep.

Brewer, E. H.; farmer; 2 m n e Monrovia. Born in Ind. 1843. Rep. Methodist.

Bray, Wm.; farmer; 1¼ m n Gasburg. Born in N. C. 1795; settled in M. C. 1825. Rep. Christian.

BRAY, WM. M.; farmer; ½ m n Gasburg. Born in Ind. 1839. Rep. Methodist.

Brewer, Henry; farmer; 1½ m n e Monrovia. Born in Tenn. 1812; settled in M. C. 1830. Rep.

BREWER, CHRIS.; farmer; Monrovia. Born in Ind. 1833. Rep. Methodist.

Bundy, J. E.; farmer; 1 m s w Monrovia. Born in N. C. 1853; settled in M. C. 1858. Rep. Friend.

Benton, M. W.; merchant; local minister; Monrovia. Born in N. Y. 1818; settled in M. C. 1857. Rep. Methodist.

Bishop, Joseph; huckster; 1½ m e Monrovia. Born in Va. 1802; settled in M. C. 1874. Rep. Methodist.

Baldwin, Jesse; farmer; 1¼ m e Monrovia. Born in N. C. 1804; settled in M. C. 1828. Rep. Friend.

Brannon, John; farmer and trader; 1½ m s Monrovia. Born in Ohio 1820; settled in M. C. 1827. Rep.

Bayliff, J. C.; farmer; 3½ m s e Monrovia. Born in Ind. 1845. Rep. Friend.

Bray, I. M.; farmer and trader; 2 m n w Monrovia. Born in Ind. 1840. Indp't. Protestant.

Brown, Edward; farmer; 3½ m n w Monrovia. Born in Ind. 1846. Dem. Christian.

MONROE TOWNSHIP. 321

Brewer, D. W.; farmer; Monrovia. Born in Ind. 1835. Rep. Methodist.

Bundy, J. M.; carriage maker, Monrovia. Born in N. C. 1837; settled in M. C. 1860. Rep. Friend.

Belles, M. E. Miss; Monrovia. Born in Del. 1829; settled in M. C. 1863. Methodist.

Bartholomew, S. E.; farmer; Monrovia. Born in N. C. 1847; settled in M. C. 1869.

Buck, C. M.; spinning; Monrovia. Born in Ind. 1832; settled in M. C. 1851. Rep. Protestant.

Blunk, Brice; farmer; 1¾ m n Hall. Born in M. C. 1835. Dem. Christian.

Cox, Joseph K.; farmer; 3½ m n e Monrovia. Born in N. C. 1823; settled in M. C. 1872. Rep. Friend.

Carter, Joseph; carpenter; Monrovia.

Clark, Alfred; farmer; ½ m s Monrovia. Born in Ind. 1826; settled in M. C. 1853. Rep. Friend.

Cooper, J. G.; farmer; 2 m s e Monrovia. Born in Ohio 1822; settled in M. C. 1856. Rep. Friend.

Cosand, Wm.; farmer and harness maker; Gasburg. Born in N. C. 1841; settled in M. C. 1865. Rep. Methodist.

Chambers, Wm. A.; farmer; 1 m s e Gasburg. Born in Ind. 1853. Rep.

CHAMBERS, BAXTER K.; farmer and trader; 1 m e Gasburg. Born in N. C. 1825; settled in M. C. 1849. Rep. Meth.

Cruse, H. L.; farmer; 4½ m n w Monrovia. Born in N. C. 1845; settled in M. C. 1864. Dem. Christian.

Cruse, T. J.; farmer; 4½ m n w Monrovia. Born in N. C. 1823; settled in M. C. 1856. Granger. Christian.

Doan, Jonathan; farmer; 3 m e Monrovia. Born in Tenn. 1803; settled in M. C. 1828. Rep. Friend.

DOAN, JAMES; farmer; 2 m e Monrovia. Born in Ind. 1837. Rep. Friend.

Davis, J. M.; tile factory; Monrovia. Born in Ind. 1836; settled in M. C. 1870. Rep. Friend.

Dane, D. H.; saw milling; Monrovia. Born in Ind. 1847; settled in M. C. 1865. Indpt. Methodist.

DILLEN, OLIVER A.; farmer; 3 m n e Monrovia. Born in N. C. 1846; settled in M. C. 1867. Rep. Methodist.

Dillen, W. C.; farmer; 3 m n e Monrovia. Born in N. C. 1823; settled in M. C. 1867. Rep. Friend.

DAFFORD, WM. R.; farmer; 2 m s w Monrovia. Born in N. C. 1827; settled in M. C. 1862. Rep. M. Baptist.

Dane, J. B.; farmer and agent for agricultural implements; 1 m s Monrovia. Born in Ind. 1852. Rep. Methodist.

Dane, Henry S.

Dewees, Leander; farmer; 2 m s e Monrovia. Born in Ohio 1847; settled in M. C. 1855. Indp't. Friend.

Dewees, D. B.; farmer; 2 m s e Monrovia. Born in Ohio 1808; settled in M. C. 1855. Rep. Friend.

DEWEES, H. G.; of the firm of Dewees & Son; 2½ m s e Monrovia. Born in Ind. 1852. Rep. Friend.

Dawees, J. C.; 2½ m s e Monrovia. Born in Ind. 1854. Rep. Methodist.

Dewees, Ellis; farmer; 2 m s e Monrovia. Born in Ohio 1814; settled in M. C. 1864. Rep. Friend.

Davis, Jessie W.; farmer; 1 m s e Monrovia. Born in N. C. 1840; settled in M. C. 1868. Rep.

Demoss, James; farmer; 3½ m e Monrovia. Born in Ky. 1803; settled in M. C. 1827. Rep. Methodist.

Doan, T. C.; farmer; 3 m e Monrovia. Born in Ind. 1841. Rep. Friend.

Dewees, E. L.; farmer; 3 m s e Monrovia. Born in Ohio 1814; settled in M. C. 1864. Rep. Friend.

Elliott, J. S.; merchant; Monrovia. Born in Ind. 1838. Rep. Friend.

FAULKNER, LEMUEL; trader; 1¼ m e Monrovia. Born in N. C. 1836; settled in M. C. 1857. Rep. Methodist.

Farmer, G. W.; merchant; Monrovia. Born in Ind. 1847. Rep. Friend.

Fogleman, W. H.; livery stable; Monrovia. Born in Ind. 1827. Rep. Methodist.

Ferree, Daniel; farmer; Monrovia. Born 1807; settled in M. C. 1830. Rep. Friend.

Guyer, Joseph; farmer; 2 m n e Monrovia. Born in N. C. 1784; settled in M. C. 1868. Rep.

Gregory, John; farmer; Gasburg. Born in Ind. 1842. Rep. Methodist.

Gillespie, M. W.; music teacher; Monrovia. Born in Ky. 1824; settled in M. C. 1852. Rep. Methodist.

GUYER, J. M.; farmer; 1 m s e Monrovia. Born in N. C. 1847; settled in M. C. 1860. Rep. Friend.

Gregory, Richard M.; farmer; 3 m s w Mooresville. Born in N. C. 1825; settled in M. C. 1833. Rep. Friend.

Grave, Thos. C.; farmer and stock raiser; 1½ m n w Monrovia. Born in Ind. 1840; settled in M. C. 1853. Rep. Friend.

Giles, John; farmer; Monrovia. Born in Ky. 1843; settled in M. C. 1873. Rep. Methodist.

HADLEY, ZIMRI; farmer; 1¼ m e Center Valley. Born in Ind. 1831. Rep. Friend.

Hayworth, James; 2½ m w Mooresville. Born in Ohio 1818; settled in M. C. 1873. Rep. Friend.

Hayworth, Wm.; farmer; 2½ m w Mooresville. Born in Ind. 1846. Rep. Protestant.

Hadley, Samuel J.; farmer and trader; 3 m w Mooresville. Born in Ind. 1838. Rep. Friend.

HADLEY, E. A.; farmer and trader; 3 m w Mooresville. Born in Ind. 1846. Rep. Friend.

Hadley, N. K.; farmer; 3 m w Mooresville. Born in Ind. 1852. Rep. Friend.

HADLEY, NATHAN; farmer; 3 m w Mooresville. Born in Ind. 1832. Rep. Methodist.

HADLEY, LOT M.; farmer; 4 m w Mooresville. Born in N. C. 1811; settled in M. C. 1823. Indpt. Friend.

Hadley, James D.; farmer; 3 m w Mooresville. Born in N. C. 1807; settled in M. C. 1823. Rep. Friend.

Hadley, Eli; farmer; Monrovia. Born in Ind. 1838. Rep. Friend.

HORNADAY, T. R.; hardware merchant; Monrovia. Born in Ind. 1841. Rep. Methodist.

Hornaday, Wm.; blacksmith; Monrovia. Born in 1819; settled in M. C. 1835. Rep. Methodist.

Hubbard, John S.; farmer; Monrovia. Born in N. C. 1811; settled in M. C. 1830. Rep. Friend.

Hobson, Stephen; farmer; Monrovia. Born in N. C. 1832; settled in M. C. 1869. Rep. Friend.

Hubbard, Nathan E.; farmer and stock dealer; ½ m e Monrovia. Born in Ind. 1840. Rep. Friend.

Henson, Calvin; carpenter; Monrovia. Born in N. C. 1827; settled in M. C. 1856. Rep. Methodist.

Hinshaw, J. A.; farmer; Monrovia. Born in N. C. 1844; settled in M. C. 1870. Rep. Methodist.

Hadley, Evan; farmer and merchant; Monrovia. Born in N.C. 1816; settled in M. C. 1820. Rep. Friend.

Holaday, T. P.; physician; Monrovia. Born in Ohio 1835; settled in M. C. 1872. Rep. Friend.

Hornaday, J. S.; blacksmith; Monrovia. Born in N. C. 1827; settled in M. C. 1838. Rep. Methodist.

Hadley, Jonathan; farmer; Monrovia. Born in Ind. 1836. Rep. Friend.

Hubbard, Sanders; farmer and stock raiser; 1½ m n w Monrovia. Born in Ind. 1844. Rep. Friend.

Hobson, J.; farmer; 2½ m n w Monrovia. Born in N. C. 1814; settled in M. C. 1869. Rep. Friend.

Hobson, J. J.; farmer; 2½ m n w Monrovia. Born in N. C. 1838; settled in M. C. 1838. Rep. Friend.

Hutchens, H. C.; farmer; 2½ m n w Monrovia. Born in N. C. 1838; settled in M. C. 1871. Rep. Methodist.

Hammonds, William; farmer; 4½ m n w Monrovia. Rep. Christian.

Hammonds, Elizabeth; farmer; 3 m w Monrovia. Born in Ind. 1834; settled in M. C. 1856. Christian.

Hunt, Jesse M.; farmer; 2¼ m s w Monrovia. Born in Ohio 1851; settled in M. C. 1865. Rep. Friend.

Hunt, Amos; farmer; 2¼ m s w Monrovia. Born in Va. 1814; settled in M. C. 1865. Rep. Friend.

Hadley, Samuel; farmer; ½ m s Monrovia. Born in N. C. 1811; settled in M. C. 1835. Rep. Friend.

Hobson, Wm. S.; farmer; 1½ m e Monrovia. Born in N. C. 1839; settled in M. C. 1849. Rep. Friend.

Hobson, N.; farmer; 1½ m e Monrovia. Born in N. C. 1845; settled in M. C. 1849. Rep. Friend.

HENLEY, NIXON; farmer and short-horned cattle and long-wool sheep breeder; 1 m s e Monrovia. Born in N. C. 1846; settled in M. C. 1849. Rep. Friend.

Hadley, Solomon; farmer and stock raiser; Monrovia. Born in Ind. 1844. Rep. Friend.

Hinshaw, Barzillia; farmer; ½ m e Monrovia. Born in N. C. 1834; settled in M. C. 1870. Rep. Friend.

Hite, Sanford; farmer; Gasburg. Born in Ky. 1840; settled in M. C. 1850. Rep. Methodist.

HADLEY, T. E.; farmer and trader; ½ m e Monrovia. Born in N. C. 1814; settled in M. C. 1821. Rep. Friend.

Hadley, Hiram; farmer; Monrovia. Born in N. C. 1810; settled in M. C. 1833. Rep. Friend.

Hadley, D. C.; farmer and trader; Monrovia. Born in Ind. 1834. Rep. Friend.

Hobson, Stephen; glove maker; Monrovia. Born in Ind. 1824; settled in M. C. 1871. Rep. Christian.

Johnson, Calvin; farmer; 1½ m n e Monrovia. Born in Ind. 1833. Friend.

Johnson, Philip; farmer; Monrovia. Born in N. C. 1804; settled in M. C. 1828. Rep. Friend.

Johnson, Ashley; farmer; Monrovia. Born in Ind. 1843. Rep. Friend.

Johnson, Mahlon; farmer; Monrovia. Born in Ind. 1835. Rep. Friend.

Johnson, J. H.; farmer; 1¼ m s e Monrovia. Born in Ind. 1840. Rep.

Johnson, Joseph; farmer; ¾ m e Monrovia. Born in N. C. 1854; settled in M. C. 1873. Rep. Methodist.

Johnson, Thomas A.; farmer; ¾ m n w Monrovia. Born in N. C. 1804; settled in M. C. 1836. Rep. Friend.

Johnson, David B.; fire and life insurance; ¾ m n w Monrovia. Born in Ind. 1851. Rep. Friend.

Johnson, Elisha; farmer and produce shipper; ¾ m n w Monrovia. Born in Ind. 1843. Rep.

Johnson, Mary A.; farmer; 3 m n w Monrovia; Born in N. C. 1816; settled in M. C. 1839. Friend.

Johnson, B. R.; druggist; Monrovia. Born in Ind. 1851. Rep. Methodist.

Johnson, James; farmer; 3 m n w Monrovia. Born in N. C. 1838; settled in M. C. 1872. Dem. Christian.

Johnson, Sanford; farmer; 3 m n w Monrovia. Born in Ind. 1845. Rep. Methodist.

Jackson, Z. W.; farmer; 3½ m n w Monrovia. Born in N. C. 1839; settled in M. C. 1873. Dem.

Johnson, Levi; farmer; 4½ m n Monrovia. Born in N. C. 1840; settled in M. C. 1871. Dem. Methodist.

Keller, Michael; farmer; 3 m w Mooresville. Born in Baden, Germany, 1823; settled in M. C. 1849. Rep. Meth.

Latta, J. C.; farmer; 3 m n e Monrovia. Born in N. C. 1819; settled in M. C. 1845. Rep. Methodist.

Long, Wm. K.; farmer; 1 m e Gasburg. Born in Ky. 1821; settled in M. C. 1833. Dem. Christian.

Long, Esther, Miss; farmer; Gasburg. Born in Ind. 1831. Methodist.

Lindley, David; farmer; 1 m n e Monrovia. Born in N. C. 1799; settled in M. C. 1833. Rep. Friend.

Lindley, Aaron; farmer; 1 m n e Monrovia. Born in N. C. 1827; settled in M. C. 1833. Rep. Friend.

Lindley, Jephthah; farmer; 1 m s Monrovia. Born in N. C. 1829; settled in M. C. 1832. Rep. Christian.

Langstaff, Laban; fruit grower; Monrovia. Born in Ohio 1835; settled in M. C. 1865. Rep. Friend.

Langstaff, Benjamin P.; farmer; Monrovia. Born in N. J. 1806; settled in M. C. 1865. Rep. Friend.

Lewallen, Alonzo; farmer; 2 m s w Monrovia. Born in Ind. 1844. Rep. Christian.

Lewallen, Charles; farmer; 2 m s w Monrovia. Born in Ind. 1851. Rep. Christian.

Lewallen, John T.; farmer; 2½ m s w Monrovia. Born in Ind. 1839. Rep. Christian.

Lindley, O. W.; farmer; ¼ m s Gasburg. Born in N. C. 1815; settled in M. C. 1855. Rep. Friend.

Lane, Jasper; farmer; ½ m s Gasburg. Born in Ohio 1840; settled in M. C. 1871. Rep.

Larrance, Wm.; farmer; 4 m s e Monrovia. Born in N. C. 1818; settled in M. C. 1863. Rep. Friend.

Lindley, A. E.; farmer; 1¾ m n w Monrovia. Born in N. C. 1831; settled in M. C. 1839. Rep. Methodist.

MARLEY, DAVID F.; farmer; 1½ m e Center Valley. Born in N. C. 1836; settled in M. C. 1851. Rep. Friend.

McCRACKEN, W. R.; druggist; Monrovia. Born in Ind. 1839. Rep. Christian.

McCracken, Robert; farmer; Monrovia. Born in N. C. 1816; settled in M. C. 1819. Rep. Christian.

McCall, Josiah; engineer; Monrovia. Born in Ohio 1849; settled in M. C. 1865. Rep.

Marker, Curtis; chair maker; 1½ m s Monrovia. Born in Del. 1805; settled in M. C. 1855. Rep. Methodist.

McCracken, Samuel; farmer; 1½ m s w Monrovia. Born in Ind. 1847. Rep. Christian.

McCracken, James; farmer; 1 m s Monrovia. Born in Ind. 1842. Rep. Christian.

Marley, John W.; farmer; 1½ m s e Monrovia. Born in N. C. 1829; settled in M. C. 1857. Rep.

MYRRICK, A. G.; farmer; 3 m e Monrovia. Born in N. C. 1817; settled in M. C. 1852. Rep. Methodist.

Myrrick, Mrs. Mary; farmer; 2½ m e Monrovia. Born in N. C. 1818; settled in M. C. 1828. Methodist.

MYRRICK, CHAS. W., Jr.; book agent; 3 m e Monrovia. Born in N. C. 1850; settled in M. C. 1852. Rep. Prot.

Mull, W. H.; Monrovia; carpenter and undertaker. Born in Tenn. 1819; settled in M. C. 1829. Rep. Methodist.

Metcalf, Rev. W. H.; 3 m e Monrovia. Born in Va. 1812. Present resident.

Marlett, J. T.; carpenter; Monrovia. Born in N. C. 1819; settled in M. C. 1840. Rep. Methodist.

Marlett, D. T.; wagonmaker; Monrovia. Born in N. C. Rep. Methodist.

Nicholas, J. F.; farmer; 4½ m n w Monrovia. Born in Ind. 1842. Rep. Methodist.

Nicholas, Thos.; farmer; Monrovia. Born in Ky. 1806; settled in M. C. 1826. Rep. Methodist.

Odel, T. K.; farmer; ½ m n Monrovia. Born in N. C. 1849; settled in M. C. 1874. Dem. Methodist.

Osborn, J. M.; blacksmith; Monrovia. Born in Ind. 1844; settled in M. C. 1860. Rep. Christian.

OVERMAN, JAMES; farmer; 3 m w Monrovia. Born in N. C. 1851; settled in M. C. 1860. Rep. Protestant.

PERRY, EDWARD; farmer; 3 m n e Monrovia. Born in N. C. 1842; settled in M. C. 1864. Rep. Methodist.

POE, W. S.; dry goods; firm of Ballard & Poe; Monrovia. Born in Ind. 1841. Dem. Independent.

Painter, Thos.; farmer; 1 m s w Monrovia. Born in Ohio 1833; settled in M. C. 1845. Rep. Friend.

PEARCE, ELISHA; farmer and trader; 3½ m n e Monrovia. Born in Ohio 1829; settled in M. C. 1832. Rep. Meth.

Pray, Joseph; tanner; ¼ m s Monrovia. Born in Pa. 1808; settled in M. C. 1835. Rep. Friend.

Pike, Losen; farmer; ½ m e Monrovia. Born in N. C. 1851; settled in M. C. 1873. Rep. Friend.

Plummer, Wm.; farmer; ½ m w Gasburg. Born in Ind. 1823; settled in M. C. 1845. Rep. Methodist.

Parish, David; farmer; 1 m w Monrovia. Born in N. C. 1819; settled in M. C. 1857. Rep. Protestant.

Pruitt, Mordecha; farmer; 4 m n w Monrovia. Dem. Christ.

Philips, Samuel; Merchant; Monrovia. Born in Ind. Rep. Protestant.

Portis, Silas; engineer; Monrovia. Born in N. C. 1833; settled in M. C. 1870. Rep. M. Baptist.

Reames, John; log hauler; Gasburg. Born in Ohio 1836; settled in M. C. 1858. Rep. Methodist.

Reed, Moahtt; harness maker; Monrovia. Born in Ohio 1841; settled in M. C. 1872. Rep. Methodist.

MONROE TOWNSHIP. 333

Reagan, Jesse; physician and surgeon; Monrovia. Born in Ind. 1826; settled in M. C. 1860. Rep. Christ. Temp.

Rushton, George W.; farmer; 2½ m n w Monrovia. Born in Ind. 1847. Rep. Protestant.

Rug, T. J.; clerk in store; Monrovia. Born in Ind. 1839. Rep. Friend.

STANLEY, ELWOOD; 1¼ m e Center Valley. Born in Ind. 1836; settled in M. C. 1861. Rep. Friend.

Scotten, J. A.; farmer; 2 m s e Center Valley. Born in N. C. 1827; settled in M. C. 1862. Dem.

Stanton, Chalkley; farmer; Monrovia. Born in Va. 1806; settled in M. C. 1850. Rep. Friend.

Shover, W. K.; farmer; 2½ m s e Monrovia. Born in Ind. 1850. Rep. Methodist.

Stanton, Elwood; farmer and Berkshire hog breeder; ¾ m e Monrovia. Born in Ind. 1844; settled in M. C. 1874. Rep. Friend.

Steel, Wm.; farmer; 2 m n w Monrovia. Born in N. C. 1823; settled in M. C. 1851. Rep. Methodist.

Scotten, Sol.; farmer; 3½ m n w Monrovia. Born in N. C. 1836; settled in M. C. 1866. Dem. R. Baptist.

Scotten, Enoch; farmer and shoemaker; 2½ m n w Monrovia. Born in Ind. 1838. Dem. R. Baptist.

Sawyer, Dayton; laborer; Monrovia. Born in Ind. 1847. Rep. Protestant.

Smith, E. J.; farmer; 3½ m n w Monrovia. Born in Ind. 1840; settled in M. C. 1869. Dem.

Shields, Elias; farmer; 4 m w Monrovia. Born in Ind. 1836; settled in M. C. 1841. Rep. Christian.

Sawyers, J.; farmer; Monrovia. Born in N. C. 1824; settled in M. C. 1849. Rep. Friend.

THATCHER, JOSEPH K.; farmer; 1½ m n Hall. Born in Ind. 1846; settled in M. C. 1868. Rep. Protestant.

TANSEY, B. E.; carpenter; Monrovia. Born in Ind. 1845. Rep. Methodist.

Thompson, John S.; farmer; 2 m of Center Valley. Born in N. C. 1842; settled in M. C. 1868. Rep. Methodist.

THOMPSON, WM. O.; farmer; 1 m n w Gasburg. Born in N. C. 1825; settled in M. C. 1847. Rep. Methodist.

Thompson, Wm. B.; farmer; Monrovia. Born in N. C. 1813; settled in M. C. 1844. Rep. Methodist.

TAYTOR, J. N.; farmer; ¼ m s w Monrovia. Born in Va. 1813; settled in M. C. 1849. Rep. Friend.

Taylor, Dr. George; ½ m Monrovia. Born in east part of Ireland 1798; settled in M. C. 1873. Rep. Friend.

TINCHER, J. D.; farmer; 3½ m e Monrovia. Born in Ind. 1841. Methodist.

Townsend, T.; farmer; 3 m s w Mooresville. Born in Ind. 1851; Rep. Friend.

Tansey, T. Z.; shoe and boot maker; Monrovia. Born in Ind. 1833. Rep. Methodist.

Thompson, W. H.; saddle and harness maker; Monrovia. Born in Ohio 1838; settled in M. C. 1865. Methodist.

Tansey, Daniel; carpenter; Monrovia. Born in Ind. 1833; settled in M. C. 1845. Rep. Methodist.

Tudor, W. W.; farmer; 4 m w Monrovia. Born in Ky. 1843; settled in M. C. 1859. Dem. Christian.

TURNER, J. B.; farmer; 3½ m n w Monrovia. Born in N. C. 1832; settled in M. C. 1834. Dem. Christian.

Thomas, R. W.; farmer; Monrovia. Born in N. J. 1835; settled in M. C. 1858. Rep.

Taylor, J. A.; proprietor flouring mills; Monrovia. Born in Ind. 1840; settled in M. C. 1849. Rep. Friend.

Williams, Jesse; teamster; Monrovia. Born in Ind. 1850. Indpt.

WOODWARD, BENJ.; farmer; 3½ m w Mooresville. Born in Tenn. 1806; settled in M. C. 1850. Rep. Friend.

Ward, Stephen; farmer; 1¼ m n e Gasburg. Born in N. C. 1811; settled in M. C. 1834. Rep. Methodist.

Ward, David W.; carpenter; 1½ m n e Gasburg. Born in Ind. 1849; settled in M. C. 1857. Rep. Methodist.

WARD, WM. T.; merchant; Gasburg. Born in Ill. 1837; settled in M. C. 1857. Rep. Methodist.

WEESNER, JOHN; carpenter and P. M.; Gasburg. Born in N. C. 1835; settled in M. C. 1838. Rep. Friend.

Welman, J. L.; farmer and carpenter; 2½ m s w Monrovia. Born in Ky. 1831; settled in M. C. 1845. Rep. Christ.

WILSON, DAVID; farmer and granger; 1 m e Monrovia. Born in N. C. 1835; settled in M. C. 1850. Rep.

Weesner, Wm.; farmer and tanner; ½ m e Monrovia. Born in N. C. 1791; settled in M. C. 1838. Rep. Friend.

Weesner, Josiah; farmer; Gasburg. Born in N. C. 1813; settled in M. C. 1838. Rep. Friend.

WELMAN, CHAS.; farmer; 1¾ m e Monrovia. Born in Ind. 1857. Rep. Christian.

WILSON, JEREMIAH; prop'r Wilson House; Monrovia. Born in Va. 1793; settled in M. C. 1861. Rep. Meth.

Warmoth, Wm.; farmer; 4½ m n w Monrovia. Born in Ky. 1844; settled in M. C. 1856. Dem. Christian.

Warmoth, B. B.; farmer; 4½ m n w Monrovia. Born in Ky. 1819; settled in M. C. 1857. Dem. Christian.

Warren, Jesse W.; Monrovia. Born in Ind. 1821; settled in M. C. 1849. Rep. Meth.

York, E. F.; farmer; 1 m e Monrovia. Born in N. C. 1844; settled in M. C. 1866. Rep. Methodist.

York, T. T.; boot and shoe maker; 2 m s Monrovia. Born in N. C. 1838; settled in M. C. 1872. Rep. Methodist.

York, Aaron; shoemaker and tollgate keeper; 1 m e Monrovia. Born in N. C. 1815; settled in M. C. 1866. Rep. Methodist.

York, J. M.; shoe and boot maker; Monrovia. Born in N. C. 1835; settled in M. C. 1872. Rep. Methodist.

RAY TOWNSHIP.

Ray Township is located in the southwest part of the county, and contains about 26 square miles. It is bounded on the north by Ashland township, on the west by Owen county, on the south by White River (it being the line between Ray and Baker townships), and on the east by Jefferson township. The surface of this township is generally broken, but along the river bottoms are some good farms. The rest of the township is good grass lands, and is generally well timbered.

Paragon, a small station on the I. and V. Railroad, about 10 miles southwest of Martinsville, is the only village in the township of any note. Church and school privileges are tolerably good. The Freemasons and Odd Fellows have each a Lodge in Paragon. There are 4 churches in the township, and also 4 school houses, valued at $2850.

The township was once very large but now is quite small, having been divided in the centre, east and west, and Ashland township made. The citizens are generally clever and sociable, and a church-going people. The vote of the township is 204; Republican, 121; Democrat, 83.

CHURCH, LODGE AND SCHOOL STATISTICS.

Christian Church, Paragon; pastor, Wm. A. Hough; Sabbath school superintendent, Wm. A. Hough; membership, 100; average attendance of Sabbath school, 75; value of church property, $3000.

Lutheran Church, Mt. Zion, 3½ miles west of Paragon;

membership, 12; pastor, —— Hinkle; Union Sabbath school superintendent, Wm. Anderson; average attendance of Sabbath school, 50; value of church property, $1000.

Paragon Lodge, U. D., F. and A. M., membership, 23.

Paragon Lodge, No. 406; I. O. O. F.; membership, 43; value of Lodge property, $600.

Paragon Grange, No. 1243; organized, January 30, 1874; No. of members, 25; H. C. Hodges, Master; W. H. Farr, Sec'y.

DIRECTORY OF RAY TOWNSHIP.

Abbedd, Charles; wagon maker; Paragon. Born in Germany, 1815; settled in N. C. 1859. Dem. Lutheran.

Alexander, H. B.; farmer; 2½ m w Paragon. Born in Ind. 1839. Dem. Meth.

Asher, Wm. H.; farmer; 3½ m s e Alaska. Born in Ind. 1846; settled in M. C. 1872. Dem. Protestant.

Baker, J. C.; carpenter and wagon maker; Paragon. Born in Ky. 1828; settled in M. C. 1849. Rep. Christian.

Byram, Anna; boarding house; Paragon. Born in Ind. Christian.

Blankenship, P. M.; farmer; Paragon. Born in Ind. 1846. Rep. Protestant.

Butler, Tobias; farmer; 4 m n w Paragon. Born in Md. 1790; settled in M. C. 1828. Methodist.

Bourn, Elijah; farmer; 5½ n w Paragon. Born in Ky. 1809; settled in M. C. ——. Rep. Christian.

COLLIER, JAMES; farmer; Paragon. Born in Ind. 1829; settled in M. C. 1853. Rep. Christian.

Collier, J. H.; farmer; 1½ m w Paragon. Born in Ind. 1840; settled in M. C. 1856. Dem. M. Baptist.

Cracraft, Reuben; farmer and mechanic; 2½ w Paragon. Born in Ind. 1823; settled in M. C. 1830. Dem. Methodist.

Costton, Harrison; farmer; 4 m n w Paragon. Born in Ky. ——; settled in M. C. 1857. Dem. Protestant.

DUNNAVANT, WM. T.; blacksmith; Paragon. Born in Tenn. 1830; settled in M. C. 1865. Rep. Christian.

Dallins, S. F.; farmer; 2 m w Paragon. Born in Ky. 1849; settled in M. C. 1854. Protestant.

DOW, A. R.; farmer; 3 m n Paragon. Born in Ind. 1834. Dem. Christian.

Eaton, H. C.; farmer; Paragon. Born in Ind. 1843. Protest.

Farr, U. H.; druggist and farmer; Paragon. Born in Ind. 1846. Rep. Protestant.

FREDRICK, L. W.; saw milling and farmer; Paragon. Born in N. C. 1839. Dem. M. Baptist.

Goss, H. C.; farmer; 4½ m n w Paragon. Born in Ind. 1838. Rep. Protestant.

Goss, G. H.; farmer; 4½ m n w Paragon. Born in Ind. 1825. Rep. Protestant.

Goss, Elisha; farmer; 2½ m w Paragon. Born in Ind. 1825; settled in M. C. 1868. Rep. Protestant.

Gaulding, A. E.; hotel keeper; Paragon. Born in Ky. 1845; settled in M. C. 1871. Rep. Protestant.

Gaulding, Abel; machinist; Paragon, Born in Mass. 1821; settled in M. C. 1869. Spiritualist.

Ground, Hiram; farmer; 4 m n e Gosport. Born in N. C. 1823. Dem. Protestant.

Goss, W. J.; farmer; 1 m w Paragon. Born in Ind. 1838; settled in M. C. 1869. Rep. Protestant.

*Goss, George; farmer; 3 m n w Paragon. Born in Ind. 1845; settled in M. C. 1870. Rep. M. Baptist.

GALLEMORE, HENRY; farmer and stock raiser; ¾ m e Paragon. Born in Ind. 1848. Christian.

Gallemore, Noah; farmer; ¾ m e Paragon. Born in Ind. 1846. Rep. Christian.

Hudson, George; farmer; Paragon. Born in Ind. 1842. Dem. Protestant.

Hodges, Eph.; farmer; 1 m w Paragon. Born in Ind. 1820; settled in M. C. 1824. Rep. Christian.

Hodge, H.; farmer; 2 m w Paragon. Born in Ind. 1845. Rep. Protestant.

Haase, J. J.; farmer; 3½ m w Paragon. Born in Ind. 1831.
Dem. Protestant.

Haase, H. H.; farmer; 3 m w Paragon. Born in Ind. 1839;
Dem. Protestant.

Haugh, Wm. A.; pastor Christian church; Paragon. Born in
Ind. 1835; settled in M. C. 1874. Rep.

HODGES, PHILIP; farmer; Paragon. Born in N. C. 1797;
settled in M. C. 1824. Rep. Christian.

Knight, J. H.; physician and surgeon; Paragon. Born in Ind.
1838; settled in M. C. 1854. Rep. Christian.

KENNEDY, JOHN; physician and surgeon; Paragon. Born
in Ind. 1833. Rep. Christian.

Kennedy, D. P.; physician and surgeon; firm of J. & D. P. Kennedy. Born in Ind 1845. Rep. Protestant.

Kennedy, Wm. R.; engineer; Paragon. Born in Ind. 1849;
settled in M. C. 1871. Dem. Protestant.

Lingle, Wm.; farmer; 3 m w Paragon. Born in Ind. 1849.
Rep. Methodist.

Lingle, John; farmer and apiarian; 3 m n e Gosport. Born in
Ind. 1847. Rep. Methodist.

Lingle, Casper; farmer; 3 m n e Gosport. Born in N. C. 1823;
settled in M. C. 1829. Rep. Methodist.

Letterman, Baker; farmer; 4 m n Paragon. Born in N. C. 1820. Dem. Methodist.

Letterman, Joseph; farmer; 4 m n Paragon. Born in Ind. 1847. Dem. Methodist.

McCord, J. D.; merchant; Paragon. Born in Ind. 1845; settled in M. C. 1872. Rep. Protestant.

Marsh, Wales; dealer in saddles and harness; Paragon. Born in N. Y. 1816; settled in M. C. 1859. Protestant.

Mason, Charles; general saw mill; Paragon. Born in Iowa 1840; settled in M. C. 1874. Protestant.

McFarling, L. L.; express agent; Paragon. Born in N. C. 1813; settled in M. C. 1869. Rep. Methodist.

Miller, J. C.; farmer; 7 m n e Gosport. Born in Ind. 1846. Dem. Protestant.

Miller, Robert; farmer; 4 m n w Paragon. Born in Ind. 1841. Dem. M. Baptist.

MORRISON, JAMES; farmer; 2 m n Paragon. Born in Ind. 1844; settled in M. C. 1873. Rep. Protestant.

Marsh, Fielding; farmer; ½ m n Paragon. Born in Ind. 1826; settled in M. C. 1833. Rep. M. Baptist.

Newton, H. H.; farmer; ½ m e Paragon. Born in Ind. 1840. Dem. Protestant.

Neal, S. M.; farmer; ½ m w Paragon. Born in Ind. 1832; settled in M. C. 1866. Dem. Protestant.

Newton, M. J.; farmer; Paragon. Born in 1842. Dem. Prot.

OLIVER, ELBERT W.; saw mill hand; Paragon. Born in Ind. 1834; settled in M. C. 1840. Rep. Methodist.

Owens, B. W.; farmer on Owens' Island; 2 m s w Paragon. Born in Tenn. 1842; settled in M. C. 1871. Rep. Baptist.

Pierson, G. H.; barber and painter; Paragon. Born in Ind. 1841; settled in M. C. 1865. Rep. Protestant.

Pierson, J. M.; confectioner; Paragon. Born in Ind. 1833. Rep. Christian.

PARKER, WM.; carpenter; 4 m n w Paragon. Born in Tenn. 1837; settled in M. C. 1869. Rep. Atheist.

RUSS, DAVID; farmer; 1½ m n Paragon. Born in Ind. 1835; settled in M. C. 1871. Rep. Christian.

Rosengarten, S.; merchant; Paragon. Born in Germany 1812; settled in M. C. 1872. M. Baptist.

Rosengarten, Miss; music teacher; Paragon. Born in Ind. 1857; settled in M. C. 1872. Christian.

Rosengarten, C. O.; merchant; Paragon. Born in Ind. 1852; settled in M. C. 1872. Rep. Protestant.

Ross, J. M.; carpenter; Paragon. Born in Ind. 1847; settled in M. C. 1868. Rep. Protestant.

Ross, Absalom; carpenter; Paragon. Born in Ind. 1839; settled in M. C. 1852. Rep. Protestant.

ROBINSON, E. J.; Eclipse Planing Mill; Paragon. Born in Pa. 1817; settled in M. C. 1867. Rep. Christian.

Robinson, Gabriel; blacksmith; Paragon. Born in Ky. 1828; settled in M. C. 1864. Rep. Christian.

Ross, H. C.; carpenter; Paragon. Born in Ind. 1841; settled in M. C. 1864. Protestant.

Rule, John; teamster; 4½ m n w Paragon. Born in Ind. 1838; settled in M. C. 1873. Dem. Protestant.

Stierwalt, Kener; carpenter; 3 m w Paragon. Born in N. C. 1847. Rep. Christian.

Stierwalt, J. A.; farmer; 3 m n w Paragon. Born in Ind. 1849. Dem. M. Baptist.

Secrest, William A.; engineer; Paragon. Born in Ind. 1852. Rep. Protestant.

Stierwalt, Kenner; farmer; 3½ m n e Gosport. Born in Ind. 1849. Dem. Protestant.

Stierwalt, Adam; farmer; 4 m n w Paragon. Born in N. C. 1800; settled in M. C. 1825. Dem. M. Baptist.

Stapp, W. H.; clerk in Eclipse saw mill; Paragon. Born in Ind. 1843; settled in M. C. 1873. Rep. Protestant.

SECREST, WM. A.; farmer; 1¾ m n Paragon. Born in N. C. 1830; settled in M. C. 1845. Rep. Protestant.

Thompson, P. F.; constable; Paragon. Born in Va. 1847; settled in M. C. 1872. Protestant.

Thompson, J. P., boot and shoe maker; Paragon. Born in Va. 1844; settled in M. C. 1871. Rep. Protestant.

Tackett, Wm.; farmer; 3 m n e Gosport. Born in Ky. 1820; settled in M. C. 1832. Dem. Protestant.

Voshell, D. H.; farmer; 1⅓ m n Paragon. Born in Ind. 1826. Christian.

Vickrey, H. C.; farmer; 3 m s w Paragon. Born in Ind. 1828. Rep. Christian.

Vickrey, C. W.; farmer; 3½ m w Paragon. Born in Ind. 1838. Rep. Christian.

Voshell, L. J.; farmer; 5 m n w Paragon. Born in Ind. 1838. Dem. M. Baptist.

Voshell, J. M.; farmer; 3 m n w Paragon. Born in Ind. Dem. Protestant.

Voshell, John; farmer; 3 m n w Paragon. Born in Ind. 1848. Dem. M. Baptist.

Whitaker, Bland; farmer; 2½ m s e Alaska. Born in Ind. 1829; settled in M. C. 1869. Rep. M. Baptist.

Whitesett, A. J.; Justice of Peace; Paragon. Born in Ind. 1817; settled in M. C. 1847. Rep. Christian.

WALTZ, ABSALOM; saw milling; Paragon. Born in Ohio 1838; settled in M. C. 1872. Dem. Protestant.

Wilson, J. C.; farmer; Paragon. Born in Ind. 1841; settled in M. C. 1856. Rep. Christian.

Wilson, T. O.; farmer; Paragon. Born 18—; settled in M. C. 1860. Dem. Christian.

Whitesett, W.; farmer and teamster; Paragon. Born in Ind. 1838. Rep. Protestant.

WHITAKER, ED.; farmer; 2½ m w Paragon. Born in Ind. 1834. Dem. Protestant.

Whitaker, Bland; farmer; 6 m n w Paragon. Born in Ind. 1847. Christian.

Whitaker, J. K., Sen.; farmer; 2 m s e Alaska. Born in Ky. 1819; settled in M. C. 1843. Protestant.

Whitaker, Levi; farmer; 8 m n e Gosport. Born in Ky. 1804; settled in M. C. 1833. Dem. Protestant.

Whitaker, B. B.; farmer; 2½ m s e Alaska. Born in Ind. 1847. Dem. Christian.

WARTHEN, J. J.; farmer; 3 m n Paragon. Born in Ind. 1834. Dem. Christian.

Warthen, W. S.; farmer; 3 m n Paragon. Born in Ind. 1831. Rep. Protestant.

Walters, R. S.; farmer; 1¼ m n Paragon. Born in Ind 1817; settled in M. C. 1828. Dem. M. Baptist.

Young, Hannibal; farmer; 7 m n e Gosport. Born in Ind. 1839. Rep. Protestant.

Young, J. H.; farmer; 7 m n e Gosport. Born in 1846. Rep. Christian.

WASHINGTON TOWNSHIP.

WASHINGTON TOWNSHIP is the largest civil township in the county, and also contains a greater population and more wealth. Although there is perhaps more broken or waste land in this than can be found in either of the other townships, the surface of the central part generally lies well for cultivation, and the soil is very rich, especially the river bottoms. The south part of the township, and also the north, is more or less broken and rough. The broken land of this township is not very profitable for growing grain, but just the place for fruits, provided that there could be some arrangements made to transport fruit to market in sufficient time after being gathered.

Martinsville, the county seat of the county, is located in this township, and so is also Hastings Station. This township is watered by White River, Indian Creek, and their tributaries. Indian Creek empties into White River about 5 miles southwest of Martinsville. I would give here the names of some of the first settlers, but they have already been mentioned in the historical sketch of the county. The church and school privileges of this township are good, as will be shown by the annexed statistics.

CHURCH, LODGE AND SCHOOL STATISTICS.

M. E. Church, Martinsville; pastor, Rev. H. Hays; membership, about 350; value of church property, $15,000; Sabbath school superintendent, Prof. French; average attendance of Sabbath school, 140.

Christian Church, Martinsville; pastor, N. J. Major; membership, 260; value of church property, $2,000; superintendent of Sabbath school, A. M. Cunning; average attendance of Sabbath school, 120.

Cumberland Presbyterian Church, Martinsville; pastor, W. T. Ferguson; membership, 185; value of church property, when complete, $5,000; Sabbath school superintendent, W. T. Ferguson; attendance of Sabbath school, 101.

St. Martin's Catholic Church; pastor or priest, Henry Kessing; membership, 50; value of church property, $2,000.

Martinsville Lodge, No. 274, I. O. O. F.; membership, 100; value of Lodge property, $2000.

Martinsville Encampment, No. 93; membership, 25.

Martinsville Lodge, No. 74, F. and A. M.; membership, 113; value of Lodge property, $300.

Martinsville Grange; organized, April, 1874, with 17 members; fixtures and furniture not bought; at the time of gathering these statistics the Lodge had held but one meeting; Secretary, H. R. Stevens.

Martinsville school trustees, R. V. Marshall, B. D. Blackstone, E. M. Woody.

Township trustee, Perry F. Douglass; number of school houses in township, 15; value of school property, $8000.

Little Indian Creek M. Baptist Church; located 6 miles southwest of Martinsville; pastor, Rev. John Goodman; membership, 65; value of property, $200.

Ridge Chapel M. E. Church; located 6 miles south west of Martinsville; Rev. Mr. Burge, pastor; membership, 30.

Roberts Creek M. Baptist Church; located 6 miles south east of Martinsville; pastor, Rev. John Goodman; membership, 30; Sabbath school superintendent, Joseph Pollard; attendance of Sabbath school, 20; value of school property, $200.

Sand Creek M. Baptist Church ; 3 miles east of Martinsville ; pastor, J. B. Cox ; membership, 65 ; value of church property, $1000.

Christian Church, Lower Liberty; pastor, Joseph H. Baxter; membership, 75 ; value of property, $1200 ; Sabbath school superintendent, W. K. Hastings ; attendance of Sabbath school, 50.

M. E. Church ; 2 miles west of Mahalasville ; class No. 2 ; pastor, Rev. H. C. Woods ; membership, 10 ; Sabbath school superintendent, Thos. Singleton ; average attendance of Sabbath school, 75.

Sand Creek Grange, No. 1222 ; located 3 miles south east of Martinsville; organized 1874; membership, 52; Master, Nelson Cramer ; Secretary, David Bothwell.

Mahalasville Grange, No. 1365 ; located at Mahalasville ; organized Feb. 10, 1874; membership, 47; Master, Joseph Taggart; Secretary, David M. Gibbs.

Indian Creek Grange ; located 4½ miles south west of Martinsville; organized 1874; membership, 76; Master, John Sheerer ; Secretary, J. C. Duncan.

Clear Creek Grange ; located 5 miles north east of Martinsville; membership, 40; Master, John Williams ; Secretary, M. Hammond.

DIRECTORY OF WASHINGTON TOWNSHIP.

ARMSTRONG, M. E. Miss; dress maker and milliner; Martinsville. Born in Ind. 1842; settled in M. C. 1866. M. Baptist.

ASHER, J. E.; constable; Martinsville. Born in Ky. 1828; settled in M. C. 1835. Rep. Protestant.

Allen, John; stone cutter; Martinsville. Born in Scotland 1820; settled in M. C. 1843.

Acton, W. G.; manager for Singer S. M. Co.; Martinsville. Born in Ind. 1830; settled in M. C. 1872. Rep. Christ.

Axt, F. G.; tanner; Martinsville.

Avery, Monroe; farmer; 3 m s e Martinsville. Born in M. C. 1842. Dem. Protestant.

Avery, Madison; farmer and horticulturist; 3 m s Martinsville. Born in M. C. 1833. Rep. M. Baptist.

AYERS, JOSEPH S.; farmer and machinist; Martinsville. Born in Ga. 1841; settled in M. C. 1866. Dem. Prot.

Allen, W. W.; farmer; 3 m e Martinsville. Born in Ind. 1842; settled in M. C. 1862. Dem. M. Baptist.

Avery, Geo.; farmer; 4 m e Martinsville. Born in N. C. 1801; settled in M. C. 1841. Dem. Protestant.

Avery, Elijah; farmer; 4 m e Martinsville. Born in Ind. 1833; settled in M. C. 1841. Dem. Protestant.

Avery, Jesse; farmer; 3¼ m e Martinsville; Born in M. C. 1829. Dem. M. Baptist.

Askew, M. M.; farmer; 4 m n e Martinsville. Born in N. C. 1821; settled in M. C. 1834. Christian.

ARMSTRONG, DANIEL M.; farmer; 6 m s w Martinsville. Born in Pa. 1824; settled in M. C. 1871. Rep. M. Bap.

Adkins, Jacob; farmer; 6 m s Martinsville. Born in Ky. 1819; settled in M. C. 1833; Rep. Methodist.

Branch, R. H.; clerk in store; Martinsville. Born in Ind. 1852; settled in M. C. 1872. Rep. Christian.

Bucker, John; marble business.

Bales, J. M.; farmer; Martinsville. Born in Ind. 1851; settled in M. C. 1873. Rep. Christian.

Borders, J. M.; blacksmith; Martinsville. Born in Ind. 1839; settled in M. C. 1839. Dem. Methodist.

Branhan, George; clerk; Martinsville. Born in Ind. 1848; settled in M. C. 1869. Rep. Protestant.

Boswell, Scott; sewing machine business; Martinsville. Born in Ind. 1849; settled in M. C. 1873. Rep. Christian.

BROUGHTON, JOHN; farmer; 1½ m s w Martinsville. Born in Ky. 1824; settled in M. C. 1851. Rep. M. Baptist.

BAKER, HENRY C.; teamster; Martinsville. Born in Ind. 1844; settled in M. C. 1844. Rep. Christian.

BURNS, A. J.; farmer; 4 m s Martinsville. Born in M. C. 1844. Rep. Christian.

BLACKLER, Miss E. A.; dress maker; Martinsville. Born in N. J. 1834; settled in M. C. 1856. Dem. Presb.

BURTON, DAVID P.; farmer and granger; Martinsville. Born in M. C. 1848. Rep. Methodist.

Barriard, Sylvanus; farmer; Martinsville. Born in Ohio 1833; settled in M. C. 1846. Rep. Friend.

Baxter, J. H.; school teacher; Martinsville. Born in Ind. 1848; settled in M. C. 1870. Rep. Christian.

Brown, L. J.; farmer; 2 m w Martinsville. Born in M. C. 1844. Rep. Christian.

BALEY, A. M.; marshal; Martinsville. Born in Ind. 1837; settled in M. C. 1842. Rep. Methodist.

WASHINGTON TOWNSHIP. 353

Barnett, W. C.; proprietor marble works; Martinsville. Born in Pa. 1849; settled in M. C. 1871. Rep. Protestant.

Busbee, G. W.; jeweler and watch repairer, and groceries; Martinsville. Born in Ind. 1826; settled in M. C. 1856. Rep. Protestant.

BRANCH, E. F.; dealer in clothing, groceries, seeds and grain; Martinsville. Born in Ind. 1846; settled in M. C. 1865. Rep. Protestant.

BISHOP. W. E.; restaurant; Martinsville. Born in Ind. 1853; settled in M. C. 1873.

BLANKENSHIP, PERRY, Jr.; farmer; Martinsville. Born in M. C. 1850. Rep. Christian.

BAIN, J. G.; firm of Bain & Smock, editors and proprietors of the Morgan Co. Republican. Born in M. C. 1844. Rep. C. Presbyterian.

Bargman, Andrew; farmer; 4 m n Martinsville. Born 1831; settled in M. C. 1858.

Buckner, Jehu; retired farmer; Martinsville. Born in Tenn. 1799; settled in M. C. 1820. Rep. Christian.

Buckner, J. P.; physician; Martinsville. Born in Ind. 1850; settled in M. C. 1866.

Bailey, L. W.; merchant; 5 m n e Martinsville. Born in Ind. 1852; settled in M. C. 1860. Dem. Protestant.

Blackburn, Robert; farmer; 6½ m n e Martinsville. Born in Ind. 1848. Rep. Methodist.

BEISSWEENGER, CHARLES; farmer; 4 m n e Martinsville. Born in Germany 1821; settled in M. C. 1855. Dem. Protestant.

Beissweenger, George; farmer; 4 m n e Martinsville. Born in Germany 1807; settled in M. C. 1856. Rep. Prot.

Baker, T. J.; farmer; 5 m n Martinsville. Born in Ky. 1832; settled in M. C. 1850. Rep. Christian.

Barley, Lewis; farmer; 4½ m n e Martinsville. Born in N. J. 1813; settled in M. C. 1860. Protestant.

Burton, D. P.; farmer; 3 m s w Martinsville. Born in M. C. 1848. Rep. Methodist.

Bullington, W. J.; farmer; 3 m s w Martinsville. Born in Ind. 1828; settled in M. C. 1828. Rep. Christian.

Baker, Dila; farmer; 3 m s w Martinsville. Born in Ky. 1808; settled in M. C. 1828. Christian.

Burton, J. L.; farmer; 4¼ m s w Martinsville. Born in M. C. 1844. Rep. Methodist.

Bothwell, David; farmer; 2 m s e Martinsville. Born in M. C. 1841. Dem. Protestant.

Burns, Wm.; farmer; 7 m s Martinsville. Born in Ky. 1824; settled in M. C. ———. Protestant.

BAKER, G. M.; farmer; 5½ m s Martinsville. Born in Ky. 1814; settled in M. C. 1828. Rep. M. Baptist.

Baker, Absalom; farmer; 5½ m s Martinsville. Born in Ind 1850. Rep. Protestant.

BURNS, GEO. W.; farmer; 4 m s Martinsville. Born in Ky. 1828; settled in M. C. 1828. Rep. Christian.

Buckner, Robert; 3 m s Martinsville. Born in Ind. 1825. Rep. Christian.

Buntel, E.; boot and shoe maker; Martinsville. Born in France 1828; settled in M. C. 1874. Neutral.

Branham, Daniel; proprietor hotel; Martinsville. Born in Ky. 1804; settled in M. C. 1869. Temp. Rep. Christian.

Cain, Patrick; farmer; 6 m s Martinsville. Born in Ireland 1824; settled in M. C. 1853. R. Catholic.

COX, WM.; farmer and granger; 2 m n w Martinsville. Born in Ohio 1820; settled in M. C. 1826. Rep. Protestant.

CLARK, JOHN M.; carpenter; Martinsville. Born in Ind. 1850; settled in M. C. 1850. Rep. Christian.

Clendene, Joseph; farmer; 6 m s e Martinsville. Born in Ind. 1835; settled in M. C. 1835. Rep. Protestant.

CLINGLER, E. W.; Cooper; Martinsville. Born in Ohio 1827; settled in M. C. 1868. Rep. Universalist.

CORDELL, J. E.; hotel keeper; Martinsville. Born in Ind. 1851; settled in M. C. 1867. Rep. Christian.

Cramer, W. S.; blacksmith; Martinsville. Born in N. J. 1851; settled in M. C. 1858. Rep. Methodist.

Cramer, Arch; farmer and blacksmith; Martinsville. Born in N. J. 1803; settled in M. C. 1839. Rep. Methodist.

CARVER, GEO.; railroader; Martinsville. Born in N. J. 1854; settled in M. C. 1858. Rep. Methodist.

Cordell, R. H.; groceries and produce; Martinsville. Born in N. C. 1841; settled in M. C. 1864. Indpt. Protestant.

CRAIG, HIRAM T.; recorder of M. C.; Martinsville. Born in Ky. 1798; settled in M. C. 1819. Dem. O. S. Bapt.

COLEMAN, J. M.; firm of Coffey & Coleman, attorneys; Martinsville. Born in Ind. 1848; settled in M. C. 1852. Dem. Protestant.

Cunningham, N. T.; merchant, farmer and trader; Martinsville. Born in M. C. 1832.

Craytor, A. H.; tailor; Martinsville. Born in M. C. 1833. Rep. Methodist.

CARSON, S. F.; justice of peace; Martinsville. Born in Ohio 1836; settled in M. C. 1858. Rep. Protestant.

Crary, C. S.; insurance agent; Martinsville. Born in Ind. 1845; settled in M. C. 1866. Rep. Protestant.

Cure, H. W.; physician; Martinsville. Born in Ind. 1830; settled in M. C. 1869. Christian.

Carver, A.; cabinet maker; Martinsville. Born in Pa. 1827; settled in M. C. 1857. Rep.

Clark, W. P.; firm of Hardwick & Clark, grist mill; Martinsville. Born in M. C. 1835. Rep. Christian.

Clingler, Pleasant; engineer; Martinsville. Born in Ind. 1849; settled in M. C. 1873. Rep. Protestant.

Clapper, G. W.; firm of Clapper & Co., woolen mills; Martinsville. Born in Pa. 1817; settled in M. C. 1844. Rep. Christian.

CRAMER, WM. S.; farmer and saw milling; 3½ m s e Martinsville. Born in M. C. 1841. Rep. Methodist.

CRAMER, LEWIS P.; carpenter and stone mason; 5 m s e Martinsville. Born in N. J. 1826; settled in M. C. 1857. Rep. M. Baptist.

CANDLER, J. D.; farmer; 2½ m n Martinsville. Born in Ind. 1843; settled in M. C. 1860. Rep. Protestant.

Crank, John; farmer; 5 m n Martinsville. Born in Va. 1811; settled in M. C. 1840. Dem. Protestant.

Crawford, T. M.; farmer; 1 m e Martinsville. Born in Ind. 1845; settled in M. C. 1867. Rep. Protestant.

CLARK, JOHN B.; brick maker; 1½ m s Martinsville. Born in Scotland 1838; settled in M. C. 1860. Rep. Protest.

Crider, Lewis; farmer; 4½ m s w Martinsville. Born in Ky. 1830; settled in M. C. 1846. Rep. Protestant.

CRAMER, D D.; farmer; Martinsville. Born in N. J. 1836; settled in M. C. 1839. Rep. Methodist.

CRAMER, G. W.; farmer; 3½ m s e Martinsville. Born in N. J. 1829; settled in M. C. 1839. Rep. Methodist.

Davidson, James; house painter; Martinsville. Born in Ind. 1812; settled in M. C. 1861. Union. Christian.

DIXON, NORMAN L.; carpenter; Martinsville. Born in N. Y. 1820; settled in M. C. 1868. Rep. Methodist

DAVIS, JOSHUA; carpenter and builder; Martinsville. Born in Ind. 1831; settled in M. C. 1857. Rep. Christian.

Davis, R. T.; harness maker; Martinsville. Born in Ky. 1850; settled in M. C. 1870. Rep. Methodist.

DOUGLAS, PERRY F.; trustee of Washington township; Martinsville. Born in Ohio 1833; settled in M. C. 1857. Indpt. Protestant.

Deturk, L. P.; firm of Deturk Bros., planing mill; Martinsville. Born in Pa. 1836; settled in M. C. 1839. Dem. Prot.

Deturk, A.; firm of Deturk Bros., planing mill; Martinsville. Born in Pa. 1831; settled in M. C. 1839.

DIXON, J. W.; groceries; Martinsville. Born in Ky. 1852; settled in M. C. 1867. Rep. Methodist.

Davee, Joseph; keeper of fine stock and farmer; Martinsville; Born in Ohio 1810; settled in M. C. 1822. Dem. R. Bap.

Danley, G. A.; firm of G. W. Clapper & Co., woolen mills; Martinsville. Born in N. Y. 1837; settled in M. C. 1869. Rep. Christian.

DODD, WM. A.; railroad fireman; Martinsville. Born in N. C. 1835; settled in M. C. 1841. Rep. Protestant.

Davis, J. R.; farmer; ¼ m n w Mahalasville. Born in N. C. 1822; settled in M. C. 1853. Dem. Protestant.

DAVIS, THOS. W.; farmer; ¼ m n w Mahalasville. Born in N. C. 1854; settled in M. C. 1871. Dem. Protestant.

Dyre, Geo.; farmer; 6 m n e Martinsville. Born in M. C. 1834. Dem. Protestant.

DYRE, WASHINGTON; farmer; 6 m n e Martinsville. Born in Ind. 1846; settled in M. C. 1855. Dem. Protestant.

DILINGER, M. L.; farmer; 4 m n e Martinsville. Born in N. C. 1838; settled in M. C. 1865. Dem. Protestant.

Day, Charles; blacksmith; 1 m e Martinsville. Born in Ohio 1828; settled in M. C. 1843. Rep. Protestant.

Duncar, J. C.; farmer; 4¾ m s w Martinsville. Born in Ind. 1838; settled in M. C. 1861. Lib. Methodist.

Downey, John; farmer; 2½ m s w Mahalasville. Born in Ireland 1806. Rep. Methodist.

EVANS, J. R.; marble cutter; Martinsville. Born in Ky. 1850. Rep. Methodist.

Elliott, J. R.; blacksmith and wagon maker; Martinsville. Born in Ky. 1829; settled in M. C. 1831. Rep. Methodist.

EDWARDS, SAM'L E.; farmer; 6 m s Martinsville. Born in Ind. 1834. Dem. M. Baptist.

EGBERT, G. W.; farmer and druggist; Martinsville. Born in Ohio 1824; settled in M. C. 1838. Dem. Protestant.

Endicut, J. W.; barber; Martinsville. Born in Ind. 1845; settled in M. C. 186–. Rep. Protestant.

Edmunds, R. H.; farmer and trader; Martinsville. Born in Ind. 1833; settled in M. C. 1852. Indpt. Methodist.

Eudaly, N. E.; saw milling; Martinsville. Born in Ind. 1842; settled in M. C. 1869. Rep. Christian.

Elliott, Josiah; farmer; 1 m e Paragon. Born in Ind. 1828; settled in M. C. 1833. Protestant.

Egbert, Tiglman H.; druggist; Martinsville. Born in Ind. 1849; settled in M. C. 1849. Dem. Protestant.

ECHOLS, JOHN W.; farmer; 1½ m s Martinsville. Born in M. C. 1849. Rep. Protestant.

ELGIN, NATHAN; farmer; 2¼ m s e Martinsville; Born in M. C. 1851. Rep. Christian.

EDWARDS, WM. S.; farmer and mechanic; 6 m s Martinsville. Born in E. Tenn. 1825; settled in M. C. 1853. Rep. M. Baptist.

Edwards, Thomas; retired farmer; 7 m s Martinsville. Born in Tenn. 1808; settled in M. C. 1830. Dem. Christian.

FAULKNER, S. W.; confectionery and restaurant; Martinsville. Born in Ind. 1832; settled in M. C. 1865. Rep. Methodist.

FRETTS, J. W.; carriage painter; Martinsville. Born in Mich. 1848; settled in M. C. 1872. Indp. Protestant.

Forgeay, John; butcher; Martinsville. Born in Va. 1829; settled in M. C. 1859. Rep. Christian.

FRANC, J. N.; farmer; Martinsville. Born in N. C. 1839; settled in M. C. 1843. Rep. Friend.

FARR, CAM.; deputy sheriff; Martinsville. Born in M. C. 1848. Rep. Christian.

Fowler, H. D.; farmer and trader.

FISHER, CHARLES; blacksmith; Martinsville. Born in Ind. 1851; settled in M. C. 1852. Rep. Presbyterian.

Ferguson, W. T.; Pastor Presbyterian Church; Martinsville. Born in Ky. 1836; settled in M. C. 1870. Rep.

Freeman, A.; hardware, wall paper, saddles and harness; Martinsville. Born in Ind. 1828; settled in M. C. 1845. Dem. Methodist.

Farley, Thomas; farmer and wagonmaker; 3½ m s e Martinsville. Born in Ind. 1820; settled in M. C. 1822. Dem. Protestant.

FARR, WM.; farmer; 5 m n e Martinsville. Born in N. C. 1805; settled in M. C. 1827. Rep. Christian.

Farr, R. C.; farmer; 1 m s e Martinsville. Born in N. C. 1847; settled in M. C. 1865. Dem. Christian.

Ferrin, Isaac; farmer; 6 m s w Martinsville. Born in M. C. 1835. Dem. M. Baptist.

FULKERSON, WM. L.; farmer; 1¼ m n Martinsville. Born in Va. 1824; settled in M. C. 1873. Rep. Methodist.

Fuselman, John; blacksmith; Martinsville. Born in Pa. 1826; settled in M. C. 1845. Dem. C. Presbyterian.

GRUBBS, G. W.; firm of McNut & Grubbs, att'ys; Martinsville. Born in Ind. 1841; settled in M. C. 1868. Rep. M. Baptist.

Gillig, T. M.; barber; Martinsville. Born in Prussia 1847 ; settled in M. C. 1868.

GRAVES, ORANGE; finisher in woolen factory; Martinsville. Born in N. Y. 1821; settled in M. C. 1871. Rep. Presbyterian.

Gilpin, Israel; engineer and machinist; Martinsville. Born in Ind. 1831; settled in M. C. 1848. Dem. Protestant.

Gould, H. S.; conductor on C. & M. R. R. Born in Ind. 1835; settled in M. C. 1871. Rep.

Graves, Preston; sup't woolen mills; Martinsville. Born in N. Y. 1842; settled in M. C. 1866. Rep. Presbyterian.

Gilpin, Scott; engineer; Martinsville.

GREGORY, J. N.; treasurer and collector M. C.; Martinsville. Born in M. C. 1828. Dem. Presbyterian.

Graham, Robert; clerk in store; Martinsville. Born in M. C. 1840. Dem. Presbyterian.

Garner, Henry; farmer; Martinsville. Born in Ind. 1832; settled in M. C. 1874. Dem. Christian.

Gurley, Joseph; carriage maker; Martinsville. Born in Md. 1834; settled in M. C. 1856. Rep. Protestant.

Gurley, J. D.; farmer; Martinsville. Born in Md. 1843; settled in M. C. 1857. Rep. Protestant.

Goodman, Rev. John; 6 m s w Martinsville. Born in Ky. 1826; settled in M. C. 1870. Dem. M. Baptist.

Gose, Philip; farmer; 6 m s w Martinsville. Born in Ind. 1827; settled in M. C. 1846. Dem. M. Baptist.

Gibbs, D. M.; farmer; 1½ m n w Mahalasville. Born in Ind. 1834. Rep. Methodist.

GEYER, G. S.; blacksmith; Martinsville. Born in Pa. 1835; settled in M. C. 1856. C. Presbyterian.

Geyer, J. M.; carriage maker; Martinsville. Born in Pa. 1850; settled in M. C. 1865. Dem. Protestant.

Gilpin, George; carpenter; Martinsville. Born in Ind. 1829; settled in M. C. 1851. Rep. Protestant.

GARRETT, ABSALOM; farmer; 4 m s e Martinsville. Born in N. C. 1803; settled in M. C. 1835. Dem. Lutheran.

Garrett, Michael; farmer; 4 m s e Martinsville. Born in M.C. 1837. Dem. M. Baptist.

GLADDEN, ISAAC T.; farmer; 5 m s e Martinsville. Born in M. C. 1850. Rep. Protestant.

Goss, Winter; farmer; 6½ m s w Martinsville. Born in M. C. 1828. Rep. Protestant.

Harris, J. F.; merchant tailor; Martinsville. Born in France 1820; settled in M. C. 1866.

Hunt, Aaron D.; farmer; 3 m e Martinsville. Born in N. J. 1816; settled in M. C. 1853. Dem. Protestant.

HUNT, H. A.; farmer and carpenter; 3 m e Martinsville. Born in N. J. 1848; settled in M. C. 1853. Dem. Prot

Hoover, M.; firm of Hoover & Renner, flouring mill; Mahalasville. Born in Ind. 1833; settled in M. C. 1872. Prot.

Henderson, E.; farmer and pork packer; Martinsville. Born in M. C. 1833. Dem. R. Baptist.

Hatry, L.; clothing store; Martinsville. Born in Germany 1841; settled in M. C. 1865.

Hardwick, John; miller; Martinsville. Born in Ind. 1840. Rep. Protestant.

Headley, Hillary; boot and shoe business; Martinsville. Born in Ohio 1848; settled in M. C. 1869. Rep. Protestant.

Headley, J. M.; boot and shoe business; Martinsville. Born in Ohio 1844; settled in M. C. 1869. Rep. Methodist.

HAMMOND, WM.; farmer; Martinsville. Born in M. C. 1836. Rep. Methodist.

Hammond, A. J.; 2½ m e Martinsville. Born in M. C. 1851. Rep. Methodist.

Hart. J. H.; clerk in drug store; Martinsville. Born in Pa. 1852; settled in M. C. 1868. Rep. Christian.

Harrison, W. R.; firm of Harrison & Sherley; Martinsville. Born in Tenn. 1822; settled in M. C. 1848.

Hite, Milt., Jr; firm of Stevens & Hite, general merchandize; Martinsville. Born in Ind. 1848; settled in M. C. 1855.

Harryman, Byron; barber; Martinsville. Born in M. C. 1850. Rep. Protestant.

Huxley, C. B.; farmer and stock raiser; Martinsville. Born in Ohio 1838; settled in M. C. 1866. Rep. Indpt.

Hite, M.; Pres't First National Bank; Martinsville. Born in Ky. 1815; settled in M. C. 1855.

Hooten, I. A.; farmer; 4 m s w Martinsville. Born in Ind. 1849; settled in M. C. 1862. Rep. Protestant.

HASTINGS, REES; farmer; 5 m s w Martinsville. Born in Pa. 1815; settled in M. C. 1835. Rep. Christian.

Hastings, W. K.; farmer; 5 m s w Martinsville. Born in M. C. 1840. Rep. Christian.

Hovious, Rachel; 6 m s w Martinsville. Born Ky. 1791; settled in M. C. 1873. M. Baptist.

HASTINGS, ISAAC; farmer; 2 m s w Martinsville. Born in Pa. 1815; settled in M. C. 1833. Rep. Christian.

Hastings, E. J.; farmer; 2 m s w Martinsville. Born in Ind. 1819; settled in M. C. 1833. Rep. Christian.

HASTINGS, WM. K.; farmer; 2 m s w Martinsville. Born in M. C. 1849. Rep. Christian.

Hastings, Wm.; farmer; 2 m s w Martinsville. Born in Pa. 1785; settled in M. C. 1833. Rep. Christian.

Hastings, N. T.; farmer; 2 m s w Martinsville. Born in M. C. 1845. Rep. Christian.

Hawk, John S.; farmer; 3 m n Martinsville. Born in N. J. 1802; settled in M. C. 1853. Rep. Christian.

HAWK, SAMUEL T.; farmer; 3 m n Martinsville. Born in N. J. 1844; settled in M. C. 1868. Rep. Christian.

Hendricks, Thompson; farmer; 2 m n Martinsville. Born in Tenn. 1814; settled in M. C. 1829. Rep. Christian.

Hull, E. E.; farmer; 2¼ m s e Martinsville. Born in N. J. 1823; settled in M. C. 1866. Protestant.

Hanna, J. W.; farmer; 3 m s e Martinsville. Born in Ky. 1834; settled in M. C. 1867. Dem. Protestant.

HARRYMAN, G. W.; brick mason; Martinsville. Born in M. C. 1842. Rep. Methodist.

Hastings, N. T.; farmer; 2 m s Martinsville. Born in M. C. 1845. Rep. Christian.

Haywood, Benjamin; blacksmith; Martinsville. Born in N. J. 1816; settled in M. C. 1840. Dem. Presbyterian.

Helton, W.; farmer; 4 m s e Martinsville. Born in M. C. 1841. Dem. Protestant.

Hutoon, Henry; farmer; 5 m s e Martinsville. Born in Ohio 1810; settled in M. C. 1855. Dem. Protestant.

Hatley, Wm.; farmer; 5 m s e Martinsville. Born in M. C. 1830. Dem. M. Baptist.

Hammons, John; farmer; 1½ m e Martinsville. Born in Va. 1809; settled in M. C. 1830. Rep. Christian.

Hammons, Winfield S.; 1½ m e Martinsville. Born in M. C. 1849. Rep. Protestant.

Hammons, Matilda; farmer; 2½ m e Martinsville. Born in Ind. 1814; settled in M. C. 1829. Methodist.

HAMMONDS, HARVEY; farmer; 3¼ m e Martinsville. Born in M. C. 1848. Rep. Protestant.

Huff, Geo. M.; farmer; 5 m n e Martinsville. Born in Ind. 1852; settled in M. C. 1873. Rep. Protestant.

WASHINGTON TOWNSHIP.

Hall, C. W.; miller; 5 m n e Martinsville. Born in Ohio 1836; settled in M. C. 1840. Liberal. Protestant.

Hatley, L. S.; farmer; Martinsville. Born in M. C. 1840. Rep. M. Baptist.

Hatley, Austin; farmer; 4 m s Martinsville. Born in N. C. 1822; settled in M. C. 1850. Dem. M. Baptist.

Hobbs, I. C.; farmer; 5 m s e Martinsville. Born in N. C. 1816; settled in M. C. 1842. Protestant.

Harper, Branson; farmer; 4 m s Martinsville. Born in N. C. 1824; settled in M. C. 1830. Protestant.

JONES, JONATHAN; farmer; 1½ m n w Mahalasville. Born in M. C. 1836. Dem. Protestant.

Jackson, Jeremiah; farmer; 5 m n Martinsville. Born in Tenn. 1816; settled in M. C. 1828. Dem. Protestant.

JARRETT, MICHAEL; farmer; 3½ m s e Martinsville. Born in Ind. 1837. Dem. Protestant.

Johnson, W. C. W.; wagon maker; Martinsville. Born in N. J. 1827; settled in M. C. 1843. Rep. Methodist.

Jacobs, James; feed and sale stable; Martinsville.

Jerman, A. P.; wagon maker; Martinsville. Born in Ohio 1833; settled in M. C. 1850.

Johnson, J. J.; firm of Johnson & Long, druggist and physician; Martinsville. Born in Ind. 1828; settled in M. C. 1850. Rep. Methodist.

Jordan, James H.; attorney; Martinsville. Born in Ind. 1832; settled in M. C. 1871. Rep. Presbyterian.

JOHNSON, I. S.; teamster; Martinsville. Born in N. C. 1828; settled in M. C. 1828. Rep. Presbyterian.

Jordan, J. H.; firm of Mitchel & Jordan, attorneys; Martinsville. Born in Va. 1842; settled in M. C. 1871. Rep. Protestant.

KENNEDY, WM. W.; high sheriff M. C.; Martinsville. Born in M. C. 1843. Rep. Protestant.

King, James; boot and shoe maker; Martinsville. Born in Pa. 1818; settled in M. C. 1850.

Kennedy, J. E.; grocery and silversmith; Martinsville. Born in Ohio 1837; settled in M. C. 1866. Rep. Methodist.

Keneday, J. G.; dentist; Martinsville.

KISER, C. W.; carpenter; Martinsville. Born in Mo. 1854; settled in M. C. 1866. Dem. Protestant.

KRINER, B. F.; wagon maker; Martinsville. Born in Pa. 1849; settled in M. C. 1858. Rep. Methodist.

Kiefer, J. C.; blacksmith; Martinsville. Born in Germany 1842; settled in M. C. 1856. Rep. Christian.

Kent, Isaac; farmer; 4 m s e Martinsville. Born in Va. 1786; settled in M. C. 1826. Dem. Protestant.

Kent, Joseph; farmer; 3¼ m e Martinsville. Born in Ky. 1824; settled in M. C. 1837. Dem. Methodist.

Kent, John; farmer; 3¼ m e Martinsville. Born in Ky. 1813; settled in M. C. 1837. Dem. Methodist.

Koons, Manford; farmer; 3 m n e Martinsville. Born in M. C. 1851. Dem. Protestant.

LEE, JOHN F.; farmer; 1 m n w Mahalasville. Born in M. C. 1852. Dem. Protestant.

Leonard, Charles; farmer; 2 m s Cope. Born in Ind. 1844; settled in M. C. 1869. Dem. Protestant.

Leonard, J. W.; farmer and merchant; 5 m n e Martinsville. Born in Ind. 1850; settled in M. C. 1869. Dem. Christ.

Laughlin, L. A.; farmer; 3 m n e Martinsville. Born in M. C. 1832. Dem. Protestant.

Long, Charles; farmer; 4 m s Martinsville. Born in Ind. 1829. Rep. Protestant.

Long, J. R.; firm of Johnson & Long, druggists; Martinsville. Born in M. C. 1827. Rep. Methodist.

LAUBACH, LEVI; stoves and tin ware; Martinsville. Born in Pa. 1832; settled in M. C. 1873. Indpt. Methodist.

LEONARD, J. P.; machinist; Martinsville. Born in N. C. 1836; settled in M. C. 1836. Dem. Methodist.

Lipp, H.; carpenter; Martinsville. Born in Pa. 1837; settled in M. C. 1870. Dem. Presbyterian.

LOYD, W. G.; timber man; Martinsville. Born in Ky. 1828; settled in M. C. 1873. Rep. Christian.

Lash, Marshall; bricklayer; Martinsville. Born in N. J. 1848; settled in M. C. 1859. Rep. Protestant.

Lee, B. J.; physician and surgeon; Martinsville.

Lewis, Jacob; plasterer; Martinsville. Born in N. C. 1830; settled in M. C. 1836. Indpt. Methodist.

Logan, Luke; boot and shoe maker; Martinsville. Born in Europe 1843; settled in M. C. 1872. Indpt. Catholic.

LOCKHART, A.; wine, liquor, tobacco and cigars; Martinsville. Born in Europe 1832; settled in M. C. 1861. Dem. Episcopal.

LEWIS, J. A.; furniture and undertaker; Martinsville. Born in N. J. 1833; settled in M. C. 1855. Dem.

Ledrow, Geo.; farmer; 7 m s w Martinsville. Born in Ohio 1823; settled in M. C. 1868. Rep. Methodist.

LOUTT, CHARLES; sawmilling; 2½ m s w Mahalasville. Born in Europe 1844; settled in M. C. 1871. Rep. Prot.

Mast, Harry; clerk; Martinsville. Born in N. C. 1840; settled in M. C. 1872. Dem. Protestant.

Michael, H. Gone from home.

Manderville, J. H.; stone mason; 4½ m s e Martinsville. Born in N. J. 1798; settled in M. C. 1866. Rep. Protestant.

McKENEY, WM. J.; farmer; 5¼ m s Martinsville. Born in Ky. 1841; settled in M. C. 1869. Dem. Protestant.

Miles, W. T.; teamster; 1½ m e Martinsville. Born in M. C. 1848. Dem. Christian.

MABEE, WM.; carpenter and contractor; 3 m e Martinsville. Born in N. J. 1822; settled in M. C. 1854. Dem. Prot.

Mabee, J. L.; carpenter; 3 ·m e Martinsville. Born in N. J. 1851; settled in M. C. 1854. Dem. Protestant.

Mills, W. E.; carpenter; Martinsville. Born in M. C. 1837. Rep. Protestant.

MILLER, L. A.; farmer; 3 m n e Martinsville. Born in Prussia 1833; settled in M. C. 1848. Rep. Protestant.

Mullins, S. R.; farmer; 5 m n Martinsville. Born in N. J. 1839; settled in M. C. 1863. Dem. Christian.

MULLINS, MARY A. M.; dress maker; 5 m n Martinsville. Born in M. C. 1843. Protestant.

Major, Sylvanus; farmer; 4 m n Martinsville. Born in M. C. 1849. Rep. Christian.

Mains, Mary C.; farmer; 1 m e Martinsville; Born in Ohio 1817; settled in M. C. 1867. Methodist.

Moore, Geo. W.; brick maker; 1½ m s Martinsville. Born in N. C. 1818; settled in M. C. 1840. Rep. Christian.

Maxwell, J. J.; farmer; 4 m s w Martinsville. Born in M. C. 1839. Lib. Protestant.

McCracken, S. G.; Deputy Treasurer of M. C.; Martinsville. Born in M. C. 1849. Rep. Christian.

MITCHELL, THOS. B.; in Clerk's office; Martinsville. Born in M. C. 1837. Rep. Protestant.

McNUTT, C. F.; firm of McNutt & Grubbs, att'ys; Martinsville. Born in Ind. about 1836; settled in M. C. 1862. Dem. Protestant.

Mason, L. P.; saw milling and dealer in lumber; Martinsville. Born in Ohio 1842; settled in M. C. 1873. Rep. C. Pres.

McHale, Anthony; boot and shoe business; Martinsville. Born in Europe 1848; settled in M. C. 1870. Ind. Catholic.

MATTHEWS, L. B.; grocery and bakery; Martinsville. Born in Md. 1825; settled in M. C. 1856.

McCracken, C. A.; clerk and book-keeper; Martinsville. Born in M. C. 1846. Rep. Presbyterian.

Marshall, L. P.; printer; Martinsville. Born in Florida 1856. Rep. Presbyterian.

Moran, John; pump manufacturer; Martinsville. Dem. Meth.

Mitchell, G. S.; M. D.; Martinsville. Born in Ind. 1852. Rep. Christian.

MORAN, EDWARD; firm of Olds & Moran, sawmill; Martinsville. Born in M. C. 1852. Presbyterian.

Morrison, Wm.; plasterer and contractor; Martinsville. Born in Ireland 1836; settled in M. C. 1847. Rep. Presbyterian.

MILLER, PETER; boots and shoes, billiards, etc.; Martinsville. Born in Prussia 1817; settled in M. C. 1852.

McMILLAN, JOHN; driven well business; Martinsville. Born in Ohio 1840; settled in M. C. 1873. Dem. Pres.

McCracken, D. F.; tinner; Martinsville. Born in Mo. 1837; settled in M. C. 1866. Rep. What is to be will be.

MITCHELL, I. M.; farmer, merchant and banker; Martinsville. Born in Ky. 1809; settled in territory 1810; settled in M. C. 1829. Rep.

Morrison, Thos.; firm of Morrison Bros.; Martinsville. Born in Ireland 1832; settled in M. C. 1843. Rep. Presb.

Maxwell, J. J.; 4½ m s w Martinsville. Born in Ind. 1839; settled in M. C. 1839. Liberal. Protestant.

Masters, John; farmer; 2¼ m s e Martinsville. Born in S. C. 1798; settled in M. C. 1838. Rep. Christian.

MORRISON, JAMES; farmer; Martinsville. Born in Ireland 1802; settled in M. C. 1857. Rep. Presbyterian.

Miller, Wm. H.; hardware, tinware and stoves; Martinsville. Born in Ind. 1819; settled in M. C. 1837. Rep. Christ.

Mitchell, E. V. drugs; Martinsville. Born in Ind. 1852.

Mitchell, John K.; dry goods; Martinsville. Born in Ind. 1840.

Mitchell, James M.; dry goods; Martinsville.

Marshall, R. V.; assistant P. M.; Martinsville. Born in Ind. 1821; settled in M. C. 1865. Rep. Methodist.

MITCHELL, S. M.; firm of Mitchell & Son, merchants and bankers; Martinsville. Born in Ind. 1814; settled in M. C. 1832. Rep. Christian.

Mitchell, W. C.; firm of Mitchell & Son; Martinsville. Born in M. C. 1842. Rep. Christian.

Marshall, A. H.; physician; firm of Marshall & Co.; Martinsville. Born in Ind. 1852; settled in M. C. 1865.

Martin, James; farmer; 5½ m s w Martinsville. Born in Ohio 1819; settled in M. C. 1827. Dem. Christian.

McClure, Robert; farmer; 3 m s Martinsville. Born in Ind. 1841. Dem. Methodist.

Mann, K. K.; mechanic; Martinsville. Born in Ky. 1832 settled in M. C. 1865. Rep. Methodist.

NUTTER, C. H.; farmer, carriage work, &c.; Martinsville. Born in Ky. 1820; settled in M. C. 1829. Rep. Christ.

Nutter, I. W.; farmer; 4 m n Martinsville. Born in Ind. 1839. Rep. Christian.

Nixon, John B.; physician; 5 m n e Martinsville. Born in Ohio 1835; settled in M. C. 1871. Dem. Protestant.

Northern, W. H.; farmer; 4½ m n e Martinsville. Born in M. C. 1846. Rep. Protestant.

NORTHERN, WM.; farmer and trader; 4½ m n e Martinsville. Born in M. C. 1834. Lib. Protestant.

Northern, Tilford; farmer; 5 m n Martinsville. Born in M. C. 1849. Rep. Protestant.

Northern, John; farmer and blacksmith; 5 m n Martinsville. Born in N. C. 1799; settled in M. C. 1822. Rep. Christ.

Northern, L. G.; farmer; 5 m n Martinsville. Born in M. C. 1835. Dem. Protestant.

OLDS, F. A.; firm of Olds & Moran; saw mill; Martinsville. Born in M. C. 1850. Christian.

PHELPS, F. P. A.; attorney; Martinsville. Born in Ind. 1822; settled in M. C. 1829. Rep. Protestant.

Proctor, D. B.; farmer; Martinsville. Born in Va. 1801; settled in M. C. 1860. Neutral. Christian.

Pool, Wm.; farmer; 1 m s Martinsville. Born in Ohio 1813; settled in M. C. 1820. Rep. Protestant.

WASHINGTON TOWNSHIP.

Pratt, Wm. Y.; carpenter; Martinsville. Born in Va. 1834; settled in M. C. 1836. Rep. Methodist.

Parks, P. S.; local editor Gazette; Martinsville. Born Ind. 1833;

Parks, T. H.; dry goods merchant; Martinsville.

Parks, M. H.; attorney; Martinsville. Born in M. C. 1842.

Parks, P. M.; farmer; 1 m n Martinsville.

Parks, W. E.; student; Martinsville. Born in M. C.

PHELPS, TUELL; clerk for Cunningham; Martinsville. Born in M. C. 1850. Rep. Protestant.

POTTENGER, JOHN; firm of Jacobs & Pottenger, livery stable; Martinsville. Born in Ind. 1845; settled in M. C. 1873. Rep.

Pennington, Nelson; sawmilling and engineer; Martinsville. Born in Va. 1845; settled in M. C. 1858.

Preston, G. W.; farmer; Martinsville. Born in Ind. 1828; settled in M. C. 1828.

PAYNE, JAMES M.; farmer; 3 m s e Martinsville. Born in Ind. 1837; settled in M. C. 1865. Dem. Protestant.

PAYNE, THOS. J.; farmer; 3 m s e Martinsville. Born in Ind. 1833; settled in M. C. 1865. Dem. Protestant.

Payne, J. W.; farmer; 3 m s e Martinsville. Born in N. C. 1803; settled in M. C. 1865. Dem. Methodist.

Parker, Charles; farmer; 5 m s e Martinsville. Born in N. C. 1820; settled in M. C. 1824. Dem. Protestant.

Pearcy, George; farmer; 3 m e Martinsville. Born in Ind. 1842; settled in M. C. 1846. Dem. Protestant.

Pearcy, Van. B.; farmer; 2½ m e Martinsville. Born in Ind. 1843; settled in M. C. 1846. Dem. Protestant.

PEARCY, MADISON; farmer; 5 m n e Martinsville. Born in Ind. 1845; settled in M. C. 1859. Dem. Protestant.

PARKER, CHARLES; farmer; 3½ m s e Martinsville. Born in M. C. 1851. Protestant.

Parker, Jacob; farmer; 3 m s e Martinsville. Born in Ind. Dem. Protestant.

Quackenbush, Benj.; farmer; 5 m n Martinsville. Born in Ind. 1853; settled in M. C. 1867. Rep. Protestant.

RAWLINGS, JAS. P.; farmer; 2 m s Martinsville. Born in Ind. 1836; settled in M. C. 1856. Rep. Methodist.

Reynolds, L. D.; chair maker; 3½ m n e Martinsville. Born in Ohio 1824; settled in M. C, 1852. Rep. Protestant.

RAINAR, JOHN; farmer and blacksmith; 4 m n e Martinsville. Born in Germany 1819; settled in M. C. 1852. Dem. Protestant.

Russell, Ezra; farmer; 4 m n e Martinsville. Born in N. C. 1798; settled in M. C. 1831. Dem. Christian.

Russell, Wm.; farmer; 4 m n e Martinsville. Born in M. C. 1840. Dem. Christian.

RUSSELL, ISRAEL; farmer; 5 m n Martinsville. Born in M. C. 1848. Dem. Protestant.

Rudicel, M. S.; farmer; 5 m n Martinsville. Born in M. C. 1843. Dem. Christian.

Ritter, L. W.; manager of Indian Creek mills; 2 m s Martinsville. Born in Ind. 1832; settled in M. C. 1874. Rep. Methodist.

Reed, James; farmer; 3 m s w Martinsville. Born in M. C. 1825. Rep. Methodist.

Rose, Aaron; farmer; 1 m n Martinsville. Born in N. J. 1829; settled in M. C. 1838. Rep. Methodist.

Robinson, Y. J.; farmer; 1 m w Martinsville. Born in Tenn. 1828; settled in M. C. 1871. Methodist.

ROBINSON, J. L.; laborer; ½ m w Mahalasville. Born in N. J. 1829; settled in M. C. 1865. Dem. Protestant.

REED, NAAMAN; farmer; 3½ m s Martinsville. Born in Ky. 1813; settled in M. C. 1831. Rep. Methodist.

Reed, Noah; farmer; 3½ m s Martinsville. Born in Ind. about 1850. Rep. Methodist.

Ryan, J. W.; musical instruments; Martinsville. Born in Ind. 1847. Rep. Protestant.

RILEY, EDWARD; clerk in butcher shop; Martinsville. Born in N. J. 1852; settled in M. C. 1868. Rep. Protestant.

RADFORD, WM.; agricultural implements; Martinsville. Born in Ky. 1833; settled in M. C. 1838. Ind. Meth.

Rothwell, John; farmer; 1¼ m s Martinsville. Born in Ireland 1803; settled in M. C. 1839. Dem. Presbyterian.

ROWE, MERWIN; grocery; Martinsville. Born in N. Y. 1830; settled in M. C. 1871. Rep. Methodist.

REINHART, G. W.; farmer; Martinsville. Born in M. C. 1853. Rep. Protestant.

Ray, James; cabinet maker; Martinsville. Born in Va. 1784; settled in M. C. 1833. Rep. Protestant.

ROOKER, J. S.; painter, grainer and paper hanger; Martinsville. Born in Ind. 1835; settled in M. C. 1867.

RECORD, WILLIS; Clerk of M. C.; Martinsville. Born in Ind. 1826; settled in M. C. 1836. Rep. Protestant.

Robinson, H. C.; physician and surgeon; Martinsville. Born in Ky. 1849; settled in M. C. 1865. Rep. Protestant.

Richey, E. P.; physician and surgeon; Martinsville. Born in Ind. 1845; settled in M. C. 1873. Rep. Protestant.

Ray, J. F.; Deputy Auditor; Martinsville. Born in Ky. 1830; settled in M. C. 1832.

Reed, W. F.; printer; Martinsville. Born in Ind. 1851. Rep. Methodist.

REESE, J.; artist and ornamental painter; Martinsville.

Ryan, G. W.; firm of Ryan Bros., music dealers; Martinsville. Born in M. C. 1845. Rep. Protestant.

Smith, Sallie; milliner and fancy hair goods; Martinsville. Settled in M. C. 1860. Methodist.

SMOCK, H. A.; firm of Bain & Smock, editors and proprietors of Morgan Co. Republican. Born in Indiana 1846; settled in M. C. 1870. Rep. Christian.

WASHINGTON TOWNSHIP. 379

Sherley, W. S.; firm of Harrison & Sherley, attorneys; Martinsville. Born in Ky. 1836; settled in M. C. 1858.

Stevens, John; firm Stevens & Hite, general merchants; Martinsville. Born in M. C. 1832. Rep. Protestant.

SHORT, H. N.; Superintendent of schools; Martinsville. Born in Ind. 1842; settled in M. C. 1871.

Sims, Henry; farmer, stock dealer and broker; Martinsville. Born in N. J. 1819; settled in M. C. 1821. Rep. Lib.

Stout, A.; farmer; Martinsville. Born in Ind. 1815; settled in M. C. 1839; Dem. M. Baptist.

Schofield, S. H.; physician; Martinsville. Born in Pa. 1826; settled in M. C. 1845. Dem. Methodist.

STEVENS, H. R.; farmer; Martinsville. Born in M. C. 1841. Rep. Protestant.

Sims, C. F.; proprietor harness shop; Martinsville. Born in M. C. 1833. Presbyterian.

Smith, W. P.; justice of peace and minister; Martinsville. Born in Ind. 1809; settled in M. C. 1840. Rep. Methodist.

Swawger, H. T.; boot and shoe business; Martinsville. Born in Pa. 1836; settled in M. C. 1870. Rep. Presbyterian.

Smith, J. E.; hardware, tinware and stoves; Martinsvllle. Born in Ky. 1840; settled in M. C. 1874. Rep. Methodist.

Sailors, Charles; blacksmith; Martinsville. Born in Ind. 1846. Protestant.

SAXEA, CHAS.; tanner and farmer; Martinsville. Born in Germany 1820; settled in M. C. 1868. Rep. Protestant

SCHAUB, PHILIP; tanner; Martinsville. Born in Germany 1824; settled in M. C. 1864.

Sailors, G. W.; blacksmith; Martinsville. Born in Ind. 1844; settled in M. C. 1844. Rep. Protestant.

Stipp, B. F.; farmer; Martinsville. Born in Ohio 1813; settled in M. C. 1820. Rep. Protestant.

SHIREMAN, HENRY; farmer; Martinsville. Born in N. C. 1823; settled in M. C. 1839. Dem. Protestant.

SMITH, J. S.; coal dealer; Martinsville. Born in Ind. 1842; settled in M. C. 1861. Rep. Methodist.

SHEPPARD, I. D.; firm of Sheppard & Son, saddle and harness shop; Martinsville. Born in N. J. 1811; settled in M. C. 1834. Rep. Methodist.

Sheppard, J. S.; firm of Sheppard & Son, saddles and harness; Martinsville. Born in M. C. 1839. Rep. Methodist.

Shireman, Arch; blacksmith; Martinsville. Born in Ind. 1852. Rep. Protestant.

STINSON, E. P.; farmer; ½ m w Mahalasville. Born in N. C. 1829; settled in M. C. 1859. Rep. Methodist.

Simms, Abraham; farmer and saw mill; 2 m e Martinsville. Born in N. C. 1820; settled in M. C. 1833. Dem. M. Bap.

Simms, Jasper; farmer and saw mill; 2 m e Martinsville. Born in M. C. 1849. Dem. M. Baptist.

SIMMS, NIMROD; farmer and blacksmith; 3½ m e Martinsville. Born in N. C. 1825; settled in M. C. 1834. Dem. M. Baptist.

SLOUGH, JOHN T. Capt.; farmer; 2 m e Martinsville. Born in Ind. 1836; settled in M. C. 1865. Rep. Christian.

STINE, ELIZABETH; school teacher; 4 m n e Martinsville. Born in M. C. 1844. M. Baptist.

Stine, J. M.; miller; 5 m n e Martinsville. Born in Ind. 1850; settled in M. C. 1869. Dem. Lutheran.

Stine, E.; farmer and proprietor flour mill; 5 m n e Martinsville. Born in N. C. 1814; settled in M. C. 1869. Dem. Lutheran.

STAFFORD, JAMES M.; farmer; 6 m n e Martinsville. Born in M. C. 1835. Lib. Protestant.

Stevenson, Wm.; farmer; 6½ m n e Martinsville. Born in Ohio 1824; settled in M. C. 1848. Rep. Protestant.

Stout, G. W.; farmer and carpenter; 6 m n e Martinsville. Born in Tenn. 1837; settled in M. C. 1864. Dem. Protestant.

STEWART, E.; farmer; 5 m n e Martinsville. Born in M. C. 1854. Dem. Protestant.

Stockwell, Samuel; farmer; 2½ m n e Martinsville. Born in Ohio 1805; settled in M. C. 1834. Rep. Christian.

Stewart John. Gone from home.

STRAWDER, JOHN W.; farmer; 3 m n Martinsville. Born in Va. 1845; settled in M. C. 1864. Rep. Protestant.

Sweet, A.; farmer; 1½ m n Martinsville. Born in Ky. 1831; settled in M. C. 1834. Rep. Christian.

SWEET, E. D.; farmer and carpenter; 1½ m n Martinsville. Born in Ky. 1828; settled in M. C. 1834. Rep. Christ.

SHIREMAN, MICHAEL; farmer; 1¾ m e Martinsville. Born in N. C. 1828; settled in M. C. 1835. Dem. Protestant.

SINGLETON, THOS.; farmer; 5 m s Martinsville. Born in Ireland 1820; settled in M. C. 1854. Methodist.

Satterwhite, Harvey; Cashier First Nat. Bank; Martinsville. Born in Ky. 1832; settled in M. C. 1856. Rep. Meth.

Thompson, O. N.; carpenter; Martinsville. Born in Ind. 1847; settled in M. C. 1873. Rep. C. Presbyterian.

Tilford, S. M.; boots, shoes and groceries; Martinsville. Born in Ind. 1829; settled in M. C. 1852. Christian.

Tilford, S. A.; Auditor of M. C.; Martinsville. Born in Ind. 1827; settled in M. C. 1848. Indpt. Christian.

THWING, O. O.; physician; Martinsville. Born in Ohio 1837; settled in M. C. 1866. Lib. Christian.

Tiney, Chris.; boot and shoe maker; Martinsville. Born in Germany 1841; settled in M. C. 1873. Indpt. Presb.

TURNER, WM.; carpenter and trader; 3 m n Martinsville. Born in Va. 1831; settled in M. C. 1861. Rep. Protest.

Tucker, R. H,; farmer; Martinsville. Born in Ind. 1850. Rep. Christian.

THOMAS, G. W.; cooper; Martinsville. Born in Ind. 1833. Rep. Protestant.

TUCKER, SAM'L; hotel and farmer; Martinsville. Born in Ky. 1819; settled in M. C. 1837. Rep. Christian.

TARLTON, R. H.; physician and druggist; Martinsville. Born in Ky. 1822; settled in M. C. 1847. Dem. Methodist.

THOMAS, ISAAC; prop'r Thomas House; Martinsville. Born in Ky. 1801; settled in M. C. 1848. Rep. Methodist.

TAYLOR, W. B; stock dealer; Martinsville. Born in Ind. 1819; settled in M. C. 1820. Rep. Presbyterian.

Teague, Solomon; farmer and trader; 3¼ m e Martinsville. Born in N. C. 1823; settled in M. C. 1832. Rep. Protestant.

Teague, Solomon; farmer; 3½ m s e Martinsville. Born in N. C. 1823; settled in M. C. 1835. Rep. Protestant.

TOWNSEND, THOS. J.; farmer; 4 m s e Martinsville. Born in M. C. 1840. Rep. Protestant.

Townsend, M. L.; farmer; 4 m s e Martinsville. Born in M. C. 1836. Rep. M. Baptist.

Townsend, Frank P.; farmer; 4½ m s e Martinsville. Born in M. C. 1852. Dem. M. Baptist.

TOWNSEND, WM., Jr.; farmer; 4¼ m s e Martinsville. Born in M. C. 1847. Dem. Protestant.

TOWNSEND, ANDREW J.; farmer; ¾ m n w Mahalasville. Born in M. C. 1833. Rep. Protestant.

Thomas, Harrison; farmer; 3 m n e Martinsville. Born in M. C. 1852. Dem. Protestant.

Thompson, Thomas; farmer; 4½ m n Martinsville. Born in M. C. 1849. Dem. Christian.

Thacker, Andrew; farmer; 7 m s w Martinsville. Born in Ind. 1833; settled in M. C. 1838. Dem. Protestant.

Townsend, Irvin; farmer; 2 m s e Martinsville. Born in Ind. 1819; settled in M. C. 1819. Dem. M. Baptist.

Townsend, Hueston; farmer; 4 m s e Martinsville. Born in 1818; settled in M. C. 1823. Dem. M. Baptist.

Townsend, Wm.; farmer; 2 m s e Martinsville. Born in M. C. 1847. Dem. Protestant.

Townsend, Lane; farmer; 4 m s e Martinsville. Born in M. C. 1850. Dem. Granger.

Thacker, Wm.; laborer; 3 m s Martinsville. Born in Ind. 1850. Protestant.

Taggart, Joseph; farmer; 5 m s e Martinsville. Born in Ireland 1825; settled in M. C. 1840. Dem. Granger.

Tackett, Thos. H.; farmer; 5 m n Martinsville. Born in Ind. 1842; settled in M. C. 1842. Dem. Protestant.

Ulrey, John; farmer; Martinsville. Born in Ohio 1852; settled in M. C. 1873. Dem. Christian.

Voyles, Evan; farmer; 4 m s e Martinsville. Born in Indiana 1814; settled in M. C. 1824. Dem. M. Baptist.

Voyles, Albert; farmer; 4 m s e Martinsville. Born in Ind. 1842. Protestant.

WARNER, J. C.; fireman on railroad; Martinsville. Born in Ind. 1850. Rep. Methodist.

WIGGINTON, A.; groceries and notions; Martinsville. Born in Ky. 1819; settled in M. C. 1845. Rep. Methodist.

Warner, F. M.; livery; Martinsville. Born in Ind. 1842. Rep. Protestant.

Warner, Mrs. P. B.; milliner; Martinsville. Born in Ind. 1831. Rep. Methodist.

Wilson, S. N.; S. M. agent; Martinsville. Born in Ind. 1833. Rep. Christian.

Wilson, C. A.; wagon maker; Martinsville. Born in N. C. 1842; settled in M. C. 1869. Dem. Christian.

WARNER, G. W.; farmer; Martinsville. Born in Ky. 1822; settled in M. C. 1833. Rep. Methodist.

Woody, E. M.; merchant; Martinsville. Born in Ind. 1835; settled in M. C. 1870. Rep. C. Presbyterian.

Winter, H.; clerk in store; Martinsville. Born in Ind. 1843. Rep. Presbyterian.

Watkins, J. A.; county commissioner, farmer and trader; 1¼ m s w Martinsville. Born in Ind. 1822. Indpt.

Warner, G. W ; farmer and trader; Martinsville. Born in Ky. 1822; settled in M. C. 1832. Rep. Methodist.

WILLIAMS. HENRY; butcher, firm of Williams & Son; Martinsville. Born in Ind. 1832; settled in M. C. 1871.

Wetherly, C. P.; farmer; 5 m s e Martinsville.. Born in Ala. 1843; settled in M. C. 1865. Dem. Methodist.

Williams, L. C.; carpenter; Martinsville. Born in Ky. 1822; settled in M. C. 1850. Rep. Presbyterian.

Williams, T. H.; farmer; Martinsville. Born in M. C. 1849. Dem. Christian.

WHITE, JAMES; farmer; 6 m n e Martinsville. Born in Tenn. 1824; settled in M. C. 1833. Christian.

Wagaman, J. J.; farmer; 5½ m n e Martinsville. Born in Ind. 1844; settled in M. C. 1861. Dem. Protestant.

Wills, Francis M; farmer; 5 m n Martinsville. Born in M. C. 1847. Dem. Christian.

Whitener, John; tollgate keeper; 1 m e Martinsville. Born in N. C. 1820; settled in M. C. 1839. Dem. Protestant.

Wall, Geo. W.; farmer; 2 m s w Martinsville. Born in M. C. 1837. Rep. Protestant.

Williams, Wm.; farmer; 4 m n w Martinsville. Born in Ind. 1816; settled in M. C. 1820. Dem.

Whisell, Marion; farmer; 6 m s Martinsville. Born in Ind. 1842; settled in M. C. 1871. Dem. Protestant.

YOUNG, JACOB; miller; Martinsville. Born in Pa. 1827; settled in M. C. 1871.

APPENDIX.

CONSTITUTIONAL AMENDMENTS.

The Amendment proposed to the Constitution, June 8, 1866.

ARTICLE XIV.

SECTION 1. All persons born or naturalized in the United States, and subject to the jurisdiction thereof, are citizens of the United States and of the State wherein they reside. No State shall make or enforce any law which shall abridge the privileges or immunities of citizens of the United States; nor shall any State deprive any person of life, liberty or property, without due process of law, nor deny to any person within its jurisdiction the equal protection of the laws.

SEC. 2. Representatives shall be apportioned among the several States according to their respective numbers, counting the whole number of persons in each State, excluding Indians not taxed. But when the right to vote at any election for the choice of electors for President and Vice President of the United States, Representatives in Congress, the executive and judicial officers of a State, or the members of the Legislature thereof, is denied to any of the male inhabitants of such State, being twenty-one years of age, and citizens of the United States, or in any way abridged, except for participation in rebellion or other crime, the basis of representation therein shall be reduced in the proportion which the number of such male citizens shall bear to the whole number of male citizens twenty-one years of age in such State.

SEC. 3. No person shall be a Senator or Representative in

Congress, or Elector of President and Vice President, or hold any office, civil or military, under the United States, or under any State, who, having previously taken an oath, as a member of Congress, or as an officer of the United States, or as a member of any State Legislature, or as an executive or judicial officer of any State, to support the Constitution of the United States, shall have engaged in insurrection or rebellion against the same, or given aid or comfort to the enemies thereof. But Congress may, by a vote of two-thirds of each house, remove such disability.

Sec. 4. The validity of the public debt of the United States, authorized by law, including debts incurred for payment of pensions and bounties for services in suppressing insurrection or rebellion, shall not be questioned. But neither the United States nor any State shall assume or pay any debt or obligation incurred in aid of insurrection or rebellion against the United States, or any claim for the loss or emancipation of any slave; but all such debts, obligations and claims shall be held illegal and void.

Sec. 5. The Congress shall have power to enforce, by appropriate legislation, the provisions of this article.

The amendment passed the Senate by a vote of 33 yeas to 11 nays, and the House by a vote of 138 yeas to 36 nays.

ARTICLE XV.

Section 1. The right of citizens of the United States to vote shall not be denied or abridged by the United States or by any State on account of race, color, or previous condition of servitude.

Sec. 2. The Congress shall have power to enforce this article by appropriate legislation.

ARTICLES OF CONFEDERATION

AND

PERPETUAL UNION BETWEEN THE STATES.

The Articles of Confederation reported July 12, '76, and debated from day to day, and time to time, for two years; were ratified July 9, '78, by 10 States; by New Jersey, on the 28th of November of the same year, and by Delaware, on the 23d of February following. Maryland, alone, held off two years more, acceding to them March 1, '81, and thus closing the obligation. The following are the Articles:

To all whom these Presents shall come. We, the undersigned Delegates of the States affixed to our names, send greeting— Whereas, the Delegates of the United States of America, in Congress assembled, did, on the 15th day of November, in the year of our Lord, 1777, and in the Second Year of the Independence of America, agree to certain Articles of Confederation and Perpetual Union between the States of New Hampshire, Massachusetts Bay, Rhode Island and Providence Plantations, Connecticut, New York, New Jersey, Pennsylvania, Delaware, Maryland, Virginia, North Carolina, South Carolina and Georgia, in the words following, viz:

"*Articles of Confederation and Perpetual Union between the States of New Hampshire, Massachusetts Bay, Rhode Island and Providence Plantations, Connecticut, New York, New Jersey, Pennsylvania, Delaware, Maryland, Virginia, North Carolina, South Carolina and Georgia.*

ARTICLE I. The style of this Confederacy shall be "The United States of America."

Art. 2. Each State retains its sovereignty, freedom and independence, and every power, jurisdiction and right, which is not by this confederation expressly delegated to the United States in Congress assembled.

Art. 3. The said States hereby severally enter into a firm league of friendship with each other, for their common defense, the security of their liberties, and their mutual and general welfare, binding themselves to assist each other against all force offered to, or attacks made upon them, or any of them, on account of religion, sovereignty, trade, or any other pretense whatever.

Art. 4. The better to secure and perpetuate mutual friendship and intercourse among the people of the different States in this Union, the free inhabitants of each of these States—paupers, vagabonds, and fugitives from justice excepted—shall be entitled to all privileges and immunities of free citizens in the several States; and the people of each State shall have free ingress and regress to and from any other State, and shall enjoy therein all the privileges of trade and commerce, subject to the same duties, impositions and restrictions as the inhabitants thereof respectively, provided that such restriction shall not extend so far as to prevent the removal of property, imported into any State, to any other State of which the owner is an inhabitant; provided, also, that no imposition, duties or restriction shall be laid by any State on the property of the United States or either of them.

If any person guilty of or charged with treason, felony or other high misdemeanor in any State, shall flee from justice, and be found in any of the United States, he shall, upon demand of the Governor, or executive power of the State from which he fled, be delivered up and removed to the State having jurisdiction of his offense.

Full faith and credit shall be given in each of these States, to the records, acts, and judicial proceedings of the courts and magistrates of every other State.

Art. 5. For the more convenient management of the general interest of the United States, Delegates shall be annually appointed, in such manner as the Legislature of each State shall direct, to meet in Congress on the first Monday in November in every year, with a power reserved to each State to recall its Delegates, or any of them, at any time within the year, and to send others in their stead for the remainder of the year.

No State shall be represented in Congress by less than two, nor by more than seven members; and no person shall be capable of being a Delegate for more than three years in any term of six years; nor shall any person, being a Delegate, be capable of holding any office under the United States, for which he, or another for his benefit, receives any salary, fees or emolument of any kind.

Each State shall maintain its own Delegates in any meeting of the States, and while they act as members of the Committee of the States.

In determining questions in the United States, in Congress assembled, each State shall have one vote.

Freedom of speech and debate in Congress shall not be impeached or questioned in any court or place, out of Congress, and the members of Congress shall be protected in their persons from arrests and imprisonments, during the time of their going to and from, and attendance on Congress, except for treason, felony, or breach of the peace.

Art. 6. No State, without the consent of the United States in Congress assembled, shall send an embassy to, or receive an embassy from, or enter into any conference, agreement, alliance or treaty with any King, Prince, or State; nor shall any person holding any office of profit or trust under the United States, or any of them, accept of any present, emolument, office or title of any kind whatever from any King, Prince, or Foreign State; nor shall the United States in Congress assembled, or any of them, grant any title of nobility.

No two or more States shall enter into any treaty, confederation or alliance whatever between them, without the consent of the United States in Congress assembled, specifying accurately the purposes for which the same is to be entered into, and how long it shall continue.

No State shall lay any imposts or duties which may interfere with any stipulations in treaties, entered into by the United States in Congress assembled, with any King, Prince, or State, in pursuance of any treaties already proposed by Congress, to the Courts of France and Spain.

No vessels of war shall be kept up in time of peace by any State, except such number only as shall be deemed necessary by the United States in Congress assembled, for the defense of such State, or its trade; nor shall any body of forces be kept up by any State, in time of peace, except such number only, as in the judgment of the United States in Congress assembled, shall be deemed requisite to garrison the forts necessary for the defense of such State; but every State shall always keep up a well regulated and disciplined militia, sufficiently armed and accoutred, and shall provide and have constantly ready for use, in public stores, a due number of field-pieces and tents, and a proper quantity of arms, ammunition and camp equipage.

No State shall engage in any war without the consent of the United States in Congress assembled, unless such State be actually invaded by enemies, or shall have received certain advice of a resolution being formed by some nation of Indians to invade such a State, and the danger is so imminent as not to admit of a delay, till the United States in Congress assembled can be consulted; nor shall any State grant commissions to any ships or vessels of war, nor letters of marque reprisal, except it be after a declaration of war by the United States in Congress assembled, and then only against the Kingdom or State, and the subjects thereof, against which war has been so declared, and under such regulations as shall be established by the United States in Congress assembled, unless such State be infested by pirates, in which case vessels of war may be fitted out for that occasion, and kept so long as the danger shall continue, or until the United States in Congress assembled shall determine otherwise.

Art. 7. When land forces are raised by any State for the common defense, all officers of, or under the rank of colonel, shall be appointed by the legislature of each State respectively, by whom such forces shall be raised, or in such manner as such State shall direct, and all vacancies shall be filled up by the State which first made the appointment.

Art. 8. All charges of war, and all other expenses that shall be incurred for the common defense or general welfare, and allowed by the United States in Congress assembled, shall be defrayed out of a common treasury, which shall be supplied by the several States, in proportion to the value of all land within each State granted to or surveyed for any person, as such land and the buildings and improvements thereon shall be estimated according to such mode as the United States in Congress assembled, shall, from time to time, direct and appoint. The taxes for paying that proportion shall be laid and levied by the authority and direction of the legislatures of the several States within the time agreed upon by the United States in Congress assembled.

Art. 9. The United States in Congress assembled shall have the sole and exclusive right and power of determining on peace and war, except in the cases mentioned in the 6th article —of sending and receiving embassadors—entering into treaties and alliances, provided that no treaty of commerce shall be made whereby the legislative power of the respective States shall be restrained from imposing such imposts and duties on foreigners, as their own people are subjected to, or from prohibiting the exportation or importation of any species of goods or commodities whatsoever—of establishing rules for deciding in all cases what captures on land or water shall be legal, and in what manner prizes taken by land or naval forces in the service of the United States shall be divided or appropriated—of granting letters of marque and reprisal in times of peace—appointing courts for the trial of piracies and felonies committed on the high seas, and establishing courts for receiving and determining finally appeals in all cases of captures, provided that no member of Congress shall be appointed a judge of any of the said courts.

The United States in Congress assembled shall also be the last resort on appeal in all disputes and differences now subsisting, or that hereafter may arise between two or more States concerning boundary, jurisdiction, or any other cause whatever ; which authority shall always be exercised in the manner following :—Whenever the legislative or executive authority or lawful agent of any State in controversy with another shall present a petition to Congress, stating the matter in question, and praying for a hearing, notice thereof shall be given by order of Congress, to the legislative or executive authority of the other State in controversy, and a day assigned for the appearance of the parties by their lawful agents, who shall then be directed to appoint, by joint consent, commissioners or judges to constitute a court for hearing and determining the matter in question ; but if they can not agree, Congress shall name three persons out of each of the United States, and from the list of such persons each party shall alternately strike out one, the petitioners beginning, until the number shall be reduced to thirteen ; and from that number not less than seven, nor more than nine names, as

Congress shall direct, shall in the presence of Congress be drawn out by lot, and the persons whose names shall be so drawn, or any five of them, shall be commissioners or judges, to hear and finally determine the controversy, so always as a major part of the judges who shall hear the cause shall agree in the determination ; and if either party shall neglect to attend at the day appointed, without showing reasons which Congress shall judge sufficient, or being present shall refuse to strike, the Congress shall proceed to nominate three persons out of each State, and the Secretary of Congress shall strike in behalf of such party absent or refusing ; and the judgment and sentence of the court to be appointed, in the manner above prescribed, shall be final and conclusive ; and if any of the parties shall refuse to submit to the authority of such court, or to appear or defend their claim or cause, the court shall, nevertheless, proceed to pronounce sentence or judgment, which shall in like manner be final and decisive, the judgment or sentence and other proceedings being in either case transmitted to Congress and lodged among the acts of Congress for the security of the parties concerned ; provided that every commissioner, before he sits in judgment, shall take an oath, to be administered by one of the judges of the Supreme or Superior Court of the State where the cause shall be tried, " well and truly to hear and determine the matter in question, according to the best of his judgment, without favor, affection, or hope of reward:" provided also that no State shall be deprived of territory for the benefit of the United States.

All controversies concerning the private right of soil claimed under different grants of two or more States, whose jurisdictions as they may respect such lands, and the States which passed such grants, are adjusted ; the said grants or either of them being at the same time claimed to have originated antecedent to such settlement of jurisdiction, shall, on the petition of either party to the Congress of the United States, be finally determined as near as may be in the same manner as is before prescribed for deciding disputes respecting territorial jurisdiction between different States.

The United States in Congress assembled shall also have the sole exclusive right and power of regulating the alloy and value of coin struck by their own authority, or by that of the respective States—fixing the standard of weights and measures throughout the United States—regulating the trade and managing all affairs with the Indians, not members of any of the States; provided that the legislative right of any State within its own limits be not infringed or violated—establishing or regulating post-offices from one State to another, throughout all the United States, and exacting such postage on the papers passing through the same as may be requisite to defray the expenses of the said office—appointing all officers of the land forces, in the service of the United States, excepting regimental officers—appointing all the officers of the naval forces, and commissioning all officers whatever in the service of the United States—making rules for the government and regulation of the said land and naval forces, and directing their operations.

The United States in Congress assembled shall have authority to appoint a committee, to sit in the recess of Congress, to be denominated "A Committee of the States," and to consist of one delegate from each State; and to appoint such other committees and civil officers as may be necessary for managing the general affairs of the United States, under their direction—to appoint one of their number to preside; provided that no person be allowed to serve in the office of president more than one year in any term of three years—to ascertain the necessary sums of money to be raised for the service of the United States, and to appropriate and apply the same for defraying the public expenses—to borrow money, or emit bills on the credit of the

United States, transmitting every half year to the respective States an account of the sums of money so borrowed or emitted—to build and equip a navy—to agree upon the number of land forces, and to make requisitions from each State for its quota, in proportion to the number of white inhabitants in such State, which requisition shall be binding; and thereupon the legislatures of each State shall appoint the regimental officers, raise the men, and clothe, arm, and equip them in a soldier-like manner, at the expense of the United States; and the officers and men so clothed, armed, and equipped, shall march to the place appointed, and within the time agreed on by the United States in Congress assembled; but if the United States in Congress assembled shall, on consideration of circumstances, judge proper that any State should not raise men, or should raise a smaller number than its quota, and that any other State should raise a greater number of men than the quota thereof, such extra number shall be raised, officered, clothed, armed, and equipped in the same manner as the quota of such State, unless the legislature of such State shall judge that such extra number can not be safely spared out of the same; in which case they shall raise, officer, clothe, arm, and equip as many of such extra number as they judge can be safely spared. And the officers and men so clothed, armed, and equipped, shall march to the place appointed, and within the time agreed on by the United States in Congress assembled.

The United States in Congress assembled shall never engage in a war, nor grant letters of marque and reprisal in time of peace, nor enter into any treaties or alliances, nor coin money, nor regulate the value thereof, nor ascertain the sums and expenses necessary for the defense and welfare of the United States, or any of them, nor emit bills, nor borrow money on the credit of the United States, nor appropriate money, nor agree upon the number of vessels of war to be built or purchased, or the number of land or sea forces to be raised, nor appoint a commander-in-chief of the army or navy unless nine States assent to the same; nor shall a question on any other point, except for adjourning from day to day, be determined, unless by the votes of a majority of the United States in Congress assembled.

The Congress of the United States shall have power to adjourn to any time within the year, and to any place within the United States, so that no period of adjournment be for a longer duration than the space of six months, and shall publish the journal of their proceedings monthly, except such parts thereof relating to treaties, alliances, or military operations, as in their judgment require secresy; and the yeas and nays of the delegates of each State on any question shall be entered on the journal when it is desired by any delegate; and the delegates of a State, or any of them, at his or their request, shall be furnished with a transcript of the said journal, except such parts as are above excepted, to lay before the legislatures of the several States.

Art. 10. The Committee of the States, or any nine of them, shall be authorized to execute, in the recess of Congress, such of the powers of Congress as the United States in Congress assembled, by the consent of nine States, shall, from time to time, think expedient to vest them with; provided that no power be delegated to the said committee, for the exercise of which, by the Articles of Confederation, the voice of nine States in the Congress of the United States assembled is requisite.

Art. 11. Canada, acceding to this confederation and joining in the measures of the United States, shall be admitted into, and entitled to all the advantages of this union; bnt no other colony shall be admitted into the same unless such admission be agreed to by nine States.

Art. 12. All bills of credit emitted, moneys borrowed, and debts contracted by, or under the authority of Congress, before the assembling of the United States, in pursuance of the present confederation, shall be deemed and considered as a charge against the United States—for payment and satisfaction whereof the said United States and the public faith are hereby solemnly pledged.

Art. 13. Every State shall abide by the determinations of the United States in Congress assembled on all questions which, by this confederation, are submitted to them. And the articles of this confederation shall be inviolably observed by every State, and the union shall be perpetual; nor shall any alteration at any time hereafter be made in any of them, unless such alteration be agreed to in a Congress of the United States, and be afterward confirmed by the legislatures of every State.

And Whereas, It hath pleased the Great Governor of the World to incline the hearts of the legislatures we respectively represent in Congress, to approve of and to authorize us to ratify the said Articles of Confederation and perpetual union;

Know Ye, That we, the undersigned delegates, by virtue of the power and authority to us given for that purpose, do, by these presents, in the name and in behalf of our respective constituents, fully and entirely ratify and confirm each and every of the said Articles of Confederation and perpetual Union, and all and singular the matters therein contained. And we do further solemnly plight and engage the faith of our respective constituents, that they shall abide by the determinations of the United States in Congress assembled on all questions which, by the said confederation, are submitted to them. And that the articles thereof shall be inviolably observed by the States we respectively represent, and that the union shall be perpetual. In witness whereof we have hereunto set our hands in Congress.

Done at Philadelphia, in the State of Pennsylvania, the 9th day of July, in the year of our Lord 1778, and in the 3d year of the Independence of America.

HOMESTEAD LAW.

By act of Congress of May 20, 1862, any person who is the head of a family, or who has arrived at the age of twenty-one years, or has performed service in the army or navy, and is a citizen of the United States, or shall have filed his declaration of intention to become such, and has never borne arms against the Government of the United States, or given aid and comfort to its enemies, shall, from and after the 1st of January, 1863, be entitled to enter a quarter section (160 acres) of unappropriated public land, upon which he or she may have already filed a pre-emption claim, or which is subject to pre-emption, at $1.25 per acre; or 80 acres of unappropriated lands, at $2.50 per acre. In order to make his or her title good to such lands, however, such person must make affidavit that such application is made for his or her exclusive use and benefit, and that said entry is made for the purpose of actual settlement and cultivation, and not, either directly or indirectly, for the use or benefit of any other person or persons whomsoever; and upon filing the affidavit, and paying the sum of ten dollars to the register or receiver, such person shall be allowed to enter the land specified; but no certificate or patent is issued for the land until five years from the date of such entry, and the land must, during that time, be improved and not alienated (it can not be taken for debt).

At any time within two years after the expiration of said five years, the person making the entry, or, in case of his or her death, his widow or heirs, may, on proof by two witnesses that he or she has cultivated or improved said land, has not alienated any part of it, and has borne true allegiance to the United States, be entitled to a patent, if at that time a citizen of the United States. In case of the abandonment of the lands by the person making the entry, for a period of more than six months at one time, they revert to the United States.

RECIPES.

GOLDEN OIL.

1 pint linseed oil, 1 drachm oil organum, 1 drachm oil cedar, 1 drachm oil sassafras, 1 drachm oil hemlock, 1 drachm oil peppermint, 1 drachm tinc. laudanum, 4 drachms gum camphor.

MUTTON-BROTH.

Take three pounds of the scrag-end of a fresh neck of mutton, cut it into several pieces, wash them in cold water, and put them into a stew-pan with two quarts of cold spring-water; place the stew-pan on the fire to boil; skim well, and add a couple of turnips cut into slices, a few branches of parsley, a sprig of green thyme, and a little salt. When it has boiled gently by the side of the stove for an hour and a half, skim off the fat from the surface, and then let it be strained through a lawn sieve into a basin, and kept for use.

BEEF-TEA.

Take two pounds of the lean part of the gravy-piece of beef, and carefully pare away every particle of fat, skin, or sinew; cut this into small square pieces the size of a nut, put the beef into a stew-pan capable of containing two quarts, and pour three pints of boiling water upon it, add a little salt, put it on the stove fire, and, as soon as it boils, skim it, and then remove it to the side of the stove to continue boiling gently for an hour, after which it should be strained through a napkin for use.

PECTORAL CHICKEN-BROTH.

Cut up a young fowl into several pieces, put in a stew-pan with three pints of spring-water; set on the stove fire to boil; skim well, and add a little salt; take two tablespoonfuls of pearl-barley, wash it in several waters, and add it to the broth, together with one ounce of marsh-mallow roots cut into shreds for the purpose of better extracting its healing properties. The broth should then boil one hour, and be passed through a napkin into a basin, to be kept ready for use.

INDEX.

	PAGE
Declaration of Independence	3
Constitution of the United States	9
Constitution of Indiana	26
Emancipation Proclamation	54
Political Platforms	56
Baxter Liquor Law	85
Geological Items	93
Philosophy	104
Sketches of Astronomy	106
Pay of Government Officers	114
Religious	115
Population of States and Territories	117
Population of Principal Cities	117
Male Inhabitants	118
Vote of Each State	119
Population of Indiana by Counties	120
Population of Indiana Towns	121
Sabbath Schools	125
Recipes	127
Morgan County History	131
Adams Township	147
Ashland Township	166
Baker Township	178
Brown Township	182
Clay Township	207
Gregg Township	230
Green Township	245
Harrison Township	256
Jackson Township	263
Jefferson Township	288

Madison Township	299
Monroe Township	316
Ray Township	338
Washington Township	348
Constitutional Amendment	389
Articles of Confederation	391
Homestead Law	402
Recipes	404

TO OUR PATRONS.

We take the present mode of returning our thanks to the citizens of Morgan county for the liberal patronage we have received for this work; also for the gentlemanly treatment to our canvassers, hoping that the work will prove to be all that has been claimed for it. We have tried to make it with as few mistakes as possible, and have endeavored to insert the names of all the principal men of the county. We have met with some few men who did not wish their names inserted, and who treated the canvassers rather coolly, all of which we did not promise to insert their names, we only promised those who had no objection; therefore you may possibly not find every principal man in the county located.

Hoping that you will be satisfied with our efforts to fulfill our promise, we remain yours, as ever,

P. P. THOMAS.

CLINE & McHAFFIE,

PUBLISHERS AND PROPRIETORS OF THE

PEOPLE'S GUIDE.

Good canvassers wanted, to work on commission, to take orders. Also, territory by counties to let to good responsible men.   Address,   CLINE & McHAFFIE,
Clayton, Ind.

WM. CLINE, JR.,

DESIGNER OF A NEW MODE OF

CARD ADVERTISING,

By which from three to fifty times the amount of advertising can be done for the same money generally used, and it is more effectual.   Address,   WM. CLINE, JR.,
Clayton, Ind.

P. P. THOMAS,

Who has just finished the work for the People's Guide, or Directory of Morgan County, Ind., wishes a few good agents for canvassing in Clinton, Parke and other counties, for which he will pay a good commission to responsible men.

Address,   P. P. THOMAS, Amo, Ind.

www.ingramcontent.com/pod-product-compliance
Lightning Source LLC
Chambersburg PA
CBHW050851300426
44111CB00010B/1217